LIBRARY OF NEW TESTAMENT STUDIES

430

formerly the Journal for the Study of the New Testament Supplement series

CONTOURS IN THE TEXT

Textual Variation in the Writings of Paul, Josephus and the Yaḥad

J.D.H. NORTON

t&t clark

Copyright © Jonathan D.H. Norton, 2011

Published by T&T Clark International
A Continuum imprint
The Tower Building, 11 York Road, London SE1 7NX
80 Maiden Lane, Suite 704, New York, NY 10038

www.continuumbooks.com

British Library Cataloguing-in-Publication Data
A catalogue record for this book is available from the British Library

ISBN HB: 978-0-567-22939-7

Typeset by Pindar NZ, Auckland, New Zealand
Printed and bound in Great Britain

CONTENTS

LIST OF TABLES

ACKNOWLEDGEMENTS

My gratitude goes to a number of people who have offered help and support. A Master's thesis written in Oxford in 2002 gave rise to the questions broached in this book. Bob Morgan and Chris Roland guided my research during that year and showed kindness during difficult times. Chris Tuckett encouraged me to transform the reams of laborious text-critical analysis into a doctoral thesis, which he supervised from 2003 to 2006. Over the years this research has benefited from tuition, comments and insights of various kinds. I am grateful to Annette Steudel, Émile Puech and the late Hartmut Stegemann for their formative guidance in scrolls matters. Étienne Nodet has offered me many pleasurable hours discussing Josephus; Anders Klostergaard Petersen has shared many illuminating thoughts on Paul; and Magnar Kartviet has made valuable observations on a draft of Chapter 4. Torleif Elgvin and the late Graham Stanton recommended literature that proved indispensable. Two Oxford librarians, Libby Birchall and Louise Calder, have been enormously helpful. Regular conversations with Nick King, Hanne von Weissenberg, Kevin Sullivan, Mila Ginsburskaya and Travis Derico have provided help, support and friendship. The guidance of my examiners, John Barclay and Martin Goodman has been invaluable in the preparation of the thesis for publication. For their erudite support I am most indebted to Steve Mason, who commented on Chapters 1 and 3, and to Sean Ryan, Andrew Teeter and Reverend Pawel Rytel-Andrianik each of whom made comments on the entire manuscript.

I thank the dialogue partners with whom I have engaged in this book, in particular Dietrich-Alex Koch and Christopher Stanley, whose work has been an ongoing inspiration to me over the past eight years and with whose ideas I have tussled with admiration.

My thanks go to the AHRC for Master's and D.Phil. funding from 2001–2006, to the DAAD for funding research in Jerusalem in 2004 and to Wolfson College, particularly Martin Francis, for funding regular conference attendance between 2002 and 2007.

I thank Marianne Wade for providing weeks of sanctuary in 2005 and 2010, during which substantial writing was done. I thank Zoe McIntosh for the many crosswords and baths, and for enduring several impromptu lectures on the Pharisees. I thank Christopher Meade for supplying coffee, conversation and encouragement at times of need. I thank my brother Joe Norton for patient and expert technical aid and my father Harry for his unfailing support of my work. For her immense academic, editorial and moral guidance I thank Anastasia Norton-Piliavsky, without whom I would have produced some sort of a book much earlier, and probably would have been happy with it.

Wolfson College, Oxford
July 2010

ABBREVIATIONS

א	Codex Sinaiticus
α' σ' θ'	*Aquila, Symmachus* and *Theodotion* (see: 'The Three')
A	Codex Alexandrinus
AJ	*Antiquitates Judaicae*, Flavius Josephus (*The Jewish Antiquities*)
B	Codex Vaticanus
BHS	*Biblia Hebraica Stuttgartensia*
BJ	*Bellum Judaicum*, Flavius Josephus (*The Jewish War*)
Cont.Ap.	*Contra Apionem*, Flavius Josephus (*Against Apion*)
D	the *Damascus Document* texts from Qumran
𝔊	used by textual critics to indicate either the Greek text witnessed by LXX manuscripts, or the hypothetical Hebrew text that the Greek presupposes
G^HR	a 'hebraising revision' of the OG toward a Hebrew text akin to proto-𝔐
καιγε-Theodotion	a first-century BCE–CE hebraising revision of the OG toward a Hebrew text akin to proto-𝔐
Lat	Latin versions
Leg.	Philo, *Legatio ad Gaium* (Embassy to Gaius)
LXX	a Greek version of the Jewish scriptures, including translations from Hebrew biblical works and Jewish compositions in Greek, transmitted as part the early Christian canon
𝔐	the Masoretic Text exemplified in early medieval manuscripts (such as the Leningrad and Aleppo Codices), which contain the rabbinic canon of the Hebrew bible
M	the *Milḥamah* text from Qumran
MMT	the *Miqsat Ma`ase ha-Torah* (Halakhic Letter) texts from Qumran
Mos.	Philo, *Vita Mosis* (The Life of Moses)
MT	identical with 'M' (used occasionally)
OG	Old Greek. Works of Jewish scripture in Greek dating from c. 3rd BCE–1st CE comprising translations of Hebrew biblical works and Jewish compositions in Greek
proto-θ'	see: 'proto-Theodotion'
proto-Theodotion	a revision of the OG – apparently a precursor of θ' circulating

	in the early/mid-first century CE – related to the first century BCE–CE *kaige* project.
proto-𝔐	a Hebrew text-form in which at least some biblical works existed from the Hellenistic period onward (known from Judaean manuscript discoveries) and which became standardised in early rabbinic circles from the second century CE. Proto- M was the precursor of the early Medieval Masoretic Text.
RSV	The Revised Standard Version translation of the Canonical Hebrew Bible and the Greek New Testament
S	the *Serekh ha-Yaḥad* text from Qumran
Somn.	Philo, *De Somniis* (On Dreams, That They are Sent by God)
SP	Samaritan Pentateuch
Spec.	Philo, *De Specialibus Legibus* (The Special Laws)
Syr	Syriac versions
T	Targum
TF	The Fragment Targum
TJ	Targum Pseudo Jonathan
TN	Targum Neofiti
TO	Targum Onqelos
The Three	the three revisions of the OG toward a proto- M dating from the late second to mid third centuries CE, *Aquila*, *Symmachus* and *Theodotion*.
V	Jerome's Latin Vulgate translation of the Bible
1QpHab	the copy the *Habakkuk Pesher* found in Qumran Cave 1
1QS	the copy *Serekh ha-Yaḥad* found in Qumran Cave 1
4QD	
4QM	the copies of *Milḥamah* found in Qumran Cave 4
4QMMT	the copies of *Miqsat Ma`ase ha-Torah* (Halakhic Letter) found in Qumran Cave 4

Conventions

Isa 1:1LXX	the LXX form of a biblical verse, e.g. Isa 1:1
Isa 1:1OG	the OG form of a biblical verse
Isa 1:1G	the G form of a biblical verse
Isa 1:1𝔐	the M form of a biblical verse
Isa 1:1θ	the θ' form of a biblical verse
Isa 1:1HR	a 'GHeb' form of a biblical verse
Isa 1:1(?)	a form of a biblical verse a cited in an ancient text, deriving from an unknown tradition (textual tradition or oral)

Critical apparatus

]   *'divereges from'*. For example: M SP θ'] LXX α' – 'M, SP and Theodotion agree against LXX and Aquila'

>   *'omission'*. For example: LXX SP > M – 'feature shared by LXX and SP is absent in M'

;   *'related but distinctive forms'*. For example, LXX] M; SP; θ' – 'LXX disagrees with the rest. The readings of M SP and Theodotion are related, but not identical'

In edited text

טיכ[...]אבנ   square brackets indicate missing text

אבנ o הוז   small circle 'o' represents an uncertain letter trace

דבר {ודבר} ודבר   superlinear insertion

For Gail and Harry Norton,
whom I miss, with love

ἐπίτρεψόν μοι πρῶτον ἀπελθεῖν
καὶ θάψαι τὸν πατέρα μου

1

PAUL AND JEWISH SCRIPTURE

1.1 *The question*

Between 40 and 55 CE Paul, a missionary, cited passages from Jewish scripture in a number of letters he wrote in Greek. Some of these letters survive through Christian transmission. In 1957 E. Earle Ellis published an influential study in which he concludes that Paul made skilful and conscious use of various text-forms of Jewish scripture that were available in the first century. That is, Paul used Greek sources – the Septuagint (LXX) and Greek revisions of it – as well as Hebrew sources. In 1986 Dietrich-Alex Koch published a study of Paul's use of scripture, which has been widely accepted as the definitive work on the subject. Koch concludes that Paul used only Greek scripture and was entirely unaware of his own use of different text-forms of biblical works. Ellis and Koch represent a polarization of perspectives. They disagree entirely on the question of Paul's awareness of the textual plurality that characterized Jewish scripture during the first century CE.

Nineteenth- and twentieth-century manuscript discoveries have led to a proliferation of text-critical studies of Jewish scripture of late antiquity, giving rise to an increasing appreciation of variety within it and the extent to which the text of any given copy differed from all the others. Within the context of these developments, commentators have sought to establish the character of Paul's written sources. E. Kautzsch's 1869 conclusion that Paul's sources were largely identical with the Greek Septuagint has been widely confirmed by subsequent enquiries.

This study questions Paul's awareness and encounter with textual plurality in Jewish scripture, as well as ways in which these can be discussed. To ask 'What text-forms did Paul use?' is not the same as to ask 'Of what textual traditions was he aware?' The former is a text-critical question, which can be answered without considering the latter. Enquiries into Paul's *awareness*, however, involve a recurrent set of attended issues. With what versions of biblical works was he familiar? How did he access these versions through written copies? Did he use Hebrew or Aramaic texts as well as Greek? And did he cite from memory? These are the questions of a social historian and thus cannot be fully addressed in text-critical terms.

In Chapter 1 I examine a selection of important studies of Paul's use of scripture, arguing that the application of particular text-critical expedients to questions of Paul's perception and citation of his sources often leads commentators to subordinate historical concerns. As a result, scholars have often allowed anachronistic categories to guide analysis of Paul's perception of textual variation. In Chapter 2 I propose terms better suited to a socio-historical view of Paul's literary encounter. On this basis, an exploration of selected writings from Flavius Josephus and Dead Sea sectarians demonstrates that exegetical use of textual variation was available to Paul's contemporaries (Chapters 3 and 4). Such means were indeed used by Jews from different class, professional, ideological, and educational backgrounds. Moreover, such practices belonged to a more oral environment than usually acknowledged (Chapters 5 and 6). In Chapter 7 I show that when Paul has reason to make use of textual variation, he does.

1.1.1 *Some terms*

I use and abbreviate significant text-critical terms in the following way:

Jewish scripture: A body of traditional Jewish writings used by Jews in antiquity. The term does not describe a fixed body of literature because it is disputed which works exactly were considered authoritative in this period. 'Jewish scripture' implies no distinction based on language, recension or text-type.

LXX: The 'Septuagint' as witnessed principally by Christian manuscripts from the third century onwards.

OG: The presumed 'Old Greek' translation of individual Hebrew works, which occurred successively between the third century BCE and the first century CE. By using 'OG', I avoid the unreflected equation between the later Christian LXX texts and first-century texts, which are barely represented in extant copies.

G^{Ed}: The oldest retrievable wording of the Septuagint as reconstructed by the editors of the *Göttingen Septuaginta*.

𝔊: Used by textual critics to indicate either the Greek text witnessed by LXX manuscripts, or the hypothetical Hebrew text that the Greek presupposes. The same author (e.g. Tov 1992) can use 𝔊 in both senses. In this study I use 𝔊 when discussing particular authors, explaining in which sense it is used in each case.

Hebrew Bible: Traditional Hebrew literature deemed authoritative by first-century Jews. These include the collection of works from Genesis to 2 Chronicles fixed in the Rabbinic period (presented in *Biblia Hebraica Stuttgartensia*). In the first century these works were not equally popular. For example, Isaiah and Psalms are widely cited in Second Temple Jewish compositions and are well attested at Qumran, in contrast to Chronicles or Ezra-Nehemiah. Works, such as Jubilees, which entered neither the Rabbinic nor Christian canons, were regarded as authoritative by certain Jewish groups of the Second Temple period.

Hebrew Text (HT): Any text of traditional Hebrew literature used in the first century CE.

Masoretic Text (MT or 𝔐): The Hebrew text, exemplified by *Biblia Hebraica Stuttgartensia*.

Proto-MT, proto-𝔐: A consonantal Hebrew text, which corresponds closely to the MT, and which is witnessed in several late Second Temple manuscripts. Proto-𝔐 became gradually standardized from the mid-second century BCE and was adopted in Rabbinic Judaism. My discussion applies between the second century BCE and the mid-first century CE. Thus, proto-𝔐 is distinguished from the Samaritan Pentateuch (SP), from text-types known from Qumran, from the Hebrew text-form underlying the OG, and from non-aligned texts (see Chapters 2 and 4).

καιγε: A Hebraizing revision of the OG. That is, a revision of the OG (towards a Hebrew text akin to proto-𝔐) represented by the first-century BCE–first-century CE Greek Minor Prophets Scroll from Naḥal Ḥever (8ḤevXIIgr). Scholars also talk of 'καιγε-Theodotion', in order to indicate a supposed relationship between the earlier καιγε revision of 8ḤevXIIgr and the late second-century CE Hebraizing revision of Theodotion (θ').

G^HR: Adopted in this book to represent any Hebraizing revision of the OG of a given work towards a Hebrew version of that work. That is, the καιγε revision represented by the first-century BCE–first-century CE Greek Minor Prophets Scroll, and the second–third-century CE versions Aquila (α'), Symmachus (σ') and Theodotion (θ').

pM: Adopted in this book to represent collectively those forms of traditional works – Hebrew versions and various types of G^HR – that reflect proto-𝔐, particularly where it differs from the OG.

Work: A literary composition. This study focuses on traditional works of Jewish literature, such as Genesis, Exodus or Isaiah, as they were known and used in the first century CE.[1] 'Work' here replaces the common terms 'book' (e.g. 'Book of Isaiah') and 'text' (e.g. 'biblical texts'). I avoid 'book' because it can evoke discussions of the physical nature of written sources, discussions that play an important role in the studies considered below (for 'text', see below).

Copy: A physical copy of a literary work that was seen, read and handled by an ancient individual.

Traditional: Designates literature that was understood by ancient persons to have been both shared by a limited community and transmitted ancestrally (hence, it is endowed with a sense of historical continuity).[2] I find that the commonly used term 'biblical', with its bookish and modern canonical connotations, forestalls some questions central to this study.

Commentators use 'text' and '*Vorlage*' inconsistently. This confuses discussions of ancient perceptions of textual plurality. The meaning of 'Text/text' varies in German and English. It can mean:

---

1   Of course, some traditional works were still circulating in multiple editions at the turn of the era, e.g. Daniel, Jeremiah, Samuel/Kings/Chronicles. Hence, I cannot assume that a given work was 'known' to all first-century Jews in the same form, or in a form recognizable to us today (Chapter Two). Bearing this in mind, I assume that first-century Jews perceived individual traditional works as recognizable objects of Jewish literary heritage.

2   Rather than ascribing empirical fixity and temporal continuity to a body of literature, my use of 'traditional' designates such an idea ascribed to it by ancient text users. A number of studies have already shown certain 'traditions' to be rhetorically rather than empirically significant (see particularly Hobsbawm and Ranger 1992).

1.   A *physical object*. 'Text' can mean a physical manuscript copy of a literary work. I use 'copy' instead of 'text'.
2.   A *visible literary object*. 'Text' can indicate the words inscribed on a manuscript.
3.   An *abstract literary object*. 'Text' can mean *literary work*. For example, commentators often designate Genesis, Exodus or Isaiah as 'texts' or 'biblical texts'.[3] Instead, I use 'work'.
4.   An *abstract text-critical object*. 'Text' can indicate a modern abstract, text-critical conceptualization of an ideal or original text-form, derived from a comparison of multiple ancient copies of a literary work and the application of text-critical criteria to distinguish secondary from the earliest retrievable readings. This taxonomical process aims to describe the perceived evolution of text-forms and it presupposes inherently modern concerns. No single copy is a true representative of any text-form. Stages and branches of this evolution are often expressed in terms of text-types, recensions, revisions and textual traditions (Chapter 2).

I adopt two distinct usages of the term text. The first indicates a *visible literary object* (2, above). Any copy of a literary work presents a text. By text I mean the words inscribed on a manuscript, which the reader sees and the hearer hears read aloud. The second usage, which I designate as «text», conveys the abstract, text-critical sense of the word (4, above).[4]

The term *Vorlage* has been assimilated into English academic parlance. It is used in various ways that reflect distinct concerns:

1.   The *written text* exhibited by a manuscript or manuscripts. '*Vorlage*' is often associated with the text-critical question of the text-form available to an ancient individual.
2.   *Manuscripts* themselves. In this sense, '*Vorlage*' is often associated with socio-historical questions, such as the expense, scarcity, unwieldiness of scrolls, their public value as holy objects, or their contribution to a literary individual's authority in public perception.
3.   *Manifestation* of a literary work to its user. Scholars debate whether Paul encountered Isaiah as a copy of Isaiah, several copies of it, a Christian *florilegium*, or a collection of his own *excerpta*. All of these could be described as manifestations of Isaiah.

These three definitions represent three common (and often overlapping) uses that, however, reflect distinct areas of concern. My use of '*Vorlage*' differs throughout, always reflecting the particular usage of a scholar in question.

An 'exegete' is a person whose aspirations to interpret literature extend beyond

---

3   Ancient Jews also perceived such works as objects of their literary heritage (see Footnote 1, above). At present, however, I am concerned with modern uses of 'text'.

4   My use of «text» is similar in some respects to Tov's '*texts*' (1992; his italics).

mute perception.[5] I use 'exegete' to indicate a person of late antiquity who engages with the textual content (written or oral) of traditional literature and seeks to interpret its meaning. While I attribute a level of literary expertise to those designated 'exegetes' in this study, the term does not presuppose any ideas about sectarian affiliation, socio-linguistic background (such as 'Palestinian', 'Diaspora' or 'Hellenized'), or any particular training (such as 'scribal', 'Pharisaic' or 'priestly').

1.1.2 *Emil Kautzsch and Hans Vollmer*

In this chapter I examine a sample of studies that are representative of existing approaches to the subject. The studies by Kautzsch and Vollmer in the nineteenth century have been particularly influential.[6]

Scholars prior to Kautzsch proposed that certain Pauline citations diverge verbally from the LXX (uncials א, A or B) because Paul appealed to a Hebrew *Vorlage*.[7] Roepe,[8] on the other hand, concludes that Paul did not cite from the Hebrew, but almost exclusively from the LXX, and almost always from memory. He suggests that two divergent citations (Rom. 9.17 – Exod. 9.16; Rom. 12.19 – Deut. 32.35) stem from other Greek versions.

Kautzsch, who focuses entirely on the text-critical problem of Paul's *Vorlagen*, confirms Roepe's findings.[9] Counting eighty-four Pauline quotations, Kautzsch derives eighty-two from the OG ('Alexandrian translation') on account of their closer or remoter agreement with the Septuagint (witnessed principally by codex A, but also א, B).[10] For Kautzsch, Paul's generally loose citation from memory accounts for variable agreement with known LXX text-forms. A handful of Paul's citations of Isaiah and the two citations of 3 Kingdoms agree with later Hebraizing revisions of OG towards proto-𝔐 (Theodotion, Aquila and Symmachus). Kautzsch concludes that Theodotion often depends on NT readings in his translation.[11] For the two citations of Job, which are closer to the Hebrew and reveal no reminiscence of the OG, Kautzsch suggests that Paul had no access to a Greek form of Job. He concludes that Paul cited a Hebrew form of Job from memory, while in all other cases he had the

---

5   While a person who hears a recited text or reads a written text inevitably takes it to mean something, 'mute perception' attributes to a person no explicit aspiration to interpretive innovation, in contrast to an exegete.

6   Kautzsch 1869; Vollmer 1895. For a thorough survey of pre-twentieth-century scholarship on Paul's use of scripture, see Stanley 1992, 4–30.

7   For example, Whiston 1722; Bleek 1828, 338–587.

8   Roepe 1827.

9   Kautzsch 1869; also Vollmer 1895, 7 and Stanley 1992, 7 [13].

10   Thirty-four agree exactly with the LXX and thirty-six deviate slightly. A further twelve deviate more strongly. According to Kautzsch, all derive ultimately from the LXX.

11   Kautzsch 1869, 95–106, esp. 104 [1]; cf. Vollmer 1895, 25. Kautzsch also suggests that marginal notes to 'ἀλλ.' in Hexaplaric texts of Isa. 59.8 refer to Paul's reading in Rom. 3.17 (Kautzsch 1869, 35f.) and argues for a number of other Pauline readings entering the LXX manuscript traditions (cf. Vollmer 1895, 14–17).

OG.[12] Kautzsch also supposes that Paul could have known some 'biblical' passages from Rabbinic versions circulated in schools.[13]

Vollmer's study follows the work of Kautzsch, forming the foundation for important twentieth-century studies of Paul's use of scripture.[14] A set of his ideas and preoccupations have influenced successive discussions. Noting the appearance of the Hatch-Redpath Septuagint concordance and Lagarde's 1882 Septuagint study,[15] Vollmer calls for a new investigation of how Paul's citations would illuminate his attitude to Jewish scripture because, as Vollmer observes, the question of Paul's attitude to scripture has 'conspicuously receded behind the text-critical question in recent German monographs'.[16] However, Vollmer stresses that such investigation cannot be separated from text-critical enquiry:

> Whether Paul cites according to the Masoretic Text or the Septuagint, whether he also makes use of other versions, whether he reproduces literally or allows himself freedom when citing, whether he always draws on his own memory or occasionally uses a Jewish compilation: these are questions which cannot be ignored when assessing the apostle's view on the Old Testament.[17]

While Vollmer asserts that the text-critical problem is not identical with the question of Paul's attitude to scripture, he considers the two issues inseparable. Thus, he commences with the 'Text-Frage'.[18] Vollmer's language concerning Paul's *Vorlagen* shows that his understanding of the state of the 'biblical' text in the first century is commensurate with the text-critical assumptions and concerns of Vollmer's day. He sees the Hebrew as the 'original' text, a concrete entity accurately represented by the Masoretic Text.[19] While he observes that it seems 'alien [. . .] to our modern critical sense that one preferred uncritically to follow the version instead of keeping to the original . . .',[20] he remarks that this translation was so widely used, that Paul (like Philo) accepted its authority without question.

While Whiston[21] views the Greek as an indicator of a 'purer' Pharisaic Hebrew

---

12 Kautzsch (1869, 108–110); cf. Vollmer 1895, 7–8: 'Sein Resultat is daher, dass Paulus nusquam consulto von der alexandrinischen Uebersetzung abweiche, ihm nur hie und da neben derselben auch der masoretische Text vorgeschwebt habe, und dass die Citate sämmtlich aus dem Gedächtnis gegeben seien.' See also Koch 1986, 57 [1].

13 Kautzsch thinks that the form of Deut. 32.35 in Rom. 12.19 partly agrees with SP and Targum Onqelos against the LXX. Kautzsch (1869, 77) suggests that Onqelos and Paul's translations flowed from a 'schulmaessig verbreite rabbinische Auffassung'(Vollmer 1895, 31–32).

14 Vollmer 1895.

15 Ibid., 28; Lagarde 1882.

16 Ibid., v; my translation.

17 Ibid.

18 Ibid., 9.

19 Ibid., v, for instance.

20 Ibid., 9; my translation.

21 Whiston 1722.

text (against a 'corrupted' Rabbinic 𝔐), for Vollmer, the Greek 'version' represents a 'Diaspora Judaism' in contrast to the Hebrew of a 'Palestinian Judaism'. Accepting Acts' presentation of Paul as a Greek-speaking Diaspora Jew with a Palestinian Semitic training in 'Rabbinic' Judaism, Vollmer deems Paul at home in both 'forms' of Judaism. Vollmer emphasizes the influence of Philo and the 'Alexandrian school' on Paul's thought,[22] but notes that this Alexandrian ethos did not fully subsume Paul's Rabbinic education.[23]

Paul did not use the Septuagint for the sake of his audiences 'while he privately made use of the Hebrew original: No, he lived himself entirely in and with the Greek text'.[24] Vollmer illustrates 'Eigentümlichkeiten der Septuaginta' that pervade Paul's language and thought, both in Paul's explicit citations and 'allusions'.[25] None of the internal lexical data from Paul's citations of scripture unambiguously indicates Paul's use of Hebrew sources.[26] Vollmer cites predecessors in support.[27] Whereas Vollmer sees the HT as a fixed entity, he acknowledges that the Greek 'version' is represented by several 'recensions', represented by third- to fifth-century LXX witnesses (codices א, A or B, as well as a recension pre-dating, but related to 'die jüngere Uebersetzung'[28]). Vollmer agrees that Paul makes extensive use of the 'Septuaginta', but asks which 'Rezensionen' were available to him and whether he used them exclusively.[29] Examining Paul's citations, Vollmer identifies a series of passages apparently available to Paul in a form divergent from the LXX.[30] He writes that 'Paul knew yet other Greek versions apart from the Septuagint', such as one resembling Theodotion or a Job Targum.[31] Vollmer can imagine that Paul, while reading the OG, had another Greek version 'in mind'.[32] However, he does not believe that Paul was able to compare multiple copies of the same work.[33]

To avoid practical difficulties arising from the idea of Paul's free use of multiple

22 For Paul's perceived dependence on Philo see Vollmer 1895, 61–73.

23 Ibid., 69. For Paul's Pharisaic education in Jerusalem, after Acts 22.3, see Vollmer 1895, 43 [1]; for Paul's 'Palestinian rabbinic schooling', see ibid., 68–69; cf. 32.

24 Ibid., 10; my translation.

25 Ibid., 12f.

26 Vollmer (1895, 41–42) suggests that Paul uses a 'younger Jewish translation' akin to α' σ' θ' (cf. ibid., 19–33 and 48). A combination of three passages in 2 Cor. 9.10 presupposes the association of Hebrew 'rain', but 'Nach der Septuaginta könnte freilich diese Zummanenstellung nicht gemacht sein'. Vollmer argues that these passages were combined in a Hebrew *florilegium* prior to Paul.

27 Heinrici 1900, 598, cited in Vollmer 1895, 8; Steck, cited in Vollmer 1895, 8.

28 Vollmer postulates a recension related to α' σ' θ' circulating 'neben der Septuaginta' in the first century CE (1895, 25–26), now confirmed as καιγε-Theodotion (Barthélemy 1963).

29 Vollmer 1895, 13.

30 Ibid.,13–21.

31 Ibid., 24–26; my translation.

32 Regarding verbal mingling of Septuagint, α', and θ' in Gal. 3.13, Vollmer suggests: 'Vielleicht schwebte dem Apostle der Wortlaut einer Uebersetzung vor', which differed from the LXX (Vollmer 1895, 29). Kautzsch also envisaged Paul reading one version while recalling another; see Footnote 12, above.

33 Vollmer 1895, 33.

copies, Vollmer argues that Paul used an available *florilegium*.[34] While Vollmer implies that Paul could have different Greek versions 'in mind' when citing,[35] he is unwilling to envisage Paul citing from memory at will. For Vollmer, Paul's ability to reproduce the wording of the LXX indicates direct citation from written sources. Although he emphasizes Paul's extensive awareness of the literary context of his citations, Vollmer proposes that Paul 'looked up' his citations.[36]

Vollmer's description of the textual profile of Paul's citations is confirmed by the studies of Koch and Stanley.[37] Unlike some of his successors (such as Deissmann, Michel, Ellis, Hengel, and to some extent, Koch[38]), Vollmer's study does not presuppose a fundamental relationship between the textual character of Paul's *Vorlagen* and the 'kind' of Judaism that Paul allegedly represents. In order to establish the textual character of Paul's sources, Vollmer prioritizes lexical evidence internal to Paul's citations. Yet, he also places significant weight on circumstantial considerations, such as his exposure to 'Rabbinic Pharisaic' and 'Philonic Alexandrian' ethos (see Footnotes 22 and 23, above). Doubting that Paul selected particular text-forms by comparing copies, and remaining cautious about overstating Paul's capacity to cite scripture from memory, Vollmer attributes a limited awareness of textual plurality to Paul.

1.2 *Dietrich-Alex Koch*

I take the studies by Koch and Ellis[39] – both highly influential – to be representative of an existing polarity in conceptualizing Paul's awareness of textual plurality.[40] Perhaps the most thorough attempt yet made to locate the *Vorlagen* of Paul's citations of scripture within the *Überlieferungsgeschichte* of the LXX,[41] Koch's 1986 study is a direct descendant of Vollmer's work.

Koch does not clearly distinguish between the two projects he pursues: his text-critical analysis of Paul's citations, and his reconstruction of Paul's written sources (*Vorlagen*). On the one hand, he establishes the textual profile of Paul's explicit citations of scripture, examining the lexical relationship between each Pauline cita-

---

34 Vollmer suggests pre-Pauline Jewish *florilegia* (ibid., 38). Following Wettstein 1751, Vollmer also points to the combination of Gen. 15.6 and Hab. 2.4 in Rabbinic tractate *Shemoth Rabba* and its similarity to Rom. 1.17. Hatch 1889 had already suggested the use of 'biblical anthologies' alongside other literature (cf. Vollmer 1895, 38).

35 See Footnote 32, above.

36 See Vollmer (1895, 11 [1]) for the reproduction of the LXX. Paul's diverse use of scripture 'setzt [. . .] einen solchen Reichtum an Stellen voraus, wie ihn auch der ehemalige Schriftgelehrten schwerlich im Kopfe tragen konnte' (ibid., 38).

37 Koch 1986; Stanley 1992.

38 Deissmann 1925; Michel 1929; Ellis 1957; Hengel 1991a; and Koch 1986.

39 Ellis 1957 and Koch 1986.

40 This division of scholarship in terms of a limited issue is arbitrarily made for heuristic purposes. There are, naturally, divergences of opinion among scholars belonging to the same 'stream', which I will point out.

41 See the review, Hays 1988, 331.

tion and available ancient manuscript witnesses to Greek Jewish scripture. On the other hand, Koch makes claims about the nature of Paul's written sources – the text presented by Paul's tangible copies. Koch's analysis of the textual profile of Paul's explicit citations (relative to known ancient Greek sources) and his reconstruction of Paul's written sources flow seamlessly together, giving the impression that they are identical. Yet the two are analytically distinct.

1.2.1 *Koch's reconstruction of Paul's written sources*

Koch limits his study to explicit citations and provides criteria for distinguishing them from allusions and verbal parallels,[42] as he considers the latter two categories unsuitable for establishing the textual character of the sources to which they may allude. Koch establishes eighty-nine explicit citations in Paul's undisputed letters, which appear in Romans, 1 and 2 Corinthians and Galatians. Sixty-six citations are indicated with explicit introductory formulae (*Einleitungsformulierungen*) in Paul's text and nineteen are marked as distinct from Paul's own text by other syntactical means. Koch includes four citations lacking any such indication.[43] He argues that of the ninety passages Paul cites in his letters, twenty-nine agree entirely with the 'received *Wortlaut* of the LXX in its oldest retrievable form'.[44]

Koch believes that Paul consistently cites from one copy of each work, a scroll (see Section 1.2.2.2, below). He describes the textual character of Paul's written source for each work on the basis of his analysis of the textual profile of Paul's citations of that work.

Honing Vollmer's findings, Koch shows that the readings of Paul's Pentateuch *Vorlage* are generally closer to those of F (and hence to A) and, remoter from the readings of B. The evidence from the minuscule groups y (closer to A and F) and f (closer to B) follows this pattern.[45]

Despite the high frequency of Pauline Psalm citations (comparable to his Isaiah citations), no precise agreement emerges between Pauline Psalm citations and the LXX text groups identified by Rahlfs.[46] Paul's citations reveal to Koch, however, that Paul's Psalms *Vorlage* is generally in close verbal agreement with the OG.

Paul's citations of The Twelve are too few for Koch to establish the textual character of Paul's Minor Prophets *Vorlage*.[47]

3 Kingdoms and Isaiah occupy a special place in the history of transmission of Greek Jewish scripture. In several instances Paul's Greek citations approximate the wording and sense of the proto-Masoretic Hebrew at points where the latter diverges

---

42 Koch 1986, 9–23.

43 Joel 2.32 (Rom. 10.13), Ps. 23.1^{LXX} (1 Cor. 10.26), Isa. 40.13 (1 Cor. 2.16), Hab. 2.4 (Gal. 3.11), (Koch 1986, 23). See Section 6.3, Table 6.1, below.

44 Ibid., 102; my translation.

45 Ibid., 53.

46 Ibid., 55; Rahlfs 1931.

47 Koch 1986, 54–55.

markedly from the OG (Job 5.13; 41.3;[48] 3 Kgdms 19.10, 18;[49] Isa. 8.14; 25.8; 28.11; 52.7). This proximity led Ellis to suggest that Paul made direct use of Hebrew versions of these works.[50] Koch, affirming Vollmer's suggestion, concludes that in these cases Paul's *Vorlagen* had already undergone Hebraizing revisions, aimed at harmonizing OG with proto-𝔐.[51]

The early first-century CE Greek Minor Prophets Scroll (8HevXIIgr) represents a revision of the OG towards a first-century Hebrew source, apparently close to proto-𝔐. Indeed, this 'καιγε' project may pre-date the turn of the era.[52] According to Koch, both Paul's Job and 3 Kingdoms *Vorlagen* had undergone similar comprehensive Hebraizing revisions, each displaying its own distinct revisionist tendencies.[53]

The textual character of Paul's Isaiah *Vorlage* is more complex. Paul cites from Isaiah more than from any other work, so Koch's results for Paul's Isaiah *Vorlage* are the most comprehensive. Ziegler[54] divided Isaiah[LXX] into two dominant text groups: the older Alexandrian text (represented by majuscules A and *Q*, generally supported by S) and the younger Hexaplaric text (represented by majuscules B and V). Koch concludes that Paul's Isaiah *Vorlage* agrees chiefly with the Alexandrian.[55] So the majority of Paul's citations of Isaiah reveal a «text» corresponding to the oldest retrievable form of the OG in Isaiah.

Koch reconciles this Alexandrian Isaiah «text» with Hebraizing Pauline Isaiah citations (Isa. 8.14; 25.8; 28.11; 52.7), suggesting that Paul's Isaiah *Vorlage* had undergone a partial Hebraizing revision at precisely the points where the LXX 'sich nicht nur in der Wiedergabe einzelner Wörter gegenüber dem HT frei verhält, sondern auch die zugrunde liegende syntaktische Struktur umgestaltet hat'.[56] Koch argues, then, that discrete verses had undergone Hebraizing revision throughout this Alexandrian *Vorlage* at those points where OG and proto-𝔐 diverge most radically. Since the Hebraizing verses Paul cites span all of Isaiah (chs 8, 25, 28 and 52), Koch concludes that this revision was made at discrete points throughout Paul's copy. This

---

48 Ibid., 71–73.

49 Ibid., 73–77.

50 See Section 1.5, below. Kautzsch also wondered whether Paul knew Job in Hebrew (see Footnote 12, above).

51 Koch 1986, 57, 59.

52 Barthélemy 1950 dated 8HevXIIgr to the late first century CE, while Barthélemy 1963 dated 8HevXIIgr to the mid-first century CE. Roberts (Roberts and Skeat 1983 [1954], 45–62) dates 8HevXIIgr to 50 BCE–50 CE, while Skeat (ibid.) dates it to the second century CE (cf. Tov *et al.* 1990, 22–26; cf. Marcos 2000, 192).

53 Koch concludes (with Schaller 1980) that Paul's Job *Vorlage* was a Hebraizing recension of LXX[Job] close to those known from the Berlin papyrus fragment P 11778 and from Testament of Job (Koch 1986, 71). He also concludes that Paul's 3 Kingdoms *Vorlage* was a Hebraizing LXX recension with a distinct recensional tendency and method akin to that of Paul's Job *Vorlage* (ibid., 79).

54 Ziegler 1939.

55 Koch 1986, 48.

56 Ibid., 78.

reconstruction is reminiscent of Deissmann's suggestion that Paul 'einen Septuaginta Text benutzt hat, der an einzelnen Stellen bereits eine jüdische Revision erlebt hatte'.[57]

Koch argues that Paul never appealed to Hebrew copies.[58] Paul's Hebraizing citations (close to 𝔐 against the LXX) indicate Hebraizing revisions in Paul's *Vorlage*. He doubts that Paul used Aramaic Targums. In the few cases where Paul's citation approximates a Targum against the LXX or 𝔐 (e.g. Jer. 9.22-23[LXX]; Deut. 32.35; Isa. 64.3), Koch proposes that Paul relied on traditions that originated in the Diaspora synagogue and entered early Christian liturgy as oral traditions.[59]

It is noteworthy that, while Koch confirms the textual profile of Paul's citations established by Vollmer, he differs with respect to his evaluation of Paul's sources. That is, Koch believes that Paul cited from a scroll of each work, whereas Vollmer supposes that Paul used a *florilegium*. This telling divergence shows that a distinction must be made between the 'textual profile' of Paul's citations and the nature of his 'sources'. Textual profile is an expression of the lexical relation of any given text to taxonomically derived text-critical categories, in this case the relation of Paul's citation to the LXX recensions and revisions distilled by textual critics from the sum of ancient manuscripts and their total lexical variation. This process is distinct from considering the kind of written source Paul used on any given occasion. This distinction, which I make throughout this study, bears directly on the question of how ancient exegetes encountered literature and textual variations within it.

1.2.2 *Koch's conclusions*

Koch makes three proposals that are significant for the present study:

(a) Paul cited directly from written sources ('*Vorlagen*') rather than from memory.

(b) Between circa 48 and circa 58 CE Paul cited exclusively from one copy of each work of scripture.

(c) Paul cited from his sources uncritically with no awareness of the available variant text-forms. Paul was unaware of textual plurality.

Koch provides material arguments to demonstrate that (a) Paul predominantly cited directly from *Vorlagen* rather than memory,[60] arguments which I discuss below (Section 1.2.3). It is first important, however, to understand the role of (b) and (c) in Koch's study. In his discussion of Isaiah, Job and 3 Kingdoms *Vorlagen*, Koch explicitly presents (b) and (c) as *conclusions* arising out of his analysis. However, (b) and (c) are in fact assumptions that predicate his method and form the basis for his analysis. Koch provides only incidental justification for (b) and (c) throughout

---

57 Deissmann 1925, 80–81 (cf. Deissmann 1926, 100). See also Deissmann 1905, 69f. and Rahlfs 1921, 182ff.

58 Koch (1986, 19 [30], 57 [3], 78, 80 [112]) rejects the claim of Ellis (1957, 139 and 153) that Paul used both Semitic and Greek sources.

59 Koch 1986, 36, 77–78, 41.

60 Koch 1986, esp. 92.

his work, but offers no united argument. Here I highlight the analytical significance of Koch's assumptions.

1.2.2.1 *(a) Paul generally cited directly from written sources*

Aside from the ten instances in which Koch thinks that Paul cites from memory, he argues from lexical data within Paul's letters that Paul cited directly from written sources. Apart from these arguments from evidence internal to Paul's letters – which I survey and critique in Section 1.2.3, below – Koch appeals to general historical considerations. It would not have been prohibitively expensive for Paul to access the quantity of scrolls indicated by the number and range of citations in his letters.[61] While the private possession of eight scrolls indicates a particularly pious household in *4 Macc.* 18.10-19, Koch argues that financial support from Paul's communities would have funded his own copy of each of the works that he frequently cites.[62]

Moreover, Koch argues that, prior to composition, Paul followed the 'geläufige' ancient 'Arbeitstechnik' of consulting sources and collecting literary notes or excerpts ('selbst erstellte Exzerpte').[63] This included Paul's preparation of 'biblical' proof texts, which he incorporated into his letters.[64] 2 Tim. 4.13 refers to 'biblical scrolls' (τὰ βιβλία) and 'parchment notebooks' (τὰς μεμβράνας), suggesting to Koch that Paul used the latter for note taking and composition. Stanley develops this idea (see Section 1.3 and Section 1.8.2.1, below). Koch dismisses the view that Paul used a Jewish or a Christian *florilegium*.[65]

1.2.2.2 *(b) Paul only ever cited from one copy of each work*

Koch provides material arguments to demonstrate that (a) Paul cited predominantly from written sources in a direct manner rather than from memory. However, Koch does not address the implicit step required to move from the evidence that Paul generally used written sources to his more specific contention that (b) between circa 48 and circa 58 CE Paul only cited from one copy of each work.

Koch does make some passing statements on the matter. Having reconstructed Paul's Isaiah, Job and 3 Kingdoms *Vorlagen*, he expresses doubt that Paul made critical use of multiple copies of Isaiah: '[D]aß er sich um mehrere Texte z. B. von Jes mit unterschiedlicher Textform bemühte, diese erwarb und kritisch-abwägend benutze, ist eine abwegige Vorstellung . . .' He continues:

> Für Paulus ist es dagegen wesentlich wahrscheinlicher, 1. daß sein jeweiliger Jes-, Hi- und
> III Reg-Text alle feststellbaren vorpaulinischen Zitatkorrekturen enthielt, d.h. daß es sich

---

61 Ibid., 99–101.
62 Ibid., 101.
63 Ibid., 99.
64 Ibid., 99–100. Koch points to Pliny as exemplary of this ancient technique (see Section 1.8.2.1, below).
65 Ibid., 9, 247–256.

jeweils um eine einzige, rezensierte Textfassung des betreffenden Buches handelte; 2. daß Paulus sich der Unterschiede zwischen seinem rezensierten Jes-, Hi- und III Reg-Text und der unrezensierten Fassung dieser Bücher gar nicht bewußt war.[66]

Koch presents this pair of propositions as conclusions drawn from his reconstruction. But these propositions must properly be seen as the key assumptions that form the basis for his method of reconstructing Paul's *Vorlagen*.

Koch's reconstruction of the Pauline *Vorlagen* presupposes his proposition that (b) Paul only cited from a single copy of each work. The data assembled by Koch to show that Paul's Isaiah *Vorlage* belonged to the 'Alexandrian text-type' (rather than the Hexaplaric) are taken from three letters: Galatians ($\times$ 1), 1 Corinthians ($\times$ 2) and Romans ($\times$ 12).[67] Similarly, the Isaiah citations that reveal the partial Hebraizing revision of Paul's Isaiah source derive from 1 Corinthians (Isa. 25.8; 28.11) and Romans (Isa. 8.14 and 52.7). Because Koch's overall reconstruction of Paul's Isaiah *Vorlage* depends on data drawn from three letters, Koch must assume that Paul only cited from one copy of Isaiah. The same is true of Koch's reconstruction of Paul's Job *Vorlage*, for which he derives data from 1 Corinthians and Romans,[68] as well as his reconstruction of Paul's Pentateuch *Vorlage*, data for which is drawn from Galatians, 2 Corinthians and Romans.[69] When Koch states that it is 'wesentlich wahrscheinlicher' that Paul used a single copy of Isaiah, Job and 3 Kingdoms, his 'wahrscheinlich' is misplaced; far from being a probable conclusion derived from his analysis, the proposition is axiomatic to his method.

Koch's proposition that (b) Paul only ever cited from a single copy of each work of scripture is ultimately founded on the proposition that (c) Paul cited from his written sources uncritically, being unaware of various available text-forms. Were Koch to concede that Paul could critically select readings from various text-forms at different times, his reconstruction of a single Pauline *Vorlage* from letters written over a period of ten years would be unjustifiable. Hence, the proposition that (c) Paul cited from his written sources uncritically, being unaware of various available text-forms, is the linchpin of Koch's argument.

Koch founds his claim that Paul only referred to his own copy of each work on the assumption that Paul was unable to compare multiple copies of a given work. He rejects the possibility that Paul could have accessed synagogue scrolls on his missionary journeys because Acts reports that Paul was routinely ejected from the synagogues of Asia Minor.[70]

---

66 Ibid., 80–81.
67 Ibid., 49.
68 Ibid., 71–73.
69 Ibid., 52.
70 Ibid., 99 [42]. Although elsewhere Koch concedes that 2 Cor. 11.24 (thirty-nine strokes) shows that Paul must have performed in synagogues (ibid., 89 [7]).

1.2.2.3 *(c) Paul cited without awareness of variant versions*

By doubting Paul's awareness that some of his citations reflected Hebraizing revisions of the OG, Koch again agrees with Vollmer. To accept Paul's familiarity with variant versions of particular works, argues Koch, would be 'anachronistic' and would credit Paul with 'weit fortgeschrittener exegetischer Arbeit' of the kind later undertaken by Origen or Eusebius.[71]

Koch never explicitly presents this as a united argument, but asserts throughout his study that Paul cited unwittingly from various text-forms. I refer to this as his 'suitability argument'. Koch considers that in some cases the form of a passage cited by Paul is verbally less suitable for Paul's argument than another. This applies to Paul's citations of Job 5.13 (1 Cor. 3.19)[72]; Isa. 25.8 (1 Cor. 15.54)[73]; 28.11 (1 Cor. 14.21)[74]; 59.20 (Rom. 11.26)[75]; and Hos. 2.1^{LXX} (Rom. 9.25).[76] Had Paul been in a position to make a critical choice in these cases, reasons Koch, he would surely have chosen the more suitable form. These decisions, however, are based on Koch's own judgement about the suitability of a particular reading for Paul's argument. In Section 7.4 I argue that this argument is weak and that the examples do not contribute to a cumulative case.

1.2.3 *Paul's limited command of the literary content of scripture*

Koch credits Paul with a limited familiarity with the literary content of scripture that he learned 'in der hellenistischen Synagogue'. Koch distinguishes

> zwischen einer allgemeinen Vertrautheit mit den wichtigsten Überlieferungsinhalten der Schrift und einer sicheren Kenntnis des Textes einer nicht unbeträchtlichen Anzahl von Schriftworten [. . .], die ja erst die Anführung eines bestimmten Wortlauts aus dem Gedächtnis ermöglichte.

He credits Paul with only a general familiarity with the most important traditional contents ('die wichtigsten Überlieferungsinhalte') of scripture, denying (conversely) that Paul had 'die Fähigkeit, für einen bestimmten Zusammenhang eine geeignete Schriftaussage heranziehen und auch im Wortlaut wiedergeben zu können'.[77]

Koch does not accept that Paul could cite scripture from memory, noting that many (Ellis and Michel in particular) overestimate Paul's mental 'Schriftkenntnis'.[78] He argues from lexical data internal to Paul's letters that he cited directly from a written copy rather than from memory. However, these arguments (listed as i–v, immediately

---

71 Ibid., 80–81.
72 Ibid., 80 [113], 72.
73 Ibid., 80 [113].
74 Ibid., 80 [113], 65.
75 Ibid., 177 [34].
76 Ibid., 55 [34].
77 Ibid., 92.
78 Koch (1986, 92) cites Michel 1929 and Ellis 1957; cf. Koch 1986, 94 [15].

below[79]) presuppose that citation from memory would inevitably result in deviation from the wording of G^Ed.

(i)   Paul can accurately reproduce the wording of his *Vorlage* in 40 per cent of the passages he cites (thirty-seven of ninety-three).[80] Koch supposes that one can only do this when one cites directly from a written copy.

(ii)   Paul usually follows his *Vorlage* closely when using κύριος and θεός. Koch believes that confusion of divine titles would be inevitable if Paul cited from memory.[81] This assumption is questionable because divine titles were clearly a matter of great importance in Greek and Hebrew texts of the period.[82]

(iii) In fifty-two of Paul's citations Koch attributes distinctive wording of Paul's citations to Paul's intentional alteration of his source, not memory error.[83] Koch hereby assumes that the alterations are *only* conceivable as a result of textual work from copies.

(iv)   Hence, longer strings of combined citations (such as Rom. 3.10-18) are placed strategically in the structure of the surrounding Pauline context, pointing to a planned composition, of which Koch can only conceive as the result of sustained textual work from manuscripts. It remains an assumption that citation from memory could not have been incorporated into planned composition. One does not need to assume that memory citations could only be inserted into the composition 'erst im Augenblick des Briefdiktats', as does Koch.

(v)   Finally, in two instances where Paul cites the same verse twice (Lev. 18.5 in Rom. 10.5 and Gal. 3.11; Isa. 28.16c in Rom. 9.33 and 10.11), he does so once according to his source and once in an altered form.[84] Koch reasons that, because Paul is able to replicate the source-wording of each citation once, the change he makes to each cannot be a memory error. But this is only an argument against memory *error*, not against citation from memory as such, because there is no way to test whether each was cited *and altered* from memory.

Koch identifies nine citations that he argues were made directly from a copy,[85] and

---

79 The following arguments are presented in Koch 1986, 95–96, unless otherwise stated.

80 Koch identifies ninety-three individual passages reproduced by Paul (ibid., 33, 186, cf. 21–23) in one hundred and six separate citations (ibid., 33). Of the ninety-three, Paul modifies fifty-two (ibid., 186). In four cases Koch cannot identify the origin of the Pauline reading. Of the remaining thirty-seven: in twenty-nine Paul reproduces the earliest recoverable *Wortlaut* of the OG (G^Ed) (ibid., 102); in eight Paul's wording diverges from the OG, but that divergence is not attributable to Paul (ibid., 186 cf. 57–76).

81 Ibid., 93; cf. 86f.

82 See Marcos 2000, 311–313 and Stegemann 1969.

83 Koch 1986, 102, 186.

84 Paul also cites Lev. 19.18 twice (Gal. 5.14 and Rom. 13.9) but each citation is identical with the LXX.

85 Direct citations (Koch 1986, 96, 188–189). Eight are citations of 'Rezensionen', which, he considers, can only have existed 'in schriftlicher Gestalt' ('written form') (ibid., 96, cf. 80). These are: 3 Kgdms 19.10, 18; Job 5.13; 41.3; Isa. 8.14; 25.8; 28.11; 52.7. He adds to this a ninth, Isa. 10.22, which (along with Isa. 52.7) exhibits haplography in Paul's citation (ibid., 81–83, 96).

ten which he believes to have been made from memory.[86] He notes that seven of the nine 'direct citations' exhibit Pauline alteration, but only three of the ten 'memory citations' reveal Pauline alteration.[87] He concludes that the 'general phenomenon' ('Gesamtphänomen') of modification of citations in Paul's letters is a feature of direct citation, not an error of memory. However, given the sparseness of the evidence, his conclusion, that Paul almost always cited directly, is adventurous. Apart from the nine direct citations and the ten from memory, Koch counts a further seventy-four whose manner of citation cannot be established, conceding that in some cases errors of memory cannot be ruled out.[88]

Paul did not cite directly from written sources in the two 'Gefangenschaftsbriefe', Philippians and Philemon, and in the parts of 2 Corinthians apparently written in haste.[89] Koch infers that Paul fails to cite scripture explicitly whenever no copies are to hand. However, Paul also fails to cite scripture under other circumstances; 1 Thessalonians was not apparently written from prison. And Romans 5–8, an integral part of that letter in which Paul cites most prolifically, contains only two citations: Exod. 20.17a = Deut. 5.21a (Rom. 7.7), one of the Decalogue, which Koch considers so common for Paul to have known from memory;[90] the other is Ps. 43.23[LXX] (Rom. 8.36).

Koch's general claim that Paul primarily cited directly from written sources is a possible way of accounting for the evidence. However, problems with Koch's approach – highlighted here and in Section 1.7, below – render his claim undemonstrated.

1.3 *Others of the stream represented by Koch*

1.3.1 *Adolf Deissmann and Otto Michel*

Predecessors of Koch's work, notably the studies of Deissmann and Michel,[91] similarly belong to Vollmer's text-critical lineage. Deissmann, like Vollmer, records the profound influence that the 'Septuaginta' has on Paul's language and thought. On the basis of this influence, Deissmann doubts that Paul was educated in Judaea (Acts 22.3).[92] He writes: 'Urteilt man dann aber aus dem Gesamteindruck heraus, den der uns bekannte Paulus macht, so ist es doch wohl wahrscheinlich, dass der Sohn

---

86 Ibid., 95. Koch identifies ten cases of memory citation: (1) 1 Cor. 1.31 (= 2 Cor. 10.17); 2.9; 9.10b (passages derived from an oral text-transmission); (2) Isa. 11.10a-c; 28.16; and 59.20-21 (passages subject to pre-Pauline Christian alteration, known to Paul in oral form); (3) Lev. 19.18; Deut. 5.17-21; 19.15; 32.35 (presumed already current in early Christianity and familiar through oral tradition).

87 Ibid.

88 Ibid., 189.

89 Ibid., 96–97.

90 Koch thinks that Rom. 7.7 reproduces Exod. 20.17a (οὐκ ἐπιθυμήσεις). However, he takes Deut. 5.21 (οὐκ ἐπιθυμήσεις) to have been the common fare of memory, cf. Koch 1986, 95; see Footnote 86, above.

91 Deissmann 1925 and Michel 1929.

92 Whereas Vollmer accepts Acts 22.3. See Footnote 23, above.

von Tarsus seine Knabenzeit in der hellenistischen Vaterstadt verlebt hat.'[93] This 'Gesamteindruck' consists of Paul's mastery of 'hellenistische Umgangssprache'[94] and the profound influence which the Septuagint has on Paul's logic: 'Will man den ganzen Paulus religionsgeschichtlich verstehen, so muss man den Geist der Septuginta kennen. Nicht das hebräische Alte Testament . . .'[95]

Michel builds on Vollmer's text-critical study of Paul's citations, affirming Vollmer's observation that the language and thought of the LXX deeply pervade Paul's writing.[96] Michel further develops Vollmer's observation that Paul's sources at times reflect Theodotion against the LXX.[97] In agreement with both Vollmer before him and Koch after him, he denies that Paul cited from Hebrew scripture.

Like Vollmer,[98] but in contrast to Koch,[99] Michel accepts that Paul received a Pharisaic education in Jerusalem and spoke Hebrew (Acts 22.2-3): 'Es ist selbstverständlich, dass er imstande war, den hebraeischen Urtext seiner Bibel zu lesen, aber er lebt und arbeitet nur mit seiner griechischen Bibel.'[100] Two passages persuade Michel that Paul did not consult Hebrew copies when writing his letters. First, Michel observes that Paul's allusion to Exod. 12.40 in Gal. 3.17 follows the 'faulty' chronology of the LXX rather than that of 𝔐. 'Selbst dann hält [Paulus] an dieser [d.h. LXX] fest, wenn sie Fehler und Ungenauigkeiten aufweist.'[101] (Michel questionably assumes that Paul would share Michel's own standard of 'faultiness'.) Second, in 1 Cor. 2.16 Paul cites Isa. 40.13, according to the LXX, where according to Michel, 'der massoretiche Text seinen Worten veil günstiger wäre'.[102] By prioritizing such internal lexical evidence of Paul's letters over external evidence (in this case Acts' claims about Paul's socio-linguistic ethos), Michel's method is akin to that of Vollmer, Koch and Stanley.

While Michel allows allusions to inform his study, Koch and Stanley altogether exclude them for the sake of accuracy in establishing the textual profile of Paul's citations with reference to the LXX transmission history. Michel shares Roepe's and Kautzsch's assumption that Paul's deviations from the LXX result from erroneous citations from memory. He takes combined and mixed citations as the principal

93 Deissmann 1925, 71.
94 Ibid., 71.
95 Ibid., 79; cf. 80.
96 Michel 1929, 55–68.
97 Ibid., 63f.
98 See Footnote 23, above.
99 See Footnote 190, below.
100   For Michel (1929, 68), Paul was familiar with Palestinian synagogue practices, which Michel considers to be exemplified by later Tannaitic literature. He refers to synagogue practices mentioned in Megilla (4:2ff.): 'Paulus war Diasporajude und als solche zunächst mit den Gewohnheiten der Diaspora vertraut, aber sein aufenthalt in Jerusalem wird ihn auch mit den Gepflogenheiten Palästinas bekannt gemacht haben' (Michel 1929, 112–113).
101   Michel 1929, 68.
102   Ibid.

evidence for his argument for Paul's citation from memory,[103] assuming that passages become mixed through memory error.[104]

1.3.2 *Christopher Stanley*

Stanley's work seeks to temper Koch's approach with a scale of probability for Paul's modification of the wording of his sources.[105] Stanley examines Paul's handling of the 'wording of his biblical quotations' and the 'wording of his source text'.[106] He praises Koch for his precision in setting 'the criteria for determining what constitutes "citation"'.[107] He further commends Koch's limiting his evidence to explicit citations; that is, citations to which Paul alerts his audience, which Stanley calls a 'reader-centred' approach to Paul's citation.[108] However, Stanley argues that Koch's criteria attribute too high a literary competence to Paul's original audience. Seeking to narrow the criteria for explicit citation in Paul's letters,[109] Stanley argues:

> The strength of the [reader-centred] approach lies in its conservatism: investigation is limited to a body of texts whose status as citations is reasonably assured, thus minimising the possibility that the results will be contaminated by the accidental inclusion of heterogeneous materials.[110]

In order to argue that Paul made conscious exegetical alterations to his written sources, Koch must first establish the wording of those sources prior to Paul's alteration.[111] Stanley criticizes the rigidity of Koch's 'all or nothing' approach,[112] finding Koch's reconstructions of Paul's sources and his judgements regarding Paul's alterations of them overly confident.[113]

Stanley entirely accepts Koch's arguments for direct citation from written sources[114] (summarized in Section 1.2.3, above), taking Paul's verbal reproduction of the OG (essentially G^{Ed}) to indicate direct citation from copies, not from memory.[115] Stanley rules out Paul's preference for a particular form of a given passage because he doubts that Paul simultaneously compared multiple copies of the same work.[116]

---

103   Ibid., 10, especially 80–82, 86–87, 217. See also ibid., 71, 73.
104   Ibid., 80.
105   Stanley 1992, 56–61.
106   Ibid., 4.
107   Ibid., 35.
108   Ibid., 33–35.
109   Ibid., 37.
110   Ibid., 34 (reiterated ibid., 56).
111   See Koch 1986, 186.
112   Stanley 1992, 56.
113   Ibid., 55–56. Lim (1991) also criticizes Koch's confidence in his ability to recover the sources of Paul's citations.
114   Stanley 1992, 70.
115   Ibid., 69, 71.
116   Ibid., 71; cf. Section 2.2.3, below.

Stanley emphasizes the difficulty Paul would experience in looking up a verse in a long, unwieldy scroll.[117] He does not accept Koch's solution that Paul used a single 'eclectic' Isaiah *Vorlage*, finding such an eclectic copy unlikely.[118] Instead, observing ancient authors' use of wax tablets for drafting literary compositions and collecting literary extracts, Stanley develops Koch's hypothesis that Paul compiled his 'biblical' *excerpta* in wax notebooks (see Section 1.8.2.1, below).[119] Citing Luke-Acts' narrative of Jewish hostility to Paul in Asia Minor, Stanley rules out Paul's access to synagogue scrolls during his travels,[120] proposing instead that Paul used scrolls housed in his own communities.[121] When Paul came to cite scripture, he did not encounter the full text of each work, but rather his own *excerpta*. Such dislocation of passages from their traditional literary context explains to Stanley the semantic departure of many of Paul's citations from their literary contexts.[122] Like Koch, then, Stanley believes that Paul only used Jewish scripture in Greek[123] and had a limited command of its literary contents.

Unlike Koch, Stanley believes that Paul consulted different copies of a literary work at different times and places, which to him explains the textual diversity encountered in Paul's citations. While he denies that Paul could compare copies simultaneously in order to select a preferable reading, he notes that some citations 'reveal Paul's *familiarity* with revised editions of the Old Greek text'.[124] By accepting the possibility of Paul's access to multiple copies, and so attributing to Paul some awareness of textual plurality, Stanley diverges from Koch. This divergence does not

117   Ibid., 17: 'the difficulties associated with looking up specific verses in a bulky scroll while composing a letter are real'; cf. ibid., 69 '. . . the immense difficulties associated with looking up individual references in multiple unmarked scrolls in the process of composing a letter'.

118   He argues that, since the citations from one work (Isaiah) within the same letter (Romans) include agreements not only with 'each of the major text-families of the Septuagint', but also with a pre-Christian G^{HR}, these citations cannot derive from a single eclectic copy (ibid., 69; cf. 73 [27], 254). In a number of comments Stanley expresses his view of the limits of the eclecticism possible in a given copy. '[T]he biblical text was by no means so fluid that one has to suspend all judgement concerning its specific content.' The 'diversity' of biblical scrolls from the Judaean Desert 'is not fluid or chaotic but conforms to a clear and simple pattern consisting of distinct families limited in number' (ibid., 48, citing Cross 1966, 84). Stanley acknowledges that 'all individual manuscripts are ultimately eclectic, so that no single manuscript reflects in full the characteristics of the textual family with which it is associated' (1992, 69). However, this eclecticism is ultimately limited and thus 'Paul's biblical text can be defined more narrowly as belonging to [a] particular strand in the extant Septuagint manuscript tradition' (ibid., 68). His frequent 'standard text' indicates his view of limits of eclecticism (e.g. 31, 57, 58, 60, 70 [21]). In fact, a highly eclectic first-century copy is conceivable (see Section 2.1.1, below).

119   Paul's citations from Isa. 52.5 and 52.7 represent the OG and a G^{HR} respectively, demonstrating that Paul referred to different copies at different times and noted down isolated citations (Stanley 1992, 73–78 cf. 255 [12], 256 [15]) in wax notebooks.

120   Ibid., 17 [50], 71. In this, Stanley agrees with Koch, against Michel and Ellis.

121   Ibid., 73 [27].

122   Ibid., 74 and 78.

123   Ibid., 67, appealing to Michel's argument against Paul's use of Hebrew scripture; see Section 1.3.1, above.

124   Stanley 1992, 51 [59]; my italics.

lead to any significant disagreement with Koch, however, as both scholars rule out Paul's ability to select a preferred form of a particular passage.

1.4 *The stream represented by Koch and Paul's awareness of textual plurality*

I have called for a careful distinction between textual criticism of Paul's citations and speculation about the manifestation of his actual written sources. Vollmer, Deissmann, Koch, and Stanley's various propositions regarding Paul's sources – *florilegia*, scrolls, *excerpta* – are all compatible with the established textual profile of Paul's citations. While disagreeing about the nature of Paul's sources, they all attribute the textual diversity of Paul's citations to his sources rather than to Paul himself. Vollmer attributes this textual diversity to the early Christian compilers of the *florilegia*; Deissmann and Koch to Jewish scribes who produced Hebraizing revisions; and Stanley to the diversity of manuscripts in various early Christian communities.

These conclusions hinge on the pragmatic question of Paul's access to multiple copies of a given work. The scholars mentioned doubt that Paul could compare several copies of the same work (see Section 2.2.3). According to Koch, moreover, Paul could not know of the existence of various first-century text-forms of the OG ('revisions' and 'recensions') in circulation. An important distinction is to be made between an ancient exegete's comparison of multiple *copies* of a work and his perception of different *text-forms* of that work (see Section 2.2.3). The former is a pragmatic-historical question while the latter is a modern text-critical idea attributed to Paul anachronistically.

Regarding Paul's awareness of textual plurality, three issues are perennially significant:
1. Paul's use of Semitic sources
2. Paul's access to multiple copies of the same work
3. Paul's citation from memory

The first issue is characterized by difficulties reconciling lexical evidence internal to Paul's letters with circumstantial evidence, such as biographical details from Acts or Paul's own claim to being a 'Pharisee' or a 'Hebrew of Hebrews'. The second and third issues prove problematic within the lineage of enquiry discussed above because 'access to multiple copies' and 'memory citation' are seen to introduce ambiguity into the primary evidence – Paul's citations – for particular text-critical approaches to Paul's sources. The approach represented by Ellis throws these questions into relief.

1.5 *E. Earle Ellis*

Ellis affirms Kautzsch, Vollmer and Michel's observations of the general 'affinities' of Paul's 'style and vocabulary' with the LXX.[125] However, he finds that Deissmann 'perhaps overstates it', when he claims that 'to understand Paul . . . we must know the spirit of the LXX'.[126] Ellis, unconvinced that Kautzsch and Vollmer resolved the question of Paul's command of Hebrew,[127] thinks that Paul demonstrates considerable knowledge of Hebrew (particularly in some Isaiah citations and in his two Job citations)[128] and occasionally performs his own '*ad hoc* rendering' of the Hebrew.[129]

Ellis believes that Paul perceived Greek and Hebrew versions of Jewish scripture as distinct identifiable quantities and was aware of textual differences between them. Hence, at times Paul preferred the LXX to the Hebrew[130] and at times vice versa.[131] While some appeals to the Hebrew may be attributable to pre-Pauline Christians,[132] Ellis' Paul emerges as a bilingual first-century Jew, whose writing and thought reflect a mingling of Semitic and Greek-speaking milieus.

> It was only natural that Paul, retaining in his mind Hebrew concepts and thought-forms, should frame his Greek on the analogy of the existing theological vocabulary of the LXX. Even where the apostle quite evidently sees in a citation the underlying connotations of the Hebrew, the Alexandrian version remains his mode of expression.[133]

Ellis observes that after the translation of the OG, Greek words acquire something of the value of the Hebrew words that they represent and vice versa.[134] Ellis further envisages interaction between Paul's direct citation from a Greek copy and from his memory of the Hebrew, arguing that Paul used the LXX, correcting it according to 𝔐.[135] In this Ellis differs from Koch and Stanley, who draw a sharp distinction between direct citation from a copy and citation from memory.[136] In Sections 2.3-2.6, below, I return to the notion of Paul reading one form of a passage while thinking of another form of it.

125 Ellis (1957, 12–14) also notes similar findings of Swete (1900), Nägeli (1905) and others.
126 Ellis 1957, 13 [1], citing Deissmann 1926.
127 Ellis 1957, 19 [6].
128 For Ellis, the Isaiah citations in Rom. 10.15; 1 Cor. 14.21 and 15.54 show Paul's knowledge of the Hebrew (ibid., 12 [3]); Paul knew Job most intimately in Hebrew (ibid., 144 [3]). For further examples see ibid., 14, 19 and 20.
129 Ibid., 139.
130 For example, ibid., 143.
131 For example, ibid., 144–145.
132 Ibid., 145.
133 Ibid., 13.
134 Ibid., 13, citing Dodd 1965. See further: Bratsiotis 1966; Isaacs 1976.
135 For example, Ellis 1957, 14.
136 Vollmer envisages Paul holding one version of a passage 'in his mind's eye', while directly referring to another, the two versions consequently fusing in Paul's text (see Footnote 32, above).

According to Ellis, Paul not only distinguished between Greek and Hebrew versions, but also between various Greek versions; that is, the OG and its Hebraizing revision, 'proto-Theodotion'. Envisioning Paul performing 'an interpretative selection from various known texts',[137] Ellis implies that Paul could distinguish between distinct text-forms of given works and could privilege particular readings by comparing multiple copies of the same work. Like Koch, Ellis imagines Paul carrying scrolls around with him (on the basis of 2 Tim 4.13). Unlike Koch, he believes that Paul also read scrolls in the synagogues of Asia Minor, in which he preached, as Acts reports.[138] Ellis accepts Paul's Pharisaic education in Jerusalem (Acts 22.3, 26.4-5). '[A]part from Christianity,' he writes, 'it is probable that Palestinian Judaism was the only determinative influence in Paul's life.'[139]

Ellis credits Paul with the expert ability to cite scripture from memory. Commenting on Paul's citation of a diverse range of text-forms (i.e. 'LXX . . . Hebrew . . . Aramaic targumim . . . other Greek translations'), he writes:

> [I]t might be expected that one who knew the Scripture in several languages and had a thorough knowledge of the sense of Scripture would be less tied to any text-form. 'Memory quotation' should be understood, however, as a free rendering in accordance with literary custom, or for an exegetical purpose, rather than as a result of 'memory' lapse. The importance of scriptural memorisation for the Jews, Paul's Rabbinic training, and the verbal exactness of many of his quotations, militate against the latter explanation.[140]

Where for others exactness is a mark of 'direct' citation from a copy, for Ellis it is a sign of memorization.

Ellis' proposition that Paul combined direct citation from Greek copies with his memory of Semitic versions is attractive in that it neither rests too heavily on either model of ancient citation (citing directly from copies or from memory) nor polarizes the two approaches. Ellis' view, that exegetes' memory of variant forms supplemented their perception of written copies, is sensitive to the complexities of textual perception, memory and composition. Unfortunately, Ellis does not develop this critical point.

1.6 *The stream represented by Ellis*

Hengel accepts Koch's reconstruction of the Isaiah *Vorlage*: a copy representing OG Isaiah, which had undergone partial Hebraizing revision.[141] However, Hengel

---

137   Ellis 1957, 139.
138   Ibid., 19 [5].
139   Ibid., 38. Ellis appeals to van Unnik's (1973) argument for the reliability of Acts 22.3.
140   Ellis 1957, 14–15.
141   Hengel 1991a.

contends that Paul, as a 'Schriftgelehrte',[142] produced his own Isaiah *Vorlage* for himself – not directly from the Hebrew, as Ellis proposed – but on the basis of Paul's 'knowledge of revised versions' of the Greek.[143] Hengel criticizes Koch for claiming that 'Paul was not even aware of the differences between his revised text of Isaiah, Job and 3 Kingdoms and the unrevised versions of these books'.[144]

Appealing to van Unnik,[145] Hengel defends Acts' testimony to Paul's childhood Pharisaic education in Jerusalem.[146] Even without Acts, he argues, Paul's own auto-biographical statements prove him a Hebrew-speaking Judaean Jew: Gal. 1.22 does not show Paul's meeting with Cephas to be his first visit to Jerusalem; Rom. 15.19 shows that Paul began to preach his own gospel in Judaea;[147] and Paul's claim to be Ἑβραῖος in Phil. 3.5 proves him to be a Hebrew speaker with Judaean roots.[148]

Van Unnik, arguing that Paul was educated in Jerusalem from earliest childhood, gives priority to Aramaic as Paul's mother tongue over his Diaspora Greek. Following Luke, Hengel sees Paul as truly bilingual – equally at home in Greek and Aramaic.[149] Paul's 'idiosyncratic' Greek style proves that Paul did not move to Jerusalem as early as van Unnik proposed, but learned Greek as a youth in Tarsus.[150] Like Vollmer, Deissmann and Michel, Hengel acknowledges Paul's 'sovereign' command of Greek scripture, both OG and Hebraizing revisions of Isaiah, Job and 3 Kingdoms. 'Paul's use of scripture developed out of oral teaching' and extensive argumentation that typified the 'institution of the Jewish Palestinian *soferim*' and the 'Jewish school which centred on learning Torah by heart'.[151] Claims about Paul's ἀκρίβεια in the

142   Hengel (ibid.) refers to Paul either as 'Gelehrte' or 'Schriftgelehrte', both of which Bowden (Hengel 1991b) renders as 'scribe': 'des damals relativ jungen jüdischen Gelehrten' (ibid. 1991a, 213 – 'of the Jewish *scribe* who at the time was relatively young' – 1991b, 19); 'Pharisäer und Gelehrtenschüler' (1991a, 232 – 'a Pharisee and pupil of the *scribes*' – 1991b, 34); 'seine eigene schriftgelehrte Arbeit' (1991a, 235 – 'his own work as a scribe' – 1991b, 35). Hengel explains his term *Schriftgelehrte* thus: γραμματεύς of the synoptic gospels is a term of 'typically Palestinian coinage', referring to the group known as *soferim*. Therefore, Paul omits to mention that he is γραμματεύς (Phil. 3.5-6), because his Gentile audience would understand only its common Hellenistic meaning: 'copyist, secretary, clerk' (Hengel 1991b, 35–36).

143   'The revised texts could very well in part also derive from his own work as a scribe' (Hengel 1991b, 35), which Paul produced 'on the basis of his knowledge of revised versions' (ibid., 35 [189]). Hengel, appealing to Stanley (1990), proposes Paul's 'own critical recension of the text' (Hengel 1991b. 36 [194]). Cf. ibid., 35–36, 35 [191].

144   Hengel 1991b, 35 citing Koch 1986, 81 (Bowden's translation).

145   Van Unnik 1973.

146   Hengel 1991b, 22 and 34.

147   Because of the με in an accusative infinitive clause, Rom. 15.19 refers to Paul's own mission (ὥστε με ἀπὸ Ἰερουσαλὴμ καὶ κύκλῳ μέχρι τοῦ Ἰλλυρικοῦ πεπληρωκέναι τὸ εὐαγγέλιον τοῦ Χριστοῦ) (Hengel 1991b, 24–25 [143–145]).

148   Hengel (1991b, 117 [146]) argues that Ἑβραῖος means 'Hebrew speaker' (cf. Prologue to Sirach 22; *4 Macc.* 12.7; 16.15, and Philo *Vita Mosis* 2.31). Grintz (1960) demonstrates that when Josephus mentions one who speaks ἑβραϊστί, he means Hebrew, not Aramaic (see Section 3.4.2).

149   Hengel 1991b, 22, 34.

150   Ibid., 35.

151   Ibid., 35–36. Hengel refers to the Pharisaic schools of Hillel and Shammai and the houses of

Torah (Acts 22.3; 26.4-5 cf. Phil. 3.5-6; Gal. 1.14) suggest to Hengel that Paul was intimately familiar with Greek and Hebrew scripture.[152] Against Koch's low estimation of Paul's command of scripture, and its textual variations, Hengel says 'we may not make the apostle a dilettante and ignoramus'.[153] Hengel and Ellis both agree on Paul's great competence in the literary aspects of Greek and Hebrew scripture (including memorization) and his expert awareness of its textual plurality. Both accept the testimony of Acts. However, Hengel goes beyond Ellis in his (mis)appropriation of Tannaitic material for his discussion of first-century Pharisees.[154]

Lim also adopts an inclusive view of the variety of Paul's written sources.[155] Following Acts, he accepts that Paul spoke Greek, Hebrew and Aramaic, and that (as a result of his Palestinian Pharisaic education) he used Hebrew copies.[156] Lim argues that Paul was aware of a passage in its variant text-forms.[157] Emphasizing the difficulties involved in handling multiple 'rolls' or 'codices' and in looking up passages in a long scroll, Lim suggests that Paul used 'anthologies' of 'biblical' passages.[158]

Marcos also estimates highly Paul's command of Jewish scripture and awareness of textual plurality:

> I think that textual research alone does not resolve all the problems of Paul's quotations, as the influence of exegesis also has to be looked at. In many cases, Paul's text is closely connected with the application of that text to the present moment. Applications use common interpretations, oral or Targumic traditions and the Targum method of exegesis. Paul uses the technique of *midraš pešer*. In this method, the explanation of the text determines the text-form of the quotation. This occurs in several ways: 1. by mixing relevant verses within an express proof text; 2. by adapting the grammar to the context and application of the New Testament; 3. *by choosing suitable translations of known texts* or Targums; 4. by creating interpretations to fit the moment. All in all, Paul was capable of applying scripture to the demands of every particular situation of the Christian community like any rabbi or sage of his time.[159]

Paul could select 'suitable translations' and appeal to oral traditions. Marcos, like Ellis and Hengel, compares Paul to a Rabbi or 'sage', presumably after Acts 22.3, and equates first-century Pharisees with the Rabbis of Tannaitic literature.

---

learning in Jerusalem, one of which Paul allegedly attended under Gamaliel (ibid.; cf. 118 [157]).

152   Ibid., 37–38.
153   Ibid., 35, while citing Koch 1986, 81 (Bowden's translation).
154   Hengel accepts the modern conflation of 'scribes' in the New Testament with Rabbis of the Tannaitic literature into the category of *Schriftgelehrte* ('Torah scholar'), which Schams (1998) rightly criticizes.
155   Lim 1997.
156   Ibid., 161f.
157   Lim's evidence are Paul's two citations of Isa. 40.13 (Rom. 11.33; 1 Cor. 2.16), whose respective wording differs in each case (Lim 1997, 159).
158   Ibid., 154 (echoing Vollmer, Koch and Stanley on the difficulties of using an unwieldy scroll).
159   Marcos 2000, 329; my italics.

Michel's argument stands almost precisely between the positions of Koch and Ellis. Like Ellis, he credits Paul with sufficient command of scripture to cite routinely from memory. On the other hand (like Koch), Michel prioritizes the internal lexical evidence of Paul's letters over Paul's rhetorical statements. Arguing from this lexical evidence, he concludes that although (on the basis of Acts) Paul could have used Hebrew copies, he did not.

1.7 *Citation from memory*

A great deal is claimed about Paul's ability (or its lack) to cite from memory. This concern is based on a common assumption (particularly in the stream represented by Koch), expressed either in positive or negative terms. The negative expression supposes that citation from memory inevitably results in erroneous 'deviations' from the learned text.[160] The positive expression supposes that accurate verbal reproduction of a source is *only* possible by citing directly from a copy.

Following Kautzsch, Michel attributes many of Paul's deviations from the wording of the LXX to faults of memory, explaining Paul's mixed citations as 'erroneous memory conflations' (see Section 1.3.1, especially Footnote 103, above). Koch accounts for such deviations differently, arguing that Paul did not cite from memory. Rather, where Paul's citations diverge from G^Ed, Paul often himself altered the wording of his source for his own exegetical purposes.[161] For Koch they are intentional alterations rather than memory errors; the frequent agreement of Paul's citations with the wording of G^Ed is 'proof' of Paul's general direct citation from copies. The assertion that accurate verbal reproduction indicates direct citation from a written source inversely affirms Roepe, Kautzsch and Michel's contention that errors result from memory recall.

Koch's material is compatible with this assumption, but does not constitute evidence for it. Of Koch's types of evidence for Paul's direct citation from written sources (summarized in Section 1.2.3, above) the first, third and fifth (that is, (i) Paul's reproduction of source *Wortlaut*; (iii) Paul's exegetical modifications; (v) two independent citations of the same verse) are positive iterations of this assumption; the second ((ii) divine names) amounts to its negative assertion.[162] Koch presents this evidence as a cumulative case for Paul's substantial use of written sources. However, each type could be explained equally well in terms of citation from memory. The same applies to Koch's evidence against Paul's general citation from memory (see Section 1.2.3, above). What Koch and Stanley present as evidence is an expression

160   The term text, rather than «text» (see Section 1.1.1 above) is applicable because an individual presumably learned the text from a particular copy, at least for extended periods of time.
161   The deviations are *bewusst vorgenommene Texteingriffe* (Koch 1986, 189).
162   The same is naturally true of Stanley's summary of Koch's evidence for direct citation (see Section 1.3.2, above).

of their assumptions about the nature of direct citation from written sources. That is, their analysis follows their model rather than the contrary.

The ability to reproduce accurately the wording of a known «text» does not constitute proof of direct citation from a written source rather than memory. Pointing to Marrou and Harris,[163] Stanley acknowledges the extremely important role played by rote memorization and oral reproduction of written texts in Graeco-Roman education and the literary world in general.[164] Gerhardsson and Lieberman present similar evidence in Rabbinic Judaism.[165] Assuming that an ancient person memorized the text of a given manuscript copy verbatim, we must acknowledge that citation from memory would be indistinguishable from direct citation from the written source. I do not wish necessarily to attribute to Paul a remarkable capacity to cite from memory, but to point out the lack of reliable criteria for distinguishing between citation from memory and written text.

Stanley notes two arguments typically presented in favour of Paul's frequent citation from memory.[166] One argument emphasizes the central role of rote memorization in ancient Graeco-Roman and Jewish education. The other explains 'deviations from the precise wording of the biblical text' in terms of memory errors.[167] Stanley argues that these arguments 'cancel' each other out. However, his 1992 study goes on to demonstrate that deviations in wording are not the products of memory error, but largely a result of Paul's own exegetical alteration. Thus, Stanley cannot justifiably maintain this argument against citation from memory because the idea of 'cancellation' (to which he appeals) is dispelled by his own results.

Stanley also considers the notion that Paul routinely cited from memory to be inconsistent with the diverse textual profile exhibited by Paul's citations. I divide his statement into two parts to ease the following discussion. He writes:

[1] Had Paul relied upon a version of the Greek text that he had (presumably) memorised in childhood, one would expect to see at least a measure of consistency in the textual affinities of his various quotations, at least among those that come from the same book of scripture. The present study, in agreement with earlier investigations of Paul's biblical *Vorlage*, has found no such pattern. . . .

[2] . . . Especially troublesome for the "memory quotation" view are those places where Paul seems to have taken his quotations from an early Jewish revision of the Old Greek text. Only if one assumes that Paul has allowed these revised versions to displace the form of

163   Marrou 1956, Harris 1989.
164   Stanley 1992, 16 [47].
165   Gerhardsson 1961 and Lieberman 1965.
166   Roepe 1827; Kautzsch 1869; Ellis 1957; Toy 1884; Johnson 1895; Michel 1929; Lindars 1961; and Hanson 1974.
167   Stanley 1992, 16–17.

the text that he had known since childhood can it be maintained that these quotations, too, arose out of the apostle's memory in the moment of composition.[168]

Stanley has a particular notion of rote memorization in mind: (1) an ancient Jew learned each work by rote from a particular copy available during childhood schooling; (2) this memorized text remained the one that a person accessed throughout his lifetime. It is this idea that Stanley finds inconsistent with the diversity of the textual profile of Paul's citations. There are difficulties with this view.

Assumption (1) is predicated on Stanley's belief that there are limits to the eclecticism of copies of first-century texts.[169] In Section 2.2.1, I argue against limiting such eclecticism because the same text-critical problems of textual diversity apply to memorized as well as written texts. If we suppose that Paul had memorized a particular work and that his textually eclectic citations of that work accurately represent this memorized text, it would be impossible for us to know whether he had memorized the text of an eclectic copy, or whether he had memorized the texts of several written copies. The two are indistinguishable.

There are further problems with Stanley's argument that a memorized text is incompatible with the textual diversity of Paul's citations. According to (2), the memorized text is a rigid textual object that is practically identical with the text of the copy memorized in childhood.[170] As a corollary, he assumes that memorization of a literary work is a process by which a text is transferred from manuscript to student's mind and can be accurately recalled thereafter with no aspect of it altered through later encounters with variant forms of the text or through various uses of the text in exegetical contexts that require modifications in its wording. Stanley's vision may be true of Graeco-Roman education or Rabbinic learning. However, this pattern characterizes learning within contexts of high textual standardization that did not apply to Jewish scripture in Paul's times.[171]

The *process* of memorization, and the *memorized text* must be distinguished. While memorization of a literary work in the first century may have amounted to the rote recall of the text of a particular copy learned in childhood, the effect of subsequent encounters with variant text-forms of that literary work on an individual's perception of the memorized text cannot be established. In Chapter 2 I argue that textual

---

168   Ibid., 255–256.
169   See Footnote 118, above.
170   Stanley's '*version* of the Greek text' means 'text of a copy' as defined in Section 1.1.1 (see also Footnote 118, above).
171   Despite revisionist projects like καιγε-Theodotion or the claims made for the Septuagint in the *Letter of Aristeas*, the efforts of Alexandrian textual critics to standardize classical literature do not seem to be paralleled for Jewish scripture to the same degree in the first century. Rabbinic efforts to standardize the proto-Masoretic text-form (hence the Rabbis' interest in the variant readings of Rabbi Mier's Torah, which, according to Siegel (1975), was orthographically similar to 1QIsa.ᵃ (see Chapter 4)) seem to characterize the second and third centuries.

plurality was an important part of many first-century Jewish exegetes' encounters with traditional works.

Stanley conceives either of an entirely literary or an entirely memory-based citation strategy. When writing about Paul, he largely proposes the presence of the former and a lack of the latter. Yet when an individual makes direct use of a copy of a literary work within a textually diverse environment, the text of a passage can evoke associations with its other text-forms and various exegetical ideas connected with it (see following chapters). These associations must not necessarily be perceived as rote recall, but as an individual's cumulative knowledge of a given passage and his perception of its significance.[172] Because the ancient individuals studied here are erudite exegetes operating within conventional literary contexts, awareness of textual plurality cannot be detached from the oral exegetical environment in which they must have operated.

Notwithstanding its text-critical merits, Koch and Stanley's approach to Paul's sources exaggerates the literary aspects of Paul's encounter with scripture to the detriment of social context. Their cumulative case, reliant as it is on the assumption of direct citation from written copies, does not rule out the presence of memory in Paul's citation practice. Their appeal to this cumulative case, however, leads them to exclude the influence of memory on the practice of direct citation from written sources. While this exclusion is suited to their analysis of the textual character of Paul's written sources (which is a prerequisite to discussing how he used them), it forestalls the historical question of his awareness of textual plurality.

1.7.1 *Suppression of memory*

According to Koch, (1) Paul only refers to Greek texts when composing his letters; (2) he predominantly cites directly from copies and rarely from memory; and (3) he only cites from a single copy of each work (see Sections 1.2.2.2–1.2.2.3, above). I have argued that only point (1) actually emerges from Koch's text-critical analysis, while points (2) and (3) are presuppositions of his reconstruction of Paul's *Vorlagen*.

Whenever Paul's wording deviates from all known manuscripts of the LXX, Koch suggests whether and how Paul has modified his *Vorlage*. In order to do this, Koch must propose the original wording of the source. Therefore, Koch's analysis relies heavily on his reconstruction of Paul's written sources. Consequently, he must discard the possibilities of memory citation, multilingualism and Paul's conscious preference for one text-form – factors that would introduce too many variables into his text-critical exercise.

Stanley introduces a scale of probability for Paul's verbal alterations of a source. Like Koch's, however, Stanley's task is text-critical, and accuracy relies on awareness

---

172   Stanley is aware that Paul inhabited an oral world (1992, 338f.). However, this awareness does not affect Stanley's highly literary projection of Paul's practice. This outlook pervades especially his chs 1–3, 6, and the summaries of chs 7 and 8 (Stanley 1992, 3f., 31f., 65f., 252f., 289f., 336f.).

of the wording of Paul's sources. Memory citation is one of the 'heterogeneous materials' that he must exclude to avoid 'contamination' of his study.[173] He also excludes literary allusions and verbal parallels in Paul's composition that lack explicit indications of their use by the author, even in cases where they reproduce verbatim the OG of the passage known from an LXX manuscript. Of course, Stanley does not casually dismiss memory citation simply because it does not suit his task; he is persuaded by Koch's arguments that Paul's direct citation from written sources is evidenced by lexical data in Paul's letters (see Section 1.3.2, above), important arguments, which must be taken seriously but whose employment and implications I question. I argue that Stanley's approach does not necessarily require the exclusion of citation from memory. And there is no reason to suppose that the citation of a diligently memorized text can be distinguished from a citation made directly from a copy. When Stanley writes that 'the evidence runs wide and deep that Paul did indeed draw his quotations from some sort of written text',[174] he is referring to the cumulative observations of Kautzsch, Vollmer, Michel, and Koch (see Section 1.3, above). However, what 'runs wide and deep' is not evidence for this conclusion, but rather the shared assumptions that underpin it. As a result, such exclusion of memory from analyses of Paul's citation techniques, which attributes to Paul an almost entirely literary modus operandi, really arises from the literary mode of modern analysts.

Written sources provide our sole access to ancient citation techniques. And biblical scholars today must be wary of allowing the predominance of textual material available to us, and the contingent literary paradigms, to lead to the construction of an overly literary picture of antiquity. The role of memory in ancient citation practice can hardly be quantified through extant textual evidence and one must infer with historical sensitivity the dimensions of memory in first-century Jewish exegetical communities.

The approach that I have outlined above limits the conception of memory to rote memorization. Because, as observed, a perfectly memorized text is indistinguishable from the written text, in current discussion textual memory becomes merely another means of access to a written copy. Textual memory is thereby subsumed within the question of access to copies, a question whose urgency itself derives from the predominantly written-textual view of Paul's use of scripture. On this view, Paul's encounter with scripture emerges as a solitary process of private study restricted by limited access to scrolls and the confines of a textual memory reduced to rote memorization eclipsed within a written-textual analytical model.[175] The notion of Paul's unfamiliarity with traditional literature and his lack of awareness of textual plurality are contingent upon this picture and its presuppositions. Subsequent chapters will emphasize the use of scripture within ancient Jewish oral discourse and argue that, far from representing the private literary exercise often envisaged, written texts and

173   See Section 1.3.2, above.
174   Stanley 1992, 69; reiterated ibid., 71.
175   See Carruthers' (1992, 16–45, ch. 1 'Models for Memory') excellent discussion of different means and aims of memorization in antiquity.

their use belonged to fundamentally social interactions. I argue that an individual's awareness of textual traditions was inseparable from the interactive process.

1.7.2 *Awareness of textual plurality*

Envisaging Paul using different copies of the same work on different occasions and compiling *excerpta*, Stanley leaves open the possibility that at times Paul compared different forms of a given passage, although he does not entertain this possibility in his study.

Ellis does not reduce Paul's ability to prefer a form of a passage to Paul's simultaneous comparison of written sources. The questions of memory and access to copies are not polarized in Ellis' position. Ellis' observation, that deviations from known text-forms in Paul's citations reflect 'literary custom' and 'exegetical purpose' rather than slips of memory,[176] is borne out by Koch and Stanley's findings, who show that the distinctive readings of Paul's citations often reflect Paul's exegetical activity. However, Ellis diverges from Koch, Stanley and Vollmer in his confidence in Paul's ability to cite accurately from memory, attributing Paul's frequently precise replication of the OG wording to his 'desire to reproduce a given text'. Paul satisfied this 'desire' by appealing to written sources in some cases and to memory in others.

Nevertheless, Ellis' confidence in Paul's expert multilingual and pluri-textual citation from memory is subject to the same problems as the stance represented by Koch: (a) it lacks reliable criteria for distinguishing 'direct' citation from accurate memory citation; so that (b) the text-critical problem of identifying the memorized text – and the «text» it represents – remains. Ellis benefits from maintaining the more flexible approach to the textual problem of Paul's citations. Although by taking a 'maximal' view Ellis risks overstating Paul's literary expertise, he avoids forcing his socio-historical synthesis of Paul's use of scripture into either affirming or denying possible aspects of Paul's use of scripture, such as awareness of different oral sources or polyglossia.

1.8 *Approaches to evidence*

In the preceding discussion I have observed that a particular lineage, represented by Vollmer, Deissmann, Michel, Koch and Stanley, subordinates circumstantial data – such as rhetorical claims by Paul or Luke-Acts about Paul's Semitic ethos, or assumptions about the literary skills of Pharisees – to lexical data internal to Paul's letters. So, for example, while Vollmer, Deissmann and Michel assume Paul's Judaean Semitic ethos, they rule out his use of Hebrew scripture on the basis of the lexical evidence of his letters.[177] Koch and Stanley seek further to secure the quality of the

---

176   See Footnote 140, above.
177   See above, Footnotes 101 and 102 (Michel); 93 (Deissmann); and 36 (Vollmer).

textual data, particularly through tightening the criteria by which material is admitted for analysis (see Sections 1.2 and 1.3.2, above).

Text-critical enquiry is never independent of circumstantial historical considerations. Determining the nature of Paul's sources is done through establishing the textual profile of his citations, which is integrally bound up with the question of how Paul modified the wording of his sources. This, in turn, involves numerous judgements about Paul's own ideological and rhetorical motives for each citation and how these motives compare with agendas implied in Paul's sources.[178] Deciding on the manifestation of Paul's sources – whether *florilegia*, scrolls or collections of *excerpta* – involves further historical judgements, such as the availability, manual convenience, weight and expense of different kinds of manuscript, under various conditions conceivable for Paul, such as visits to synagogues, sojourns in churches, long foot-journeys, or incarcerations. As we saw, Koch's reconstruction of a single *Vorlage* for each work was predicated on a number of historical judgements. Historical considerations inevitably inform the premises of any study of Paul's attitudes to scripture. However, it is important to establish which kinds of premise should be given prior weight in analysis. In the following I treat some recurrent issues.

1.8.1 *Pharisees and Scribes*

It is often supposed that, having been a Pharisee (Phil. 3.5), Paul had an expert command of Jewish literature (for example, Ellis, Hengel and Lim). Josephus consistently presents the Pharisees' reputation as the most precise interpreters of Jewish laws as the distinguishing characteristic of this group;[179] the gospels broadly confirm this, presenting Pharisees as concerned with legal interpretation and violation.[180] As a voluntary association, whose membership was characterized by legal expertise, it is fair to suppose that Pharisees shared this aspiration when joining the group.[181]

---

178   Noted by Koch 1986, 9–10.

179   For instance, in *Vita* 189–198 Josephus explains the impressive legal knowledge (ἀκρίβεια) of the delegation sent to oust him from Galilee by noting that they were Pharisees. By this knowledge they claim to be Josephus' equals (cf. *Vita* 9, Josephus' own knowledge of the laws was ἀκριβής from boyhood, prior to his contact with Pharisees). He elsewhere states that Pharisees are most pious and accurate in interpreting 'the laws' (τοὺς νόμους, *BJ* 1.110); accurate in the 'legal customs' (τὰ νόμιμα, *BJ* 2.162); and in interpreting the 'laws of the fathers' (τοῦ πατρίου νόμων, *AJ* 17.41). Josephus presents the Pharisees as a φιλοσοφία, an elective group ideologically motivated to lead a certain kind of life (see Mason 1996; Saldarini 1988, 123f., 288f.).

180   e.g. Mt. 9.14; Mk 2.18; Lk. 5.33 (fasting). Mt. 12.2, 14; Mk 2.24; 3.5; Lk. 6.2, 7; 14.3f. (Sabbath). Mt. 15.2f.; Mk 7.1f.; Lk. 11.38 (hand-washing). Mt. 15.12 (food-purity). Mt. 19.3f.; Mk 10.2f.; 12.19f. (divorce). Mt. 22.15f.; Mk 12.13f. (taxes). Mt. 22.34 (greatest commandment). Mt. 23.5 (phylacteries and fringes). Mt. 23.16f. (oaths). Mt. 23.23; Lk. 11.42 (tithing). Mt. 23.24, 27 (corpse impurity). Mt. 23.25; Mk 7.4; Lk. 11.39 (purification of vessels). Lk. 5.21 (blasphemy). Lk. 11.41 (almsgiving).

181   For example, Saldarini (1988) describes the Pharisees as a 'literate, corporate, voluntary association' (ibid., 281) who 'are best understood as retainers who were literate servants of the governing class and had a program for Jewish society and influence with the people and their patrons' (ibid., 284). Saldarini thinks that the Pharisaic movement 'must have educated its members to some degree' but admits

Nevertheless, here judgements about the level of expertise generally expected of Pharisees will be given no weight. First, I argue below that exegetical use of textual variation represents an ambient literary mode,[182] which Paul shared with a number of his literate contemporaries, who were Jews of diverse social standing and ideological affiliation.[183] Second, modern uncertainty regarding Pharisees remains. Available evidence explicitly refers only to first-century Judaean Pharisees.[184] While Acts locates Paul's Pharisaic training in Jerusalem, a widespread suspicion that this narrative is a Lukan fiction renders the testimony of Acts unsuitable as a basis for analysis.[185] In line with a notion of 'Diaspora Pharisees' developed in modern times,[186] some scholars believe that Paul, an entirely Hellenized Diaspora Jew, received Pharisaic training in Tarsus rather than Judaea.[187] Suspect as we might that a variety of Pharisaism existed in the Diaspora, there is no direct evidence for its existence.[188] Paul is the only example of a 'Diaspora Pharisee' and his apostolic writings provide unreliable insights into his Pharisaic life. Thus, I will not give analytical priority to Paul's 'Pharisaism' with regard to presuppositions about his literary competence.

In the canonical gospel narratives Pharisees are often closely associated with γραμματεῖς, commonly translated as *Schriftgelehrten*, 'Torah scholars' or 'scribes'. Hengel, for instance, considers Paul both a Pharisee and a scribe.[189] Because in Phil. 3.5-6 Paul fails to designate himself a γραμματεύς, Koch counsels against overestimating Paul's command of Jewish scripture. He presupposes that, having

that this remains hypothetical (ibid., 285), adding that Josephus 'implies that all learned their own traditions and some were highly educated' (ibid., 288).

182   See Section 1.8.4, below.

183   For Josephus and Dead Sea sectarians, see Chapters 3–5, below. For Paul himself, see Chapter 7, below.

184   e.g. Vermes 1973a, 56; Goodman 1983, 78 and 93; Sanders 1985, 198, 390 [90]; 1992, 535[45].

185   For example, Deissmann 1925; Strecker 1976; Schoeps 1959; Haenchen 1968, 553; Koch 1986, 92–93 (see Footnotes 186 and 190, below); cf. Pervo 1987. Paul's letters do not help to resolve the question of Paul's Judaean schooling (*pace* Hengel 1991, 23–39).

186   The roots of this notion lie in earlier studies, for example, Whiston (1722), Vollmer (1895, 61–73). While Deissmann (1925) accepts Jerome's report of Paul's Gischalan ancestry, Deissmann (1925, 71f.) believes that Paul – a fully Hellenized Jew – received Pharisaic training in Tarsus. Hengel (1991, 29–34) argues that Strecker (1976) and Schoeps (1959) in particular developed the notion of 'Diaspora Pharisaism'. For Schoeps, Diaspora Pharisaism, of which Paul's thought is indicative, was a product of a highly Hellenized Diaspora Judaism and fundamentally non-Palestinian (1961, 22–47). Strecker (1976, 482) builds squarely on Deissmann and Schoeps. More cautious, Sanders still speaks of 'Diaspora' and 'Palestinian Pharisaism' as distinct (1991, 1; 1992, 536 [2], 538 [51]). Assuming that Phil. 3.5 must be intelligible to the Philippian audience, Saldarini posits Pharisees active in Macedonia, and speculates also Cilicia or Syria (1988, 292–293).

187   Koch (1986, 92 [4]) seems to accept this view, considering Gal. 1.15-24 to contradict Luke's picture (in Acts) of Paul's activities in Judaea prior to the visit reported in Gal. 1.18.

188   Hengel (1991, 29–34) reviews and rejects evidence commonly presented in favour of Diaspora Pharisaism. On Mt. 23.15, a *locus classicus* for arguments in favour of Diaspora Pharisees (converting Gentiles), see Goodman (1994a, 70–71), who interprets it differently.

189   See Footnotes 142 and 143, above. Hengel may be influenced by Jeremias' claim that Paul was a *Schriftgelehrte* (Jeremias 1923–1937 II B, 101–103).

inevitably received 'intensive rabbinische Schulung', all γραμματεῖς had the capacity to reproduce scripture from memory; in contrast, Paul lacked this capacity because he was not a scribe.[190] Koch implies that scribes alone were capable of memorizing the ancestral literature. However, in an oral world, it is dubious to assume that the rare skill of writing was the sole credential for reciting text from memory. Moreover, Schams (1998) argues that ancient references to 'scribes' represent different groups of professionals performing a wide variety of tasks (including civic or military clerks, copyist-technicians, scribal exegetes, and priests), and thus against the simple equation of 'scribes' with expert Torah scholarship (see Chapter 5, below). As with his Pharisaic identity, decisions about Paul's 'scribal' or 'non-scribal' status cannot form the premises for this analysis.

1.8.2 *Access to copies*

I have identified doubts concerning access to copies as an important factor in widespread reluctance to credit Paul with an awareness of textual plurality. This issue similarly arises out of prior decisions regarding circumstantial data. Ellis supposes that Paul routinely compared multiple scrolls of the same work in the synagogues, which he entered in order to debate with compatriots, *before* he was ejected (according to Acts Paul was often ejected from synagogues). Koch supposes the opposite, reasoning that, *because* Paul was routinely ejected, he was not able to study synagogue scrolls. Thus Ellis predicates his argument (that Paul compared copies in order to select preferred variant readings), and Koch predicates his argument (that Paul, consulting one copy of each work for ten years, was unable to make a preference) on divergent inferences from certain circumstantial evidence.

Responses to the question of Paul's awareness of textual plurality cannot rest upon speculation about Paul's access to copies at various stages in his lifetime, which scholars divide into childhood, youth, Pharisaic and apostolic periods. The presentation of Paul's debates in Diaspora synagogues in Acts may be a narrative fiction,[191] and Paul's ejection may be influenced by Luke's polemic against 'the Jews' who reject the gospel. One cannot, however, be certain that Paul never debated with other Jews, nor compared different copies of the same work during his pre-apostolic or apostolic phases. The visits to Jerusalem, reported in Galatians 1–2, were opportunities for viewing scrolls and discussing readings. Stanley assumes that Paul uses different scrolls at different times. Analysing the textual profile of Paul's explicit Isaiah citations and their distribution throughout the letters, Wilk concludes that Paul used various copies of Isaiah ('verschiedene Jesajarollen') over this period. Wilk argues

---

190   Koch (1986, 92–93), citing Haenchen (1968, 553) and Conzelmann (1972, 67), doubts Paul's Rabbinic education, considering the report of Paul's Pharisaic education (Acts 22.3) to be a fabrication fitting Luke's desire to present Paul as an authentic Judaean.
191   Cf. Pervo (1987), who compares Acts with the historical fiction of some ancient novels.

that Paul used *various* copies representing Isaiah[OG], *one* partial Hebraizing revision of Isaiah[OG], and *one* thorough Hebraizing revision of Isaiah[OG].[192]

The question of access to scrolls is circumstantial and conclusions on the matter inevitably speculative. Throughout his lifetime it is conceivable that Paul saw different scrolls at different times. Perhaps he had occasional chances to compare multiple copies of the same work or to compare a passage recorded in a notebook with the same passage in another copy (see Section 1.8.2.1, below). Perhaps at times he carried his own scrolls and perhaps he referred to *florilegia*. He may have discussed the different readings of a verse with fellow worshippers, Pharisees, elders, rabbis, apostles of Christ, or his own Gentile believers, at times consulting one or multiple copies, at times working from memory. Because all of these possibilities are attested in antiquity, any combination of them is conceivable for Paul. Therefore, prior judgement regarding this issue cannot be allowed to determine conclusions.

1.8.2.1 Excerpta

Both Koch and Stanley argue that Paul compiled his own *excerpta* in notebooks or wax tablets.[193] Koch notes that the author of 2 Timothy considered the use of notebooks as 'geläufig' in a late-first-century Christian mission. Koch argues that αἱ μεμβράναι – distinct from τὰ βιβλία containing traditional works – are the notebooks in which Paul collected *excerpta*.[194] Stanley develops this argument with a survey of ancient authors' compilations of *excerpta* in Greek, Latin and Hebrew milieus. Xenophon, Aristotle and Athenaeus all use cognates of ἐκλέγειν, in reference to extracting desired literary passages.[195] Plutarch selected from his own written notes (ὑπομνήματα).[196] Cicero prepared to write a book on rhetoric by excerpting (*excerpsimus*) 'the most suitable precepts' from various works.[197] Pliny the Elder compiled numerous volumes of excerpts and notes. An author was read aloud while the Elder Pliny, or his secretary (*notarius*), made 'extracts and observations' (*adnotabat excerpebatque*) on wax tablets (*pugillares*).[198] Pliny the Younger made extracts while a volume of Livy was read aloud (*Epistles* 6.20.5). Papyri show that selections from

---

192   Wilk (1998, 41–42) shows that: Paul used the Isaiah[OG] scrolls and the partial Hebraizing revision during composition of Galatians, 1 and 2 Corinthians, and Romans; Paul used the thorough Hebraizing revision when specifically composing Romans 9–11. Hübner (1993, 317f.), cited by Wilk (ibid.), had already suggested that Paul studied a new Isaiah scroll when writing Romans 9–11.

193   Koch 1986, 99 [40]. Stanley 1992, 74–79. Stanley surveys a helpful range of literature. On Pliny the Younger, see Chadwick 1969. On Aristotle and Athenaeus, see Knox and Easterling 1985. On Plutarch, see Helmbold and O'Neill 1959. For Hellenistic and rhetorical schools, see Marrou 1956 (153–154); Turner 1968 (91–92); and Hani 1972 (30–50).

194   Koch 1986, 99 [40]. However, according to Stanley 2 Tim 4.13 is 'questionable' because 'μεμβράνα as a Latin loan word can only mean parchment' (1992, 46).

195   Xenophon *Memorabilia*, 1.6.14; Aristotle *Topics*, 1.14; Athenaeus *Deipnosophists*, 8.336d. See Stanley 1992, 74.

196   Plutarch *Peri Euthumias* 464F. Helmbold and O'Neill (eds.) 1959, ix.

197   Cicero *De Inventione*, 2.4.

198   Pliny the Younger, *Epistles* 3.5. Hutchinson (trans.) 1923.

classical authors and thematic collections of classical citations were used in school exercises in the Hellenistic period and in the rhetorical schools.[199]

Several Judaean Hebrew manuscripts present compilations of extracts, in some cases with interpretive comments appended to them.[200] These include 4Q158 (Reworked Pentateuch), 4Q175 (Testimonia), 4Q176 (Tanhumim), 4Q174 and 4Q177 (Florilegium; Midrasch zur Eschatologie).[201] To these can be added 4Q339 (List of False Prophets, Aramaic), 4Q340 (List of Netinim) and 4Q559 (Biblical Chronology),[202] all of which thematically gather excerpts from various traditional Jewish sources. 4Q175, 339, and 340 were written on single sheets,[203] suggesting private use.

Stanley takes Pliny the Elder in particular as a model for Paul's collection of *excerpta*,[204] referring to studies on the use of 'parchment notebooks' and 'wax tablets' in the ancient world.[205] Having established the general currency of the practice, Stanley treats it as Paul's primary mode of operation. Accordingly, Paul was more closely acquainted with his own 'highly familiar anthology'[206] than with the traditional literature from which it was drawn, which explains for Stanley why 'a number of Paul's citations are used in a sense quite foreign to their original context'.[207] However, this is unconvincing. The dislocation of a passage from its traditional literary context is common among Paul's exegetical contemporaries.[208] In Sections 7.1–7.2.3 I discuss a number of Paul's uses of scripture, to which the 'dislocation' of a passage from its traditional literary context is intrinsic.

It remains unclear to what extent Paul's situation was comparable to the scenarios represented in this survey. Pliny the Younger and his uncle received the attentive assistance of slaves both for recitation and inscription. Besides, the literary enterprises of Plutarch, Pliny or Cicero (and their level of education) are not immediately comparable with the circumstances of Paul's itinerant mission.[209] Nor is his situa-

199   See Stanley (1992, 75), citing Marrou 1956, 153–154; Turner 1968, 91–92.

200   Stanley 1992, 76–77.

201   4Q158 (Reworked Pentateuch) collects extracts from Exodus 20 and Deuteronomy 5 and 18 (cf. Allegro 1968, 3–6; Fishbane 1988, 352–353). 4Q175 collects passages which the interpreter apparently took to refer to eschatological figures (Allegro 1968, 57–60). 4Q177 gathers and comments on extracts from various sources, including Deuteronomy, Exodus, Psalms, Isaiah, Jeremiah, Zephaniah, Hosea, Joel, Nahum, and Ezekiel (Allegro 1968, 69–73). 4Q174 (Florilegium; cf. Allegro 1968, 53–57) and 4Q177 (Catena A; cf. Allegro 1968, 67–78) contain anthological collections of excerpts interspersed with comment (Steudel 1994). For 4Q176, see Allegro 1968, 60–66.

202   VanderKam and Flint, 2002, x.

203   Tov 2008, 431.

204   Stanley (1992, 75–76); cf. Koch (1986, 99 [40]).

205   Stanley 1992, 78 [46], citing Knox and Easterling 1985, 18; Kenyon 1932, 91–92; and Harris 1989, 194.

206   Stanley 1992, 74; 'highly familiar collection' (ibid., 79 [49]).

207   Ibid., 74 and 78.

208   The authors of continuous *pesharim* preserve the traditional literary context of contiguous passages and simultaneously interpret adjacent passages in radically different ways.

209   Although Paul at times worked with collaborators and co-authors, and was assisted by an amanuensis (cf. Randolph Richards 2004 and Murphy-O'Connor 2005).

tion necessarily comparable to Hellenistic schools. Stanley's treatment of *excerpta* compilation as Paul's *primary* mode of operation is to allow a speculation about Paul to determine analysis. Rather, the ancient practice of compilation of excerpts should be included among the possibilities open to Paul, but not presented as Paul's primary method.[210]

1.8.3 *Linguistic milieu*

The lexical evidence of Paul's Greek letters does not entail Paul speaking τῆ Ἐβραΐδι διαλέκτῳ (Acts 22.2) or using Semitic sources. While Paul's claim to be Ἐβραῖος ἐξ Ἐβραίων (Phil. 3.5) may suggest he was a Hebrew speaker,[211] it is impossible on linguistic grounds alone to verify from the letters his knowledge of Semitic languages.[212] On the other hand, his predominant use of Greek scripture does not necessarily speak against his use of Hebrew texts during his lifetime. Paul's appeal to the OG and his Hellenistic tone and style all reflect the life-setting of his extant writing: Greek letters to Greek-speaking audiences. Any apparent Semitism in his Greek can be attributed to Semitisms deriving from the Greek Jewish literature (OG and Hebraizing revisions) that permeates his language, and perhaps because it permeated Diaspora synagogue vernacular. Therefore, I will limit my discussion to Paul's awareness of textual plurality in Greek scripture.

1.8.4 *Ambient literary modes*

No prior conclusions regarding Paul's literary expertise can be predicated on the level of expertise generally expected of any given *kind* of ancient Jew, such as Palestinian Pharisee, Diaspora Pharisee, Jewish scribe or itinerant missionary. While a certain general literary competence might be attributed to each type, applying such rules to an individual, such as Paul, risks predetermining outcomes of analysis by affirming generalizations that pre-emptively confine analysis.

However, studies show that ancient literate people in general participated in certain ambient literary modes, not restricted to sectarian affiliation or professional class. Such modes can be considered open to Paul, as a literate person, without predicating judgements on his political, sectarian, professional or linguistic background. For example, surveying a variety of ancient literary material, Stanley establishes that ancient authors (Jewish and non-Jewish[213]) frequently altered the wording of traditional literature in order to make their citations better suit their own syntax, writing

---

210   Stanley must admit that 'there is nothing in Paul's letters to indicate the physical form that such an anthology might have taken' (1992, 78 [46]).

211   See Footnote 148, above.

212   Inconclusive indications exist. For example, Vollmer (1895, 41–42) notes the allusory combination of three passages in 2 Cor. 9.10, which share a common term ('rain') in Hebrew, but none in Greek. Vollmer proposes that these Hebrew passages were already combined, and Paul later found them gathered in a Christian Greek *florilegium*.

213   See Stanley's surveys of this practice among Dead Sea sectarians (1992) and Greek authors (1990).

style and rhetoric. Since this practice was ambient, there is nothing remarkable in Paul's frequent alteration of the wording of his sources. According to Stanley, Koch's view, that Paul's tendency to alter the traditional wording was unique, derives from Koch's conviction that Paul's citations are generally indispensably constitutive of Paul's own arguments.[214] Stanley shares the latter conviction about the constitutive role of Paul's citations,[215] but finds that Paul was participating in ambient practice when he integrated his literary sources through verbal alteration.

If a particular literary mode was ambient, it can be considered open to Paul in his context. No particular ambient mode should be arbitrarily excluded from a construction of Paul's literary practice. Neither should a particular ambient mode be made indispensable to such a construction to the arbitrary exclusion of other modes. Both situations nevertheless arise. For example, studies have amply shown that memory citation was widespread among a wide variety of ancient people, literate and illiterate. However, I have shown that, because of axiomatic efforts to control textual material in analysis, memory citation is forcibly excluded from influential studies of Paul's use of written sources. On the other hand, the ambient practice of compiling *excerpta*, presumably open to Paul, becomes Paul's primary modus operandi in Stanley's 1992 study in order to account for the diverse textual profile of Paul's citations, while ruling out memory citation and awareness of textual plurality, both factors that Stanley considers to contaminate his own project. In these cases presuppositions are circularly confirmed through the very analyses whose premises these presuppositions determine, without advancing historical insight.

In this study, I explore the awareness and use of textual plurality within a variety of ancient Jewish exegetical practices, working towards a better understanding of Paul's literary engagement within that context. I propose that this literary mode, ambient among Paul's literate Jewish contemporaries, was open to Paul.

1.9 *Conclusions*

A study of ancient exegetes' awareness and attitudes is a historical project. While we work in a literary paradigm, we must not conceptualize ancient Jews' exegetical practice as residing entirely in a written world. Although Paul's citation practice was significantly literary, citation from memory and from written sources cannot be polarized. In this chapter I have assessed some influential arguments against Paul's use of textual plurality. I have not argued the opposite. Instead, I have reconsidered the framing of the question at hand. I argue that awareness and use of text-forms must be understood as belonging to an ongoing exegetical discussion.

In the following chapter I examine evidence for textual variation in first-century

---

214   For Koch, Paul's citations are 'ein konstitutiver Bestandteil der Argumentation des Paulus, die gar nicht unter Absehung von den Zitaten erfaßt werden kann' (1986, 284).
215   Stanley (1992, 78 [47]).

Jewish scripture and suggest a model for ancient exegetes' perception of it. I then outline a range of ways in which some of Paul's peers perceived such textual variation. In the final two chapters I draw on these insights in order to re-examine our evidence for Paul's awareness of textual plurality.

PAUL AND TEXTUAL CRITICISM

2.1 *Textual criticism and textual plurality in ancient Jewish scripture*

The majority of extant ancient Septuagint manuscripts date from the third century CE onwards. Along with other literary works transmitted by early Christians, they broadly represent the old Alexandrian translation (OG) of the Pentateuch and translations of the Prophets and Writings. Despite a tendency towards textual standardization in the first centuries CE, the Christian LXX manuscripts exhibit various recensions and revisions of the OG in individual works, including the Hexaplaric and Lucianic recensions.[1] Pre-Christian fragments of Greek scripture from the Judaean Desert and Egypt reveal a great deal of textual variety within Greek manuscripts in the Hellenistic and Roman periods. Revisions of the OG towards the Hebrew and inner stylistic revisions within Greek apparently began before the turn of the era.[2]

Most works of Jewish scripture are Hebrew compositions, whose translation into Greek began in the third century BCE. The Letter of Aristeas (first century CE or earlier) places the translation of the Pentateuch under Egyptian royal patronage in the mid-third century BCE. Translations of works, such as the Historical Books, the Prophets and Psalms, appeared in the following two centuries alongside the composition of other Jewish Greek literature, which later entered the Christian canon, apocrypha or pseudepigrapha. Greek translations of Hebrew works and Greek compositions are usually dated by internal historical indications.[3]

The Judaean manuscripts attest to considerable textual variation in ancient Hebrew scripture. Scholars distinguish various Hebrew text-types. Three Pentateuch text-types are often identified: 𝔐 is often considered Palestinian; the Hebrew source

---

1 Marcos 2000. The Hexaplaric recension, most evident in codex B, derives from Origen's comparison of the OG with proto-𝔐, the Three (α' σ' θ') and other revisions of the OG.

2 Ziegler 1959 and 1939; Gooding 1976; van der Kooij 1992; Ulrich 1999b; Marcos 2000; Tov 1981 and 2008.

3 See Dorival, Harl and Munnich (1988, 110–111) on dating Greek translations of Hebrew works; Marcos (2000, 326) for the antiquity of LXX Isaiah, XII, Psalms. See Williams (2001, 249–252, 261, 275–276) on dating of LXX Psalms before the first century CE and just after 161 BCE; on homogeneity (ibid., 253–260). Seeligmann (1984, 76–94) dates LXX Isaiah to 170–150 BCE; cf. Seeligman *et al.* 2004, 222–250. The Prologue to Greek Sirach mentions the Law and Prophets in Greek, which would date the Greek version of Isaiah to 132 BCE or earlier (cf. Marcos 2000, 54).

underlying the OG is considered an Egyptian text-type separated from the Palestinian in the fourth and fifth centuries BCE; and SP is thought to originate in Babylon.[4] Tov distinguishes five types of Hebrew '*text*' (his italics) in the late Hellenistic and early Roman periods.[5] Ulrich writes: 'most evidence points toward pluriformity at the time when both Christianity and Rabbinic Judaism were in the formative stages.'[6]

For a number of Hebrew works, considerable fluidity persisted into the first century CE. There are multiple textual traditions of Exodus, Numbers, Deuteronomy and Samuel.[7] 'Double traditions' are known for Exodus, Jeremiah, Daniel and 1 Samuel.[8] However, forms of Genesis and Leviticus seem to have stabilized earlier.[9] Although Hebrew Isaiah manuscripts from Qumran exemplify a relatively stable proto-𝔐 «text» in the second century BCE, they exhibit numerous minor multivalent textual affinities towards the Hebrew presupposed by the OG and non-aligned textual traditions.[10] LXX-like readings appear in numerous Hebrew manuscripts[11] and scriptural citations in exegetical compositions.[12] The proto-𝔐 and OG traditions of most works were far more stable by the late second century CE. Judaean manuscript discoveries, dating to the Bar Kokhba Revolt (circa 135 CE), reveal the stable proto-𝔐 «text» presupposed by Origen's Hexapla and by The Three (α', σ', θ').[13]

Textual critics organize fragmentary data into 'text-types', 'text groups', 'families' or 'recensions'. These text-critical categories are applied as analytical tools in discussions of diverse manuscript evidence. The nineteenth-century 'tripartite' model of 𝔐, LXX and SP ultimately results from the Rabbinic preservation of proto-𝔐, Christian preservation of LXX, and the Samaritan adoption of SP.[14] These

4   For example, Talmon 1975; Davila 1993; Tov 1992; Ulrich 1998, 1999b.

5   These are: a type in Qumran orthography; proto-𝔐; pre-SP; texts akin to 𝔊 (i.e. the Hebrew text presupposed by the LXX); non-aligned '*texts*' (originally set out in Tov 1992, 114–115 and modified in recent years. Compare Tov 2001).

6   Ulrich 1999b, 12.

7   Ibid., 25–26. For example, while 4QNum.[b] and 4QSam.[a] witness Hebrew «texts» presupposed by the LXX, other Numbers and Samuel manuscripts from Qumran are closer to 𝔐 (cf. Tov 1992, 20).

8   Ulrich 1999b, 36–41.

9   Ibid., 25.

10 Which Ulrich (1999b, 29) takes to show 'that the LXX faithfully transmitted an existing Hebrew text'. Successive layers in Isaiah 1–12 existed in the second century BCE or earlier (Kaiser 1983). The old form of LXX Isaiah, relatively stable in the first century CE, was not identical with the Christian uncials of the fourth and fifth centuries CE (Marcos 2000, 326 and 328–329).

11 For example, in: 1QIsa.[a] (Kutscher 1974, 547); 4Q252 (Brooke *et al.* 1996); supralinear glosses to 4QGen.[j] (Davila 1993) and 5QDeut. frg. 1 (Baillet and Milik *et al.* 1962; but Tov (1992) deems these 'non-aligned' readings).

12 For instance, Lange 2002, 26: Hebrew LXX-like 'texts' are cited in several non-'biblical' scrolls: Pentateuch citations in 4QTestimonia (175), Joshua in CD 4.3-4, Jeremiah in 4QOrd.[a]. Identification of these Hebrew citations as LXX-like is only possible for 'biblical' works 'which allow a clear distinction between different text types' (ibid.).

13 Fragments of Exod. 13.11-16 and Psalms 25–26 are identical with 𝔐 (Aharoni 1961, 23 and 40). Cf. Marcos 2000, chs 5, 7–9.

14 Tov 1992, 161.

divisions are essentially a development of the view held from the third century by Church Fathers, such as Origen and Jerome, who encountered relatively stable Hebrew (proto-𝔐) and Greek (LXX) «texts». These text-critical categories reflect a conceptualization of ancient textual plurality, organized according to major textual lineages of transmission. While these categories provide a stable typology essential for constructing histories of textual development, they are abstract text-critical objects that do not correspond to any ancient copy. Hence, it is inappropriate to frame ancient exegetes' attitudes to their literature in terms of these objects.

The 'post-Qumran'[15] perspective acknowledges that fluid Greek and Hebrew «texts» were stabilizing in the Hellenistic and Roman periods, but not at the same rate.[16] In recent decades scholars have questioned the older view that the three 'text-types' were stable entities in the first century.[17] Tov speaks of a 'multiplicity of *texts*' (his italics), of which 𝔐, SP and 𝔊 are only three representatives.[18] From this textual 'multiplicity' 'only a few groups of closely related *texts* are discernible'.[19]

Assuming a Lagardian model of Septuagint translation and development,[20] the «texts» of the Göttingen edition of the LXX (G^{Ed})[21] are ideal constructions of the oldest retrievable Greek form of each work of Jewish scripture. As a text-critical object, 'G^{Ed}' is analytically distinct from the 'OG' that was broadly represented in ancient copies. Nevertheless, while no two copies exhibited the same «text» prior to the printing press, a «text» can be generally reflected by a sufficient number of copies. Some consider the broad consistency of the OG (and its proximity to G^{Ed}) to be demonstrated by ancient Judaean and Egyptian LXX fragments. According to Marcos, these manuscript discoveries vindicate Lagarde's notion of a single Old Greek translation of the Pentateuch, as reported in the Letter of Aristeas, from which translations of various textual traditions of the LXX derive.[22]

The same fragments, however, demonstrate the extensive divergence of any

---

15 Stanley (1992, 50), Lim (1997, 10 [29]).

16 For example, Tov 1992, 114; Brooke 2000, 116; Ulrich 1998. The discussion concerning how to identify text-types is complex. See, for example, Lange 2002, 22–25 and VanderKam 1998, 389–396 discussing Tov 1992.

17 Tov finds the classical text-critical categories to lack precision (criticizing Kahle 1915; Tov 1992, 156–157). Gooding (1976) (criticizing Lagarde 1882) and Davila 1993 criticize inconsistency in usage.

18 Tov 1992, 160. In this case, by 𝔊 Tov seems to mean the Hebrew text presupposed by the LXX.

19 Ibid., 163; his italics.

20 See Footnote 22, below.

21 Since the Göttingen *Septuagint* is a post-printing press construction, distinction between the «text» of the Göttingen edition and the text of each copy is redundant. All of its copies are identical and therefore the text of any copy is identical with the «text» that it represents. My terminological conventions – text (of a copy) and «text» (see Section 1.1.1) – are relevant to distinguish between ancient and text-critical encounters with ancient literature. I speak of the «text» of G^{Ed} because it is a conscious modern effort to represent a «text».

22 Marcos 2000, 71 (rejecting Kahle's proposal that numerous independent Greek translations of each work came to be standardized around the turn of the era into the LXX); cf. 64–5. However, Tov thinks Lagarde's model impossible in practice (1992, 183).

particular first-century OG copy from the «text» of G^Ed. Revisions of the OG towards the emerging proto-𝔐 are evident from the second century BCE.[23] However, as this early evidence is so fragmentary, the extent of systematization of these revisions remains unclear.[24] While some second-century BCE revisions are not very systematic, others (from the turn of the era) are more so. Some fragments reflect partial revisions of the OG in the Pentateuch.[25] Wevers and Schaller detect a G^HR of Job.[26] There is also evidence for a proto-Lucianic revision of the OG 'towards a Hebrew text of the Palestinian type'.[27] The Palestinian καιγε revision (8ḤevXIIgr, first century CE or earlier) is the most thorough revision known before the late second century CE, which apparently formed the basis for second-century CE recensions of Theodotion (θ'), Aquila (α') and Symmachus (σ').[28] But while 8ḤevXIIgr generally revises towards proto-𝔐 and exhibits consistent stylistic directions in its Greek, it frequently preserves OG readings.[29] While The Three (θ', α' and σ') generally concur in revising the sense of OG towards proto-𝔐, often one or more go their own way.[30]

Notwithstanding such evidence, textual critics tend to doubt that ancient exegetes could have been aware of multiple text-types. Endorsing Tov's rejection of 'text-types' in favour of talking about a multiplicity of *texts*, Ulrich observes that

> [d]espite [Tov's] decentralisation of the MT, [. . .] he continues to use the MT, the SP and the LXX as text-type categories. This does have the advantage of clear, handy labelling (although since the MT, the SP and the LXX are different from book to book, only a specialist would know the significance of the labels). *The disadvantage is that it gives the impression both (1) that the MT, the SP and the LXX were known textual categories in the Second temple period, and (2) that critical comparison of parallel text-types was an activity in the period.*[31]

23 Marcos 2000, 71. Recensional activity 'goes back to a period quite close to the origins of the translation itself' (ibid., 247). 'The variants in the pre-recensional papyri indicate that the revisions of the LXX have to be put back to a date closer to its composition' (ibid., 65).

24 Ibid., 65. For example, the proto-Lucianic revision harmonized 'the old LXX to conform to the Palestinian Hebrew text of the second-first centuries BCE' (ibid., 249). Lesser revisions, along with καιγε-Theodotion and proto-Lucian (cf. ibid., 248), reveal 'intense activity of revision carried out before Origen' (ibid., 251) – *pace* Koch 1986, 80. 7QLXX^Exod. (7Q1) is a revision towards Hebrew from circa 100 BCE (Marcos 2000, 252, referring to Wevers 1954). There is evidence of Pentateuch revisions prior to Origen (Marcos 2000, 252, referring to Gooding 1955).

25 See Marcos 2000, 251–252) for his references to Pap 967, Pap *Antinopolitanus* (pre-Origenic); 7QLXX^Exod. (100 BCE); Rylands Papyrus gr. 458 (second century BCE); and 4QLXX^Num. See also Kraft 2003.

26 Wevers 1954 (cf. Koch 1986, 71 [65]) on the Berlin fragment P 11778; and Schaller 1980 (cf. Koch 1986, 71 [65]) on the Testament of Job.

27 Marcos 2000, 248f.

28 Tov *et al.* 1990, 22–26, 103f. Barthélemy (1963) dates the scroll to the late first century CE. Roberts (Roberts and Skeat 1983 [1954], 54–62), and Kahle 1954 suggest 50 BCE–50 CE. Parsons (1990, 19–26) and Skeat (Roberts and Skeat 1983 [1954], 54–62) date it to the first century BCE.

29 Tov *et al.* 1990, 103f.

30 For example, σ' of Isa. 53.11 agrees semantically with OG against pM, α' and θ'.

31 Ulrich 1998, 9; my italics. As an alternative, Ulrich proposes successive literary editions in which

Tov, himself, has similar misgivings. While 'it is possible that a certain tendency developed to compare texts' that were in circulation 'or even to revise or correct some texts according to others', there is 'little evidence that such a process took place'.[32] In doubting that Paul consciously used multiple 'Textformen' (by which he means the OG and καιγε), Koch finds himself in agreement with Ulrich and Tov.[33]

Emphasizing the widespread availability of a variety of text-forms in antiquity, Brooke concludes that 'the plurality of texts was accepted as a matter of fact' by ancient exegetes.[34] He proposes that 'for the most part the biblical texts represented in various interpretations are what may be deemed to have been generally available at the time'.[35] Indeed, some ancient exegetes capitalized on the variability of textual readings and there is evidence of plurality 'either at the textual or interpretative level or both'.[36] However, when speaking of ancient Jews, a 'matter of fact' acceptance of textual plurality does not equal their understanding of the *nature* of that plurality. That is, their perception *that* plurality existed in their own time does not entail that they perceived «texts» in anything like the modern categorical manner. Surely, ancient Jews could not perceive the categories of modern textual criticism. It is important, then, to distinguish two kinds of ancient awareness. Koch correctly doubts Paul's awareness of 'text-types' and 'recensions'. However, he mistakenly proceeds from this judgement to conclude that Paul had no awareness of plurality at all.

2.1.1 *A multivalent encounter*

How did ancient exegetes perceive the diversity of text-forms that they encountered? How did the environment of textual and exegetical plurality in this period express itself in the ancient Jewish exegetes' relationship with their literature? I designate ancient Jewish exegetes' *encounter* with this plurality 'multivalent'.

First-century Jewish groups in general apparently neither canonized nor claimed particular text-types as ideological property. The Tannaitic idea that Temple *soferim* carefully preserved proto-𝔐 in Second Temple times probably attributes post-third-century CE Tannaitic concerns to the earlier period.[37] By then Rabbinic Judaism and Christianity had adopted proto-𝔐 and the LXX, respectively, and had begun to standardize their copying traditions. Thus, manuscripts from the Bar Kokhba Revolt, the first column of Origen's Hexapla and the Hebrew sources compared by Justin and Trypho with LXX exemplars all appear to reflect proto-𝔐.

Literature known as the 'rewritten bible' throws light onto the ancient exegetes'

---

the manuscript evidence is viewed diachronically, not according to some supposed textual norm (ibid., 84–85).

32 Tov 1992, 190.
33 See Section 1.2.2.2, above.
34 Brooke 2000, 112.
35 Ibid., 116.
36 Ibid., 114–115. VanderKam (2002, 41–42) holds a similar view.
37 Or it may represent a Rabbinic apologetic designed to legitimize the priority of proto-𝔐 in Rabbinic Judaism. Note Tannaitic polemics against the early Christian LXX (cf. Feldman 1988).

multivalent encounter with traditional literature. Most extant 'rewritten bible' compositions are in Hebrew, although a Greek paraphrase of Exodus is extant.[38] Moreover, some translations of certain traditional works paraphrase and exegetically augment those works. Indeed, in some respects the OG approximates the literature designated as 'rewritten bible'.[39] Brooke suggests that 'rewritten bible' compositions aim to supplement rather than replace or supersede traditional works. The 'rewritten bible' reveals an ancient perception that some traditional «texts» could convey different sets of meanings.

> Rewritten scriptural compositions do not seem to have been composed to replace the authoritative sources which they rework. All operate some kind of interpretative strategy (however veiled that might be). They can only offer one interpretation at a time in their representations of the scriptural text.[40]

The continuous *pesharim* also illustrate how Jewish exegetes perceived the semantic potential of a traditional work. While the work is reproduced line-by-line (in a text-critically recognizable form), the pesherist intersperses this text with interpretations of each citation. A traditional passage can be linked to a past event or an anticipated future event. The pesherist subjects contiguous passages to radically divergent interpretations, without a sense that this disrupts the cogency of the traditional work. He seems comfortable with the idea that any traditional passage can simultaneously generate a variety of distinct meanings.[41]

Although first-century exegetes perceived a given traditional work as a unified literary object, they knew that textual diversity existed within copies of works[42] and were aware of the textual and interpretive flux within the discourse which they encountered. Variant copies of, for example, Isaiah, would be recognized as different expressions of a single prophetic tradition. And I suggest that ancient exegetes distinguished between copies (that is, material representations of a work) and the abstract body of the work itself, a distinction that is virtually lost in the age of the printing press.[43]

---

38 Ulrich 1990.

39 See, for example, Kooij 1981, 1989, 1989–90, 1992; Seeligman 1984, 47–48; Seeligman *et al.* 2004, 222–250; Campbell 2005.

40 Brooke 2002, 33.

41 1QpHab. 7.1-16 indicates this – that in words of scripture God would reveal meanings to the Teacher, meanings that were unknown to the prophets who uttered them.

42 Textual plurality also exists in copies of non-'traditional' Jewish literature. Copies of M, S, D and MMT from the Qumran corpus differ from each other in significant respects and yet in many cases seem to have been copied and used simultaneously. 'Traditional' works, such as Jeremiah, Daniel and Samuel/Kings, which were of sufficient general authority to be ultimately included in the Rabbinic and Christian canons, also circulated in multiple editions.

43 The «text» of Isaiah in a particular impression of the RSV, for instance, is identical with the characters inscribed in thousands of copies. See the seminal discussions of the effect of the printing press on modern thinking in Ong 1982 and Anderson 1983.

2.2 *Modern text-critical perspectives and Paul's awareness of textual plurality*

Ellis assumes that Paul was so well versed in Greek and Hebrew scripture that he could modify the «text» of the 'LXX' in light of the 'MT'.[44] Koch, on the contrary, describing such activity anachronistically as 'advanced exegetical work',[45] cannot imagine Paul working in this way.[46] Two issues are at stake here. First (as discussed in Chapter 1), Koch is probably right to doubt – on practical grounds – that an exegete like Paul could routinely compare multiple copies of the same work (see Section 2.2.3). Second, there is the question of how an individual might perceive those text-critical categories, such as 'LXX' and 'MT', known to modern scholarship as 'text-forms'. So, when discussing ancient Jewish exegetes' awareness of textual plurality it is important to distinguish between two distinct issues: (1) the practical doubts that Paul could compare different copies of each work and (2) text-critical doubt that ancient exegetes perceived various 'text-types'.

Not only were no two ancient copies identical, several Judaean manuscripts exhibit highly eclectic[47] affiliations to the categories of modern textual criticism (𝕲, 𝔐, SP, G[HR], etc.). In postulating an eclectic Pauline Isaiah *Vorlage*, Koch appreciates that any given Greek copy of a work could simultaneously reflect OG and G[HR]. It is unlikely that ancient exegetes perceived different 'text-types' from the individual copies they saw.

2.2.1 *Copies and text-forms*

Michel speaks as though comparison of '𝔐' and 'LXX' text-types was open to Paul. At times he refers to the 'Hebrew text' as the 'Urtext' and the Septuagint as the 'Übersetzung', implying that the two were fixed quantities.[48] Michel realizes that the «texts» of the LXX and that of pre-Theodotionic revisions often cannot be fully separated in eclectic copies: 'Abänderungen des LXX-Textes im Sinne Theodotions findet man ja selbst in LXX-Texten!'[49] However, since he considers the 'Hebrew text' to be identical with the 'MT',[50] he thinks it possible for a first-century exegete to distinguish between proto-𝔐 and OG «texts».[51]

Treating the Hebrew text available to Paul as identical with 𝔐,[52] Koch does

---

44 For example, Ellis 1957, 14, 139, 153. Cf. Section 1.5, above.

45 Koch 1986, 80–81, cf. Section 1.2.2.3, above.

46 Koch (1986, 19 [30], 57 [3], 78, 80 [112]) rejects Ellis' claim (1957, 139 and 153), denying that Paul used both Semitic and Greek sources; cf. Section 1.2.2, above.

47 It is, of course, 'eclectic' only with respect to modern text-critical categories.

48 Michel 1929, 64.

49 Ibid., 67.

50 Ibid., 50–68.

51 See citation from ibid. in Chapter One, Footnote 101.

52 By 'MT' Koch means Kittel's *Biblia Hebraica* and the *Biblia Hebraica Stuttgartensia* 1977 (also see Koch 1986, 57 and 24 [45]).

not need to deal with Hebrew textual plurality.[53] However, he attends closely to first-century textual variation in Greek. When Koch rejects the possibility of Paul's comparing 'mehrere Texte . . . mit unterschiedlicher Textform',[54] he implies both definitions: (1) comparing individual copies and (2) comparing the general text-forms that they represent. He views (1) as implausible on pragmatic grounds[55] and sees (2) as a primarily 'exegetisch-philologisch' undertaking inconceivable in the first century, arguing that '[b]ereits für Paulus ein derartiges exegetisch-philologisches Vorgehen anzunehmen, wäre jedoch anachronistisch'.[56]

The issue is not quite as clear in Stanley's discussion. On practical grounds, he argues that Paul could not simultaneously compare multiple copies.[57] However, his idea of Paul copying single verses into notebooks retains the possibility that Paul could compare an individual verse in multiple forms. That is, Stanley can imagine that an ancient individual could be aware of different text-forms. Although he acknowledges the state of textual plurality in the first century, he highlights the limits of eclecticism within a copy, arguing that any given first-century copy must recognizably belong to a particular strand of LXX transmission (see Section 1.3.2, especially Footnote 118, above).

However, the evidence reviewed in Section 2.1 above shows that Hebraizing revisions of the OG could be either partial or systematic.[58] Revisions could also be either Hebraizing or inner Greek revisions aimed at stylistic improvement. Extant fragments show that revisions began very soon after the translation of each work and were widespread by the first century (Footnote 23, above). Indeed, the relative stability of a standard LXX «text» for each canonical work exhibited by Christian manuscripts may well reflect the process of standardization from the second century CE onward. By contrast, the situation for first-century exegetes was one of considerable textual variation.

In light of the preceding discussion, it is important to distinguish between an ancient exegete's comparison of different copies of a work and his conscious comparison of different «texts».

---

53 Koch considers Hebrew citations in sectarian compositions in order to compare Paul's *Zitierpraxis* with that of Dead Sea sectarian exegetes (1986, 190–198). The Judaean Hebrew biblical fragments are not relevant to his text-critical study of Greek texts.

54 Ibid., 80, cf. Section 1.2.2.2.

55 Relating mainly to the expense that that would entail (see Section 1.2.2.1, above).

56 Koch 1986, 80.

57 See Section 1.3.2, above.

58 Compare Wilk (1998, 41–42), who advises against attempts to set a limit on the extent of eclecticism in ancient Greek copies of Jewish scripture. His analysis of Paul's Isaiah citations suggests that Paul used: multiple copies representing OG; one copy exhibiting a partial Hebraizing revision of Isaiah[OG]; and one comprehensive Hebraizing revision of Isaiah[OG].

2.2.2 *Paul's awareness of variant readings*

In several articles Stanley highlights the rhetorical function of Paul's citations as communicative acts.[59] He argues that Paul's expectation of his audiences' capacity to appreciate his literary references must be commensurate with the generally low literacy of his recipients. That is, Paul must have intended many of his citations to have a purely rhetorical effect without expecting his audiences to appreciate their exegetical and hermeneutical subtleties. Paul presumably expected them to follow his explicit rhetoric, but to assume that Paul presented his listeners with arguments requiring advanced exegetical appreciation of his use of scripture, would be to accuse Paul of misjudging his audience.[60]

In Chapter 7 I identify various rhetorical functions in Paul's citations and conclude that in many cases the explicit citation plays a purely rhetorical role and that his explicit argument would retain coherence without it. That is, I argue that within Paul's rhetoric many citations have an intrinsically low exegetical function. In such cases, it is important that the citation is sufficiently verbally or thematically congruous with Paul's text to produce a satisfactory rhetorical effect. Koch and Stanley have shown that Paul frequently alters the source wording in order to smooth continuity of the citation with his own writing. Since in these cases rhetorical congruence and stylistic seamlessness are a priority, the particular text-forms of passages chosen by Paul (if variants exist) are often unimportant. However, in some cases citations play more than a purely rhetorical role. The citation is indispensable to Paul's logic, that is, Paul's appeal to the passage logically structures his argument and one could not remove such a citation without disrupting the coherence of the argument. In such cases, where distinct textual traditions are characterized by semantically variant forms, Paul can only employ the form of the passage that he has indeed employed. By 'semantic' I mean 'pertaining to meaning' (see below).

Koch, Michel and Stanley argue the opposite. They point to several Pauline citations, where they believe another form of the passage would have been more suitable for Paul's purpose than the form Paul uses. (I have called this the 'suitability argument'; see Section 1.2.2.3, above). I denote such cases as 'type A'.[61] Koch and Stanley generalize these cases to argue that Paul *always* cited his sources uncritically, unaware of alternative forms of the given passage. In fact, these cases rarely support the argument invoked by Koch and Stanley, and certainly do not allow for general inferences (see Section 7.4, below). For now, it suffices to note that neither scholar attends to the converse: that in a number of cases, where the form of a Pauline citation is closer to a G[HR] than the OG, Paul can only sensibly use the form he cites. In these cases, the alternative form of the passage would make no sense for Paul's argument.

---

59 Discussed in Section 7.1.1, below.

60 Stanley 1997a, 1997b, 1998 and 1999.

61 Type A cases are: Isa. 25.8 in 1 Cor. 15.54 (Koch 1986, 80 [113]); 28.11 in 1 Cor. 14.21 (Koch 1986, 80 [113], 65); 59.20 in Rom. 11.26 (Koch 1986, 177 [34]); Job 5.13 in 1 Cor. 3.19 (Koch 1986, 80 [113], 72); Hos. 2.1[LXX] in Rom. 9.25 (Koch 1986, 55 [34]).

I denote such cases as 'type B', presenting exegetical study of particular type B cases in Chapter 7, below.

In many cases where the citation appears to have a low logical function in Paul's argument, the form of a cited passage has little bearing on his argument (see Sections 7.2–7.2.3, below). These cases frequently belong to type A. Conversely, in some instances the citation is logically indispensable in Paul's argument whereby only one form of a passage is useful to him. Some of these cases are type B. In most type A examples invoked by Koch, where another form of the cited passage would better suit Paul's argument, the citation is not indisciplinable to the logic of Paul's argument, but performs a rhetorical function. So attention to the variety of roles played by citations invalidates the generalized suitability argument (see Section 7.4).

2.2.3 *Expertise and plausibility*

The question of Paul's intentional selection of forms of traditional passages is not a text-critical question, but a historical one. However, it is routinely addressed in text-critical terms. So, Vollmer writes: 'Es ist a priori nicht eben recht glaubhaft, dass Paulus über mehrere Versionen des Alten Testaments verfügt, von denen er bald die eine, bald die andere aufgerollt hätte.'[62] Koch asserts: 'daß er sich um mehrere Texte z. B. von Jes mit unterschiedlicher Textform bemühte, diese erwarb und kritisch-abwägend benutze, ist eine abwegige Vorstellung.'[63] Stanley says:

> All in all, the evidence seems strong that the great majority of Paul's biblical quotations were taken directly from written texts of some sort. But the practical explanation would appear to be insuperable. How can such conflicting data be resolved? Clearly the answer is not to be found in casting Paul as a modern biblical scholar, scrambling through a mountain of unwieldy scrolls (in a Jewish synagogue, no less) in search of the precise wording of a passage that he is in the midst of dictating to an increasingly impatient amanuensis?[64]

Lim raises the same point.[65] The implication is that in order to select a particular form of a passage, Paul must operate like a modern textual critic, perceiving various 'text-forms' through the comparison of multiple copies. When Hengel suggests that Paul could distinguish two 'recensions', he sees Paul as a scribe producing his own copy of Isaiah from at least two copies, one resembling the OG, the other καιγε-Theodotion.[66]

Modern perceptions of ancient Jewish scribes working 'text-critically' have influenced discussions of ancient awareness of textual plurality. A number of Qumran scholars suggest that *Yaḥad* exegetes appealed to variant versions of particular

---

62 Vollmer 1895, 33.

63 Koch 1986, 80.

64 Stanley 1992, 71.

65 Lim (1997, 154) talks of the problems involved in handling multiple 'rolls or codices'. He therefore suggests that Paul used biblical 'anthologies'.

66 See Chapter One, Footnote 143.

passages. Assuming that *Yahad* members had access to multiple copies in their library at Qumran, scholars are generally comfortable with the thought of *Yahad* exegetes' awareness of variant versions.[67] Stendahl supposes the same when he writes that the exegetical work, implied by Matthew's formula citations, was done in a 'School'.[68] Whoever produced these Matthaean citations seems to have made use of the OG, a G[HR] and in some cases proto-𝔐.

These examples reveal an assumption that exegetical use of textual plurality is inherently institutional and 'scribal'. The scribal institution is thought to provide a sufficiently literary ethos and biblio-technical facilities for modern commentators to consider such an ancient literary practice plausible. On the other hand, the common view of Paul – a missionary whose writing generally suggests to scholars no more than secondary education,[69] travelling around Asia Minor, considered vagrant by many contemporaries,[70] unwelcome in some synagogues,[71] and therefore with limited access to scrolls – leads scholars to consider his circumstances irreconcilable with expert 'scribal' literary activity. However, this view is based on a conjecture that exegetical engagement is necessarily predicated on private study only possible in an institution. In Chapter 5 I argue that the *Yahad*'s engagement with literature reflects the same markers of oral discourse as Paul's writing, showing that the difference in their circumstances does not categorically divide their literary enterprises.

Scholars conflate several distinct issues relating to Paul's possible awareness of textual plurality:

(1) Bilingualism and text-types
(2) Revisions of the OG
(3) Individual 'variant readings' or 'textual variants'

(1) The old question of Paul's use of Hebrew and Greek text-types, which remains open for Michel, Ellis and Lim,[72] allows for Paul's bilingualism. Because the

---

67 See Chapter 5, below.

68 Stendahl 1954.

69 Deissmann (1925, 71) credits Paul with colloquial artisan's Greek. However, Gamble (1995) questions Deissmann's (Deissmann 1978 [1927], 69–72) view that early Christian works generally represent colloquial Greek, arguing that Paul's letters display a contemporary professional prose and reflect the style of official and philosophical letters. Porter (1997, 578–583) argues that Paul can employ various styles characteristic of exercises known from Hellenistic 'grammar schools', the middle of three tiers of classical education: primary school (*ludus litterarius*), grammar school (*schola grammatici*), and the rhetorical school (*schola rhetoric*) (cf. Marrou 1956, 186–205, 242–54; Bonner 1977, 34–75, 165–276; Clark 1957, 9–66; Morgan 1998, 21–25; Hock, 2005, 17–25).

70 2 Cor. 11.23-28 shows that Roman officials and Jewish synagogues considered Paul unwelcome. Beating with 'rods' and imprisonment (cf. Philippians 1; Philemon) reflect Roman punishment, the 'thirty-nine' strokes reflect Jewish punishment (cf. Deut. 25.3). Acts provides further anecdotal evidence.

71 This is explicitly the case in Acts, but reference to 'thirty-nine' lashes in Paul's own writings suggests the same (see previous footnote).

72 Michel 1929, Ellis 1957 and Lim 2002.

lexical evidence of Paul's letters is mute in regard to his knowledge of Hebrew, the question of Hebrew and Greek text-types has been excluded from this study.[73]

(2) This does not resolve the question of Paul's informed ability to prefer particular semantic forms of Greek passages. By the first century, individual copies of Greek Jewish scripture exhibited eclectic mixtures of OG, Hebraizing or inner-Greek revisions. Some revisions were systematic, others less so.[74] It is dubious to credit him with an awareness of distinct Greek «texts».

(3) The terms 'variant reading' or 'textual variant' recur in scholarly discussions of Paul's sources. Scholars ask whether Paul could select this or that 'reading' in preference to another. This is partly a reiteration of the second issue (relating to 'Revisions of the OG') because the 'textual variants' in question are those atomic units that text-critically characterize 'text-type', 'recension' or 'revision'. Koch's doubt that Paul knew various 'text-forms' of the same work implies his reservation regarding Paul's ability to distinguish between 'variant readings'. Origen's 'highly advanced exegetical work'[75] involved painstaking comparison of the variant readings of multiple copies in the production of his Hexaplaric text. Assertions of Paul's ignorance of various 'text-forms' predicate general doubts that he could distinguish multiple 'variant readings'. In attributing the diverse textual profile of Paul's citations to his sources rather than to Paul's informed choices,[76] scholars recoil from seeing Paul operating as a textual critic.

Koch expresses textual divergences between different text-forms in text-critical terms. In his view, Paul's Isaiah *Vorlage* had been subjected to a partial Hebraizing revision at precisely the points where the LXX 'sich nicht nur in der Wiedergabe einzelner Wörter gegenüber dem HT frei verhält, sondern auch die zugrunde liegende syntaktische Struktur umgestaltet hat'.[77] Koch rejects Ellis' proposition that Paul practised 'ad hoc rendering or an interpretative selection from various known texts'[78] because 'Paulus – gerade an den in Frage kommenden Stellen – keineswegs die für ihn geeignetste Übersetzung »ausgewählt« hätte'.[79] Here Koch is describing type A cases, as I defined them above.[80] He considers 1 Cor. 3.19 (Job 5.13a) and 1 Cor. 14.21 (Isa. 28.11) type A cases, continuing: 'Auch für 1 Kor 15:54 kann man sich fragen, ob der mit Θ übereinstimmende rezensierte Wortlaut von Jes 25:8 wirklich der geeignetste war. Nach den Futura von 1 Kor 15:54a.b wäre eine futurische Übersetzung, wie sie in A und Σ beiten, näherliegend gewesen.'[81] He assumes that

73 See Section 1.8.3.
74 See Section 2.1, above.
75 Koch, 80–81 (see Section 1.2.2.3, above).
76 See Section 1.4, above.
77 Koch 1986, 78.
78 Ellis 1957, 139; cited by Koch 1986, 19 [30], 57 [3], 78, 80 [112].
79 Koch 1986, 80.
80 Cf. Section 2.2.2, above.
81 Koch 1986, 80 [113].

the question revolves around Paul's preference for one 'variant reading'.[82] Such text-critical framing of Paul's awareness of Greek textual plurality obscures the question of Paul's own perception and predicts conclusions with text-critical formulations.

Koch expresses these textual divergences in text-critical terms that are predicated on a particular understanding of textual criticism as an objective lexical discipline that is free of socio-historical concerns. In order to clarify this point I want to make a distinction between lexical and semantic as a heuristic device within the present discussion to highlight the difference I propose between Koch's and Paul's interests. In the example cited above, Koch highlights Paul's 'inappropriate' use of Theodotion's aorist in contrast to Aquila and Symmachus' future tense, which Koch thinks would better have suited Paul's context in 1 Corinthians 15. At issue here is that judgements about the semantic value of text must be treated as a matter of Paul's arbitration, not to be conducted within the modern frame of a particular understanding of lexical text-critical concerns. On the basis of lexical temporal indicators (tense) Koch judges the aorist of θ' to be poorly suited to Paul's text.[83] However, a more significant *semantic* criterion moves Paul here, to which the importance of various lexical options is subordinated in Paul's arbitration. While in Isa. 25.8^{LXX} 'death swallows up humans once again', in the pM-stream (𝔐 θ' σ' α') God swallows up *death* (so that death can *no longer* swallow up humans). As the arbiter of his own interests, Paul is concerned with this semantic criterion, not the question of tense (as I argue fully in Section 7.4, below).

Textual critics distinguish syntactic forms of a «text» by means of variant readings. This is a linguistic exercise whose goal is the identification of textual families on the basis of shared distinctive readings in an effort to establish the oldest retrievable form of a «text». Relating the textual profile of Paul's citations to these textual families is a project that assumes the same logic. While judgements on 'variant readings' reflect modern critics' concerns, they presumably do not reflect the perspective of ancient exegetes. That Jewish exegetes, like Paul, frequently altered the wording of their sources for rhetorical, stylistic and theological purposes, suggests that a preoccupation with the meaning of a passage was not identical with a text-critical interest in its wording.

Attention to 'textual variants' is not the only way to express differences between forms of the same literary passage. In many cases, distinct forms of a passage (for example, presented by LXX and 𝔐; or LXX and Theodotion) convey the same meaning, despite lexical variation. However, often a passage conveys completely different senses in distinct text-forms. Aquila, Symmachus and Theodotion often share the sense of proto-𝔐 (against the OG), notwithstanding lexical variations ('variant readings') among themselves. That is, the pM-stream (proto-𝔐 + G^{HR}; see Section 1.1.1) is semantically united against the OG. Equally, LXX manuscripts can exhibit several

---

82 See Section 7.4, below.
83 A judgement that I question in Section 7.4, below.

lexical variations within a single literary passage, but be semantically united against the pM-stream. The semantic element upon which we judge two text-forms united against other text-forms is arbitrary (for example, does death swallow humans, or does God swallow death?). Should we select another semantic element (for example, future or past narration), the configuration of agreements and disagreements between the text-forms in question will shift. We must be sensitive to Paul's arbitration in this matter. I argue that it is not the presence of 'variant readings', but distinct 'sense contours' that distinguish type B cases, that is, cases; in which Paul has grounds to prefer one form. I work out the implications of this distinction below.

2.3 *Sense contours*

Various textual traditions reveal distinct 'sense contours' at particular points. For the ancient exegete, a particular sense contour characterized a distinct semantic form of a passage. In relation to ancient exegetical discourse (rather than modern text-critical) discourse, sense contours (rather than variant readings) should be adopted as the category by which to perceive ancient exegetes' points of intellectual purchase on literature. In the example of Isa. 25.8, above, a distinct sense contour characterizes the semantic form of Isa. 25.8, which Paul uses in 1 Cor. 15.54. The pM-form, in which God swallows up death, suits his purpose. The LXX form, in which death yet again swallows up humans, does not. For the ancient exegete these are more than 'variant readings'. They are conspicuously distinct sense contours (see Sections 7.3.4–7.3.4.1, below).

Ellis lists Paul's 'citations', counting the verbal variations between the LXX and 𝔐.[84] However, both forms of a passage may well exhibit 'variants' while still offering the same sense. I take Gen. 2.24 as an example.

Table 2.1 A sense contour in Genesis 2.24

Gen. 2.24^LXX	1 Cor. 6.16	Gen. 2.24^𝔐
καὶ ἔσονται οἱ δύο	ἔσονται γάρ, φησίν, οἱ δύο	וְהָיוּ
εἰς σάρκα μίαν	εἰς σάρκα μίαν.	לְבָשָׂר אֶחָד:
LXX 1 Cor. 6.16 οἱ δύο > 𝔐		

In Ellis' view, Paul and LXX agree against 𝔐 ([Paul = LXX] ≠ 𝔐) because Paul and the LXX share the phrase 'the *two* will be', whereas 𝔐 simply has 'they will be'. However, this divergence makes no semantic difference because Gen. 2.24 refers to two people (a man and a woman), in any case. That is, a single sense contour characterizes both forms of the passage despite lexical variations. Whereas Ellis classifies these lexically: [Paul = LXX] ≠ 𝔐, I view their relationship semantically: [Paul = LXX = 𝔐].

---

84 Ellis 1957 'Appendix I', 150–152.

Paul often employs G^HR at points where 𝔐 and OG significantly diverge. While this cannot prove that Paul *preferred* the pM sense (it may have been the only form of the passage he knew), attention to sense contours shifts the discussion from the intractable problem of Paul's awareness of distinct «texts» – through navigation of myriad variant readings – towards a historically conceived sense of his modus operandi. The issue of access to multiple copies reflects an unhelpful preoccupation with the technical means by which Paul could negotiate alternative semantic forms of a passage. An exegete could read a passage in a copy while knowing other exegetical ideas traditionally associated with that passage and being broadly aware that different sense contours can characterize the same passage (in other copies or at other performances). So when talking about sense contours, we need not envisage Paul sifting through multiple copies in search of a preferable reading. The concept of 'sense contours' removes anachronistic text-critical concerns from our conception of Paul's encounter with textual plurality and thereby avoids the question: 'Was Paul a textual critic?'(and the inevitable answer: 'No'). Sense contours provide a means to discuss cases where Paul had an exegetical or rhetorical incentive to prefer one particular semantic form of a passage. In other words, I suggest that we can envisage ancient exegetes perceiving these sense contours without suggesting that they operated like textual critics.[85]

2.4 *Passages*

Ancient exegetes encountered literature in discrete meaningful units – passages. Scribal conventions divide the text of ancient copies into such units, which are clearly marked for the reader's or hearer's aid. The ancient textual divisions in 1QIsaiah^a and 8ḤevXIIgr are broadly preserved in mediaeval manuscripts.[86] The *pesharim* divide continuous text into units and interpret each one independently of the neighbouring ones. A similar practice existed several centuries later. In synagogues, according to *m.* Megilla 4:4, one verse from the Hebrew Pentateuch was read aloud, or three verses at a time from the prophets, after which a translator gave an oral version in Aramaic.

I refer to such discrete textual units as passages. A 'passage' is that coherent piece of syntax interpreted by an exegete.
1. A literary passage can traditionally exist in various semantic forms, each form characterized by a distinct sense contour.

---

85 The idea of textual criticism did exist in antiquity. For example, the textual critics of Alexandria attempted to standardize the «text» of Homer. The Letter of Aristeas shows awareness that some Hebrew exemplars were 'excellent', implying that others were seen as corrupt. We may not assume, however, that ancient exegetes in general could be credited with Alexandrian standards of text-critical work (cf. Russell and Winterbottom 1998). The Rabbis were fascinated by variants in Rabbi Meir's Torah scroll (Siegel 1975, 8–17).

86 Oesch 1979; Revell 1984; Tov *et al.* 1990; Tov 1992 and 2004.

2. An individual exegete could know distinct semantic forms of a passage without (text-critically) perceiving variant 'text-types' of the literary work.
3. A given semantic form of a passage can give rise to a particular idea in ancient exegetical discourse.
4. In exegetical discourse, multiple exegetical ideas can be simultaneously and variously associated with the same passage.
5. An exegete may encounter (in a copy or a recital) a particular semantic form of a passage, associated with an exegetical idea, while remaining aware of other exegetical ideas commonly associated with that passage.
6. A passage in a given copy can thus function as a cue to the multiple exegetical ideas traditionally associated with that passage.

2.5 *Polyvalent texts*

A set of exegetical techniques was integral to the ancient exegetes' encounter with a traditional work. Several exegetical techniques capitalize on properties of consonantal Hebrew (for example: alternative vocalization, metathesis, splitting words, and substitution of similar letters of the root).[87] In other words, exegetical techniques were not secondary to the reading of texts. They were not merely methods of text alteration, but provided a lens for the very reading of these texts. A given passage of a Hebrew text offers multiple exegetical possibilities. So an exegete encountering a passage within an exegetical discussion could be familiar with several exegetical ideas traditionally associated with that passage, regardless of the wording within the particular written source.

In the Habakkuk Pesher 11.8-9, the pesherist cites Hab. 2.16, apparently according to the Hebrew reading presupposed by the OG and several cognate versions. However, his *pesher* in 11.12-16 presupposes the reading of proto-𝔐.

Table 2.2 Two sense contours in Habakkuk 2.16

1QpHab. 11.8-9	Hab. 2.16𝔐
שבעתה קלון מבוד	שָׂבַעְתָּ קָלוֹן מִכָּבוֹד
שתה גם אתה	שְׁתֵה גַם־אַתָּה
והרעל	וְהֵעָרֵל
Hab. 2.16𝔐	**1QpHab. 11.8-9**
You will be sated with shame	You will be sated with shame
instead of glory.	instead of glory.
Drink, you yourself,	Drink, you yourself,
and *be uncircumcised*!	and *stagger*!

---

87 See Section 5.3.

The Hebrew witnesses (𝔐 and the citation in 1QpHab. 11.8-9) show that one sense contour arises from the word ערל ('circumcise'), another arises from רעל ('stagger'). These two words occupy the same syntactical position in the passage. Thus, the words רעל/ערל represent distinct configurations of the *same* syntactical unit, which characterizes distinct sense contours of the passage. These sense contours are reflected more widely in known textual traditions (𝔐, LXX, α', 𝔗, V, Syr, cf. Section 4.2, below).

Many believe that the pesherist was conversant with both textual traditions (cf. Section 4.2, below). Perhaps the pesherist compared two copies of Habakkuk. Yet, not only is it unwise to assume that the exegete had two copies,[88] it is also unnecessary. He could have been equally aware of both exegetical ideas associated with Hab. 2.16; and his encounter with this passage within his exegetical environment accommodated both ideas. Perhaps the pesherist always associated both exegetical ideas with this passage, regardless of the wording of his copy. Certainly, the two exegetical ideas are enshrined as distinct readings in two textual traditions – proto-𝔐 and OG. Yet the exegete need not be aware of this. In a milieu of textual and exegetical flux, the pesherist's apparently intentional appeal to two traditions does not entail his knowledge of two 'text-types' nor his comparison of two copies.

2.5.1 *'Passages' and 'semantic units'*

If an ancient exegete presupposes now one textual tradition (such as OG) and now another (such as 𝔐), no case can be made for his global knowledge of two text-forms of the entire work, not only because his source could be eclectic according to text-critical categories, but also because we may not attribute to him text-critical logic. However, his awareness of two semantic forms of precisely the same syntactical unit can be seen as evidence for his awareness of textual plurality. As we have seen, in Hab. 2.16 two sense contours arise from distinct configurations of the same syntactical unit.

Thus, while a 'passage' is that coherent piece of syntax interpreted by an exegete, a 'semantic unit' is the smallest syntactical element within which verbal differences engender distinct sense contours. A distinct sense contour characterizes a particular semantic form of the passage. For the ancient exegete, a sense contour is a property of the passage as a whole; and several possible sense contours associated with a passage can become traditional properties of that passage.

I express this range of awareness of textual plurality as a continuum:

§A   A work can be perceived as a fixed literary object of interpretation. While the wording of a passage may be deemed fixed, exegetes assume that the passage can be interpreted in several ways.

§B   The text of a passage can be seen, not as a fixed, but as a multivalent object of

---

88 Aside from doubts about the 'Qumran library' and 'scriptorium' hypotheses (e.g. Eisenman 1983, 1986; Golb 1980, 1985, 1995; Crown and Cansdale 1994; Zangenberg 2000), we cannot be sure which Dead Sea sectarian documents were composed or copied at Qumran, if any (see Section 5.2, Footnote 21; cf. Norton 2009, 141–142). We should avoid, if we can, predicating our analysis on irresolvable questions.

interpretation. Multiple sense contours can characterize the passage. An interpreter can derive distinct sense contours through manipulation of a semantic unit. The exegete can perceive several semantic forms of the passage as properties of that passage.

§C   In various copies, a passage can exhibit distinct sense contours. An exegete can be familiar with various sense contours characterizing the passage.

In the following chapters I explore a range of ancient awareness of textual plurality in traditional Jewish literature. Although the entire range does not apply to Paul, the discussion opens perspectives on the breadth of possibilities open to him. Although Koch and Stanley do not believe that §C is a modus operandi open to Paul, I will give evidence for §C as a practice among some of Paul's contemporaries. Discussion of §B, begun in the preceding section, continues in the following chapters.

2.6 *Conclusions*

Paul did not distinguish among 'text-types' in the modern sense through comparison of multiple copies of a given work. Terms like 'textual variant' or 'variant reading' frame our own interests, often obscuring ancient concerns (Section 2.2.3). I have argued that in order to engage with ancient exegetes' perceptions, we need to establish the sense contours that they themselves identify (Section 2.3). Within an exegetical environment, the sense contour characterizing the form of a given passage prompts multiple exegetical ideas (Section 2.4).

3

JOSEPHUS AND TEXTUAL PLURALITY

3.1 *Textual traditions*

Josephus was a priest of the Judaean ruling class. He was influential in Judaean politics in the years immediately preceding and during the Jewish Revolt of 66–70 CE. Josephus stresses the influence of Pharisees in Judaean civil and religious life and claims to have governed his public affairs according to their practices (*Vita* 1–12).[1] In Rome, after the Revolt, he adopted the persona of a Hellenistic historian,[2] writing in Greek a history of the Judaean people for his patrons, and an extensive work presenting the Judaean constitution, ancestral customs and literature for an interested Graeco-Roman audience. Having carefully studied Greek literature and historiography, which he emulates, he shows knowledge of critical and interpretive traditions associated with this literature. Giving his audience his own detailed account of Judaean customs in the *AJ*, he presents and explains considerable portions of Jewish scripture, particularly those portions dealing with legal constitution and monarchy. Despite the unfamiliarity of his Roman audience with things Judaean, Josephus' presentation reveals his own intimate knowledge of Jewish literature in Hebrew and Greek, which is accompanied by a profound familiarity with common exegetical techniques and interpretive traditions associated with that literature.

3.2 *Assessing Josephus' awareness of textual variation*

The purpose of this chapter is to establish whether Josephus ever made conscious use of multiple forms of a passage from Jewish scripture. Indeed, many believe that Josephus referred simultaneously to Semitic and Greek sources of the same work, particularly in preparing his presentation of the Pentateuch. If this were true, it would be immediately evident that he was aware of variant forms of the same literary work, not only because his sources for a given work would vary in language, but also because his sources would inevitably exhibit the level of textual variation known from ancient Hebrew and Greek manuscripts. However, it is notoriously difficult to

---

1 It is questionable whether he was himself a Pharisee, cf. Mason 1991, 343–356.
2 Sterling 1992, 240–245; Feldman 1998a, 3–13.

demonstrate that he did use multiple copies of any given work and to establish the text-forms that these might have represented.

On the face of it, Josephus' own statements seem to affirm that he knew and used multiple versions, at least of the Pentateuch: he speaks of the Alexandrian Greek Pentateuch translation and claims to be using Hebrew sources at the same time (see Section 3.3, below). But considerable disagreement persists regarding Josephus' linguistic ability and the textual nature of his sources. Despite his writing in Greek, and his frequent elucidation of Hebrew and Aramaic words, his command of each language has been questioned in modern times. And although his Hebrew and Aramaic competence will be examined below, gaining insight into his linguistic abilities does not resolve the question of the textual character of his sources. As we shall see, because of the complexities inherent in the textual history of the so-called 'Historical' and 'Prophetic Books', this chapter focuses on Josephus' use of the Pentateuch, which was textually more stable than other Jewish literature in the first century. Yet uncertainty still abounds. Some think that Josephus used both Greek and Hebrew Pentateuch sources side by side. Others think he used only Greek sources (explaining Hebrew and Aramaic vernacular usage); still others think that the *AJ* is his own translation of the Hebrew Pentateuch, which he produced without reference to the Old Greek; but he may, as some believe, have consulted the Old Greek as a lexical aid. Finally, the very nature of his 'historical' presentation of the Pentateuch makes it very difficult to establish the text-form of his sources in any given case. To a considerable degree, then, the task of this chapter involves considering how to approach the question.

3.3 *Josephus' project*

It makes sense to start with Josephus' own stated aims in writing the *AJ*. While commentators have often treated his statements with scepticism, recent studies find that Josephus' programmatic aims in the *AJ* correspond well with the work that follows, so his statements should be taken seriously.[3]

In *AJ* 1.5 Josephus writes that his project (πραγματεία)[4] will 'encompass our entire ancient history and constitution of the state, interpreted from the Hebrew writings' (μέλλει γὰρ περιέξειν ἅπασαν τὴν παρ' ἡμῖν ἀρχαιολογίαν καὶ διάταξιν τοῦ πολιτεύματος ἐκ τῶν Ἑβραϊκῶν μεθηρμηνευμένην γραμμάτων). While μεθηρμηνευμένην here is understood as 'interpreted', some read this as 'translated'.[5] And this is quite possible. In *AJ* 1.7 Josephus goes on to say that, in his previous documentation of Jewish origins in the *BJ*, he had hesitated in 'transferring such a subject into a foreign and unfamiliar usage of language' (μετενεγκεῖν ὑπόθεσιν εἰς

---

3 See Mason's discussion (2000, XIIIf., esp. XIX–XX).

4 Thackeray (1967, *ad loc.*), 'work'; Feldman (2000, *ad loc.*), 'task'.

5 So Thackeray 1961, *ad loc.*; Feldman 2000, *ad loc.* Nodet (1997), too, sees the *AJ* as a primary translation.

ἀλλοδαπὴν ἡμῖν καὶ ξένην διαλέκτου συνήθειαν). 'Usage' here refers to his Greek. In *AJ* 10.218, referring back to *AJ* 1.5, he declares that 'right from the beginning of my history . . . I committed only to express the Hebrew works into the Greek tongue and explain these things, without adding anything of my own, or taking anything away' (ἐν ἀρχῇ τῆς ἱστορίας . . . ἠσφαλισάμην μόνον τε μεταφράζειν τὰς Ἑβραίων βίβλους εἰπὼν εἰς τὴν Ἑλλάδα γλῶτταν καὶ ταῦτα δηλώσειν μήτε προστιθεὶς τοῖς πράγμασιν αὐτὸς ἰδίᾳ μήτ' ἀφαιρῶν ὑπεισχημένος). These statements, particularly the latter (10.218), can be taken to indicate that Josephus undertook a 'translation' of the Pentateuch; Josephus uses μεταφέρω and μεταφράζω (*AJ* 1.7 and 10.218), at least in part, to indicate 'transferring' or 'putting' his account into Greek.

However, his project seems to entail more than 'translation' in any formally limited sense. First, in the introduction to Book 1 Josephus explains his aims in writing 'history', which are not merely to translate. 'This present project' (ταύτην [. . .] τὴν ἐνεστῶσαν [. . .] πραγματείαν) (*AJ* 1.5) belongs to the 'writing (of) histories' (τὰς ἱστορίας συγγράφειν), introduced in 1.1 and referred to throughout 1.1-8. This 'project' is Josephus' own 'writing of history' which 'will encompass our entire ancient history and constitution of the state'. That this 'history' is to be 'interpreted from the Hebrew writings' (ἐκ τῶν Ἑβραϊκῶν μεθηρμηνευμένην γραμμάτων) is a subsidiary thought reflecting his awareness that Judaean customs and literature represent an exotic and foreign subject for his audience. The *AJ* is a history, not simply a *translation* from Hebrew. Some write histories to show off their 'skill in composition' (λόγων δεινότητα) or 'to gratify those interested' (1.2), but Josephus seeks to present and 'clarify' those 'facts', which lie in 'obscurity' for the 'common benefit' (εἰς κοινὴν ὠφέλειαν, 1.3). It is precisely because these facts need to be 'interpreted out of the Hebrew scriptures' that Josephus has the right credentials for this task. He is an interpreter, qualified by his Judaean aristocratic education and priestly status. Indeed, Josephus could not provide the 'history' he promises to Epaphroditus & Co. (1.8) merely by *translating* the Hebrew writings, because a history requires a worthy historian's elucidation of 'facts' (1.3) and Mosaic philosophical principles (1.18-23), whereas the Hebrew Books of Moses contain principally 'our laws and constitution' (1.10), which Moses conveyed in part obscurely (αἰνιττομένου, 1.24), and which Josephus intends to explain (1.18, 24) (although he excuses himself from expounding on the underlying philosophical theory, 1.25). Josephus even distinguishes his own contribution from that of Moses, the author of the Pentateuch (1.18), thus distinguishing himself from someone who merely translates Moses' own words.

In *AJ* 10.218 too Josephus promises something other than translation. He does not set out only to express (μεταφράζω) the Hebrew in Greek; he will also *explain* (δηλόω) the Hebrew literary traditions in Greek (ἠσφαλισάμην μόνον τε μεταφράζειν τὰς Ἑβραίων βίβλους εἰπὼν εἰς τὴν Ἑλλάδα γλῶτταν καὶ ταῦτα δηλώσειν μήτε προστιθεὶς τοῖς πράγμασιν αὐτὸς ἰδίᾳ μήτ' ἀφαιρῶν ὑπεισχημένος). His 'only' (μόνος) relates to *expressing and explaining* as a single task[6] and excludes *adding or subtracting* anything. The latter claim is a common trope.[7] That Josephus, in the estimation of commentators, *does* supplement and omit traditional material tells us more about how he views his project and his role as interpreter than about his honesty; his additions and omissions belong, presumably, to his *explanation*; this is a true explanation by a qualified Judaean priest which, therefore, does not misrepresent the essence of Moses' writing.

Josephus presents himself standing in the tradition of the Judaean 'elders' who translated the Hebrew Torah into Greek for Ptolemy, stating his intention to 'imitate (μιμήσασθαι) the magnanimity (μεγαλόψυχον)' of Eleazar (*AJ* 1.12), the high priest who presided over the translation of the Pentateuch into Greek (εἰς τὴν Ἑλλάδα φωνὴν μεταβαλεῖν *AJ* 1.10).[8] Where Eleazar 'did not manage to obtain all our records' and 'only transmitted' the Pentateuch (*AJ* 1.12), Josephus' πραγματεία encompasses 'all of scripture' (πᾶσαν . . . τὴν ἀναγραφήν), which may mean the twenty-two works that Josephus lists in *Cont.Ap.* 1.40.[9] Again, this declaration could be taken to imply that he will complete the task begun by Eleazar's seventy-two translators in Alexandria; that is, to supplement their Pentateuch translation with his own translation of further Hebrew works.[10] However, the rhetorical function of Josephus' appeal to Eleazar here is to exemplify that customary Judaean generosity with prized ancestral traditions that Josephus now exhibits in his own offering to his enthusiastic patrons.[11] Finding that his forefathers had been generous in communicating ancestral traditions to others, he sets out to elucidate Jewish history for Epaphroditus and his friends, who love all kinds of learning and who have urged him to produce the *AJ* for their edification (*AJ* 1.8-10). His project, then, is one of explication and elucidation of Judaean traditions to outsiders, not merely the making of Hebrew works available in Greek.[12]

---

6   The τε . . . καί . . . construction intimately binds μεταφράζειν and δηλώσειν.

7   Sterling (1992, 255); cf. Feldman (2000, 7–8 [22]). Josephus elsewhere says that no one has changed scripture and that his copies are 'perfect' (*Cont.Ap.* 1.42).

8   Josephus praises this translation of the Pentateuch from Palestinian Hebrew copies in Alexandria (*AJ* 1.11-12, and his paraphrase of the *Letter of Aristeas* in *AJ* 12.11-118).

9   Josephus paraphrases the Pentateuch, Ruth, Judges, Samuel, Kings, Esther, 1 Esdras, Jeremiah and Daniel. He also seems to know Isaiah and the Minor Prophets (cf. Feldman 1997, 584). His naming twenty-two, rather than twenty-four works (as does the rabbinic literature; see *Ta'anith* 5a, *Baba Bathra* 14b), may indicate that he attached Ruth to Judges and Lamentations to Jeremiah (Feldman 1984, 135). The Prologue to Greek Sirach mentions 'the Law and Prophets' in Greek; Lk. 24.44 lists 'the law of Moses and the prophets and the psalms' together. See also Mason 2002.

10   Feldman (2000, 3 [4]) suggests that Josephus 'viewed himself as carrying on the tradition of the LXX in rendering the Bible for Gentiles'.

11   Cf. Mason 2001, xx. Josephus' likening of himself to Eleazar appears within the larger context of Josephus' various stated aims. He names the encouragement and support of influential associates, especially Epaphroditus, who were eager to learn more about Judaean history, politics and customs, as his primary motivation for writing the *Antiquities*. My thanks go to Professor Steve Mason for his helpful comments on an earlier version of this section, sent on 28 August 2009.

12   Since Josephus mentions that Eleazar's elders only translated the Pentateuch, *AJ* 1.10-12 might be understood as Josephus' claim to complete the task and that the *AJ* is his translation of the rest of Hebrew

Josephus' various terms encompass a range of ideas, from translation to rewriting, interpretation and elucidation.[13] Josephus applies μεθερμηνεύω both to his own *Antiquities* (*AJ* 1.5, *Cont.Ap.* 1.54) and to the work of the translators of the Pentateuch into Greek (*AJ* 12.20, 48). For Greek authors μεθερμηνεύω often means the translation from one language to another.[14] However, Josephus uses the verb to identify 'interpretation' as distinct from translation. Thus, in *AJ* 12.48 Ptolemy distinguishes between translating (μεταγράφω) the law from Hebrew to Greek and interpreting (μεθερμηνεύω) it. In *AJ* 12.20 Aristeas makes the same distinction: 'for we have decided *not only* to μεταγράψαι the laws *but also* (μόνον ἀλλὰ) to μεθερμηνεῦσαι them'. Using different terms, in *AJ* 1.10-13 Josephus describes how the translators are sent *both* to 'translate' (μεταβάλλω 1.10; also used at 12.15 of the LXX translation) and 'interpret' the Pentateuch (οἱ πεμφθέντες ἐπὶ τὴν ἐξήγησιν 1.12). In *Cont.Ap.* 1.54-55 his credentials as a translator (μεθερμήνευκα) of the sacred writings are enhanced by his hereditary priestly status and lifelong engagement in 'the philosophy in those writings'.[15] Again, in *AJ* 10.218 Josephus expresses his intention to both express (μεταφράζειν) the Hebrew works in Greek and explain (δηλώσειν) them, as noted above.[16] Josephus considers transfer from Semitic to Hellenistic idiom and explanation of the content to be part and parcel of the same exercise.

Josephus' attitude to transliterating Hebrew terms is illuminating. Sometimes he correctly glosses Hebrew names and terms. At other times he offers explanations for these, which commentators call 'loose etymology'.[17] In these latter cases, Josephus often incorporates the sen\se of a traditional literary context, in which the term appears, into his gloss. He is aware of the literary-contextual meanings of Hebrew words. Thus, while he knows that 'Eve' (חַוָּה) means 'life', Josephus states that Εὔα means 'mother of all living' (σημαίνει) (*AJ* 1.36), reflecting Gen. 3.20.

scripture into Greek. Yet later in the *AJ* Josephus apparently uses existing Greek versions of other Hebrew works, such as 1 Esdras, Daniel and perhaps Jeremiah. His promise to μεταφράζειν Hebrew sources (*AJ* 10.218) occurs within his account of Daniel, which he uses in Greek (Begg and Spilsbury 2005, 266). He cannot, therefore, be claiming to produce his own independent translation from the Hebrew.

13 See the discussions of Feldman 1988, 468–470 and 2000, 3 [4]; Sterling 1992, 252 [113]; Begg and Spilsbury 2005, 288 [938] on *AJ* 10.218.

14 Sterling 1992, 252 [113].

15 Cf. Feldman 1996.

16 In Greek authors μεταφράζω can mean to 'paraphrase' or 'restate' within the same language (e.g., μετάφρασις (2 Macc. 2.31), cf. Sterling 1992, 252 [113]). But μεταφράζω can also mean 'translate'. Josephus uses μεταφράζω ten times to denote translation: of a word (*BJ* 4.11; 5.151; *AJ* 1.52; 8.142; *Cont. Ap.* 1.167); of the LXX (*AJ* 12.20, 48); Manethon's translation (*Cont.Ap.* 1.228); Josephus' own *Antiquities* (*AJ* 10.218) (ibid., 252 [113]).

17 A) *AJ* 1.36 'Eve' (cf. Shutt 1971, 174); B) 2.278 גֵּר and גֵּרְשֹׁם in Exod. 2.22 (cf. Feldman 2000, 212); C) 3.282 Jubilee (cf. Shutt 1971, 170, 197; Thackeray 1961, *ad loc.*; Feldman 2000, 318); D) AJ 1.343 (Gen. 35.18) Josephus states that Jacob gave the name 'Benjamin' to his son because of the 'suffering' Benjamin had caused his mother; but 'suffering' derives from the name his mother gave (MT: בֶּן־אוֹנִי – LXX: Υἰὸς ὀδύνης μου), and which his father rejected in favour of Benjamin; E) 6.22 'watch tower' 1 Sam. 7.5b (cf. Begg and Spilsbury 2005, 103 [85]); F) 5.323 Ruth 1.20 *Naamis* (ναάμις) = good luck; *Mara* (μαρά) = pain (cf. Begg and Spilsbury 2005, 81).

He thereby applies the specific contextual meaning of the term to its general definition. Σημαίνει is Josephus' usual word for 'signify' when explaining the meaning
of names and terms. However, he twice uses μεθερμηνεύω to give descriptions of
names (*AJ* 1.52, 8.142). In *AJ* 1.52 he writes of Cain: Κάις κτίσιν δὲ σημαίνει τοῦτο
μεθερμηνευόμενον[18] τοὔνομα ('and this name, being interpreted, signifies acquisition').
If Josephus can employ σημαίνω synonymously with μεθερμηνεύω here, but also use
σημαίνω for definitions that substitute the general meaning of a term for its contextual
meaning, both terms must include for him the notions of translation and elucidation.

   In *AJ* 12.109, while recounting the completion of the LXX translation, Josephus
substantially changes his source. According to the *Letter of Aristeas*, 'Demetrius
ordered them to pronounce a curse, in accordance with their custom, on any who
should alter, by adding or changing, any of the words which had been written, or by
omitting anything'.[19] Apparently, the 'custom' refers to the prohibition on alteration
of the Torah (Deut. 4.2 and 12.32). Josephus says, however:

> Accordingly, when all had approved this idea, they ordered that, if anyone saw any further
> addition made to the text of the Law or anything omitted from it, he should examine it and
> make it known and correct it; in this they acted wisely, that what had once been judged good
> might remain forever.[20]

Despite Josephus' pledge to recount the precise details of scripture, promising not to
add or omit anything, he effects numerous additions, omissions and alterations to the
literary content of the works he paraphrases. His lifting of Aristeas' curse here seems
to reflect Josephus' attitude to his own interpretive alteration of traditional sources.

   Significant for the present study is Josephus' acknowledgement that one copy
(βιβλία, e.g. *AJ* 12.36) differs from another, emphasizing the accuracy of some copies
(διηκριβωμένα) in contrast to the carelessness with which others have been produced
(ἀμελέστερον) (*AJ* 12.37). Indeed, the precision of the Alexandrian Septuagint is
guaranteed not only by the accuracy of the translators' source copies, but also the
translators' experience of scripture (τοὺς ἐμπειροτάτους τῶν νόμων), which ensures
an 'accurate interpretation/translation' (e.g. *AJ* 12.39, 49, 104). The passage cited
above (*AJ* 12.108-109) reveals that Josephus' usual insistence on the accuracy and
unanimity of Jewish scripture (cf. *Cont.Ap.* 1.42) is a rhetorical claim to an ideal and
pristine text, whose accuracy (as he very well knows) resides in processes of expert
arbitration that entails textual variation, as the numerous embellishments and alterations to Jewish literature in his own *AJ* testify.

---

   18 Used in the same way in *AJ* 8.142.
   19 This curse may reflect Aristeas' effort to *establish* the LXX as the 'standard' Greek version amid
the numerous versions and revisions available in the first century.
   20 *AJ* 12.108-109.

3.4 *Languages*

3.4.1 *Greek*

Josephus learned Greek as a second language. Despite bemoaning stylistic difficulties (*AJ* 20.263) and receiving help with Greek style,[21] he diligently studied aspects of Greek rhetoric (*AJ* 20.263).[22] Mason writes: 'Josephus shows himself to possess a wide background in Greek literature and a keenly critical eye.'[23] The extant *Bellum Judaicum* is apparently an original Greek composition, whatever version Josephus previously wrote in Aramaic.[24] While complimenting Josephus' Greek in the *BJ*, Thackeray finds the Greek of the *AJ* inconsistent, attributing Attic stylistic reminiscences to literary assistants.[25] However, since the studies of Attridge and Rajak,[26] most discern Josephus' own hand throughout. Since he could thoroughly rework his sources to suit his own purposes, stylistic inconsistencies are best attributed to Josephus himself.[27] Despite Josephus' struggle with Greek pronunciation (*AJ* 20.263), he can skilfully emulate the style of Greek classics, which he had studied.[28]

3.4.2 *Hebrew*

A Judaean priest educated in Judaea, Josephus claims to be learned in ancestral Jewish literature (*Vita* 11; *AJ* 20.262), and his presentation of the ancestral literature in the *AJ* bears this out. Jerusalem was a Hellenized city and Judaea a Roman province. As an aristocrat, Josephus will have learned some Greek. However, his difficulty with Greek pronunciation and need for literary help suggest that his education was primarily Semitic. Nevertheless, some question Josephus' command of Hebrew because of 'sloppy' Hebrew 'etymologies' in *AJ*.[29] Others accept Josephus' Hebrew proficiency.[30]

---

21 *Cont.Ap.* 1.50. See Mason (1991, 48–49).

22 Ibid., 50.

23 Ibid., 78–79. Cf. Footnote 2, above.

24 The *BJ* is an 'excellent specimen of the Attic Greek' (Thackeray (1967, 102) and is an original Greek work filled with Greek motifs, concerns, themes and vocabulary (Mason 1991, 58–59). The verbs γράφω, συγγράφω, with which Josephus refers to his Greek version of *BJ*, do not suggest 'translation' (Hata 1975). Hata takes μεταβάλλω to mean 'rewrite' since it means 'change fundamentally' elsewhere in *BJ*.

25 Thackeray (1967, 100–124, esp. 104). Finding no Semitisms in *BJ* (ibid., 102), Thackeray detects a 'Sophoclean' assistant in *AJ* Books 15–16 (ibid., 115f.) and a 'Thucydidean hack' in 17–19 (ibid, 109f.). *AJ* shows Semitic linguistic influence, most obviously in proper nouns, and perhaps in some constructions, as does possibly also *Vita*. Cf. Shutt 1961, 1971.

26 Attridge 1976 and Rajak 1983.

27 Where comparison is possible, Josephus proves capable of reworking his sources himself (Attridge 1976). Josephus' hand is discernible throughout portions attributed by Thackeray to assistants (Mason 1991, 49). Rajak (1983) attributes the 'Sophoclean' and 'Thucydidean' reminiscences in *AJ* to Josephus himself (cited in Mason 1991, 50). Josephus consciously models himself as an Hellenistic historian (Sterling 1992, 240–245).

28 Josephus is influenced by Hellenistic historiographers, particularly Dionysius of Halicarnassus (Feldman 1998a, 3–13).

29 For example, Thackeray 1967, 77–78.

30 Particularly those proposing that Josephus used Hebrew sources of Jewish scripture, cf. Footnote 59, below.

Nodet points out that each of the frequently cited examples of Josephus' 'poor' command of Hebrew is either inconclusive or inappropriate.[31] I note that Josephus' explanations of Hebrew words are often inappropriately understood as 'etymologies', giving the impression that Josephus intended to perform philological exercises. Josephus often defines a word with reference to its immediate literary context, which he is paraphrasing (see Section 3.3, above). This reveals more about his approach to elucidation of literature than his philological aspirations. Moreover, Josephus often supplies correct derivations for words.[32] Some suggest that Josephus only knew Aramaic[33] and that by the 'Hebrew language', he means Aramaic.[34] However, Grintz shows that Josephus means Hebrew on account of the glosses of σάββατα, Ἄδαμος, ἔσσα and ἀδωνί, which can only derive from the Hebrew, and the phrase 'the opponent of the angel of God', which is translated from the Hebrew of Gen. 32.29.[35]

Josephus twice distinguishes Hebrew from Aramaic, contrasting speaking ἑβραϊστί with speaking συριστί ('Syriac', meaning Aramaic). 'As Rampsakes spoke these words in Hebrew (ἑβραϊστί), with which language he was familiar, Eliakias was afraid that the people might overhear them and be thrown into consternation, and so asked him to speak in Aramaic (συριστί)' (*AJ* 10.8). Referring to Hebrew scripture, Josephus writes: 'For, he said, though their [the Judaeans', 12.14] script seemed to be similar to the peculiar Syrian writing (τῶν Συρίων γραμμάτων), and their language to sound like the other, it was, as it happened, of a distinct type' (*AJ* 12.15).[36]

Marcus observes that 'Josephus, like the LXX, uses συριστί, "Syria", and "Syrian" – the Greek names for Aram, Aramaean or Aramaic'.[37] Aramaic was also known as 'Syriac' in later Rabbinic literature.[38] Speaking ἑβραϊστί in Josephus corresponds with יְהוּדִית ('Judaean language' [LXX, ιουδαϊστί] distinct from אֲרָמִית, 'Aramaic' [LXX, συριστί]) of 2 Kgs 18.26.[39] The grandson of Ben Sirach also uses ἑβραϊστί to mean

---

31 Nodet 1997, 156. See Section 3.5.1, below.

32 For example, *AJ* 5.121 (Judg. 1.5) *Adoni* (ἀδωνὶ) = 'Lord' (cf. Begg 2000, 30); 5.200-201 (Judg. 4.4-14; 5.1-15) Deborah (Δαβώρα) = 'bee' (cf. Begg 2000, 48); 5.336 (Ruth 4.14-15) Oded (Ὠβήδης) = 'servant' (cf. Begg 2000, 84–85).

33 For example, Thackeray 1967, 78.

34 For example, κατὰ [τὴν] Ἑβραίων διάλεκτον – *AJ* 1.33; 2.278; κατὰ γλῶτταν τὴν Ἑβραίων – 1.34; καθ' Ἑβραίων διάλεκτον – 1.36 τῇ Ἑβραίων διαλέκτῳ – 5.121.

35 Grintz (1960): both Josephus' σάββατα (*AJ* 1.33) and שַׁבָּת, 'Sabbath', derive from the root שבת, for which Aramaic translators use נח; the root שבת does not exist in Aramaic. Josephus derives Ἄδαμος (אָדָם) from אָדֹם 'red' (1.34). In Aramaic סומקא means 'red' and there is no root אדם. Josephus transliterates the Hebrew אִשָּׁה with ἔσσα (1.36), which in Aramaic is אנ[נ]תתא. Josephus (5.121) transliterates the Hebrew word יהוה with ἀδωνί (usually written יהוה and pronounced *adonai*, but occurring once in the form אֲדֹנִי in a direct address to God in Judg. 13.8 and used of God twelve times in the form אָדֹון throughout Joshua, Nehemiah, Psalms, Jeremiah and Zechariah) and explains that it means 'Lord'. In Aramaic 'Lord' is מרא. Grintz takes Josephus' phrase 'the opponent of the angel of God' to be a translation of the Hebrew of Gen. 32.29. (כִּי־שָׂרִיתָ עִם־אֱלֹהִים 'for you strove with God') in 1.333.

36 Marcus 1952, *ad loc.*

37 Ibid., 161 [b].

38 Grintz 1960, 43.

39 Ibid., 43.

'in Hebrew'.[40] I add that Josephus distinguishes between Hebrew and Aramaic in *AJ* 3.156, where he writes: 'Moses called it *abaneth*, but we call it *hemian*, having learned it from the Babylonians.'[41] Although Josephus uses 'Babylonian' as an alternative to 'Syrian', he clearly distinguishes Hebrew from 'Syrian' (i.e. Aramaic).[42]

Segal and Ben-Yehuda argue from later Rabbinic literature that Hebrew was a widely spoken and written vernacular in Hellenistic and early Roman Palestine.[43] Grintz confirms their conclusions with early Roman linguistic evidence; that is, from Matthew's gospel and Josephus' *AJ* and *BJ*. His claims are supported by the Hebrew of the Dead Sea corpus.[44]

I add examples indicating that Hebrew was integral to Josephus' daily language. In *AJ* 3.156 Josephus transliterates *massabazane* for Hebrew משנצת ('chequered work'). However, משנצת does not appear in Exod. 28.4 and Exodus 39, only its cognates תַּשְׁבֵּץ and כְּתֹנֶת ('chequered coat').[45] This suggests that משנצת was current in spoken Hebrew. In *AJ* 3.153 Josephus provides a transliteration of a Semitic word for 'linen', χέθον,[46] which is close to Hebrew כתנת, *ketôneth*, and Aramaic כתונא (כְּתוּנָא), *kituna*. However, these mean 'coat' rather than 'linen', and Josephus' words ἔνδυμα and χιτών (*AJ* 3.153) correspond with כְּתֹנֶת/χιτών of Exodus. Marcus believes that with χέθον Josephus transliterates the Aramaic word for linen, *kitan*, for which there is 'no Hebrew equivalent'.[47] However, Feldman considers Josephus' χέθον a transliteration of Rabbinic Hebrew כתנת ('linen'), noting that there is no such Hebrew word

40 Prologue to Greek Sirach.

41 Cf. Feldman 2000, 305.

42 Feldman notes that Josephus speaks of Aramaic as the 'language of the Hebrews'. In *AJ* 3.252 Josephus writes: 'the fiftieth day, which the Hebrews called asartha'. He transliterates Aramaic עצרתא('five'), not Hebrew עצרת. 'Josephus here speaks of the language of the Hebrews, rather than of Hebrew, and this is not inconsistent with identifying the language as Aramaic' (Feldman 2000, 305). I further note that Josephus actually writes τῇ πεντηκοστῇ ἣν Ἑβραῖοι ἀσαρθὰ καλοῦσι ('which the Hebrews call'), not one of his usual terms meaning 'in the Hebrew language' (see Footnote 34, above). In *AJ* 3.282 Josephus says something similar of the Hebrew term יוֹבֵל: 'the fiftieth year is called by the Hebrews Jôbêl' (καλεῖται δὲ ὑπὸ Ἑβραίων). Thus, Josephan formulas like: 'x, which the Hebrews call y', can refer to Hebrew or Aramaic words used by the Judaeans, rather than indicating Hebrew as such.

43 Segal 1936 and Ben-Yehuda 1939, cited in Grintz 1960, 32.

44 See Joosten 2000, Hurvitz 2000 and Fitzmyer 1970. Signs that the pronunciation of spoken Hebrew influenced the spelling of written Hebrew are found in some Judaean manuscripts (cf. Kutscher 1974, Qimron 1986. See Chapter 4, below).

45 Brown *et al.* 1979, 509 כָּתְנָת or כְּתֹנֶת feminine noun from the root כתן (apparently 'clothe' cf. Arabic and Aramaic).

46 'For we call linen *chethon* (χέθον γὰρ τὸ λίνον ἡμεῖς καλοῦμεν). This vocalization of the absolute, כְּתֹנֶת, occurs in the Hebrew of Exod. 28.39 (Brown *et al.* 1979, 509). As a construct, this vocalization occurs at: Exod. 28.4 (וּכְתֹנֶת תַּשְׁבֵּץ); Lev. 16.4. (כְּתֹנֶת־בַּד); Gen. 37.3, 23, 32; 2 Sam. 13.18 (כְּתֹנֶת פַּסִּים), 19 (וּכְתֹנֶת הַפַּסִּים); Gen. 37.31. (כְּתֹנֶת יוֹסֵף), 32 (הַכְּתֹנֶת בְּנִךָ), 33 (כְּתֹנֶת בְּנִי). Otherwise, it is vocalized as *chuton* (כֻּתֹּנֶת, כָּתְנָת) with *Qibbûṣ* or short *Qāmes-Ḥāṭûph*: Gen. 37.31; Exod. 28.40; 29.5, 8; 39.27; 40.14; Lev. 8.7, 13; Ezra 2.69; Neh. 7.71. In the Hebrew Bible מִצְנֶפֶת occurs in Exod. 28.4, 37, 37, 39; 29.6,6; 39.28, 31; Lev. 8.9,9; 16.4; Ezek. 21.31 (cf. Brown *et al.* 1979, 857).

47 Marcus 1952, *ad loc.*

in the Hebrew Bible.[48] As mentioned above, Josephus can use a *cognate* of a word that appears in traditional Jewish scripture, while discussing a passage in which that word appears, without invoking the word itself. With χέθον, his transliteration of *shewa* (of כְּתֹנֶת), not *hîreq* (of כְּתוּנָא), affirms Feldman's suggestion that Josephus is transliterating a Hebrew word for 'linen' (related to כְּתֹנֶת, 'coat') rather than Aramaic כְּתוּנָא ('linen'). When Josephus wants to transliterate the '*i*' sound of *hîreq* in an Aramaic word, he does so. This is seen, for example, in his word ἐμίαν, *hemian* (*AJ* 3.156) for Aramaic המינא.[49]

3.4.3 *Aramaic*

Josephus apparently knew Aramaic. Explaining Hebrew river names,[50] he gives the Aramaic form (Διγλάθ) for the Tigris at *AJ* 1.38-39, but clarifies its meaning, 'sharp', according to its Hebrew name, חִדֶּקֶל, used in Gen. 2.14[39].[51] In *AJ* 3.151 Josephus transliterates two Aramaic words: *chaanaeae* = *kahanya* ('priests') and *anarabaches* = *kahana rabba* ('high priest').[52] His application of the phrase '. . . which the Hebrews call . . .' to an Aramaic word (*Asartha*, ἀσαρθὰ) (*AJ* 3.252) is neither a confusion of Hebrew and Aramaic,[53] nor a 'loose etymology',[54] but simply an assertion of the Hebrews' (indicating Judaeans) knowledge of Aramaic (see Section 3.4.2, above). In 3.172 Josephus mentions Aramaic שיכרונא, *saccaron*, related to Hebrew שכר ('to become drunk').[55] In *AJ* 3.156 he distinguishes a literary Hebrew term ('Moses called it', ἐκάλεσεν) from its *spoken* Aramaic equivalent ('but we call it', ἡμεῖς δὲ [. . .] καλοῦμεν), giving the transliteration for both. Thus, in his glosses Josephus does not muddle his languages, but rather sorts familiar words and selects those best suited for his purposes.

Nevertheless, Josephus' familiarity with the Greek and Hebrew languages cannot indicate the kinds of sources he used and how he used them.[56] The diverse modern views on Josephus' sources must now be addressed.

48 Feldman (2000, 272 [390]) indicates the Rabbinic occurrences of the Hebrew word כתנת ('linen') cited by Jastrow (1903 I., 637).

49 המינא occurs for Hebrew אַבְנֵט in Targum Pseudo-Jonathan, Targum Onqelos and Targum Neofiti of Exod. 28.39 and 39.29; as well as in *Onqelos* 28.4. See Feldman (2000, 273 [401–402]) for further references.

50 Φεισών ('Ganges'); Φοράς ('Euphrates'); Γηών ('Nile').

51 Τίγρις δὲ Διγλάθ ἐξ οὗ φράζεται τὸ μετὰ στενότητος ὀξύ (*AJ* 1.39). Josephus hereby proposes that the Hebrew word, חִדֶּקֶל, combines חַד (*khad*) = 'sharp' (Brown *et al.* 1979, 292) (Josephus – ὀξύ) and דַּק (*dakh*) = 'thin' (Brown *et al.* 1979, 201) (Josephus – στενόν). Cf. Thackeray 1961, 19 [*f*]; Feldman 2000, 15 [81].

52 Ibid., 387.

53 Lapide 1972–75, 488; cited in Feldman 2000, 305.

54 Thackeray 1961, 439 [*d*].

55 Cf. Feldman 2000, 277 [459].

56 It has often been proposed that Josephus made use of an Aramaic Targum. However, Safrai (1990) and Buth (2000a, 2000b) persuasively argue that Aramaic Targums were not available in this period.

3.5 *Debates on the Textual Character of Josephus' Sources*

Debate surrounds evidence for Josephus' sources for the 'Pentateuch', the 'Historical Books' (Judges-Ruth, Samuel, Kings, Esther-Esdras, 1 Maccabees), and prophetic works (Jeremiah, Daniel).[57] Some claim that Josephus exclusively used Greek copies,[58] others that Josephus used only Semitic sources.[59] Bloch represents the most widespread view that Josephus consulted both Greek and Hebrew copies.[60]

3.5.1 *Greek Pentateuch sources*

The issue is usually framed in terms of a choice between OG and 𝔐 Pentateuch sources. Claims that *AJ* Books 1–4 presuppose the OG of the Pentateuch are supported by: verbal parallels between *AJ* and the OG; Josephus' use of proper names that appear to be based on the form of Hebrew names found in the OG; and details of literary content that Josephus shares with the OG against 𝔐. In the terms adopted here, the latter often constitute distinct sense contours characterizing the same passage (see Section 2.3).

While many apparent parallels between Josephus' *AJ* and the OG Pentateuch (against 𝔐) are often proposed, some commentators express serious doubts that such parallels can demonstrate Josephus' use of the LXX text-form. Hölscher notes coincidences between *AJ* Book 1 and the Septuagint, but Cohen argues that they are few and insignificant.[61] Schalit notes verbal coincidences implying Josephus' dependence on the Septuagint, but Feldman shows most to be invalid.[62] Nodet argues that, of the thirteen examples most frequently used to show Josephus' dependence on the OG, eleven are inconclusive. Nodet proposes that Josephus himself was translating from a Hebrew text like that presupposed by the OG (which Nodet calls Josephus' source,

---

57 The extent of the Jewish ἀναγραφή for Josephus was apparently similar to that represented in the Prologue to Greek Ben Sirach, the later Rabbinic collection of twenty-four works and the LXX, cf. Footnote 9, below.

58 Notably, Schalit 1968 and 1976. Attridge (1976, 30 [2]) mentions Splitter (1779), Scharfenberg (1780) and Mez (1895) as early advocates of this position. For subsequent advocates see Rappaport (1930).

59 Attridge (1976, 30) observes that these were mostly early scholars (Ernesti 1756, 1776; Tachauer 1871), pointing to Rappaport (1930) for subsequent ones. Nodet (1996, 1997) argues that Josephus used only Hebrew Pentateuch sources.

60 Bloch (1897, 18) thinks the LXX was the most natural source for Josephus because it had already been rendered into Greek. Thackeray (1967, 75–99) holds that Josephus mainly used a Semitic text of the Pentateuch with occasional reference to the LXX (ibid., 81); a Semitic text for Joshua, Judges and Ruth with a Targum for Judges; and a Greek text of the Lucianic type from Samuel through the Historical Books (ibid., 81–89 on *AJ* Books 6–8). Schalit (1976) offers instances where Josephus presupposes a Hebrew source (ibid., xxvii–xxxi) and the Septuagint (ibid., xxxii–xxxv). Others who generally conform with Bloch's position: Schalit 1976 and 1982, 258; Attridge 1984, 211; Schürer, Vermes *et al.* 1973–1987 I, 48–49; and Sterling 1992, 256 [132]. While Feldman (1988, 460) shows this position to be far more difficult to establish than often supposed, he ultimately agrees.

61 Hölscher 1916 and Cohen 1979, cited in Feldman 1984, 132.

62 For Schalit see Footnote 60, above. Cf. Feldman 1984, 131–132. Of Schalit's twenty proofs showing Josephus' use of the Septuagint, Cohen pronounces four valid (Feldman 1988, 455 [2]).

'H').[63] Eighteen of the 'numerous' agreements between Josephus' paraphrase and the OG against 𝔐 concern either proper names or 'content',[64] which are equally explicable if Josephus translated from 'H'.[65] On the basis of his study of proper names in Josephus' narrative, Shutt concludes that Josephus 'used Hebrew and Greek' Genesis sources for *AJ* Books 1.1–2.200.[66] However, Feldman and Nodet note that Christian copyists tended to harmonize proper names, as they found them in Josephus' text, with the LXX forms standard in their own day.[67]

Feldman explains that the problem is further complicated because in the first century

> there was greater agreement between the Greek and Hebrew texts of the Pentateuch than for other biblical works, on the one hand, while Josephus himself is freer in his paraphrase of the Pentateuch than he is of later biblical works, on the other hand. Hence, it is difficult to be sure whether he is using a Hebrew or a Greek text at any given point.[68]

Precisely because Josephus is 'paraphrasing', argues Feldman, verbal parallels between the *AJ* and the OG Pentateuch would be likely, even if the *AJ* were independent of the OG.

Feldman provides a range of possible explanations for Josephus' apparent agreements with the 'Septuagint': corrections by Christian copyists of Josephus' text may account for agreements between proper names in Josephus and the LXX; Josephus may adopt the language of Philo; Josephus may have used a glossary of terms[69] of the kind known to have existed from the papyri; Josephus and the LXX translators may be mutually dependent on a common Palestinian tradition; Josephus may have independently adopted some incorrect translation of a Hebrew term; or the apparent dependence may be due to a scribal error.[70]

---

63 Nodet 1997, 162–164.

64 Ibid., 165–169.

65 Nodet 1997.

66 Shutt 1971, 179.

67 On proper names: Nodet (1997, 158–159), Feldman (1988, 461, 463). According to Shutt, Josephus' proper names correspond with the form of 𝔐 four times, the LXX fourteen times. But Feldman (1988, 461) notes that Josephus differs from both sixteen times. Feldman (1988, 459–60) considers inconclusive Rajak's (1974, 238) list of instances that suggest Josephus' use of Hebrew and Greek Exodus sources.

68 Feldman 1988, 460.

69 Some have suggested that Josephus uses the OG as a glossary for his presentation of the Pentateuch (cf. Bloch (1897, 18); Schalit (1982, 258 col. 2)). On LXX translation technique, see Marcos 2000 ch. 3, esp. 30–31. On the use of glossaries in general, see Barr 2003. However, to suggest that Josephus used the OG as a glossary presupposes that he was *translating* from the Hebrew, which does not correspond with his stated aim of writing a 'history' (see Section 3.3, above).

70 Feldman 1988, 460–461.

3.5.2 *Hebrew Pentateuch sources*

Nodet has argued that Josephus, when preparing the *AJ*, used only Hebrew Pentateuch sources,[71] which reflected the text presupposed by the OG, having no access to the OG (at least 'not before the last stages of his work').[72] Nodet suggests that no copy of the LXX of the Pentateuch was available in Rome in the 80s and 90s and that Josephus intended the *AJ* to be the first Greek version of Jewish scripture available in Rome.[73] However, as argued above, neither Josephus' claim to be writing a 'history' for the edification of his patrons nor his treatment of sources (see Section 3.3), suggest his intention to produce a Greek *translation* of the Pentateuch.

Nevertheless, Josephus' frequent explanations of Hebrew names and terms, especially in the early books of the *AJ*, represent the principal evidence for his use of Hebrew sources.[74] Perhaps Josephus consulted Hebrew copies at these points, but he may know these Hebrew terms simply because they were commonly used in spoken vernacular. However, the consistently close association of the words in his text with their traditional literary context suggests Josephus' use of Hebrew copies of Genesis and Exodus representing 𝔐.

For example, in *AJ* 3.148 Josephus adds 'crowns', which is not found in any known Hebrew literary tradition. Nodet suggests that Josephus read עשית for ועשית of Exod. 30.3 and thus understood: 'You shall make its corners with a crown of gold round about.'[75] In *AJ* 3.121 Josephus may have taken the phrase והבריח התיכון ('and the middle bar', Exod. 26.28) to mean ובריח התיכון ('the bar of the intermediate [wall]').[76] In *AJ* 3.171 Josephus uses the same word, ζώνη, for חֵשֶׁב ('belt')[77] of Exod. 28.8 and 39.20 as he does for the אַבְנֵט ('belt') of Exod. 28.4, which the high priest wears around his tunic (*AJ* 3.159). Feldman notes that 'Josephus is clearly using the Hebrew text,

---

71 Nodet 1997, 157.

72 Ibid., 155. From Josephus' numerous agreements with OG against 𝔐 (where they differ), 'they show a strong dependence of Josephus on 𝔊 or his source 'H', but never (necessarily) of the Greek wording of 𝔊. On the contrary, he is sometimes likely to depend directly on the Hebrew' (ibid., 169). Nodet finds Josephus generally closer to OG (and/or its Hebrew source) than to 𝔐 for matters of what Nodet calls 'content', but for the transcriptions of the proper names Josephus 'stands somewhere in the middle, which suggests that 𝔊 has serious misspellings' (ibid., 174).

73 Nodet 1997.

74 Schalit (1976, xxvii–xxxi) offers examples showing Josephus' use of a Hebrew source; but see Attridge's reservations (1976, 31 [3]). Sterling notes the following etymologies: 1.33, 34, 36, 333; 2.278; 5.121, 200-201, 323, 336; 6.22, 302; 7.67 (1992, 256 [133]). He notes terms deriving from the Hebrew text of Exodus, Leviticus and Numbers: *erôn AJ* 3.134 (אָרוֹן – Exod. 25.10; cf. Feldman 2000, 267 [317]); *meeir AJ* 3.159 (מְעִיל – Exod. 28.31 cf. Feldman 2000, 274 [412]); *asosra AJ* 3.291 (חֲצוֹצְרָה – Num. 10.2 cf. Feldman 2000, 320 [887]); *AJ* 9.290. To these examples I add: 3.142 *assarons* (עֶשְׂרֹנִים Lev. 24.5); 3.144 *kinchares* (ככר Exod. 25.31); 3.152 *machanases* (מִכְנְסֵי־בָד Exod. 28.42); 3.156 *abaneth* (אַבְנֵט Exod. 29.9); 3.157 *massabazane* (מִצְנֶפֶת Exod. 28.4, 39); 3.162 *ephod* (אֵפֹד Exod. 28.6).

75 Nodet 1996, *ad loc*; cited in Feldman 2000, 270 [370].

76 Ibid., 263 [277].

77 Brown *et al.* 1979, 368 חֵשֶׁב – '*ingenious work*, name of the girdle or band of the ephod (*cunningly woven band* RV)'. Exod. 28.27, 28; 29.5; 39.20, 21.

inasmuch as the LXX (Exod. 28.8; 36.27) does not refer to a belt here at all'.[78] In *AJ* 1.54 Josephus has γάλα, implying Hebrew חֲלֵב ('milk'), whereas Gen. 4.4$^{\mathfrak{M}}$ vocalizes חֵלֶב ('fat') and LXX reads στεάτων ('fat').

Josephus' use of Hebrew copies is corroborated by another example. According to Josephus, the name *Gersos* (*AJ* 2.278, Γῆρσος; Exod. 2.22$^{\mathfrak{M}}$ גֵּרְשֹׁם; LXX Γηρσαμ) 'signifies in the language of the Hebrews that he had come to a foreign land'. He omits the word 'sojourner' inherent in the explanation of Exod. 2.22$^{\mathfrak{M}\& LXX}$ ('I have been a sojourner (גֵּר/πάροικος) in a foreign land'). Yet Josephus shows his awareness that the Hebrew name גֵּרְשֹׁם derives from the root גרש ('to drive out, banish'), something not conveyed in the LXX, because in Josephus' previous sentence (*AJ* 2.277) Moses' flight from Egypt explains why Moses had 'come to a foreign land' in the first place. These examples suggest Josephus' use of a Hebrew source reflecting $\mathfrak{M}$ at these points.

3.5.2.1 *Manipulations of a Hebrew semantic unit*

Josephus appears to know that a Hebrew semantic unit could be manipulated and give rise to distinct sense contours. I will discuss similar manipulations in some compositions of the Dead Sea sectarians further (see Chapter 4).[79] While he knows one vocalization of אדם, namely אָדֹם ('red') (*AJ* 1.34), his awareness of the traditional alternative אָדָם ('human') is reflected in ἄνθρωπος, which he uses twice in 1.34.[80] These are, of course, very basic words. But Josephus seems to exhibit familiarity with more complex Hebrew in his treatment of 2 Samuel–1 Kings.[81] According to Nodet, for example, Josephus combines both meanings of an unpointed Hebrew word, one followed by $\mathfrak{M}$ and one by the OG. He combines 'we will show ourselves' (ונגלינו from נגלה) of $\mathfrak{M}$ with 'we will attack', reflecting LXX's 'we will roll down on them' (implying ונגלנו from גָּלַל).[82] Josephus maintains both meanings at the expense, according to Nodet, of narrative coherence.

These examples suggest a particular kind of awareness of textual plurality. That is, Josephus knows that multiple semantic forms of a passage can exist within a Hebrew text, and can be derived through the manipulation of a semantic unit (see Section 2.5.1, above).

---

78 Feldman (2000, 277 [453]) notes that Targum Onqelos and Targum Neofiti use the same word in both passages, like Josephus.

79 Nodet (1997, 192) suggests that Josephus obtained an official Hebrew Pentateuch copy from the temple archive (possibly a present from Titus after the fall of Jerusalem), which bore annotations and glosses akin to the Masoretic *kethib-qeré*, which Josephus combined. Were this the case, his very use of the annotated copy would in itself be a form of awareness of textual plurality.

80 Shutt 1971, 175; Feldman 2000, 13.

81 Nodet (2006) provides nearly a dozen such examples.

82 For גָּלַל, meaning: 'roll, roll away', cf. Brown *et al.* 1979, 164.

3.6 *Josephus' appeal to sense contours in Pentateuch passages*

In the following case study I focus on Josephus' paraphrase of the Pentateuch, particularly Genesis and Exodus, in *Jewish Antiquities* Books 1–3. Unlike the case of Kings, Samuel, Jeremiah or Daniel, there is no evidence that Pentateuchal works existed in strongly variant editions in the late Hellenistic and early Roman periods, a level of stability that lends a degree of control to discussion. While Feldman rightly emphasizes the problems inherent in trying to decide the *overall text-form* of Josephus' Pentateuch source according to text-critical categories (that is, 𝔐 or LXX),[83] in certain cases Josephus' appeal to distinct sense contours shows his conscious use of multiple forms of *a single passage*. In what follows, the relative textual stability of the Pentateuch is important for analysis because correspondences of Josephus' *AJ* with details of the OG and 𝔐 indicate that his sources were close to OG and 𝔐 at least at the point of comparison.

3.6.1 *Weights and measures*

Josephus' apparently poor working knowledge of weights and measures[84] betrays his use of the OG as an aid for translating metric terms. In *AJ* 3.144 Josephus transliterates the Hebrew word כִּכָּר (Exod. 25.39), saying, '[t]he Hebrews call [these weights] *kinchares*, which translated (μεταβαλλόμενον) into the Greek language, signifies a talent (τάλαντον)'. Exod. 25.39^LXX has τάλαντον. In *AJ* 3.321 he says that 'seventy *kors*' (κόρους) is equivalent to '41 Attic *medimi*'; that is, a ratio of just under two *kors* to one *medimus*. But in *AJ* 15.314 he says that 'one *kor*' is equivalent to '10 Attic *medimi*'.[85] According to Feldman, one *kor* actually equals about seven Attic *medimi*.[86]

In *AJ* 3.142 Josephus makes an 'error of about one half' in his equation of Attic κοτύλας with Hebrew *assarons*.[87] An *assaron* equals approximately six and a half pints; and seven κοτύλας, which Josephus claims equals an *assaron*, actually equals three and a half pints.[88] The Greek talents equal sixty *minas*, rather than one hundred, as Josephus implies in *AJ* 3.144.[89]

While Josephus is bad at converting Hebrew into Attic measures, his chosen terms for Attic equivalents derive from the OG Pentateuch. In *AJ* 3.142 he transliterates *assarons* (עֶשְׂרֹנִים 'tithes', LXX δεκάτων – e.g. Lev. 24.5), translating it for his audience as κοτύλας. In *AJ* 3.29, 142 and 320 he also mentions *assarons*, substituting *assaron*

---

83 See Feldman's comments in Footnote 68, above.
84 Marcus (1952, 475 [e]) points out that 'Josephus is usually inconsistent' in his statements on measures.
85 Marcus and Wikgren 1980, *ad loc.*
86 Feldman 2000, 329 [962].
87 Marcus 1952, *ad loc.*
88 Ibid., 383 [d].
89 Ibid., 383 [e].

for *ômer* (עֹמֶר) of Exodus (LXX γόμορ[90]) in this and other instances.[91] This substitution is reasonable because an עִשָּׂרוֹן equalled an עֹמֶר,[92] each being a tenth of an *ephah*.[93] Leviticus[LXX] uses κοτύλη for the liquid measure לֹג, which equalled approximately half a litre (and, according to the Talmud, one twelfth of a *hin*).[94] According to Lev. 14.21 one לֹג of oil should be offered with one tenth of an *ephah*; and, according to Lev. 14.10, with three tenths of an *ephah*. So Josephus seems simply to have inferred that a לֹג, which was translated as κοτύλη in the OG, was roughly comparable in relative quantity to an *ômer*, an *ephah* or an *assaron*. This inference depends upon his appeal to the OG.

In *AJ* 3.321 Josephus mentions κόρους. However, it is not clear whether he means the Hebrew measure כֹּר or חֹמֶר. The term חֹמֶר is paralleled by κόρος only in Leviticus[LXX], Numbers[LXX], and (once) in Ezekiel[LXX].[95] Only in 1 Kings, 2 Chronicles and Ezra is κόρος consistently used for כֹּר rather than חֹמֶר.[96] Josephus paraphrases Leviticus and Numbers from *AJ* 3.204 to *AJ* 3.322; and, as noted, he avoids the term חֹמֶר, preferring *assaron*. I think, therefore, that Josephus' terms for weights and measures derive from the OG of the Pentateuch, which in this respect serves as his glossary.[97]

Josephus' inaccuracy regarding weights and measures is important because it removes any suspicion that he is using the OG while explaining vernacular Hebrew usage. He is trying to harmonize his Greek and Hebrew *sources*, with no practical sense of how to quantify these weights and measures. His use of Attic terms will give his audience a feel for these exotic Hebrew terms, but Josephus does not expect

---

90 In Exodus γόμορ always parallels עֹמֶר (Exod. 16.16, 18, 22, 32, 33, 36; Hos. 3.2). Only in Ezek. 45.11, 13, 14 is חֹמֶר translated as γόμορ; in 1 Sam. 16.20 it is erroneously used for 'donkey' (חֲמוֹר); in 1 Sam. 25.18 it parallels '100 bunches of grapes'.

91 Thackeray 1961, *ad loc.* (*AJ* 3.29, 142, 320).

92 Exod. 16.36, an *ômer* is the tenth part of an *ephah*. (וְהָעֹמֶר עֲשִׂרִית הָאֵיפָה הוּא).

93 Num. 28.5 וַעֲשִׂירִת הָאֵיפָה and LXX Num. 15.4 δέκατον τοῦ οιφι (cf. Brown *et al.* 1979, 798).

94 Lev. 14.10, 12, 15, 21, 24. Ibid., 528.

95 Cf. Hatch *et al.* 1998, *ad loc.*

96 Often the MT term כֹּר is paralleled with κόρος in the LXX: 1 Kgs 5.2 כֹּר ₓ₂ (LXX κόροι ₓ₂); 5.25a כֹּר (κόρους); 2 Chron. 2.9 כֹּרִים ₓ₂ (κόρων ₓ₂); 27.5 כֹּרִים (κόρων); Ezra 7.22 כֹּרִין *Aramaic* (Ezra 7.22 κόρων; 1 Esdras 8.20 κόρων). It is not found in Exodus[MT]. Or חֹמֶר is paralleled by κόρος: Lev. 27.16 חֹמֶר (κόρου); Num. 11.32 חֳמָרִים (κόρους); Ezek. 45.13b מֵחֹמֶר (ἀπὸ τοῦ κόρου). Brown *et al.* 1979, 499 states that the *kor* equals the *homer* on the basis of Ezek. 45.11[MT], which states that the *bat* (בַּת) and the *ephah* (אֵיפָה) are equal, that both are one tenth of a *homer* (חֹמֶר), and that the *homer* is the standard measure. Ezek. 45.14[MT] states that the 'oil statute' will be the 'tenth bath from each kor', where 'ten baths [are] a homer'. Ezek. 45.14[LXX] translates בַּת (bath) as κοτύλη ('cup'), stating that the statute is: 'one cup of oil out of ten cups; for ten cups are a gomor' (κοτύλην ἐλαίου ἀπὸ δέκα κοτυλῶν ὅτι αἱ δέκα κοτύλαι εἰσὶν γομορ). Ezek 45.13[LXX] confirms this: where Ezek. 45.13[MT] has *homer* twice, LXX transliterates חֹמֶר with γομορ in the first instance and offers κόρος in the second. κοτύλη otherwise parallels a *log* (לֹג), a liquid measure of oil, occurring only in Lev. 14.10, 12, 15, 21, 24.

97 In *AJ* 3.234, 197 Josephus transliterates *hin* (ἕιν) and writes that it is equivalent to 'two Attic χόες. The Bible has הִין (LXX ιν), which is always transliterated as ιν in Exodus, Leviticus, Numbers and Ezekiel. Josephus may be either Hellenizing the LXX transliteration or translating himself. So, this example does not help here.

them to check on his metric accuracy. If Josephus were practically familiar with the equivalence of these Greek and Hebrew terms, he would presumably display more consistency and accuracy in his explanations, in which case, we would have to reckon with the possibility that he used the OG and invoked the Hebrew terms from vernacular experience, not literary endeavour.

3.6.2 *Sacrifices*

Here Josephus seems to rely on the OG, but prefers his Hebrew source for some sacrificial terms. However, while he was apparently not perturbed by inaccuracies in his metric equivalents, correct usage regarding sacrifices moves him. His preference for certain Hebrew sacrificial terms arises from his expert judgement – born of his priestly experience – that some OG terms are inadequate.[98]

AJ 3.222 shows that Josephus knows both proto-𝔐 and OG forms of Lev. 7.12-13. Leviticus describes three types of offering: the individual burnt offering (Lev. 1.4); the related sin and guilt offerings (Leviticus 5); and the *shelem* offering, which can be translated 'peace' offering. The Greek translators commonly equate Hebrew *shelem* with Greek *sōtērion*, 'welfare'.[99] The peace-offering was further bifurcated into 'thank-offering' (Lev. 7.12f.) and 'freewill-offering' (7.16f.; 22.1-3); and the OG renders Hebrew *tôdah* (תּוֹדָה), 'thanks',[100] as *ainesis* (αἴνεσις), 'praise'.[101]

Josephus happily uses OG's *sōtērion* ('welfare') to render *shelem* ('peace').[102] But for the 'thank-offering' (*tôdah*), the first division of the peace-offering, Josephus rejects OG's loose rendering of *ainesis* ('praise'), supplying his own word, χαριστήριος (*AJ* 3.225; cf. χαριστηρίους θυσίας *AJ* 3.228). Josephus, however, follows the OG in his use of ὁλοκαυτεῖται (*AJ* 3.225f.), which echoes OG's τό ὁλοκαύτωμα ('burnt offering'), not an obvious translation for עֹלָה ('that which ascends'). In *AJ* 3.217 he has ἐσσῆνα λόγιον; and *essên* is a transliteration of חֹשֶׁן ('breastplate'). In Exod. 28.15, 29 and 30 it is called the 'pouch of judgement' (חֹשֶׁן מִשְׁפָּט/τό λογεῖον τῆς κρίσεως) because of the decision given by the *Urim and Thummim*.[103] Josephus replaces the OG translation of חֹשֶׁן מִשְׁפָּט (that is, τό λογεῖον τῆς κρίσεως) with his own ἐσσῆνα λόγιον, attaching a Hebrew term to the Greek one most familiar to him and combining OG and proto-𝔐 terms.[104] Feldman notes that λόγιον, 'would be readily intelligible to Greeks, for whom oracles were so vital a part of their religion'.[105] Finally, Josephus' interpretation of the *Urim* (δηλώσων, *AJ* 3.205; δῆλον 214-217) has been influenced

---

98 Compare Sanders 1992, 112.
99 Only the translators of Samuel and Kings rendered *shelem* with εἰρήνη.
100 Lev. 7.12 אִם עַל־תּוֹדָה יַקְרִיבֶנּוּ ('if one offers it for thanks').
101 Lev. 7.12 ἐὰν μὲν περὶ αἰνέσεως προσφέρῃ αὐτήν ('if one offers it for praise').
102 *AJ* 3.222 θυσίας σωτηρίους (compare הַשְּׁלָמִים דָּם/τὸ αἷμα τοῦ σωτηρίου θυσία σωτηρίου Num. 7.14; זֶבַח שְׁלָמָיו Lev. 17.18; זֶבַח שְׁלָמָיו/θυσίαν σωτηρίου Lev. 17.29).
103 Brown *et al.* 1979, 365.
104 Marcus 1952, *ad loc*; Feldman 2000, 289 [571].
105 Feldman 2000, 289.

by OG's translation of אוּרִים as δήλωσις (Exod. 28.30) and מִשְׁפַּט הָאוּרִים as τὴν κρίσιν τῶν δήλων (Num. 27.21).

3.6.3 *Josephus follows the OG for some priestly terms, translating others himself*

Josephus' description of the priests' vestments in *AJ* 3.151-158 principally depends on two passages: Exod. 28.40-42 and 39.27-29. In several details in *AJ* 3.151f. Josephus prefers proto-𝔐 Exodus to OG. However, he also diverges from proto-𝔐 Exodus passages, adding some details of his own found neither in 𝔐 or OG. These changes suggest that Josephus is describing what he did and wore as a priest.[106] Proto-𝔐 and OG forms of these passages do not differ significantly, so the RSV translation of 𝔐 suffices initially.[107]

Exod. 28.40-42[RSV]

[40] And for Aaron's sons you shall make *coats* and *girdles* and *caps*; you shall make them for glory and beauty. [41] And you shall put them upon Aaron your brother, and upon his sons with him, and shall anoint them and ordain them and consecrate them, that they may serve me as priests. [42] And you shall make for them linen *breeches* to cover their naked flesh; from the loins to the thighs they shall reach.

Exod. 39.27-29[RSV] (36.34-36[LXX])

[27] They also made the *coats*, woven of fine linen, for Aaron and his sons, [28] and the *turban* of fine linen, and the *caps* of fine linen, and the linen *breeches* of fine twined linen, [29] and the *girdle* of fine twined linen and of blue and purple and scarlet stuff, embroidered with needlework; as the Lord had commanded Moses.

These passages list four (or five in Exodus 39) items: coats, girdles, (turban – Exodus 39 only), caps, and breeches.[108]

---

106   Sanders (1992, 92–102) notes that Josephus embellishes descriptions of the fabrics of priestly garments and assimilates the *turban* and the *cap* of Exod. 39.27 into unified headgear. Similarly: Thackeray (1961, 390–391 [*b*]) on 'headgear'; Feldman (2000, 272 [387]) on 'breeches'. Feldman (1998b, 545–546) discusses Josephus' priestly concerns.

107   𝔐 and OG Exod. 39.27-29 exhibit two minor differences. First, there is the case of מַעֲשֵׂה אֹרֵג ('work of a weaver'), ἔργον ὑφαντὸν ('a woven work') in Exod. 39.27; the active participle of אֹרֵג ('weave') is usually used as a substantive noun = 'weaver' (Brown *et al.* 1979, 70). Greek ὑφαντός is an adjective, 'woven' (Lust *et al.* 1992–1996, 640). Second, there is וְאֶת־הָאַבְנֵט שֵׁשׁ מָשְׁזָר ('and the girdle of twined fine-linen'), καὶ τὰς ζώνας αὐτῶν ἐκ βύσσου ('and their girdles of fine-linen') (Exod. 39.29). שֵׁשׁ and βύσσος ('fine linen') are consistent parallels and OG does not render מָשְׁזָר (twined) of the Hebrew *hophal* (שׁזר for 'twist').

108   Sanders (1992, 92–93) substitutes 'tunic' for RSV's 'coat'; and 'sash' for RSV's 'girdle'. He replaces the 'turban' and 'cap' of Exodus 39, which Josephus assimilates into one item (*AJ* 3.157), with 'headgear'. Because I am concerned with the forms of these passages that Josephus presupposes, it is more useful here to maintain RSV's terms. I adopt Sanders' 'headgear' when there is no need to distinguish between the 'turban' and the 'cap' of Exodus 39.

Table 3.1 Words used by 𝔐, LXX and Josephus for priestly garments

coat	כֻּתֹּנֶת or כְּתֹנֶת[109]	Exod. 28.40f.𝔐 and 39.27f.𝔐
	χιτών	28.40f.LXX and 36.34f.LXX
	χιτών	*AJ* 3.153
	ἔνδυμα	*AJ* 3.153
girdle	אַבְנֵט	Exod. 28.40f.𝔐 and 39.27f.𝔐
	ἀβανήθ	*abanêth* = אַבְנֵט – *AJ* 3.156
	ζώνη	28.40f.LXX and 36.34f.LXX
	ζώνη	*AJ* 3.154
cap	מִגְבָּעָה	Exod. 28.40f.𝔐 and 39.27f.𝔐
	κίδαρις	Exod. 28.40f.LXX
	μίτρα	36.34f.LXX
turban	מִצְנֶפֶת	Exod. 39.27f.𝔐
	κίδαρις	Exod. 36.34f.LXX
	μασναεφθῆς	*masnaephthes* = מִצְנֶפֶת – *AJ* 3.157
	πῖλος[110]	*AJ* 3.156, 172, 186
breeches	מִכְנָסַיִם[111]	Exod. 28.40f.𝔐 and 39.27f.𝔐
	περισκελῆ[112]	Exod. 28.40f.LXX and 36.34f.LXX
	μαναχάση	*machanases* = מִכְנְסֵי[113] – *AJ* 3.152
	συνακτήρ	'binders'[114] – *AJ* 3.152
	διάζωμα	'drawers'[115] – *AJ* 3.152
	ἀναξυρίδες	'breeches' – *AJ* 3.152

Josephus derives his descriptions both from proto-𝔐 and OG Exodus 28 and 39. First, he transliterates Hebrew terms from Exodus 28 and 39. He provides terms for three of the four priestly garments. For 'breeches' he offers μαναχάση, a translitera-

---

109   Brown *et al.* 1979, 509. Abs. כְּתֹנֶת Exod. 28.39.
110   Πῖλος refers to 'anything made of felt', especially a 'close fitting cap' (Liddell-Scott 1992, 1404). Josephus may use πῖλος because it had parallels in descriptions of priestly garments in classical writers (Sanders 1992, 505 [4]).
111   'Gather, collect' (Brown *et al.* 1979, 488).
112   'Around the leg, underpants, leggings', Lust *et al.* 1992–1996, 487.
113   מִכְנְסֵי הַבַּד שֵׁשׁ מָשְׁזָר ('breeches of fine twined linen').
114   Josephus' translation of συνακτήρ ('binder') suggests that his '*machanases*', μαναχάση (trans-literation) of the dual form *miknesayim* (מִכְנָסַיִם) derives from כנס (to 'gather' or 'collect') (Thackeray 1961, 387 [*e*]).
115   Josephus may use the phrase *diazōma peri ta aidoia* because of its parallels in descriptions of priestly garments in classical writers (Sanders 1992, 505 [4]).

tion of מִכְנָסַיִם (*AJ* 3.152).[116] For 'girdle' he gives ἀβανὴθ (*abanêth*), a transliteration of אַבְנֵט (*AJ* 3.156).[117] For 'turban' he offers μασναεφθῆς, a transliteration of מִצְנֶפֶת (*AJ* 3.157). Conversely, he adopts χιτών and ζώνη, used in the OG for 'coat' and 'girdle'. He also adopts OG's βύσσινος for 'linen'.[118] Notably, for 'girdle' he provides both proto-𝔐's אַבְנֵט (ἀβανὴθ) and OG's ζώνη. His use of OG and proto-𝔐 terms for the same item suggests his reference to both Greek and Hebrew forms of these passages. Although Josephus may be using OG Exodus alongside spoken Hebrew terms, an accumulation of further considerations suggests that Josephus is using two text-forms of this passage.

Josephus transliterates the Hebrew for 'turban' and 'breeches' and translates them with non-OG Greek terms, thus preferring proto-𝔐 to the OG and producing his own translation independently of the OG. This case is akin to his treatment of the sacrifice terms in *AJ* 3.222f. (above), where he follows neither the OG sense nor its vocabulary. His reasons for rejecting OG terms and producing his own definitions appear to reflect experiential rather than linguistic concerns.

For 'coat' Josephus gives not only OG's χιτών, but also his own synonym ἔνδυμα. Whereas Hebraizing revisions of the OG known to us tend to use terms consistently, Josephus gives no fewer than three of his own synonyms for 'breeches' (see Table 3.1, above), none of which corresponds with the OG, and one of which (συνακτήρ) he seems to translate himself (see Footnote 114, above). His account of the way in which breeches were worn exceeds the detail of prescriptions in Exodus and Leviticus:

> This has as its meaning a pair of drawers. It is a loin-cloth covering the genitals, artfully fashioned, sewn from finely spun linen, with the feet fitting into it just as though into trousers. It ends above the waist and terminates at the flank, around which it is drawn tight (*AJ* 3.152; Feldman 2000).

The same occurs in his descriptions of priestly headgear. Proto-𝔐 talks of the 'caps' (מִגְבָּעוֹת), which, according to Exod. 28.40, were the headgear of common priests, and the 'turban' (מִצְנֶפֶת) of the high priest (Aaron), according to Exod. 28.4 and Exodus 39.[119] Josephus, on the contrary, transliterates only מִצְנֶפֶת of the high priest

---

116   Exod. 28.40 מִכְנְסֵי־בָד ('breeches of white linen') and Exod. 39.28 שֵׁשׁ מָשְׁזָר מִכְנְסֵי הַבָּד ('breeches of white linen, fine-linen twined'). בָּד is used of the white linen of priestly vestments, of angelic attire (Ezekiel, Daniel), and once of David (Brown *et al.* 1979, 94 I.). שֵׁשׁ denotes 'fine linen', material woven from thread (Brown *et al.* 1979, 1058).

117   He also provides the Aramaic word for the same item (see below).

118   βύσσινος ('[made] of fine linen') in Exod.LXX 28.39, 36.34; βύσσος ('fine linen') in Exod.LXX 28.40f. and 36.34-36 (cf. Lust *et al.* 1992–1996, 114); βυσσίνος (*AJ* 3.153). However, Josephus does not provide the Exodus term שֵׁשׁ ('fine linen' in 𝔐 Exod. 28.40f. and 39.27f., cf. Brown *et al.* 1979, 1058) for this, but offers the transliteration χέθον in relation to the word כֻּתֹּנֶת ('coat'). He states that it means 'linen' and hence, he is more likely transliterating a Hebrew word for 'linen' not used in the proto-𝔐 of Exodus, or possibly an Aramaic term (see below).

119   Cf. Thackeray 1961, 390–391 [*b*]. Note that Exod. 39.28 does not contradict this distinction by

and conflates the two items, stating that the resultant headgear is worn by the ordinary priests (*AJ* 3.158). In using the term πῖλος ἄκωνος ('peakless cap')[120] and in his highly detailed description of the headgear, he assimilates the cap and the turban of Exodus, describing both in combination. Again, the detail in Josephus' description of the sash (*AJ* 3.154) exceeds the description in Exodus. Josephus gives very detailed descriptions of the types of fabric from which the tunic and the girdle were made.[121] Although Exodus and Josephus only mention linen and 'scarlet stuff' in descriptions of the priestly girdle ('sash' in Sanders 1992), Sanders recognizes that Josephus knew that this 'stuff' was wool, a detail he shares with *Mishnah Kilaim* 9.1. Moreover, the order in which Josephus describes the items follows neither Exodus 28 nor Exodus 39.[122]

Table 3.2 Order of appearance of priestly garments (*AJ* 3; Exodus 28; 39)

Josephus:	breeches,	tunic,	sash,	headgear		
Exod. 28.40f:		tunic,	sash,	headgear,	breeches	
Exod. 39.27f. (36.34f.[LXX]):		tunic,		headgear,	breeches,	sash

Josephus' descriptions apparently correspond with his own experience of the order in which a priest dressed himself.[123]

Because in most cases Josephus' narrative agrees with the OG, which often diverges from proto-𝔐, the instances when he prefers proto-𝔐 are significant. Josephus' decisions in such cases indicate the importance of priestly Temple service. Although his practical expertise extends beyond a purely literary interest in the text of Exodus, his interest is ultimately rooted in text. After all, priestly practice was founded in Pentateuchal prescriptions, making the distinction between orthopraxy and orthodoxy a false dichotomy. His presentation of practices that exceed the textual prescriptions of the Pentateuch demonstrates his conviction that *because* those practices are rooted in the ancestral texts he is duty-bound to represent them.

His conscious dependence on Exodus 𝔐 at these points is supported by indications that OG Exodus 28 and 39 lack terminological consistency regarding the headgear of the high priest and lesser priests. The OG renders מִצְנֶפֶת variously with κίδαρις[124]

saying 'the turban of fine linen, and the caps of fine linen' because they are made 'for Aaron and his sons' (Exod. 39.27).

120   Thackeray (1961, 390–391 [*b*]) and Feldman (2000, 273 [405]): the term 'peakless cap' contradicts Exod. 28.40, which states that ordinary priests' caps were peaked.

121   Sanders 1992, 94–95.

122   Sanders 1992, 94–95. 'Breeches' (*AJ* 3.152), 'tunic' (*AJ* 3.153), 'sash' (*AJ* 3.154), and 'headgear' (*AJ* 3.157). Exod. 28.4, 28.39 and Lev. 16.4 describe the garments of Aaron only, not his sons' or the priests', whom Josephus is discussing in *AJ* 3.151-158. Josephus begins with the high priest at *AJ* 3.159.

123   Philo and Aristeas imply that first-century priests did not wear all four garments during Temple service. Josephus states that they did. Sanders (1992, 93–94) takes Josephus, as a priest, to be reliable.

124   Singular accusative κίδαριν for singular מִצְנֶפֶת: Exod. 28.4, 39; 39.31; 16.4.

or with μίτρα.[125] It equally renders מִגְבָּעוֹת variously with κίδαρις or with μίτρα.[126] The Hebrew provides consistent terminology, which explains Josephus' preference for the Hebrew in *AJ* 3.151f.

But Josephus also relies on the OG, as is evident from his use of the word ᾤα ('fringe'), for which Exod. 28.32⁹ᵗ has no lexical equivalent.[127] He also follows OG in *AJ* 3.159, designating the high priest's garment (that reaches down to his feet) with OG's singular term, ποδήρης.[128] Josephus states that the priest's robe (χιτών – a transliteration meaning 'linen') descends to the feet (*AJ* 3.153). Elsewhere, the high priest is said to wear all of the above, but over these he dons a robe (χιτῶνα) of blue reaching to the feet called a μεείρ (*AJ* 3.159) (= מְעִיל).[129] Josephus' reference to the blue colour derives principally from Exod. 28.31 (תְּכֵלֶת/ὑακίνθινος).[130] However, Josephus' language concerning the style of the cloak (χιτῶνα ποδήρης δ' ἐστὶ καὶ οὗτος) is closer to Exod. 29.5ᴸˣˣ (τὸν χιτῶνα τὸν ποδήρη).[131] He has adopted the word ποδήρης from the OG of Exodus.

This term usually indicates women's garb in extant pre-second-century CE Greek literature. Applied to men, it is usually a ridicule of effeminate, outlandish customs. Strabo (*Geography* 3.5.10-11) describes men who inhabit a desert island and wear bizarre 'long cloaks' (ποδήρεις ἐνδεδυκότες τοὺς χιτῶνας) and belts around their breasts. He also describes peculiar customs of Babylonians (*Geography* 16.1-20), who have effeminate long hair and cloaks down to their feet. Dio Chrysostom (*77th/78th Discourse* 32-33) describes a man who wears a 'long robe' in order to fill its 'womanish, deep fold' with loot. In Euripides' *Bacchae* (810-840) Dionysus' suggestion that Pentheus dresses himself as a woman elicits Pentheus' indignation.[132] In Callimachus' *Iambi* (193) the speaker seems to lament his youth 'inclined to the muses' and associates tossing long hair in a trailing robe with ecstatic states and

---

125   Singular accusative μίτραν for singular מִצְנֶפֶת: Exod. 28.37, 37; 29.6, 6; 39.28, 31; Lev. 8.9, 9.

126   Exod. 39.28ᴸˣˣ reverses the order of מִצְנֶפֶת and מִגְבָּעוֹת as they appear in proto-𝔐. However, the plural κίδαρεις corresponds with the plural מִגְבָּעוֹת, and the singular μίτραν corresponds with the singular מִצְנֶפֶת.

127   Feldman 2000, 273 [403].

128   Cf. Liddell-Scott 1992, 1426. Ποδήρης, an adjective meaning 'reaching to the feet', often qualifies πέπλοι or χιτών to indicate a robe 'that falls over the feet'. Later ποδήρης alone means 'long robe', used of the high priest's robe, e.g. Exod. 25.6ᴸˣˣ, *Aristeas* 96, alongside χιτών. Liddell-Scott 1992, 1363 πέπλος can mean 'any woven cloth, sheet, carpet, curtain, veil' or an 'upper garment, or mantle' in one piece worn by women; in Athens it was an embroidered 'robe' worn in procession at the Panathenaea; it is less frequently used of 'a man's robe', but then especially of long Persian dress.

129   Exod. 28.31; 29.5; 39.22. The robe had underskirts to the floor, שׁוּלֵי הַמְּעִיל, Exod. 28.34; 39.24, 25, 26 (Brown *et al.* 1979, 591).

130   Blue is also mentioned in Exod. 39.29 among other colours.

131   Three times מְעִיל = ποδήρης: Exod. 28.4 τὸν ποδήρη; 28.31 ὑποδύτην ποδήρη; 29.5 τὸν χιτῶνα τὸν ποδήρη. Twice 'breast plate' (חֹשֶׁן) = τὸν ποδήρη at Exod. 25.7 and 35.9.

132   Dionysius' suggestions include Pentheus: wearing a 'long linen robe' (βυσσίνους πέπλους), letting his hair grow long (by Dionysian magic), and donning a dress that reaches to his ankles (πέπλοι ποδήρης). Pentheus protests repeatedly that he will not 'dress like a woman'.

prophetic bliss characteristic of the 'worship of the Cybele' and 'ecstatic Bacchic rapture'.[133] Dionysius of Halicarnassus (*Roman Antiquities* 7.8.4-10.2) describes an attempt to effeminize boys by raising them as girls, suppressing gymnasiums and arms training and dressing them in women's garb with long hair decorated with flowers, hair nets and 'embroidered robes reaching down to the feet'. He once refers to Atreus, who served a feast of toes and fingers of his own children.[134] The term, when applied to objects other than garments, can mean 'long': a long 'shield',[135] a 'pillar',[136] and the 'ears of strange people' (the Ocypodes) that 'reach down to their feet'.[137]

If we are to believe Josephus' claim to have studied Greek literature (see Section 3.4.1, above), then the term ποδήρης, so frequently associated with Greek derision of the exotic, seems an odd choice for presenting the Judaean priesthood to a Gentile audience. While Josephus may at times exoticize Judaeans for his Roman audience,[138] it is unlikely that he would present the Judaean priesthood, of which he is so proud, as bizarre. I argue, therefore, that Josephus uses ποδήρης for the high priest's מְעִיל because it arises in his Greek copy of Exodus.

One further point supports this claim.[139] Josephus and Philo both understand the Pentateuch in terms of a Platonic tradition that identifies blue with the sky. Taking the temple as a microcosm,[140] each explains in his own way that the blue (*hyacinthine*) colour of temple paraphernalia[141] and high-priestly garb[142] (particularly the ποδήρης[143]) represents the air, sky or heavens. Each author also associates the ποδήρης with earth, although they differ in detail.[144] Philo, explaining that the ποδήρης is entirely 'blue (ὑάκινθος) in colour since air also is black',[145] draws on a Platonic idea that the blue of

---

133   Callimachus, *Iambi*, 117.

134   Aeschylus, *Agamemnon*, 1590.

135   Xenophon, *Cyropaedia*, 2.2.9-11; *Anabasis*, 1.8.6-11.

136   Aeschylus, *Agamemnon*, 985.

137   Strabo, *Geography*, 15.1-57.

138   Some passages seem to exoticize the virtuous Essenes.

139   My thanks go to Steve Mason for drawing my attention to the following issue and Sean Ryan for his bibliographical advice and valuable comments.

140   e.g. *Somn.* 1.214-215; *Spec.* 1.84; *Mos.* 2.100-133; *AJ* 3.179-187; *BJ* 5.212-214. For Philo, the priest's blue garb is integral to the trappings of the tabernacle, which symbolize all aspects of the universe (*Mos.* 2.100-133, esp. 109). See further Chyutin 2006.

141   The blue of the Temple veils symbolizes 'air' (*AJ* 3.183; *BJ* 5.213).

142   The blue of the priest's cap (ὁ πῖλος) represents the heaven (οὐρανός) (*AJ* 3.186).

143   The blue (ὑάκινθος) colour of the high priest's robe (ποδήρης) (Exod. 28.31; 39.29) represents 'air' (e.g. *Mos.* 2.118, 133; *Spec.* 1.85; *BJ* 5.232, cf. 5.212-214), 'heaven' (e.g. *Mos.* 2.122; *Somn.* 1:214-215) or 'sky' (e.g. *AJ* 3:184, πόλος, 'firmament').

144   For Josephus, the linen flax of the ποδήρης represents earth (e.g. *AJ* 3.183-184; cf. *BJ* 5.213, 232). For Philo the blue ποδήρης is an under-mantle (*Mos.* 2:109) whose lower fringe, touching the ground, is decorated with pomegranates and flowers that represent earth and water in their lowly cosmic position (*Mos.* 2:120-121, 133). Over the ποδήρης is a shoulder-mantle, ἡ ἐπωμίς (compare Josephus' μεεὶρ, *AJ* 3.159), which symbolizes heaven (*Mos.* 2:122, 133) and is decorated with signs representing the universe (e.g. *Mos.* 2:143).

145   *Spec.* 1.94, cf. 1.85; *Mos.* 2.118. The ποδήρης, worn beneath the ἐπωμίς (see previous footnote), 'is placed in the second classification next in honor to the heaven' (*Spec.* 1.94).

the sky results from the mingling of black (μέλαν) and white (λευκόν), corresponding to the illumination of darkness (σκότος) by light (φῶς).[146] For Plato the deep black (μέλαν κατακορές) of the night sky turns blue when mixed with brilliant (λαμπρόν) white (λευκόν) light; even more white light produces the light blue (γλαυκόν) of the daytime sky.[147] Considering the influence of Plato's *Timaeus* on Philo's *De Opificio Mundi*,[148] Philo's reading of the Septuagint invokes Platonic terms.[149] Josephus and Philo's association of ὑάκινθος with the heavens and the Greek zodiac suggests that they share a Jewish Greek philosophical reading of the OG. Nevertheless, Josephus expresses this tradition quite independently and does not seem to rely directly on Philo.[150] Significantly, neither uses Plato's word γλαυκόν, but rather the ὑάκινθος of the Septuagint, which translates תְּכֵלֶת (Exod. 28.31; 39.29), indicating violet-dyed wool.[151] Josephus' application of ὑάκινθος, used in the Septuagint for the priestly ποδήρης, to the sky suggests his use of a Greek source akin to the OG here.[152]

3.7 *Conclusions*

Josephus' discussion of weights and measures, sacrifices, and priestly garments (Sections 3.6.1–3.6.3) reflects his awareness and use of different forms of a given passage. The last two examples (sacrifices and priestly garments) represent matters of personal importance to Josephus-the-priest, who grounds their daily significance in the literature that he esteems. Thus, his appeal to two forms of a passage relating

---

146   Timaeus 68C. Colour mixture 7a: bright (λαμπρόν) + white (λευκόν) + deep black (μέλαν κατακορές) = blue (κυανοῦν); 7b blue (κυανοῦν) + white (λευκόν) = light blue (γλαυκόν). This is developed by Aristotle (*De Anima* 418b4-420; *De Sensu et Sensibilibus* 439a 17f.) and Ps-Aristotle (*De Coloribus* 793b34-794al5).

147   See Struycken 2003, 301-302.

148   Cf. Runia 1986; 2005.

149   Note also that the blue of the sky results from the celestial changes that divide time. For Philo the high priest's attire (like the Temple decor in general) not only symbolizes the elements of the cosmos, but also their dynamic interactions and the resulting division of times and seasons (*Mos.* 2:120). The illumination of darkness also has a moral import for Philo (e.g. *Somn.* 1.218).

150   Josephus differs from, and even contradicts, Philo in numerous details. For example, Philo associates the decorative pomegranates on the fringe of the ποδήρης with the earth, while Josephus associates the linen material of the ποδήρης with the earth and the pomegranates with thunder and lightning (see Footnote 144, above). Josephus' linen under-garment (λινοῦν τε ὑποδύτην, BJ 5.231; cf. AJ 3.159) lies beneath the blue ποδήρης (is this the 'skirt' (שׁוּל) of Exodus? See Footnote 129, above) whereas for Philo the ποδήρης is the blue under-mantel representing air, which is subordinate to the shoulder-mantel (ἐπωμίς); cf. Footnotes 144 and 145, above. Sanders finds Josephus more reliable; see Footnote 123, above.

151   Brown *et al.* 1979, 1067.

152   Greeks are not the only ancient people to associate blue with the heavens. For example, in Akkadian text (KAR 307) the middle heaven is of *saggilmut*, a bluish stone (cf. Wright 2000, 34–35, 56–58; Horowitz 1998). Compare Exod. 24.10, which depicts God standing in heaven on a platform of lapis lazuli or sapphire (מַעֲשֵׂה לִבְנַת הַסַּפִּיר/πλίνθου σαπφείρου). There may, then, be a traditional Hebrew association of the high priest's garb with the heavens, since סַפִּירִים also adorn the high priest's breastplate (Exod. 28.18; 39.11). However, sapphire blue is distinct from תְּכֵלֶת (violet wool) (ὑάκινθος, Exod. 28.31; 39.29) of the high priest's robe.

to these matters is no abstract textual exercise, but a choice that reflects the concerns of his daily life.

In Section 2.5.1 I have placed three types of awareness of textual plurality on a continuum. Josephus' work displays all three: §A 'ordinary' interpretation of a text considered 'fixed'; §B exegetical manipulation of semantic units in Hebrew, or awareness of two readings in one copy; and §C awareness of discrete forms of some passages appearing in distinct copies. In his references to the Pentateuch in Hebrew and Greek, Josephus was not only aware of distinct versions of the same work in the two languages, but also differentiated among copies. He moreover recognized distinct sense contours contained within a single passage, invoking one or both in his writing.

4

Dead Sea Sectarians and textual plurality

4.1 *Textual plurality in sectarian exegetical compositions*

Exegetical compositions of the Qumran corpus reveal ways in which some Palestinian Jewish exegetes made use of Hebrew textual plurality.[1] In their references to a literary passage, exegetes often make deliberate use of associated sense contours, which manifest themselves as lexically distinct forms, known in textual criticism as the 'variant readings' constitutive of textual traditions.

4.1.1 *'Passages' and 'semantic units'*

As mentioned earlier, a 'passage' is a piece of syntax, identified by an exegete as semantically coherent for interpretation (see Section 2.5.1). A 'semantic unit' is the smallest syntactical unit whose particular configuration defines distinct sense contours. A distinct sense contour characterizes a particular semantic form of the passage. For the ancient exegete a sense contour is a semantic property of the passage as a whole. Several possible sense contours associated with a passage can become traditional semantic properties of that passage.

4.2 *Habakkuk 2¹⁶ in 1QHabakkuk Pesher (1QpHab.) 11⁹*

This is a well-known example.[2] The citation of Hab. 2.16 in 1QpHab. 11.9 reads והרעל ('and stagger'). This reading is supported by the double reading of Hab. 2.16 OG, καὶ διασαλεύθητι καὶ σείσθητι ('shudder and tremble') against 𝔐 וְהֵעָרֵל ('be uncircumcised') (*niphal* imperative of ערל). The *pesher* following the citation continues: כיא לוא מל את עורלת לבו ('for he did not circumcise the foreskin of his heart'). The pesherist was apparently aware that two sense contours characterize this passage, one referring to 'staggering' and another to 'being uncircumcised'. In this case, as in others, distinct sense contours derive from the same semantic unit (ערל – רעל).

---

1 The compositions treated below are considered sectarian or *Yahad* compositions. Hereafter 'Sectarian' (capitalized) designates 'Dead Sea sectarian'.

2 Elliger 1953, 56; Brownlee 1959, 76–78 variant 120a; Horgan 1979, 19–20, 50; Lim 1997, 50.

Table 4.1 Textual evidence for Habakkuk 2.16

Hab. 2.16ᴸˣˣ	1QpHab. 11.8-9	Hab. 2.16ᵐ
πλησμονὴν ἀτιμίας ἐκ δόξης	שבעתה קלון ³מבוד	שָׂבַעְתָּ קָלוֹן מִכָּבוֹד
πίε καὶ σύ	שתה גם אתה	שְׁתֵה נַם־אַתָּה
καὶ διασαλεύθητι καὶ σείσθητι	והרעל	וְהֵעָרֵל
ἐκύκλωσεν ἐπὶ σὲ	תסוב עליכה	תִּסוֹב עָלֶיךָ
ποτήριον δεξιᾶς κυρίου	כוס ימין xxxx⁴	כּוֹס יְמִין יְהוָה
καὶ συνήχθη		
ἀτιμία ἐπὶ τὴν δόξαν σου	וקיקלון על כבודכה	וְקִיקָלוֹן עַל־כְּבוֹדֶךָ

Sense contour I   Sense contour II

1QpHab והרעל (*niphal* רעל 'stagger, totter')   ᵐ וְהֵעָרֵל (*niphal* 'be uncircumcised')

LXXi   διασαλεύθητι (διασαλεύω 'shake violently')   ℭ ואיתערטל 'bare thyself'⁵

LXXii   σείσθητι (σείω 'shake, tremble (with fear)')

α'   καί καρώθητι (καρόω 'be stupefied'⁶)

V   *et consopire* (*consōpiō*, 'lull into sleep', 'stupefy')

Syr   ואתטרף (טרף 'snatch, seize')

Hab. 2.16ᴸˣˣ	Hab. 2.16ᵐ	1QpHab. 11.8-9
Also you! drink (your) fill of shame instead of glory!	You will be sated with shame instead of glory. Drink, you yourself, and be uncircumcised!	You will be sated with shame instead of glory. Drink, you yourself, and stagger!
And shake and tremble! The cup of the Lord's right hand has come round upon you and shame has gathered upon your glory	The cup in the Lord's right hand will come around upon you and shame (will be) upon your glory	

Sense contour I derives from the reading רעל (see below). Some witnesses display discomfort with this verb. V and α' interpretively convey a sense of drunkenness, expressed in the previous verse, Hab. 2.15, and by the phrase כוס ימין יהוה.

---

3   מ(כ)בוד, García Martínez and Tigchelaar 1998, *ad loc.*

4   The *tetragrammaton* in paleo-Hebrew script.

5   Rabin 1955, 158.

6   Brownlee (1959, 77) misspells χαρώθητι, intending καρόω; Liddell-Scott (1992, 879) καρόω – 'plunge into deep sleep or torpor; of stupor, drunken sleep; be stupefied'.

> Woe to him who makes his neighbour drink of the cup of his wrath, and makes them drunk,
> in order to gaze on his nakedness (לְמַעַן הַבִּיט עַל־מְעוֹרֵיהֶם)!

The LXX suppresses the notion of nakedness in v. 15:

> Woe to him that gives his neighbour to drink the thick lees *of wine*, and intoxicates *him*, that
> he may look upon their secret lairs (τὰ σπήλαια).[7]

Τό σπήλαιον means 'a robber's cave' or 'hideout'.

An entirely different sense contour, deriving from עָרֵל, characterizes 𝔐 and 𝔗. 'Uncircumcision' or 'displaying the foreskin' relates to the 'nakedness' of Hab. 2.15.

4.2.1 *Excursus: The Greek Minor Prophets Scroll (8ḤevXIIgr)*

According to Ulrich's *Index of Passages in the Biblical Scrolls*,[8] 8ḤevXIIgr is the only ancient manuscript from the Judaean Desert to preserve Hab. 2.16.[9]

Table 4.2 Textual restoration of 8ḤevXIIgr column 18, lines 21-24

21	[ΤΗΝΑΣΧΗΜΟΣ]ΥΝΗΝΑΥ[ΤΩ]Ν_ΕΝΕΠΛΗΣ	27 characters
22	[ΘΗΣΑΤΙΜΙΑΣΕ]ΚΔΟΞΗΣ[Π]ΙΕΚΑΙΓΕΣΥΚΑΙ	30 characters
23	[ ]ΚΥΚΛΩΣΕΙΕΠΙΣΕΠΟ	[c.12] + 15 characters
24	[ΤΗΡΙΟΝΔΕΞΙΑΣ] *xxxx*[10]_ΚΑΙΕΜΕΤΟΣ	26 characters

Unfortunately, the text of line 23, corresponding to καὶ διασαλεύθητι καὶ σείσθητι/ והערל, is not preserved. Tov *et al.* note: 'In the lacuna at the beginning of l.23 of col. 18 there is probably room for only one of the two verbs of the LXX (καὶ διασαλεύθητι καὶ σείσθητι) representing one word in 𝔐, והערל.'[11]

This estimation is fair, but can be further refined. There is an average of twenty-seven characters per line (including spaces) in 8ḤevXIIgr column 18 (a maximum of thirty characters, i.e. line 22).[12] If line 23 contained thirty characters (as does line 22, the longest preserved line in the column), there would be room for only the fifteen characters of ΚΑΙΔΙΑΣΑΛΕΥΘΗΤΙ (καὶ διασαλεύθητι). However, the photograph (*edition princeps*, plate XII, cf. Footnote 9, above) shows that line 23 is about two

---

7 LXX ὦ ὁ ποτίζων τὸν πλησίον αὐτοῦ ἀνατροπῇ θολερᾷ καὶ μεθύσκων ὅπως ἐπιβλέπῃ ἐπὶ τὰ σπήλαια αὐτῶν.

8 Ulrich 1999a; reissued in Tov *et al.* 2002.

9 See 8ḤevXIIgr column 18: the fragments, Tov *et al.* 1990, plate XII; transcription, ibid., 54; textual restoration, ibid., 55.

10 The *tetragrammaton* in paleo-Hebrew script.

11 Tov *et al.* 1990, 93.

12 I base this average on the number of characters in lines 21-22, 24-40 of the reconstructed text of col. 18 in Tov *et al.* 1990, 55. The total five hundred and fifteen characters are divided by the nineteen lines to give an average of 27.1 characters per line.

and a half letter spaces shorter than line 30. Thus, fifteen very cramped characters would fit only awkwardly in the non-extant portion of line 23. However, there is comfortable space for the eleven characters of ΚΑΙΣΕΙΣΘΗΤΙ (καὶ σείσθητι). There would alternatively be comfortable room for the eleven characters of Aquila's καί καρώθητι ('be stupefied').

All this assumes that *kaige*'s Habakkuk source reads רעל. Elliger and Brownlee are persuaded of this in light of 1QpHab.'s citation and of the argument (based on the readings of LXX, α' V and Syr) that 𝔐's reading ערל is a late error, whereas רעל is original.[13] Stylistically, there is barely any precedent for *kaige* revisionists. The verb רעל appears only once in 𝔐 in the *Hophal* (Nah. 2.4), where the LXX offers the passive of θορυβέω ('throw into confusion, worry').[14] The LXX renders the cognates of רעל variously: תַּרְעֵלָה (feminine noun, 'a staggering') is πτῶσις (feminine noun, 'a stumbling');[15] יַיִן תַּרְעֵלָה ('wine of reeling') is οἶνον κατανύξεως ('wine of stupor, numbness');[16] סַף־רַעַל ('a cup of reeling') is πρόθυρα σαλευόμενα ('trembling door-posts')[17]. The nouns πτῶσις and κατάνυξις, as well as the participle σαλεύω ('shake') give the same range of meaning – from 'staggering' to 'stupefaction' – as the nuances of רעל in Hab. 2.16. The verb διασαλεύω is a *hapax legomenon* in the LXX at Hab. 2.16 and, as already noted, is too long for the space in line 23, column 18 of 8HevXIIgr. The above survey shows that either σείω, σαλεύω or καρόω are more plausible in this context and follow the LXX precedents.

If, on the other hand, *kaige*'s source read ערל with 𝔐, it is difficult to imagine what *kaige* might have offered at this point. The LXX always circumlocutes the verb ערל, which the translators apparently did not find easy to translate.[18] α', σ' and θ' render the verb ערל with ἀκροβυστίζειν in Lev. 19.23.[19] However, καὶ ἀκροβυστίσθητι is far too long for the available space of seventeen letters. While we may never be certain, it is probable that *kaige*'s source read רעל (following Brownlee and Elliger)[20] and that *kaige* rendered καὶ σείσθητι.

---

13 Brownlee 1959 and Elliger 1953.

14 Nah. 2.4 is in the context of the tumult of warfare. 𝔐's וְהַבְּרֹשִׁים הָרְעָלוּ is obscure, but seems to refer to the trembling of war horses (LXX καὶ οἱ ἱππεῖς θορυβηθήσονται).

15 Isa. 51.17 'the cup of [the Lord's] wrath and cup of reeling' (אֶת־קֻבַּעַת כּוֹס הַתַּרְעֵלָה are 'the cup of stumbling, the bowl of wrath' (τὸ ποτήριον τῆς πτώσεως τὸ κόνδυ τοῦ θυμοῦ). Note that verb עוּר means: I. 'rouse oneself' in Isa. 51.17 (הִתְעוֹרְרִי הִתְעוֹרְרִי), but can also mean II. 'be laid bare, expose oneself', whence comes the cognate מָעוֹר ('nakedness'). Note the presence of מָעוֹר, apparently along with רעל in Hab. 2.15-16. The context of מָעוֹר in Hab. 2.15 may have led to the 𝔐 reading ערל from רעל in Hab. 2.16.

16 Ps. 60.3 (LXX Ps. 59.5). Note the similarity of LXX Ps. 59.5 κατάνυξις to Aquila's κορόω in Hab. 2.16.

17 Zech. 12.2. The noun רַעַל is suitably expressed by the participle of σαλεύω ('shake'). The noun סַף has two meanings: I. bowl basin, II. threshold, sill > סָפַף ('stand on a threshold'). The LXX has understood the second meaning of סַף.

18 LXX offers a range of loosely contextual renderings (cf. Hatch *et al.* 1998), often ἀκροβυστία εἶναι.

19 Wevers 1986, 216.

20 Brownlee 1959 and Elliger 1953.

4.2.2 *1QHabakkuk Pesher*

The Hebrew verb presupposed by the LXX is apparently רעל (to 'stagger, stumble, totter'). Prior to the discovery of 1QpHab., scholars had already suggested that 𝔐 should be amended to רעל on the basis of the retroverted LXX reading.[21] Rabin renders: LXX and Peshitta 'be agitated'; Aquila 'be plunged into torpor' (i.e. הרעל).[22] Brownlee proposes that the senses of 'reeling, stupefaction, or swooning of a drunk-ard' are suggested by LXX, α' and V.[23] Contextually, the sense of drunkenness is sensible in proximity with 'the Lord's cup' (see Footnote 15, above, for the phrase כוס התרעלה in Isa. 51.17, 22).

Only 𝔐 and 𝔗 give the sense of revealing one's uncircumcision; and both of these are late in their available forms. Elliger notes that 𝔐's 'Falschlesung הערל' relates contextually to מְעוֹרֵיהֶם ('nakedness') in Hab. 2.15b, which appears in the context of inebriation in Hab. 2.15a.[24] He claims that Hab. 2.15b is a gloss relating to Hab. 2.15a, but argues that 1QpHab. and LXX show Hab. 2.15b to be older than the Masoretic misreading. Targum's 'bare thyself' (ואיתערטל) for 𝔐's ערל) also relates to מְעוֹרֵיהֶם ('nakedness') in Hab. 2.15b.

Brownlee and Elliger, among others, are primarily interested in establishing the more original reading for the Hebrew «text» of Habakkuk. Brownlee also asks whether the pesherist knew two 'readings'. Some suppose that the pesherist's source copy of Hab. 2.16 agreed with 𝔐 and that the pesherist introduced the reading himself (whether intentionally or not).[25] Brownlee writes that 'other scholars . . . accept the variant as correct and suppose that the interpretation attests merely to the commentator's acquaintance with another reading'.[26] He further notes that the interpretation in the *pesher* is 'based upon the reading of the MT', but also suggests that the phrase עורלת לבו of the *pesher* (1QpHab. 11.13) may derive from a Targum,[27] or from 'simple verbal play', citing Ginsberg.[28] Apart from Ginsberg's proposition, discussions generally seek to establish which textual versions the pesherist knew. For Vermes, the pesherist has 'knowledge of both textual traditions', 'acquaintance with the variants' and 'shows his unwillingness to choose between them' because he 'held

---

21 According to Brownlee (1959, 77): Ehrlich 1912; König 1881–85; Marti 1904; Horst and Robinson 1938; Duhm 1906; Nowack 1897; Procksch 1937; Driver and Neubauer 1876–1877; Smit 1900; Stonehouse 1911; Wellhausen 1892.

22 Rabin (1955, 158) admits: 'I cannot account for Vulgate's *conspire* [*sic*].' His confusion appears to reside in the misspelling of *consopire* that he cites as '*conspire*'.

23 Brownlee 1959, 76.

24 Elliger 1953, 56.

25 Van der Ploeg (1951) thinks that הרעל is a scribal error in 1QpHab. 11.9; van't Land and van der Woude (1954) hold that the pesherist intentionally substituted רעל for ערל of his source, finding the latter offensive (following Molin 1952). However, Brownlee (1959, 78) notes that the pesherist did not avoid the supposedly offensive word in the following commentary.

26 Brownlee 1959, 77.

27 Brownlee (1948, 18 [76]; 1959, 77) believes that 'the Targum' had a 'strong influence [. . .] on the interpretations of the scroll'. But this is unlikely, cf. Chapter Three, Footnote 56, above.

28 Brownlee 1948, 18 [76]; 1959, 77 and Ginsberg 1975.

in profound esteem every witness of what in his view was the sacred record of the word of God'.[29] (See further Section 5.2, below, where the context of this exegetical process is discussed in more detail.)

To say that the pesherist knew two 'traditions' of this passage begs the question because 'tradition' must still be defined. It could mean 'textual tradition', implying that the scribe had access to two copies of Habakkuk, presenting two «texts» at this point. However, it is neither possible nor necessary to prove that the pesherist consulted two copies. In displaying awareness of two distinct sense contours, the pesherist displays a multivalent awareness of the semantic range of the passage (Hab. 2.16b). The pesherist cited הרעל as he found it in his Habakkuk source-copy; his manipulation of רעל (in order to derive עורלת לבו in the *pesher*) shows that he is capable of manipulating the semantic unit to yield a new sense contour. That 𝔐 and 𝔊 adopt this latter sense contour according to the same configuration of this semantic unit does not mean that the pesherist knew 𝔐 or 𝔊, or that the later tradents of 𝔐 and 𝔊 knew 1QpHab. The same is true of other examples of awareness of textual plurality in the Habakkuk Pesher.[30] A more sensitive vision suggests that the various ancient versions collectively testify to (at least) two exegetical approaches to Hab. 2.16, and that 1QpHab. itself witnesses a traditionally multivalent perception of this passage. This 'tradition' may be described as 'textual' in that it has to do with a traditional literary work, but it need not be an exclusively or an essentially literary one. The multiple sense contours characterizing this passage give rise to multiple exegetical ideas – ideas which perhaps existed in the dialogical environment of the exegetical community that produced 1QpHab.[31] Manipulation of this semantic unit may have been part and parcel of habitual rehearsal and oral performance of Habakkuk within the group that produced the *pesher*.[32]

In fact, the *pesher* not only cites הרעל, which relates to the 'staggering' of the intoxication described in Hab. 2.15-16 as a whole, but also explicitly associates the 'cup of the Lord's right hand' of the passage with the wicked priest's 'excessiveness to slake his thirst' (הרויה למען ספות הצמאה, 1QpHab. 11.14). The sense of 'staggering'

29 Vermes 1976, 441a.

30 I give two further examples from 1QpHab. A) The citation of Hab. 1.8 in 1QpHab. 3.6-7 agrees with LXX in its failure to represent of יָבֹאוּ; however, the *pesher* reads יבואו (1QpHab. 3.11) (Brownlee 1959, 11–17 esp. 15, Horgan 1979, 29–30). B) The citation of Hab. 1.11 in 1QpHab. 4.9-10 reads וישם זה ('and this one made') against 𝔐 זוּ וְאָשֵׁם ('guilty men'); however, the occurrence of בית אשמ[ים] ('house of guilty men') in 1QpHab. 4.11 reflects the 𝔐 reading; see: Rabin 1955, 158; Brownlee 1948, 17 (but see Brownlee 1959, 22); Horgan 1979, 31; Brooke 1985 (esp. 39 [181], 286 [33] and 288 [46]). Finkel (1963–1964) collects examples of the use of 'textual variants', although he argues that the Habakkuk pesherist's exegesis in these cases exceeds the mere recognition of variants. For further examples: Elliger 1953; Brownlee 1948, 1949, 1951, esp. 1959 and 1979; Horgan 1979; Lim 1997 and 2002.

31 By 'exegetical community' I do not invoke particular historical notions of 'the Qumran community' nor imply a 'group' necessarily related by locality and socio-economic structure, but persons inhabiting a distinct sphere of exegetical discourse, united by a common exegetical interest in a literature.

32 By '*pesher*' I mean both this particular exegesis of Hab. 2.16 and the Habakkuk Pesher as a composition.

approximates the sense of the V and α' readings, which suggest stupefaction from drinking. Moreover, the following clause (*ll.* 14-15) reads: וכוס חמת [אל תבלענו] ('the cup of the Lord's anger will consume him'). This 'consumption' in the Lord's anger may also have been interpreted as a figurative description of stupefaction. Similarly, 1QpHab. 11.13 incorporates the 'uncircumcision' sense contour characterizing 𝔐 and 𝔗. Thus, we find several interpretive traditions in this *pesher*. Yet it is unnecessary to suggest that the pesherist had as many as four copies of Hab. 2.16 before him, each representing a different «text», perhaps in several languages. Rather, the pesherist was aware of different ways of reading this passage – resulting in two distinct sense contours – and these various readings survive in a number of copying traditions represented in copies. I do not argue that the pesherist was not aware of multiple copies, but that such knowledge was not the sole condition for awareness of textual plurality.

4.3 *Amos 5²⁶⁻²⁷ in the Damascus Document: CDᴬ 7¹⁴⁻¹⁵ and 4QDᴬ (4Q266)*

Both Rabin and Vermes assume that the mediaeval CDᴬ accurately represents the text of an ancient copy of D. While the remains of the first-century BCE manuscript, 4Q266, are incomplete, the physical dimensions of these remains and the correspondence of the preserved text (two and a half fragmentary columns) with that of CDᴬ, suggest that the mediaeval copy indeed preserves an early Roman exegetical composition.[33]

While there is no guarantee that the lost portions of 4Q266 3iii corresponded with the text of CDᴬ 6.20–8.3, all the indications suggest that the two texts correspond with each other.[34] The orthographical variant שוכת (3iii$_{17}$) for סוכת (CDᴬ 7.16), which this correspondence would entail, finds an orthographical parallel שר for סור of Isa. 7.17 CDᴬ 7.13.

The exegetical and textual similarities between the respective reproductions of Amos 9.11 in 4Q174 and in CDᴬ 7.16 (והקימותי את סוכת דוד הנפלת; compare ἀνοικοδομήσω of Acts 15.16; contrast אָקִים of 𝔐, ἀναστήσω of OG) support the antiquity of the text of CDᴬ.[35]

---

33 Baumgarten *et al.* 1997, 26: 'The script of 4Q266 is a semi-cursive hand from about the first half or the middle of the first century BCE.'

34 Except for 3iii$_{17-18}$. The divergence is apparently an *aporia* in CDᴬ 7.17, where a scribe omitted a full fifty-character line.

35 For 4Q174, CDᴬ 7.16 and Acts 15.16 representing 'a common textual tradition' (cf. Rabin 1958, 29; Brooke 1985, 114).

4.3.1 *Textual evidence*

Table 4.3 Amos 5.26-27

LXX	θ'	CDᴬ 7¹⁴⁻¹⁵	𝔐
26 καὶ ἀνελάβετε	και ηρατε	והגליתי	26 וּנְשָׂאתֶם
τὴν σκηνὴν	την ορασιν	את סכות	אֵת סִכּוּת
τοῦ Μολοχ	του βασιλεως υμων	מלככם	מַלְכְּכֶם
	<και την> αμαυρωσιν	ואת כיון צלמיכם	*וְאֵת כִּיּוּן צַלְמֵיכֶם
	ειδωλων <υμων>		
καὶ τὸ ἄστρον	αστον		כּוֹכַב
τοῦ θεοῦ ὑμῶν	του θεου υμων		אֱלֹהֵיכֶם
*Ραιφαν τοὺς τύπους			
αὐτῶν			
οὓς ἐποιήσατε ἑαυτοῖς			אֲשֶׁר עֲשִׂיתֶם לָכֶם:
27 καὶ μετοικιῶ ὑμᾶς			27 וְהִגְלֵיתִי אֶתְכֶם
ἐπέκεινα Δαμασκοῦ		מאהלי לדמשק	מֵהָלְאָה לְדַמֶּשֶׂק
λέγει κύριος			אָמַר יְהוָה
ὁ θεὸς ὁ παντοκράτωρ			אֱלֹהֵי־צְבָאוֹת
ὄνομα αὐτῷ			שְׁמוֹ

LXX	CDᴬ (trans. Rabin 1958)	𝔐
And you took up	*And I will exile*	You shall take up
the tent	the Sikkuth	Sikkuth,
of Moloch,	of your king,	your king,
and the Kiyyun of your images	*and Kaiwan, your images*	star of your god(s),
and the star of your god, Raephan,	<and the star of your God>³⁶	
their images		
which you made		which you made
for yourselves.		for yourselves;
And I will carry you away	from my tent (to) Damascus	*And I will exile* you
beyond Damascus,		beyond Damascus
says the Lord,		says the LORD,
the Almighty God		the God of hosts
is his name.		is his name.

36 Rabin notes that the phrase <and the star of your God>, which is missing from the citation in CDᴬ 7.15, '[m]ust be supplied, as it is interpreted' (1958, 29). However, Vermes writes that the exegete obtained the new meaning from Amos 5, not only by interpreting the god 'Sakkuth' and 'tabernacle' (*sukkath*) and the star god 'Kaiwan' as 'bases' (*kene*), but also 'by omitting all mention of the star god, which would have made it impossible for him to apply the interpretation he intended. He introduces it later, however, when it serves his purpose . . .' (1975a, 45).

Contours in the Text

Table 4.4 Damascus Document^A 7

14	. . . כאשר אמר והגליתי את סכות מלככם
15	ואת כיון צלמיכם מאהלי דמשק ספרי התורה הם סוכת
16	המלך כאשר אמר והקימותי את סוכת דוד הנפלת המלך
17	הוא הקהל וכיניי הצלמים וכיון הצלמים הם ספרי הנביאים
18	אשר בזה ישראל את דבריהם והכוכב הוא דורש התורה
19	הבא דמשק . . .

4Q226 3iii

17	ש]וכת דויד הנפלת המלך הוא [
18	צ] הק]הל [וכיניי הצלמי]ם המה ספר]י הנביאים]
19	אשר בזה ישראל א]ת ד]בריהם והכוכב] הוא דור]ש ה]תורה
20	הבא אל] דמשק

Composite translation

> . . . as He said: (Amos 5.26-27) I shall exile Sakkuth/Sikkuth, your king, and Kaiwan, your images, from my tent (to) Damascus. The books of Torah: these are the *sukkath* of the king, about whom He said: (Amos 9.11) I will establish that tottering *sukkath* of David. The king: he is the assembly. And the bases of the images: these are the books of the prophets whose words Israel despised. . . .

The consonantal text cited in CD^A 7.14, סכות, matches 𝔐's סֻכּוּת. The citation in CD^A modifies the traditional מֵהָלְאָה, 'from beyond',[37] to אהל ('tent'), matching OG's σκηνή for סכות. The interpretation that follows in D refers to the 'tabernacle of the king' (סוכת המלך). This citation and interpretation exhibit an exegetical use of textual plurality.

In Amos 5.26^𝔐 סכות (סֻכּוּת) and כיון (כִּיּוּן) are proper names for foreign Gods. This is clear from the context of the passage: *Sikkuth* and *Kaiwan* are synonymous with 'your images'; the final clause of v. 26 reads אֲשֶׁר עֲשִׂיתֶם לָכֶם ('that you made for yourselves'). Although both the OG and CD 7 interpret the proper name *Sikkuth* in terms of the construct form סֻכָּה (that is, סֻכַּת), neither identifies the proper name as the noun 'tabernacle'. First of all, the respective *plene* forms of the proper name and construct noun (סכות and סוכת) are morphologically distinct and cannot be confused. This is evident in CD^A 7.14-15 and will have been the case in the Hebrew source presupposed by OG. Similarly, CD^A 7.15 cites כיון and then interprets it as the plural of כֵּן (masculine noun, 'base' or 'pedestal')[38] in CD^A 7.17 (= 4Q266 3iii 18). While

---

37 הָלְאָה 'further, onwards'.
38 Root כנן (Brown *et al.* 1979, 487).

the OG exegetically renders the proper name סכות with σκηνή, by rendering מלככם ('of your king') with Μολοχ, the translator shows that the verse is referring to the proper name of a God.[39]

Amos 5.26-27 contains a polemic against Babylonian deities.[40] In 𝔐 the names סכות and כִּיּוּן are both pointed as in שִׁקּוּץ ('abomination').[41] Such a polemical vocalization was apparently current in the late Hellenistic period – Daniel similarly uses שִׁקּוּץ polemically against Zeus Olympus.[42] OG and CD are both aware that foreign gods are the prophet's subject in these verses.

CD and OG contain a common interpretation of סכות as סוכה. OG achieves a double reading of the semantic unit סכות by rendering σκηνή directly, while maintaining a proper name for a foreign deity. This double reading configures two sense contours from the single semantic unit. CD configures the same two sense contours, but manipulates the passage differently. CD maintains סכות in the citation (introducing the term סוכת, 'tabernacle of', in the following interpretation as a means of linking Amos 5.26 with Amos 9.11), but simultaneously introduces אהל ('tent') by rearranging the letters of הלאה ('beyond') of Amos 5.27. The exegete can thereby interpret סכות as 'my (God's) tent' in line with the positive interpretation of other parts of the prophecy (the Torah, the Royal Messiah, the *Doresh ha-Torah* and the Books of the Prophets) while opening the way to introduce Amos 9.11 shortly afterwards.

The CD exegete is aware that Amos 5.26-27 refers to foreign Gods. His decision to identify his *own* group with these abominable deities, and to interpret them as Torah and Prophets, is explicable in the context of a common Sectarian polemic vis-à-vis 'Israel'. CD^A 7.17-18 identifies the 'pedestals of the images' as 'the books of the prophets whose words Israel despised'. The exegete expresses his feeling of marginalization from Israel (perhaps marking an ascendant Judaean priesthood) as a whole, together with his confidence in vindication for his group. He thus reverses the traditional understanding of a passage that mounts an Israelite polemic against pagan neighbours. The מִדְבָּר language refers to Israel's wandering. The exegete sees his group as suffering an enforced marginalization from 'Israel', which he expresses in terms of exile, but an exile that actually vindicates his group and indicates its salvation. Israel is perceived from within the group as despising the group's teachings and readings of the Torah. That is, the polemic conveys the following sentiment: 'That

---

39 Even if the second plural masculine suffix was missing from the Hebrew source of the OG, he nevertheless did not render it with βασιλεύς.

40 סכּוּת is a divine proper name, probably to be read סַכּוּת as the Assyrian god *Sakkut* (the 'epithet of Adar-Ninip = Saturn'; Brown *et al.* 1979, 696). The proper name of the Babylonian deity סכּוּת בְּנוֹת (2 Kgs 17.30) is an 'Assyrian-Babylonian deity worshipped by Babylonians in Samaria' (ibid.). כִּיּוּן is a proper name probably for the Assyrian deity *Keivânu* = planet *Saturn*. Brown *et al.* 1979 (475b-476a) suggest that כִּיּוּן has been pointed so as to suggest the root כון ('something established, firm').

41 My thanks go to Professor Magnar Kartveit for drawing my attention to this point.

42 שִׁקּוּץ שֹׁמֵם (> שָׁמֵם *be desolated, horrified*) in Dan. 12.11 (cf. 11.31) is a polemical pun on the title for Zeus Olympios – בעלשמם (בעל שמים), '*lord of heaven*', to whom Antiochus Epiphanes erected an altar in the Jerusalem Temple (Brown *et al.* 1979, 1055).

which you find abominable about our teachings is actually the true interpretation of scripture. We have understood the prophets while ironically you, Israel, still wander in the desert.' The standard judgement oracle formula כי or לכן, which is consistently present in the oracles of Amos 4–5, is absent from Amos 5.25-27. Perhaps the Sectarian exegete therefore viewed this oracle as ambiguous, leading to his inventive interpretation of it.

4.4 *4QCommentary on Genesis A (4Q252)*

Table 4.5 Genesis 49.10

Gen. 49.10^LXX	Retroverted 𝔊	Gen. 49.10^SP	4Q252 frg. 6, col. 5	Gen. 49.10^𝔐
a οὐκ ἐκλείψει	לוא יסור	לא יסור	[לוא] יסור שליט	לֹא־יָסוּר
ἄρχων ἐξ Ιουδα	שבט מיהודה	שבט מיהודה	משבט יהודה [. . .]	שֵׁבֶט מִיהוּדָה
b καὶ ἡγούμενος	ומחוקק	ומחקק	המחקק [. . .]	וּמְחֹקֵק
ἐκ τῶν μηρῶν αὐτοῦ	מבין רגליו	מבין דגליו	הדגלים [. . .]	מִבֵּין רַגְלָיו
c ἕως ἂν ἔλθη	עד כי יבוא	עד כי יבא	עד בוא [. . .]	עַד כִּי־יָבֹא
τὰ ἀποκείμενα αὐτῷ	שלו	שלה	(שילה/שלו)	שִׁילֹה [שִׁילוֹ]
d καὶ αὐτὸς	והוא	ולו	(ולו)	וְלוֹ
προσδοκία ἐθνῶν	יקהת עמים	יקהת עמים (Tal 1994, 51)	יקהת עמים)	יִקְּהַת עַמִּים

Square italicized brackets, *[. . .]*, indicate my own omission of 4Q252-text for clarity. Text in parentheses represents canonical readings apparently presupposed by the 4Q252 exegesis.

Notes on the readings of LXX
מִבֵּין רַגְלָיו 𝔐] ἐκ τῶν μηρῶν αὐτοῦ LXX. Μηρός can parallel רֶגֶל, 'foot' (cf. Deut. 28.57 – τὸ ἐξελθὸν διὰ τῶν μηρῶν αὐτῆς – הַיּוֹצֵת מִבֵּין רַגְלֶיהָ). Μηρός can also parallel 'loins/reproductive organs' (cf. Gen. 46.26 יָרֵךְ); 'knee' (cf. Gen. 50.23 בֶּרֶךְ); 'thigh' (cf. Exod. 28.42 'they shall reach from the loins to the thighs', ἀπὸ ὀσφύος ἕως μηρῶν

ἔσται – וְעַד־יְרֵכַיִם יִהְיוּ מִמָּתְנַיִם), as distinct from 'loins'.[43] It is unnecessary to propose any reading but רגליו for the Hebrew of Gen. 49.10 presupposed by the LXX.

שִׁילֹה 𝔐; cf. שלה SP^mss][44] τὰ ἀποκείμενα αὐτῷ LXX – the Greek translator may have read שֶׁלֹו (i.e. a contraction of אשר לו).[45] Either his copy had שלו, or he inferred it from שילה, שלה, שלוה or similar. Syriac and Targum imply the same reading.

וְלֹו 𝔐] καὶ αὐτός (representing והוא?) LXX. If the Hebrew source presupposed by LXX read עד כי יבוא שלוה לוא יקהת ('until Shiloh comes, to him is the obedience of . . .'), the לוא being spelled *plene*, the Greek translator or a previous scribe may have attached the *he* (ה) of Shiloh to the following word, dropping the *lamed* (ל), producing: עד כי יבוא שלו הוא יקהת.

Table 4.6 Genesis 49.10 LXX and 𝔐

LXX		𝔐
a	A ruler shall not fail from Judah,	The sceptre shall not depart from Judah,
b	nor a leader from his (Judah's) loins,	nor a ruler's staff from between his feet,
c	until the things stored up for him come;	until Shiloh comes;
d	and he is the expectation of nations.	and to him (shall be) the obedience of peoples.

Table 4.7 4Q252 fragment 6 (column 5)

1	לו[א יסור שליט משבט יהודה בהיות לישראל ממשל [
2	לוא י[כרת יושב כסא לדויד כי המחקק היא ברית המלכות [
3	ואל]פי ישראל המה הדגלים *vacat* עד בוא משיח הצדק צמח[
4	דויד כי לו ולזרעו נתנה ברית מלכות עמו עד דורות עולם אשר
5	שמר o[ ]התורה עם אנשי היחד כי
6	היא כנסת אנשי [ ]o

1. A leader '*shall [n]ot depart from* the tribe/sceptre of *Judah*' (Gen. 49.10*a*). When Israel rules

---

43 ὀσφύς is the usual word for מָתְנַיִם ('loins'), cf. Isa. 11.5.

44 Shiloh is variously spelled שִׁלֹו (Judges, 1 Samuel, Jeremiah, Psalm 78), שִׁילֹו (Judges, Jeremiah) or שִׁלֹה (Joshua, Judges, 1 Samuel, 1 Kings, Jeremiah). Note: 1 Sam. 3.21 gives two spellings (שִׁלֹה, שִׁלֹו) in the same sentence. LXX always offers Σηλωμ, or Σηλω(ν), cf. Brown *et al.* 1979, 1017–1018.

45 Hence 'Until comes what is his', τὰ ἀποκείμενα αὐτῷ. Cf. *BHS, ad loc.*; Zimmerman (1998, 118), citing Pérez-Fernández (1981, 130–133).

2. [*there will not*] *be cut off an occupant of the throne for David* (Jer. 33.17). For
    '*the staff*' (Gen. 49.10*b*) is the covenant of the kingship;
3. the [thousa]nds of Israel are the '*standards*' (Gen. 49.10a) *vacat* '*until the coming*'
    (Gen. 49.10*c*) of the messiah of righteousness, the shoot of
4. David. For to him and to his seed has been given the covenant of the kingship of
    his people for everlasting generations, which
5. he kept . . . [   ] the Law with the men of the community, for
6. [   ] . . . it is the congregation of the men of

The text of Gen. 49.10 is implied in the commentary, although it is not quoted con-
tinuously as it would be in a continuous *pesher*. The following presents in square
brackets the continuous traditional text of Genesis, which is missing from 4Q252.

[10a *The sceptre (reign) shall not depart from Judah*]
    A leader '*shall [n]ot depart from* the *tribe/sceptre* of *Judah*'. When Israel rules
'*There will not be cut off an occupant of the throne for David*' (Jer. 33.17)

[10b *nor the staff from between his (Judah's) feet/standards*]
    For '*the staff*' is the Covenant of Dominion; the [thousa]nds of Israel are the
'*standards*'

[10c *until he comes to whom it belongs/ until that which belongs to him comes*]
    '*until the coming*' of the messiah of righteousness, the shoot of David.

[10d *and to him shall be the obedience of the peoples*]
    For *to him* and to his seed has been given the Covenant of Dominion of his *people*
for everlasting generations

This exegesis configures distinct sense contours through manipulation of individual
semantic units: רגלים and שילה. These sense contours characterize two distinct traditional text-forms of this passage.

4.4.1 *Sense contours arising from* שילה
In 𝔐 the שבט is the 'reign' that will not depart from Judah. It is most natural to
understand the 'feet' as Judah's, who appears as a masculine person throughout Gen.
49.8-12.[46] Thus, 'between Judah's feet' seems to indicate a reign 'in Judah'. Modern
translations translate מחקק with 'ruler's staff', which seems to represent a synonym
for שבט, 'reign'.[47] The subject of בוא – in the phrase עד כי יבוא שלה – is שלה ('until

---

46 While the שבט is masculine, it can hardly have 'feet'. If the מחקק is taken to be a person (see
following footnote) then the feet could belong to him.
47 Older translations, such as the Geneva Bible (1599), the Webster Bible (1833), the King James
version (1611-1769), the Darby Bible (1884-1890), translate מחקק with 'lawgiver'. That is, the מחקק is

Shiloh comes').[48] In 𝔐 Shiloh is a person, introduced in v. 10c, whose arrival is awaited.[49] Later, Shiloh is interpreted as the messiah in the Targums. Isa. 11.10[LXX] seems to relate Gen. 49.10d to the 'root of Jesse' (cf. Isa. 11.1), who was abundantly interpreted messianically in late Second Temple Jewish literature, stating that 'he will rise up to rule the nations; in him the nations will hope' (ὁ ἀνιστάμενος ἄρχειν ἐθνῶν ἐπ' αὐτῷ ἔθνη ἐλπιοῦσιν).[50] Gen. 49.10d[LXX] says of the (messianic) person 'to come' that αὐτὸς προσδοκία ἐθνῶν ('he is the expectation of the nations').[51]

The LXX translates שבט ('reign', 'royal sceptre', 'a mark of rule') loosely as ἄρχων ('ruler') in 10a. By presenting שבט as a person, the translator introduces a distinct sense contour into the Greek not present in 𝔐. The ἄρχων of 10a can be identified as the ἡγούμενος (= מחקק) 'leader' of 10b.

'That which is stored up for *him*' (10c) is to come. '*He*' may be either Judah or the ἄρχων/ἡγούμενος ('ruler/leader') of 10a-b, because no new person (i.e., Shiloh) is introduced in v. 10c in the LXX form of this passage. This is in contrast to 𝔐, where Shiloh appears in v. 10 as a new person in the narrative.

The LXX phrase τὰ ἀποκείμενα αὐτῷ ('the things stored up for him') derives from שלה, which the translator apparently vocalized as שֶׁלֹה in order to read שֶׁלֹּו. The term שֶׁלֹּו can appear as a contraction of אשר לו ('that which is/belongs to him').[52] The LXX translator of Gen. 49.10c apparently understood שלה to represent אשר לו and then rendered the resultant phrase עד כי יבוא אשר לו with ἕως ἂν ἔλθῃ τὰ ἀποκείμενα αὐτῷ.

The Hebrew can be understood in one of two ways:

(1) 'until the-stored-up-things, which belong to him, come'

    i.e. *until* | *it comes* | *which* | *(it is) to him*

    לו | אשר | יבוא | עד כי

---

a *person* (מחקק can mean 'commander', 'governor', 'lawgiver in other contexts, cf. Footnote 67, below). These translations may have been influenced by the LXX, whose translator understood the מחקק as a person; that is, the ἡγούμενος – one who leads or guides (from ἡγέομαι). If the מחקק is thus understood to be a person, the LXX suggests that the ἡγούμενος (מחקק) rules in the interim; that is, he is taken to wield the שבט in Judah until Shiloh comes. In fact, the idea that a 'leader' shall not be lacking 'between his thighs' may suggest a hereditary succession of leaders because the 'thighs' can represent the sexually reproductive loins (cf. Footnotes 53 and 68, below). Note also that some Targums and Aquila understand the מחקק to be a person; that is, one who interprets the law, cf. Section 4.4.2 and particularly Footnote 69, below).

48 Aberbach and Grossfeld (1982, 286) suggest the following possibilities: 'until [or: so that] tribute shall come to him'; 'until Shiloh comes'; or 'until he comes to Shiloh'; cf. McNamara 1992, 220 [24].

49 Even if the מחקק were taken to be a person (with the LXX see Footnote 47, above), Shiloh would still not be identical with this person (מחקק, 'lawgiver'), because according to this understanding of the verse the מחקק would rule in the interim; that is, *until* Shiloh comes.

50 Compare Isa. 11.10[𝔐], עֹמֵד לְנֵס עַמִּים אֵלָיו גּוֹיִם יִדְרֹשׁוּ ('he will stand as an ensign of peoples, and the nations will seek him').

51 Compare Gen. 49.10d[𝔐], וְלוֹ יִקְּהַת עַמִּים ('to him is the obedience of the peoples').

52 In his copy he may have found שׁילה, שׁלה, or שׁלוה. Cf. 𝔐 שִׁילֹה.

(2) 'until he comes, for whom the (things) have been stored up'

i.e. *until* | *he comes* | *who* | *(it is) to him*

עַד כִּי | יָבוֹא | אֲשֶׁר | לוֹ

According to reading (1),[53] the Greek translator took the relative pronoun, אשר, to refer to '*that which* (belongs to him)' rather than '*him* (to whom it belongs)'. While it is syntactically possible in the Greek that 'he' ('to whom it belongs') of v. 10c is the ἄρχων/ἡγούμενος (the 'ruler/leader' of vv. 10a-b), the 'he' of 10c most naturally refers to Judah. The Greek is sensible only if all of the masculine pronouns refer to Judah: Ιουδα (10a); αὐτοῦ (10b); αὐτῷ (10c); αὐτὸς (10d).[54] Some witnesses express the phrase with the optative ἔλθοι τὰ ἀποκείμενα αὐτῷ (mss. 54-551 56'). Another manuscript resolves the syntax differently: τὸ ἀποκείμενον αὐτοῦ ὅ ἀπόκειτα (ms. 72). Unlike 𝔐, no new person (namely, 'Shiloh') is introduced into 10c in these Greek forms.

Some Greek witnesses of Gen. 49.10c offer (2): ἔως ἂν ἔλθη ᾧ ἀπόκειται,[55] 'until he comes to whom it has been stored up'. This may not represent an independent translation of a Hebrew text, but rather an inner Greek improvement of the OG. However, it may also reveal the influence of the proto-𝔐 sense contour on Greek revisionists, namely, that a new person (other than Judah) comes in 10c (who in 𝔐 is 'Shiloh').

𝔐 and the OG offer distinct sense contours. In the former, a new person (Shiloh) appears in 49.10c. In the latter, no new person appears in addition to the ἄρχων/ ἡγούμενος of 10a-b. Aquila's rendering of Gen. 49.10 reveals conscious exegetical use of the two sense contours arising from שׁל(ו)ה (49.10c), which characterize OG and 𝔐. Gen. 40.10α':

οὐκ ἀναστήσεται σκῆπτρον ἀπὸ Ἰούδα καὶ ἀκριβαζόμενος ἀπὸ μεταξὺ ποδῶν αὐτοῦ ἔως ἂν ἔλθη καὶ αὐτῷ σύστημα λαῶν.

Aquila's future middle of ἀνίστημι ('he shall not arise') need not presuppose קום in his Hebrew Genesis source, but rather reflects his messianic association of Gen. 49.10 with the Num. 24.17[LXX]:

δείξω αὐτῷ καὶ οὐχὶ νῦν μακαρίζω καὶ οὐκ ἐγγίζει ἀνατελεῖ ἄστρον ἐξ᾽Ἰακώβ καὶ

---

53 Cf. Brenton 1844, *ad loc.*, 'A ruler shall not fail from Juda, nor a prince from his loins, until there come the things stored up for him; and he is the expectation of nations'; Hiebert (2007, 41), 'A ruler shall not be wanting from Ioudas and a leader from his thighs /until the things stored up for him come, and he is the expectation of nations'.

54 The translator clearly did not take אשר to indicate 'him who will come' (יבוא). Otherwise, he would have rendered the clause like the translator of Ezek. 21.32: עַד־בֹּא אֲשֶׁר־לוֹ הַמִּשְׁפָּט 'until he comes whose right it is'); LXX ἔως οὗ ἔλθη ᾧ καθήκει. The clause of Ezek. 21.32b is often pointed to as a parallel construction to that of Gen. 49.10c (cf. Zimmermann 1998, 118).

55 Wevers 1974, 460.

ἀναστήσεται ἄνθρωπος (𝔐 שֵׁבֶט וְקָם) ἐξ'Ισραήλ καὶ θραύσει τοὺς ἀρχηγοὺς Μωάβ καὶ προνομεύσει πάντας υἱοὺς Σήθ

Num. 24.17 is frequently interpreted messianically in Second Temple Jewish exegetical compositions.[56] The 'sceptre'[57] of Num. 24.17𝔐 becomes the messianic 'man' of Num. 24.17^LXX.[58] Symmachus has σκῆπτρον for שֵׁבֶט in Num. 24.17, where Aquila has ἄνθρωπος.

Aquila reframes Gen. 49.10 thus:

> *no* sceptre will arise from Judah, *nor* an accurate one from between his feet, until He comes; and his shall be the government[59] of peoples.

This reading of Gen. 49.10 agrees semantically with 𝔐 in that v. 10c depicts a person expected to come in the future. In 𝔐 this is Shiloh. This is unlike the OG, where the ἄρχων/ἡγούμενος of 10a-b rules in the interim until 'the-stored-up-things come to him (Judah)'. While Aquila maintains OG's ἕως ἂν ἔλθῃ, he modifies the second part of the OG clause '. . . τὰ ἀποκείμενα αὐτῷ' with 'καὶ αὐτῷ σύστημα λαῶν'.

In 𝔐 a 'sceptre' and a 'ruler' will 'not fail' in Judah until Shiloh comes. Aquila's οὐκ ἀναστήσεται departs from 𝔐 here. Yet, Aquila thereby intensifies 𝔐's sense that someone is to come, and in doing so he intensifies the tradition (not evident in Gen. 49.10) that this someone is the messiah. Aquila persuades that 'he-who-is-to-come' is the messiah by substituting ἀναστήσεται (from Num. 24.17) for the OG reading ἐκλείψει (= יָסוּר, 'fail', 'depart', of 𝔐). Aquila preserves שבט of 𝔐 with σκῆπτρον, and represents a tradition close to the Targums by supplying ἀκριβαζόμένος for the מחקק of 𝔐 (see Section 4.4.2, below).[60] Aquila imports a common messianic interpretation of Gen. 49.10 into his revised form of the passage itself. This move

---

56 For example: 1QSb V (with further messianic allusions to Gen. 49.10, Isa. 11.1-5, Ps. 2.7-9, Mic. 4.13-5.2; cf. Barthélemy and Milik (eds.) 1955, 126–127); Testament of Judah 24.1-6 (allusions to Gen. 49.10 and Isa. 11.1-5); Testament of Levi 18; Psalm of Solomon 17; Rev. 2.28 (καὶ δώσω αὐτῷ τὸν ἀστέρα τὸν πρωϊνόν, cf. the ἄστρον cf. Num. 24.17 and the ἑωσφόρος, 'morning star', of the messianically interpreted Ps. 110.3, cf. Isa. 14.13-14); Rev. 11.1 κάλαμος ὅμοιος ῥάβδῳ ('a measuring rod like staff', possibly an allusion to the שבט and מחקק of Gen. 49.10).

57 Examples of the messianic interpretation of:

a. שבט cf. 1QSb V_{25-26} (Gen. 49.10, Isa. 11.1-5, Ps. 2.7-9, Mic. 4.13), 4Q252 frg. 6 (Gen. 49.10), CD^A 7.19-21 = 4Q266 frg. 3iii _{23-24} (Num. 24.17);

b. ῥάβδος (= שבט), cf. Psalm Solomon 17.23-24 (Ps. 2.7-9 with Isa. 11.1-5); Rev. 2.27, 12.5 (Ps. 2.9); Testament of Judah 24.1-6.

c. σκῆπτρον (= שבט), cf. Testament of Judah 24.1-6 (Num. 24.17) *and* ῥάβδος, cf. Testament of Judah 24.1-6 (= שבט of Isa. 11.4^{at}, or possibly חֹטֶר, 'shoot' of Isa. 11.1).

58 The messianic ἄνθρωπος was associated with the phrase ὡς υἱὸς ἀνθρώπου of Daniel 7. See Horbury 1985 and 1998, esp. 33–34; and Collins 1995, esp. 34–38, 175–187.

59 σύστημα, 'government' – 2 Sam. 23.15 (2 Kgdms 23.15); 3 Macc. 7.3.

60 This 'accurate one' indicates an interpreter of חוקים ('statutes', a common Pentateuchal term for Mosaic laws), thus a 'scribe' or 'a teacher of Torah' (so the Targums, see below). Note that CD^A 6.3-7 interprets the מחקק of Num. 21.18 as דורש התורה.

gains exegetical warrant when it is observed that the identification of Judah as the 'lion' in Gen. 49.9 finds an echo in Num. 23.23-24, where Israel is identified as a 'lioness', the only other verse in Numbers[LXX] where the form ἀναστήσεται occurs.

The 4Q commentator combines the two sense contours that characterize 𝔐 and OG, derived from the semantic unit שׁל(ו)ה. He implies the sense of 𝔐, that a new person, Shiloh, comes in Gen. 49.10c. The commentator takes שׁל(ו)ה to designate the messiah.[61] This sense cannot be taken from the LXX as it stands, nor (apparently) from its supposed Hebrew source, in which שׁלה/שׁילה denotes 'that which is to him', where 'he' could designate either Judah himself or the 'ruler/leader'. On the other hand, the 4Q commentator understood שׁל(ו)ה to mean 'which to him' in the same way that the LXX translator understood his Hebrew source, because the ברית המלכות (4Q252 frg. 6 line 4) is 'that which will be given' to the messiah.

The commentator makes exegetical use of the multiple sense contours derivable from the semantic unit שׁל(ו)ה. Whether Aquila's version is considered an inner-Greek revision of an earlier καιγε source, an independent revision of OG towards proto-𝔐, or a new Hebraizing translation,[62] textual critics consider his revision to present a form of the traditional work of Genesis. The above example shows that a revisionist reading of a traditional work can apply the same exegetical techniques as an author of exegetical compositions.

---

61 Cf. Collins (1995, 61–63). While Gen. 49.10 was often interpreted 'messianically' in antiquity, says Collins, usually 'the messianic reference hangs on the phrase עד כי יבא שׁילה, "until Shiloh comes", taking Shiloh as a name for the messiah. An allusion to the "assembly of the peoples", without reference to Shiloh, has no obviously messianic implications . . .' (ibid., 1995, 87). I argue that 4Q Commentary interprets the semantic unit שׁ(י)ל(ו)ה in two distinct ways (enshrined, respectively, in 𝔐 and OG and mirrored in Targums and LXX cognate versions). This unit is subjected to distinct interpretations in the 4Q Commentary, despite the absence of the word שׁ(י)ל(ו)ה in the 4Q text; Shiloh lurks in 4Q252. While a discussion of 'messianism' is beyond the scope of this study, I use the term 'messianic' in a narrow sense. I speak of the 4Q252 interpretation as 'messianic', not only because the 'righteous messiah' occurs in fragment 6, line 3, but also in light of other ancient messianic interpretations of Gen. 49.10 that expect a person, usually of Davidic Royal lineage, with divine sanction to carry out God's divine eschatological (usually military) work. The distinct sense contours, enshrined in 𝔐, OG, 𝔗, and other versions are present in the 4Q Commentary.

62 Καιγε (see Section 1.1.1, above), the Hebraizing revision of the OG towards the proto-𝔐 (Barthélemy 1963 and Tov 1990), apparently formed the basis of Theodotion, Aquila and Symmachus, thought to be progressive revisions of each other (Salvesen 1991). Lindars (1992, 3) designates καιγε a revision proper, and Symmachus a stylistic revision of καιγε (that is, an inner-Greek undertaking), and Aquila a 'fresh translation'. Grabbe (1992) deems α' and σ' to be independent translations located within the harmonizing LXX tradition (not revisions, as Barthélemy (1963) proposed), and α' σ' θ' nevertheless to belong to a later stage in the harmonizing movement. Lindars' (1992) and Grabbe's (1992) suggestions find little support among contemporary commentators.

4.4.2 *Sense contours arising from* מחקק *and* רגלים

Targums take various approaches to Gen. 49.10. Table 4.8 displays synoptic parallels.[63] The Fragment Targum[64] ($\mathfrak{T}^F$) interprets the singular noun שבט as מלכין ושלטנין ('kings and rulers') and the singular noun מחקק, as ספרין ומלפי אורייא ('scribes and teachers of the Torah').[65] Both singular nouns are pluralized in the translation. The Aramaic preserves double meanings inherent in each Hebrew noun. While $\mathfrak{T}^F$ maintains the royal sense of the Hebrew שבט with the Aramaic 'kings and rulers', $\mathfrak{T}^F$ also conveys the other Hebrew sense, 'tribe', with the Aramaic מדבית יהודה ('from the tribe/house of Judah'). While $\mathfrak{T}^F$ interprets מחקק as 'scribes and teachers of the Torah', the Aramaic phrase מבני בנוי ('from among his children's children') preserves the sexual-reproductive imagery of the traditional Hebrew phrase ומחוקק מבין רגליו ('nor a staff from between his feet'), acknowledged in LXX by 'loins' (ἐκ τῶν μηρῶν αὐτοῦ).[66]

$\mathfrak{T}^F$ presupposes a «text» akin to $\mathfrak{M}$, עַד כִּי־יָבֹא שִׁילֹה. The targumist takes 'Shiloh' to be an individual who is the King-Messiah. Unlike some Targums, 4Q252 and OG of Genesis 49, $\mathfrak{T}^F$ does not interpret שִׁילֹה as אשר לו because $\mathfrak{T}^F$ makes no reference to anything that 'belongs to him-who-will-come'.

A double interpretation of מחקק occurs in all of the Targums. Firstly, the word can mean 'teacher' or 'law-giver'; Deuteronomy constantly associates the related term חק with *mitzva'oth*, indicating Israel's covenantal agreement to keep the Torah.[67] Onqelos ($\mathfrak{T}^O$) simply has 'scribe', reflecting the same interpretive tradition. Secondly, all Targums introduce 'his descendants', thereby pursuing the sexual-reproductive imagery of מחקק (מ)בין רגליו.[68] In Gen. 49.10 'his feet' are most expediently understood as Judah's feet (see Section 4.4.1, above). This pertains to $\mathfrak{T}^N$, $\mathfrak{T}^J$ and $\mathfrak{T}^F$ because the 'kings' or 'kings and rulers' are in the plural, and the singular masculine suffix of the implied traditional Hebrew רגליו must refer to '[the house of] Judah' in the

---

63 While I make no anachronistic claim to literary dependence between 4Q252 and the much younger Targums, exegetical parallels regarding Gen. 49.10 point to the continuity of this interpretive tradition. Targums sometimes preserve ancient exegetical traditions also found in Second Temple literature. Cf. McNamara 1966, Flesher 1992.

64 Klein 1980 vol. 1, 31; vol. 2, 67.

65 Note that the מחקק of Num. 21.18 is interpreted as the דורש התורה in CD^A 6.3-7.

66 The morphological proximity of the Hebrew words בין and בן (Gen. 49.10) may have aided this association. For 'feet' as a euphemism for genitals, see Footnote 68, below.

67 מחקק means either 'commander/governor' (Gen. 49.10; Num. 21.18), or 'law-giver' (Deut. 33.21; Isa. 33.22), cf. Zimmermann 1998, 116 [221]. Note that the ancient CD^A 6.3-7 interprets מחקק of Num. 21.18 as the דורש תורה. Neofiti ($\mathfrak{T}^N$), Jonathan ($\mathfrak{T}^J$) and $\mathfrak{T}^F$ of Gen. 49.10 introduce, variously, 'scribes teaching the Law' or 'scribes and teachers of the Law' ($\mathfrak{T}^F$).

68 Cathcart *et al.* (1992, 159 [30]) suggest that $\mathfrak{T}^J$ derives the phrase 'the youngest of his sons' from Deut. 28.57, where a similar wording to that of Gen. 49.10 occurs: וּבְשִׁלְיָתָהּ הַיּוֹצֵת מִבֵּין רַגְלֶיהָ וּבְבָנֶיהָ אֲשֶׁר תֵּלֵד ('and her afterbirth that comes out from between her feet and her children whom she bears'). 'Feet' can be a Hebrew euphemism for genitals (of the *seraphim* in Isa. 6.2, for example), cf. Veenker 1999–2000, Pope 1992, 721.

Table 4.8 Targums of Genesis 49.10

Neofiti*	Onqelos†	Jonathan Targum‡	Fragment§	4Q252
		10 "It shall not depart":		
10 *Kings*	10 The ruler	10 *Kings and rulers*	Kings and rulers	ll. 1-2 *The* שלׁיט
shall not cease	shall never depart	will not cease	shall not cease	*shall [n]ot depart*
from among those of	from	*from those of*	from	*from*
the house of Judah	the house of Judah,	*the house of* Judah,	the house of Judah,	the tribe of Judah (+*Jer. 33:17*)
nor scribes	nor the scribe	nor scribes	nor scribes	l. 2 For '*the staff*' is the covenant of the kingship
teaching the Law	(or: teachers)	*teaching the Law*	and teachers of the Law	(l. 4 his seed …
from his sons' sons	from his sons' sons	*from his descendents,*	from among his sons' sons,	… for everlasting generations)
for evermore –				
until *the time the*	until the	until the time the	until the time that	l. 3 until the coming
King Messiah comes,	Messiah comes,	*King Messiah comes,*	the King Messiah comes,	of the Messiah of Righteousness
to whom	whose is			For to him and to his seed has been given
the kingship belongs,	the kingdom,			the covenant of the kingship of his people
to him shall all	and him shall			

Neofiti*	Onqelos†	Jonathan Targum‡	Fragment§	4Q252
the nations be subject.	the nations obey.			
	the youngest of his sons,			
	because of whom the			
	people will pine away.			
11 *How beautiful is*		11 *How beautiful is*		
the King Messiah		*the King Messiah*		
who will arise		*who will arise*	who is destined to arise	
from among those		*from among those*	from	
of the House of Judah.		*of the House of Judah.*	the house of Judah	

* Translation: McNamara 1992.
† Aberbach-Grossfeld 1982; Berliner 1884.
‡ Text: Clarke 1984; Rieder 1980; cf. Ginsburger 1899. Translation: Maher 1992.
§ Klein 1980 vols 1 and 2.

* Translation: McNamara 1992.
† Aberbach-Grossfeld 1982; Berliner 1884.
‡ Text: Clarke 1984; Rieder 1980; cf. Ginsburger 1899. Translation: Maher 1992.
§ Klein 1980 vols 1 and 2.

Targum texts. In 𝒯ᵒ it is possible to take 'him', whose feet/descendants they are, to be either Judah or the 'ruler'.

The 4Q Commentary already exhibits a double interpretation of מחקק. First, the מחקק is identified as the ברית המלכות, described as a 'covenant of the kingship of his [God's or the messiah's] people'. In this, the Commentary diverges from the interpretations of the Targums, CD and Aquila, which all pursue a sense of an individual person, the 'law-giver/teacher'. Nevertheless, Torah observance and dominion over nations are traditionally closely related.[69] Secondly, the Commentary pursues the sexual-reproductive imagery of the traditional phrase מחקק (מ)בין רגליו in line 4, where the progeny of the messiah is introduced: כי לו ולזרעו.[70] The later Targums share this interpretation of Gen. 49.10c with the early Commentary, which represents its earliest known occurrence.

The commentator knows two possible readings of the traditional text that produce two sense contours. And he makes use of both contours. By deriving the notion of the messiah's progeny in line 4 from the sexual-reproductive interpretation of the phrase מחקק (מ)בין רגליו, the commentator presupposes רגליו ('his feet') (cf. LXX τῶν μηρῶν αὐτοῦ, 'his thighs/loins'). Lines 2-3 of the commentary read:

המחקק היא ברית המלכות [ואל]פי ישראל המה הדגלים

His use of דגלים ('standards') corresponds to the reading of the Samaritan Pentateuch.[71] The readings רגליו and דגליו arise from the visual similarity of *resh* and *dalet*. Either the commentator knows two copies witnessing these divergent readings or he substitutes *dalet* for *resh* himself as an exegetical tool. But he associates both 'feet' and 'standards' with Gen. 49.10c and, reading both, adduces traditional literary support for his commentary. In 1QM 3.15-18 and 4.15-17, the אות האלף ('banner of the thousand') occurs fifth in the list of banners (אותות)[72] and the 'fifth banner' in 1QM

---

69 The 4Q Commentary, identifying the מחקק as the royal covenant related to the rule of the royal messiah, differs from CD and the Targums, which identify the מחקק with a 'teacher/expounder of Torah' (cf. ἀκριβαζόμενος, α' Gen. 49.10). The Commentary's royal ברית is nevertheless closely related to the keeping of the Torah. Dominion over other nations, implicit in the royal covenant (see also the Covenant of David renewed for the *Nasi ha-Edah* in 1QSb V and the *Nasi*'s dominion over the nations) is hinted at in Gen. 49.10d, which envisages the 'obedience' (LXX 'hope') of the peoples. It is also in line with covenantal passages from Deuteronomy, such as Deuteronomy 28, where covenantal keeping of מצות and חקים of the Torah results in Israel's dominion over other nations (for example, Deut. 28.1, 10, 12).

70 See Footnote 68, above.

71 For the reading דגלים on 4Q252, fragment 6, see Brooke *et al.* 1996, 205.

72 'If 1QM III ₁₅₋₁₈ and IV ₁₅₋₁₇ are suitably restored' (ibid.). I note that, while the lines of 3.15-18 and 4.15-17 are partly broken, the sequence in both cases proceeds in an order that endorses Yadin's reconstruction (Yadin 1962, *ad loc.*). 1QM 3.15-18 proceeds: 'All the nation, the chiefs of the three tribes, the tribe, the princes of the ten thousand, [the thousand], [the hundred . . .].' 1QM 4.15-17 proceeds: 'The whole congregation, the th[ree tribes], [the tribe], the ten thousand, [the thousand], [the hund]red.' The sequence, 'ten thousands, thousands, hundreds, tens' is replicated throughout 1QM, according to the pattern of Pentateuch war rules.

4.10 is inscribed: דגלי אל ('God's standards').[73] It is not at all clear that 1QM should be deemed a Dead Sea sectarian or a *Yaḥad* composition. However, it was prolifically copied and preserved by scribes of E. Tov's Qumran 'scribal practice' (see Section 5.2, Footnote 21, below) and, therefore, may have belonged to the 4Q commentator's literary repertoire. He certainly identifies the ואל[פי ישראל] ('[thous]ands of Israel') as הדגלים, like the author of *Milḥamah*.

4.5 *A continuum of awareness of textual plurality*

In Section 2.5.1 I have identified three kinds of awareness of textual plurality. *Yaḥad* exegetical compositions contain evidence for at least types §A and §B. Type §A represents a common understanding of interpretation whereby the fixed text is understood within a context determined by the reader. Thus, for example, applying Habakkuk's prophecies to his own context, the pesherist understands certain elements of the text as references to a 'Wicked Priest' and others as references to a 'Teacher of Righteousness' (Section 4.2.2).[74] Similarly, the CD exegete can understand elements of Amos 5 and 9 to refer to subjects of his own contemporary interest, such as the Royal Messiah, the *Doresh ha-Torah* or the moral relation of his audience to the rest of Israel (Section 4.3.1).

Some Jewish exegetes in Hellenistic and early Roman Palestine, working in a Hebrew linguistic milieu, negotiated multiple semantic forms of a traditional passage (Type §B). They achieved distinct sense contours in each case by manipulating different forms of a single semantic unit: (1) רעל/ערל (1QpHab); (2) סוכת/סכות (CD^); (3) שלו/שלה (4Q252 #1); (4) דגלים/רגלים (4Q252 #2).[75] It is not necessary to decide whether exegetes consulted multiple copies of a passage. The distinct sense contours they produce echo known textual traditions, showing that they are working with known alternatives.

---

73 Brooke *et al.* 1996, 205. Note also that in 1QM 4.9-11 שבט, in third place, precedes דגלים, in fifth place, in the *serekh* of the eight banners.

74 'Wicked Priest': 1QpHab. 8.8; 9.9; 11.4; 12.2, 8. 'Teacher of Righteousness': 1.12; 2.2; 5.10; 7.4; 8.3; 9.9; 11.5.

75 For semantic units, see Sections 2.5–2.5.1, above.

5

SCRIBES AND TEXTUAL PLURALITY

5.1 *Scribes and other text users*

To what extent can Dead Sea sectarian exegetical practice illuminate that of Paul? In a broad sense evidence that the Sectarians made use of textual variation, as did Josephus, shows that this practice belongs to Paul's world. However, the Sectarians are often viewed as an exclusive and marginal group of expert scribes, whose literary (and devotional) pursuits were extraordinary. Can Paul be helpfully compared with the Sectarian exegetes? While distinctions between expert scribes and non-scribal text-users are essential in historical enquiry, the literary encounter of these two groups was comparable in important respects. Like ordinary illiterate folk and literate non-scribal text-users, those Sectarian exegetes who were professional scribes nevertheless encountered Jewish scripture to a large degree through oral performance, either through dictation or a scribe reading aloud to himself. I argue that despite their literary and chirographic practice, scribes' encounters with scripture, like that of ordinary people, were orally patterned. Moreover, Paul and the Sectarian exegetes participated in a common exegetical heritage.

5.2 *'Scribal exegesis'*

Many scholars accept that Dead Sea sectarians use multiple text-forms, as I have already noted (Section 4.2.2, cf. 2.2.3, above) and discuss in more detail elsewhere.[1] Here two examples will suffice. Vermes writes that the pesherist's treatment of Hab. 2.16

> not only implies an *acquaintance* with the variants; it also shows an inability to or unwilling-
> ness *to choose* between them. Both readings are cleverly *mingled*, revealing that, far from
> being free with the biblical text, the interpreter held in profound esteem every *witness* of what
> in his view was the sacred record of the word of God.[2]

---

1   See Norton (2009, 138) and the references there (ibid., 138 [10]) to: Rabin 1955, 158–159; Brownlee 1959, 7, 45–49, 76–78; Bruce 1959, 12–13; 1961, 61–69; 1983, 81f.; Horgan 1979, 245; Dimant 1984, 505 [103]; Brooke 1985, 288; 1987, 86; 2000, 112–113; Lim 1997 50, 191–192.
2   Vermes 1976, 441a; my italics. Cf. Section 4.2.2, above.

Counting the 'use of textual variants' among the 'hermeneutical principles' used by the Habakkuk pesherist,[3] Brownlee envisages the pesherist comparing copies, including 'the scroll of the teacher of righteousness', referring to later Rabbis who 'compared' readings in several 'Torah scrolls'.[4]

There is a pervasive notion that the Sectarian exegetical compositions in the Qumran corpus are inherently 'scribal'.[5] In a single article Brownlee applies the following terms to Dead Sea sectarians, referring to their exegetical activity: 'the study groups of Qumran'; '[t]he scribes of Qumrân [*sic*]'; '[t]he people of Qumran'; 'Qumran's folk'.[6] G. Vermes describes the '*scribal* creative freedom' at Qumran in biblical and non-biblical manuscripts: 'the *redactor-copyists* felt free to improve the composition which they were reproducing'.[7] Brooke speaks of the 'Qumran scribes' performing exegesis,[8] which in the case of 1QpHab. 'may appear "difficult" to obtain', and 'was only done by experts'.[9]

The *pesharim* are often considered 'autographs', suggesting that scribes who produced the extant copies were responsible for the exegeses therein.[10] Even when their status as autographs is doubted,[11] it is often assumed that the exegesis they present is inherently scribal; that is, integral to and inseparable from the act of writing. For example, describing how the 'Qumran expositor . . . separated his interpretation from the scriptural text with a word or phrase such as "its interpretation concerns"', VanderKam portrays the pesherist's exegetical work as an intrinsically written act, taking place at the moment of inscription.[12]

I have already noted that Paul's use of textual variation is often framed in terms

---

3 Brownlee (1951, 60–62) identified thirteen hermeneutical principles by which the pesherist interpreted scripture. Some involve direct lexical manipulation of the source text (e.g. '*rearrangement of the letters in a word*' (#9), '*substitution of similar letters*' in a word (#10), 'the *division of one word into two or more parts*' (#11), '*interpretation of words, or parts of words, as abbreviations*' (#12). Others involve interpreting the text as it stands, e.g. '*[a]llegorical propriety*' (#6), '*equation of synonyms*, attaching to the original word a secondary meaning' (#8), reading the passage in light of '*[o]ther passages of scripture*' (#13) (his italics). Brownlee (1964, 66 [7]) later withdrew the thirteenth principle. Elliger (1953, 157ff.) and Horgan (1979, 250) deem Brownlee's list of thirteen artificial. Brooke (1985, 283ff.) notes Brownlee's failure to distinguish hermeneutic from exegetical techniques.

4 Brownlee 1951, 73–76. Rabbis compared their own Torah scrolls with that of Rabbi Meir. Siegel (1975, esp. 8–17) concludes that Rabbi Meir's was a late Hellenistic copy since its orthography is like that of 1QIsa.ᵃ.

5 See Norton 2009.

6 Brownlee 1987, 188, 188, 191–193, respectively. A similar range of terms can be found in Brownlee 1964: 'scribes gathered about a table [. . .] in the Qumrân scriptorium' (158); 'the Qumrân community' (188); 'some scribe of the Qumrân community' (198); 'the Essenes' (199); 'the society at Qumrân' (203).

7 Vermes 1997, 24–25; my italics.

8 Brooke 1985, 5.

9 Ibid., 284.

10 Milik 1957, 37; Cross 1958, 84f; VanderKam 1994, 96; Tov 2004, 28.

11 Hammershaimb (1959, 417) doubts that our copies of the *pesharim* are autographs on account of 'such errors as point to a written original'; also Elliger 1953, 70; so Brooke 2000, 115; and Lim 2002, 27.

12 VanderKam 1994, 44.

of his access to scrolls, or lack of access. It will be recalled, for example, that Hengel and Koch's disagreement on this point revolves precisely around whether Paul was a scribe.[13] Yet where the question of access to multiple copies of a work is acute in Pauline studies, it raises no eyebrows in the context of the 'scribal community at Qumran'. The assumption is that trained scribes – who had access to a library, engaged in the expert copying of literary works in their scriptorium,[14] and were professionally involved in the collection and preservation of the scrolls on which these works were copied – would be in a position to consult multiple copies of a given work. Stendahl's proposal that the gospels of Matthew and John arose in scribal 'schools' also implies this idea.[15]

Scribes had considerably better access to multiple copies of a work than non-specialists. However, one cannot assume that access to multiple copies is the absolute prerequisite for making exegetical use of multiple semantic forms of a traditional passage. In no instance examined in Chapter 4, above, does the exegete need to consult two copies in order to identify two forms of a passage. The exegete's use of distinct sense contours may equally well result from his use of a single copy. The knowledge of the sense contours, which informs his interpretation of the text, arises in an oral environment of exposition of the passage. This knowledge lies on a spectrum of awareness, which includes both the recognition that a semantic unit in a passage *can* yield distinct sense contours, and that distinct sense contours *are* enshrined in particular copies. Exegetes who made use of multiple semantic forms of a passage – Sectarians, Paul, Josephus – operated to significant degree in a like manner, which did not necessarily involve comparison of manuscripts at the moment of exegesis.

At stake is the extent to which the exegesis of scribes is an essentially chirographic phenomenon, inseparable from the act of writing and particularly the production of manuscript copies. Elsewhere I have identified two broad modern modes of constructing ancient Jewish scribes.[16] One is a socio-historical model focusing on scribes as social groups, their relations to other ancient persons and institutions, their status, and how they are presented in various kinds of historical sources.[17] The other is a '*realia*' model, which seeks to construct the work of scribes and their literary and communicative habits in terms of data observable from manuscripts and scribal equipment, both

13 Access to copies, cf. Sections 1.8.2 and 2.2–2.2.3; Paul as scribe? (Hengel), cf. Section 1.6, above.
14 For example, Brownlee 1950; 1951; 1987, 188; Bruce 1961, 47–48 (referring to Metzger 1958–1959, 509ff.); Vermes 1975b, 16–17; 1997, 11, 20 (referring to Reich 1995 and Tov 1988); Dimant 1995, 35 [31], 36; Lim 2002, 9; Brooke (1985, 5) ('the Qumran scribes'); Stanley (1992, 39) (the *scriptorium*); ibid., 51 (the 'scribal ethos' of Qumran manuscripts). De Vaux 1961 classically depicts the scriptorium.
15 Stendahl 1954.
16 Norton 2009, 140–143.
17 Exemplified, for example, by the studies of: Schürer 1886–1911 vol. II; Jeremias 1923–1937 vol. IIB; Hengel 1969; Schürer *et al.* 1973–1987; Orton 1989; Davies 1995; Schams 1998. Unlike many of her predecessors, Schams helpfully restricts her discussion to sources where a term for 'scribe' (ספר, סופר, לבלר, γραμματεύς and λιβλάριος) occurs, or where the person(s) is identified as scribe through the act of writing.

lexical data (such as, textual characteristics of the inscribed text, palaeographical or orthographical conventions, scribal markings and marginalia) and material data (such as, preparation of leather, ruling of lines, stitching, ink, calligraphic conventions). This latter approach to constructing scribes, exemplified by M. Martin, E. Tov, and to some extent E. Kutscher,[18] has, since the 1950s, been foundational to the notion of the scribal community at Qumran. It is a notion of scribes deriving from products of writing.[19] Martin, Tov and others have observed the close collaboration of a small group of scribes in copying scrolls and correcting each other's work.[20] Tov has identified a 'Qumran Scribal Practice', which he associates with this scribal group, which has adopted particular orthographical conventions and special scribal markings in the paleo-Hebrew and a cryptic script.[21]

In fact, not all Jewish 'scribes' (according to the socio-historical model) were necessarily exegetes; some were technicians who did not engage in exegesis.[22] Scribes, according to the *realia* model, are people who write in the professional pursuit of transmitting literature. Exegesis performed by a 'scribe' is not necessarily intrinsically 'scribal'.[23] Conversely, certainly not all exegetes were 'scribes'. Although they could write, neither Josephus nor Paul is generally considered to have been a professional scribe.[24] I argue that literate non-scribal exegetes participated in the same exegetical

---

18 Norton 2009, 141–142.

19 The classical 'Schürer-Jeremias' notion of late Second Temple *Schriftgelehrten* (or: 'Torah scholars' – Schürer, Vermes *et al.* 1973–1987) seems to play no significant role in the studies by Martin (1958), Kutscher (1974) and Tov (2004). This may be because the Sectarians appear to have auto-marginalized from the Temple cult. Their practices should, therefore, be incorporated into models of Second Temple Jewish scribal practices only with caution. Equally, Schams' survey covers almost none of the material studied by Tov and their data hardly intersect. Tov (2004) does note a few of the historical references examined by Schams (1998). However, these are relatively few and only supplement observations made from physical manuscript evidence.

20 See, for example, Martin 1958, 65f., 72–73, 81–96, 495–585, 687; Tov 1997, 150–151; 2004, 21–23. For further discussion and references to further studies, see Norton 2009, 141–142.

21 Tov has developed the idea of the Qumran Scribal Practice in a number of studies (for example, Tov 1986; 1988, 7; 1997; 2004, 5, 203–209, 261–273, 277–289; see Norton 2009, 141 for further references). Although some of the Qumran scribal practitioners collaborated directly, emphasizing that the term 'Qumran Scribal Practice' does not exclusively locate the practice at Khirbet Qumran (Tov 1992, 108), Tov argues for a wider Palestinian provenance for most Qumran scrolls (e.g. Tov 1986; 1988, 7; 2004, 5; on the Qumran scriptorium, Tov 1988, 9–10). He associates this distinct scribal practice with a palaeographical period, 150 BCE–68 CE, rather than a geographical location (ibid., 15 [39]). He argues that the Greek, Aramaic, and paleo-Hebrew scrolls were probably imported to Qumran (ibid., 19; on the importation of Aramaic scrolls, ibid., 11). Brooke (2000, 109) has questioned Tov's designation Qumran Scribal Practice on the grounds that no biblical manuscript from Qumran is narrowly Sectarian. See further Norton 2009, 142 [17].

22 Norton 2009, 143–145.

23 While a kind of 'scribal' exegesis can be identified – that is, exegesis conducted at the moment of inscription (Norton 2009, 146–148 and see Section 5.4, below), this does not particularly advance the present discussion.

24 Schürer coined the common term *Schriftgelehrten*, or 'Torah scholars' (cf. Schürer *et al.* 1973–1987; Schams 1998, 18) and Jeremias (1923–1937 IIB, 101–103) included Paul and Josephus in his list of

heritage as Sectarian exegetes. Awareness and use of multiple semantic forms of a given passage belongs to this heritage.

Exegetical use of multiple semantic forms of a passage does not necessarily entail an exegete's special access to multiple copies. Much ancient Jewish exegetical work arose within a context of exegetical oral practice, rather than the solitary pursuits of copying and altering texts in accord with scribal syntactical conventions. Many manipulations of semantic forms of traditional scripture passages arose within common discursive structures and practices. The exegetes may have been priestly, Levitical[25] or lay. However, an exegesis (or a *pesher*) is often a communal product, generated within an oral-performative environment, rather than an intrinsically chirographic one. This is as much the case for *Yahad* exegetes as for Josephus and Paul, who are not commonly considered to be professional scribes.[26]

5.3 *A common exegetical heritage*

A range of exegetical methods abroad in antiquity was employed by Jewish text-users and interpreters across cultural, linguistic and geographical milieus of Jewish antiquity. Much of the exegetical work seen in the Sectarian scrolls engages in a common exegetical heritage, open to a number of ancient Jews who, while writers of one kind or another, were not scribes. The exegetical techniques in Sectarian compositions, including exegetical use of textual plurality, belong to this common exegetical heritage.

According to Fishbane, intertextual exegetical methods represented in the Rabbinic *middôt*, attributed in the *Mishnah* to Hillel's first-century school, and seen in Second Temple exegetical literature (such as that of the Dead Sea sectarians, Jubilees, or the Temple Scroll) are already present in the traditional Jewish literature that became the Hebrew canon.[27] This 'inner-biblical aggadic exegesis' pervades the redactional stages of early traditional Hebrew works, such as the Pentateuch, as well as the composition of later works, such as Samuel, Kings, Chronicles or Daniel.[28] Although Fishbane assumes that 'traditions and teachings were transmitted orally throughout the biblical period' as well as 'long afterwards' as 'non-Scriptural oral traditions', he believes that 'scribal practice provides the most concrete context for the transmission of a *traditum*' and the proper basis for studying 'the diverse exegetical dynamics of *traditium* and

---

Schriftgelehrten, along with many Rabbis and priests. I suspect that this approach accounts for Hengel's (1991a) affirmation that Paul was a γραμματεύς. See also Section 1.8.1, above.

   25 Levites and Temple scribes are connected in ancient literature (Sanders 1992). Vermes (1975b, 22–24) explains the possible Levitical status of the *Yahad Maskil* (cf. Levitical associations of the verbform *haskil* in Daniel, Ezra-Nehemiah, Psalms).

   26 See Footnote 24, above.

   27 Fishbane 1985.

   28 Ibid., 408f.

traditio in the Hebrew Bible'.[29] Notably, Fishbane does not equate exegetical tradition exclusively with its chirographic manifestation.

Second Temple exegetical works in Greek, such as Josephus, Philo, Matthew's gospel, or pseudepigrapha, display the same array of exegetical techniques as the Hebrew exegetical literature discussed above.[30] D. Daube finds techniques akin to Hillel's *middôt* in late antique Jewish Greek exegetical literature, which are associated with Alexandrian textual criticism. He also notes that Hillel's techniques resemble those of Aristotle, Cicero and others.[31] Comparing exegetical textual variations among 𝔐, the OG, cognate versions, and Targums, A. Salvesen identifies 'midrash in Greek' in Aquila, Symmachus and Theodotion.[32]

Brooke argues 'that exegetical techniques akin to the *middôt* were used widely, if not universally, in Jewish exegesis of the late Second Temple period'.[33] He indicates the dependence of the *middôt* on Alexandrian philology in the first centuries BCE and CE, giving examples of individual *middôt* used by Philo and Targums that he dates to before 70 CE.[34] Philo reproduces traditional Hebrew phrases in his exegesis and applies methods closely akin to techniques discussed and applied in Rabbinic literature. It is impossible 'to confine Philo solely to the role of an exponent of Greek philosophy in the Alexandrian Jewish community', says Brooke, and Philo's methods 'included but also went beyond those attributed in formulation to his near contemporary [Hillel]'.[35] Brooke's conclusion, that the exegetical techniques employed by Philo belong as much to first-century Palestine as to Alexandria, is supported by Kister, who speaks of a 'common heritage' of Jewish exegetical techniques in the Hellenistic and Roman periods.[36]

There are cases in Philo's discussion of Greek Jewish scripture where (as in the Sectarian examples reviewed above), his citation of a traditional *lemma* witnesses one reading (usually agreeing with the Christian LXX), while his exposition presupposes another. Whether Philo knew two forms of these passages has been subject to an ongoing debate. Katz doubts this, proposing that later Christian copyists verbally harmonized Philo's citations with the standardizing LXX, while leaving his expositions unaltered, which originally applied to first-century Greek texts available to

---

29 Ibid., 23.

30 Chapters 3 and 4, above, have presented Josephus' and *Yaḥad* exegetes' manipulation of semantic units and appeal to distinct forms of the same passage. For Josephus see Nodet 1996, 1997, 2000–2001, 2006. For Matthew see Stendahl 1954; Gundry 1967; Marcos 2000, 325f. For Philo see Footnotes 37–38, below.

31 Daube 1973. On Alexandrian textual criticism and exegesis see Russell and Winterbottom 1972 and 1998.

32 Salvesen 2004.

33 Brooke 1985, 2.

34 Ibid., 17–36.

35 Ibid., 25.

36 Kister 1998.

Philo.[37] Others propose that Philo himself made exegetical use of variant text-forms in the first century.[38]

Exegetical methods employed in Sectarian compositions belong to a wider exegetical environment spanning a range of ancient Jewish contexts. That is, these methods are neither intrinsically nor exclusively scribal. While Brooke's language occasionally ascribes an expertly scribal character to Sectarian exegesis, his study shows that these techniques were widely current in ancient Judaism. '[T]he Qumran scribes', he writes, 'were not acting independently of contemporary Judaism.' Sectarian exegetical practice should therefore not be considered to be an exclusive domain of professionally scribal communities.[39]

5.4 *Scribal awareness of textual plurality*

Scribes arbitrated the range, availability and form of Jewish ancestral literature.[40] As principal transmitters of this literature – the producers and keepers of copies – scribes were in a better position than non-scribal text-users to compare multiple copies of a work.[41] The alteration of the text of one copy on the basis of another by means of marginal and interlinear insertions indicates such awareness, at least at the moment of comparison between copies.[42] Tov and others designate these alterations as 'corrections', attributing to scribes a notion of a pristine, 'correct' text-form. This conception restricts textual variation to 'standard' and 'aberrant' text-forms, ascribing a false sense of uniformity to the literature. The term 'alteration' better acknowledges that some readings are scribal or exegetical, rather than corrective. Some scribal markings

37 Katz 1964.

38 Colson 1940; Knox 1940; Howard 1973.

39 Brooke 1985, 5.

40 While scribes copied diverse kinds of literature (bills, accounts, deeds, and contracts; political or military orders; court records; private letters; public addresses; liturgical texts; traditional narratives, poems or songs; and private devotional documents (cf. Bowman and Woolf 1994; Davies 1995; Schams 1998)), I focus exclusively on Jewish exegetical work in this study.

41 Literate text-users encountered traditional works as inscribed copies much less frequently than scribes. Male Jews heard the Pentateuch read out weekly (Philo, *Leg.* 156; Josephus, *Cont.Ap.* 2.175; Acts 15.21; cf. Juvenal, *Satires* 14, 100f.; cf. Goodman 1994b. Further: Hengel 1991a, 236 [197]; Levine 2000; Mann 1940). But this equates neither to regular private reading nor copying by hand. Most 'text-users' were illiterate hearers (Bar-Ilan 1988, 164 [8]: 3 per cent literacy in rural Palestine; up to 20 per cent for urban adult Jewish males; cf. Harris 1989; Gamble 1995, 165 [13]; Jaffee 2001, 164 [7]). However, because this discussion focuses on Paul, I restrict my present definition of 'text-user' to literate Jewish text-users, who could both read and hear traditional Jewish works.

42 Tov (2004, 223) thinks that scribes made some 'corrections' to the base text (i.e. copy) on the basis of external written sources, 'possibly because those sources were considered to be superior or more authoritative that the base text'.

in 1QIsa.[a][43] and cancellation dots found in a number of the Qumran scrolls[44] indicate the scribes' awareness of variant readings in other manuscripts.[45]

If it can be shown that a scribe has made an exegetical change to the text of a biblical work he is copying, one might designate this act as 'scribal' in the limited sense that it is intimately connected with the practice of writing. Some scholars, such as J.V. Chamberlain, W.H. Brownlee, A. van der Kooij and P. Pulikkotil, have argued that scribes made exegetical changes to the text of Isaiah.[46] Stegemann and S. Talmon observe 'dual readings' in some biblical copies, which display an exegetical approach to variant readings in different copies of the same work.[47]

I have argued that the only workable definition of 'scribal' exegesis is exegetical work carried out at the moment of inscription, and in cases where a literary product is most easily explained as the work of a scribe.[48] 4QTestimonia, 4QTanḥumim, and 4QList of False Prophets, and Blessing of *Nasi ha-Edah* (1QSb V) might provide such examples, if they are autographs.[49] However, 'autograph' only indicates the *first* or *only* copy of a written text; it cannot indicate that the scribe is responsible for the intellectual work within it.

Thinking in terms of 'scribal' exegesis does not seem useful for the present study. In none of the cases of exegetical use of textual variation presented in Chapter 4, above, must the intellectual exegetical work be that of the scribe who wrote down our copies. In the next section I will show that, despite their chirographic training, scribes' encounters with literature were to a large degree still oral and therefore closer to that of ordinary non-literate Jews than is often supposed.

---

43 For example, the *circular sign* (Cryptic A *kaph* (Tov 2004, 205 and fig. 10.4, 363)) in 1QIsa.[a] XVII₁ (cf. Trever 1950, xvi; Martin 1958, 180f.; Tov 2004, 205) is written above שלוש of Isa. 21.16 in the upper margin. 𝔐 reads בְּעוֹד שָׁנָה, whereas 1QIsa.[a] reads בעוד שלוש שנים. Tov (2004, 205) states that '[t]his sign possibly indicates the lack of שלוש in 𝔐'. The inscriber of the *kaph* was apparently aware that another *copy* (which reflected 𝔐) lacked שלוש here. This awareness can be seen as 'scribal' because it predicates the comparison of multiple copies.

44 Correction of the base text by scribes A and B, done on the basis of other copies, is witnessed by cancellation dots (dots flanking a word or phrase marked for omission) in 1QIsa.[a]: 1QIsa.[a] XIII₁₄ (Isa. 15.7) ופקדותיה corrected text = 𝔐; XXVIII₂₈ (Isa. 35:10) ישינובה corrected text = 𝔐; ישינו: XXIX₃ (Isa. 36:4) מלך יהודה lacking in 𝔐 Isaiah and 2 Kgs 18.19; XXIX₁₀ (Isa. 36.7) לפני המזבח הזההתשיחוו בירושלים the longer text is identical with 2 Kings and versions, the shorter text agrees with the 𝔐 of Isaiah. See, Tov 2004, 189, table 10.

45 See Footnote 47, below.

46 Pulikottil: exegetical alterations to 1QIsa.[a] (2001, 205–215); criteria for distinguishing errors from innovations (2001, 22–23). 'Messianically' motivated alterations: at 1QIsa.[a] 1.24 (Chamberlain 1955, 367); in Isaiah 52 (Brownlee 1964, 155–215). Van der Kooij (1981, 90–97) argues that the 1QIsa.[a] scribe was the Teacher of Righteousness who made autobiographical alterations to 1QIsa.[a] 1.24-25.

47 Stegemann (1969, 94 [512]) believes that cancellation dots to the right and left of the superlinear word in 1QIsa.[a] 49.14 mark this word as a variant. Talmon (1964, 107) finds 'parallel readings by conscious conflation' from two *Vorlagen*. However, Tov is doubtful (2004, 234).

48 Norton 2009, 146–147.

49 Ibid. The 1QS scribe, who made corrective interventions into the text of 1QIsa.[a], copied 4QTestimonia. Stegemann suggests that this scribe also added the Blessing of *Nasi ha-Edah* in 1QSb V.

5.5 *Oral performance of traditional literature*

In previous chapters I have proposed that the copy of a traditional work functions as a cue for the multiple exegetical ideas associated with given passages, rather than a rigid verbal record of, or monolithic monument to, a single semantic form (Sections 2.4–2.5.1). I find some support for this idea in the writing of M. Jaffee, according to whom Second Temple scribes, priests and laity alike encountered traditional works more commonly through oral performance than private reading or study.[50] Jews also encountered a complex of orally mediated interpretive traditions that 'were internalised in the context of public instruction'.[51] Literacy exists within encompassing oral structures. 'The orally mediated interpretive traditions associated with written texts became perceptible as cultural realities "outside of" the texts themselves and thus required some sort of ideological legitimation in relation to the written texts.'[52] Ginsberg (1975), Vermes (1973b), Daube (1973), Davies (1970, 1983) and Brooke (1998) also deal with such orally mediated interpretive traditions that span diverse Jewish literature.

Jaffee argues that the image of Jewish scribes routinely copying sacred literature by dictation is a 'ubiquitous' trope in Second Temple Jewish literature.[53] The 'scribes' Ezra and Baruch anticipate divine revelations by preparing to write.[54] Philo presents Moses as a scribe, receiving and writing down revelation, and the LXX translators of the Pentateuch.[55] Prophets are depicted as scribes and 'the scribes who transmitted [a prophet's] work continued the chain of representing his persona as their texts were passed on'.[56]

Of course, Jaffee's pseudepigraphical evidence may only reveal an idealized notion of scribes arising simply because oral performance was an important part of most ancient Jews' encounters with literature. Yet if Jaffee is correct that scribes routinely copied by dictation, it would show that scribes' encounters with traditional literature were more like those of ordinary text-users than often acknowledged. And indeed lexical manuscript evidence corroborates Jaffee's contention that Jewish scribal copying was frequently an oral mode.

5.5.1 *Chirographic practices in an oral world*

Judaean manuscript evidence shows that scribes copied both aurally (by reader's dictation) and visually (from a physical copy). Yet even while copying visually,

---

50 Jaffee 2001.

51 Ibid., 10.

52 Ibid., 7.

53 Jaffee 2001, 23–28, particularly 24.

54 Ibid., 24, 26. One also thinks of Hab. 2.2 and Rev. 1.11 – John's revelations are sent as written letters, even within the text.

55 Philo *Vita Mosis* 2.37 (Jaffee 2001, 24, 26).

56 Ibid., 25–26.

scribes seem to have uttered aloud the words they read in a copy. That is, despite their chirographic praxis, scribes inhabited a pervasively oral and aural structure.

5.5.2 *Copying by dictation*
Achtemeier has influentially argued that in late antiquity, literature in general, and traditional Jewish literature in particular, was generally recited or dictated.[57] Even when a person read to himself, he almost always read aloud. Similarly, Martin, Bruce, Burrows, Orlinsky, Siegel and Louw argue that ancient scribes copied visually,[58] aurally[59] and by citation from memory, variously combining these techniques.[60] Burrows demonstrates the omission of ה through weak pronunciation by the reader, aural confusion of מ-ב-ב and ח-כ, confusion of ד and ת, and substitution of א for ה. In 1QIsa.ᵃ Kutscher finds aural errors occurring through the scribe's uttering what he read in his own dialect.[61]

While dictation from one scroll to a group of copyists is known from ancient depictions, Hammershaimb does not believe that groups of Qumran scribes copied *en masse* by dictation in the scriptorium because he finds no Qumran copies sharing a common prototype.[62] Tov cites Hammershaimb with approval.[63] However, Tov's observation that most of the 'biblical' scrolls did not originate at Qumran, but exhibit diverse provenance, invalidates Hammershaimb's argument, which predicates the copying of all Qumran scrolls at Qumran.

Tov argues against copying by dictation in this period, appealing to a Talmudic insistence that scribes copy directly from a written source rather than from memory (*b. Meg. 18b*).[64] However, this evidence reflects much later Rabbinic efforts to standardize the proto-Masoretic Text and to develop textual guidelines for arbitrating between variant readings,[65] a context implied by the Rabbinic fascination with the special readings of the Severus scroll (Rabbi Meir's Torah).[66] This ethos, however,

---

57 Achtemeier 1990, 15–19. However, silent reading is attested, cf. Slusser 1992; Gilliard 1993.

58 Burrows 1948, 18; 1949a, 25–26; Orlinsky 1950. See Delitzsch 1920, 123–126 for the same phenomena in Masoretic manuscripts.

59 For 1QIsa.ᵃ, see Burrows 1948, 20, 22; 1949a, 25–26; 1949b, 203. For 1QIsa.ᵃ, see Bruce 1961, 63. For 1QIsa.ᵃ and the Severus scroll of Rabbi Meir, see Siegel 1975, 36–37. Louw (2008) has most recently argued that the translators of the OG translated an orally dictated Hebrew text, recited by a reader.

60 Martin 1958 I, 6–7, 688.

61 Phonological explanations for the scribe's idiosyncratic orthography: noun patterns (Kutscher 1974, 375, 474–476); verb patterns (ibid., 477). For other errors resulting from the scribe's pronunciation (ibid., 498–499). The scribe's dialect was influenced by Western Aramaic (ibid., 23ff., 54–55, 61–62, 68f., 483).

62 Hammershaimb 1959, 415–418.

63 Tov 1997, 137; reproduced in Tov 2004.

64 Tov 2004, 11.

65 See Siegel 1975; Tov 1992; and Orlinsky 1960 on the development of Kethib-Qere arbitration on the basis of the three 'Azarah' scrolls.

66 Siegel 1975. Manuscripts from the Bar Kokhba period witness the stabilization of proto-מ. Fragments of Exod. 13.11-16 and Pss. 25–26 are identical with מ (Aharoni 1961, 23, 40). See further Marcos 2000, chs 5, 7–9.

was distinct from the acceptance of textual plurality witnessed in the Judaean manuscripts. The Rabbinic ruling, which should not be projected back to the early Roman period, itself implies that some scribes *did* copy from memory in the Rabbinic period.

Hammershaimb believes that a Qumran scribe would follow his source with his eyes, while reciting it aloud,[67] and the scribe's own pronunciation influenced his orthography,[68] which suggests that scribes' chirographic work belongs in a fundamentally orally patterned world. The scribal 'sloppiness' and 'freedom' observed in the Judaean manuscripts[69] indicates that these documents were not set text-critical objects, but mnemonic prompts that aided the performance of literature within primarily oral practices.[70]

Tov acknowledges the role of the manuscript copy as a tool for a variety of oral performances. He writes that 'the Qumranites used the scrolls in different circumstances. In that case, they would have chosen a certain type of text during the official reading of the Bible, and another one for study purposes, both communal and individual'.[71] And special conventions for writing the *tetragrammaton* show that written manuscripts played a role within wider oral contexts. Writing The Name in paleo-Hebrew characters was a convention limited to Tov's Qumran scribal practice.[72] The practice was surely followed, not because it was considered wrong to write The Name, but because it was wrong to utter it (see my discussion of 1QS 7.1, Section 5.6.1, below). As Goodman notes, although some Judaean manuscripts (such as contracts and deeds) reveal the secular use of Hebrew, '[t]he sound of spoken Hebrew became itself sacred, and therefore worrying (and indeed dangerous), only when the Divine Name was pronounced'.[73] This concern makes sense only if the literary copies were primarily meant to be read aloud.

Beyond Qumran the oral nature of literary pursuit is also evident. For instance, Pliny had his sources read aloud to him, and dictated his own compositions to secretaries (see Section 1.8.2.1, above). Josephus may well have employed his literary assistants in like manner and it is hard to imagine that the privileged Philo did not work in this way. Even the 'vagrant' Paul dictated letters.[74]

---

67 Here Hammershaimb points to Acts 8.30.

68 Hammershaimb 1959, 418. The same is observed by Kutscher (1974) in 1QIsa.ᵃ (see Footnote 61, above) and by Delitzsch (1920, 123 [1]) in Masoretic manuscripts.

69 Tov 1988, 15; cf. Brownlee 1964, 216; Trever 1950, xv; Orlinsky 1950, 165, 338.

70 Compare Jaffee (2001, 16–17), who sees the scroll in the Second Temple period as a 'mnemonic safety device – a storage system for texts already held substantially in the memory'.

71 Ibid., 33.

72 See Footnote 21, above.

73 Goodman 1994b, 101.

74 Rom. 16.22 and 1 Cor. 16.21; but did he write Galatians himself? (cf. Norton 2009, 153).

5.6 *Orality, chirography and authority*

The writings of Josephus, the *Yaḥad* and Paul (see Chapter 7) display exegetical uses of textual plurality. While a literary pursuit, this practice exists within structures that are essentially oral. To frame in purely literary terms the question of these exegetes' work is to ignore pervasive oral thought structures.

While oral creations are often regarded as variants of written productions, Ong has argued that language is ultimately an oral phenomenon: writing can never dispense with orality.[75] Chirographic forms were not ends in themselves, but modes of storage and means for delineating the common content of traditional literary property. A shared heritage of exegetical techniques comprised the instruments of engagement with traditional literature. A given hermeneutic was the expression of a community's subjective perception of its relation to traditional literature, where, as Ong suggests, '[o]riginality consists not in the introduction of new materials but in fitting the traditional materials effectively into each individual, unique situation or audience'.[76]

Ong further points out the special weight of individual authority and charisma in oral societies. A fundamentally oral culture situates knowledge within a context of discussion among authoritative, charismatic speakers.[77] Oral patterning of authority is intrinsically situational, arising in an environment where the personal authority of individual protagonists plays a substantial role in their performative strategies and their persuasive success.[78] These insights are important to understand the work of Jewish exegetes considered here.

5.6.1 *Orality, chirography and authority in the* Yaḥad

1QS rhetorically defines social boundaries through legislation of ritual purity, internal hierarchy, as well as eschatological and cultic ideologies supported by peculiar hermeneutical approaches to traditional literature. This and other *Yaḥad* literature, such as the *pesharim*, distinguishes the *Yaḥad* from other groups (both Jewish and not), as well as maintaining communal boundaries between various branches of the wider ideological movement to which the *Yaḥad* belonged. Studies reveal the ideological and geographical proximity of some chirograph-members of the *Yaḥad*.[79] This need not imply, however, that Dead Sea sectarians were isolated from contemporary Jewish life. Their unusual practices were their own solutions to questions of calendar, purity and worship, issues common to many of their Jewish contemporaries. The *Yaḥad* did not inhabit the social vacuum of a Dead Sea 'scroll-jar', but was part of broader intellectual, social and literary discussions.

---

75 Ong 1982, 7–9. See also Lord 1960 and Parry 1971, who have established what has come to be known as the 'oral formulaic hypothesis'.

76 Ong 1982, 59.

77 Ibid., 43.

78 Ibid., 56.

79 See Footnote 20, above.

The language of *Serekh ha-Yaḥad* reveals a pervasion of oral structures. In Wernberg-Møller's terms, 1QS presents the *Yaḥad* as a 'community of Torah study'. He may overstate this in translating בתורה (5.2) as 'with Torah study' and לתורה (5.3; 6.22) as 'concerning Torah study'.[80] Nevertheless, Torah study was clearly important to community life. Lay members of The Many (הרבים) gathered nightly to 'read the book aloud, explain the regulation[81], and bless together'[82] (לקרוא בספר ולדרוש משפט ולברך ביחד). The verbs קרא, דרש and ברך indicate oral practice. While דרש *could* point to a private and silent pursuit, here it indicates publicly 'explaining' or 'expounding'. Lay members *darashed* (דרש) the 'regulation' or 'Law' (משפט) by reading aloud (קרא) from the *sefer*. Of the three occurrences of קרא in 1QS, two indicate reciting Torah in communal study (in 6.7, 'read the book aloud; 7.1, קורה [קורא] בספר או מברך, 'reciting the Torah or saying benedictions') and one refers to calling on God in the hope of a response (2.8 in the curse on the 'lot of Belial').[83]

Jaffee suggests that the 'man expounding the Torah' (איש דורש בתורה) of 1QS 6.6 is the priest of 6.3-4, which accounts for the reformulation in CD 13.2-4 of 'priestly man' (איש כוהן).[84] This priest presides over study sessions where at least ten members gather to constitute a 'community in miniature'.[85] In 1QS 6, not only does the 'man' expound the Torah, but The Many also spend a third of nights 'reading the book' (לקרוא בספר) and 'expounding the ruling' (לדרוש משפט). Jaffee concludes that in this group '[t]he interpretive study of texts was not confined to priestly leaders or scribal professionals. Rather, it extended beyond them to become part of the ethos of the collective'.[86]

---

80 Wernberg-Møller 1975. Compare Vermes (1997): 'they shall unite with respect to law . . .'; García Martínez and Tigchelaar (1997): 'in order to constitute a Community in law . . .'.

81 Vermes (1997) and Wernberg-Møller (1957) agree that משפט here refers to the Mosaic law (they translate, respectively: 'Law' and 'commandment(s)'. García Martínez and Tigchelaar (1997) translate it as 'regulation'. The close connection between משפט and תורה is clear at 5.16, where it is said that no member of the *Yaḥad* should acquiesce to the authority (על פי) of the אנשי העול (5.10) in any תורה or משפט. Conversely, the members *should* acquiesce to the authority (על פי) of the Zadokites 'in Torah' (בתורה) in 5.2. The phrase לדרוש משפט of 6.6 is paralleled by the phrase מדרש התורה in 8.15.

82 1QS 6.7-8 García Martínez and Tigchelaar (1997); compare Vermes (1997), 'to read the Book, to study the Law and to bless together'; Wernberg-Møller (1957), 'reciting from the Book and studying the commandment(s) and saying benedictions together'.

83 In the Hebrew Bible קָרָא generally indicates public speech – often with בְּאָזְנֵי or לִפְנֵי – and when it pertains to reading it usually means 'read aloud'. Only rarely might it indicate private reading. See Brown *et al.* 1979, 895b, '*read* to oneself'. Some cases suggest private use. Deut. 17.19 decrees that the king will 'write *for himself* a copy' of the book of Torah, held by the priests, and will 'read in it' (קָרָא בוֹ/ἀναγνώσεται ἐν αὐτῷ) all his life. Here the emphasis on private use highlights the normality of public recital. In 2 Kgs 19.14 = Isa. 37.14 Hezekiah receives and reads a letter. In 2 Kgs 22.8 Shaphan the scribe reads a book that Hilkiah the high priest hands to him. In other cases, although לִפְנֵי, בְּאָזְנֵי, or similar is lacking, private reading is possible but not self-evident (Neh. 8.18; Hab. 2.2; Isa. 34.16). However, silent reading is attested, cf. Slusser 1992; Gilliard 1993.

84 Jaffee 2001, 32–38.

85 Ibid., 34.

86 Ibid., 36.

It is *uttering* The Divine Name while 'reciting from the scroll or saying blessings' (1QS 7.1) that is punishable; this is no chirographic concern. The inscription of the *tetragrammaton* in paleo-Hebrew script in Tov's 'Qumran Scribal Practice'[87] is a device for reminding a reader not to utter The Name. The written copy works as a tool for oral performance, the chirographic operating within a wider encompassing oral structure.

Chirographic practice was located within oral structures of thought.

> Whoever enters the council of the Community enters the covenant of God (ברית אל) in the presence of all who freely volunteer. He shall swear a binding oath to revert to the Law of Moses (תורת מושה) according to all that he commanded, with whole heart and whole soul, in compliance with all that has been revealed (הנגלה) to the sons of Zadok, the priests who keep the covenant and interpret his will (ודורשי רצונו) . . . (5.7-10)

The Torah of Moses is stored in written copies. Yet the entire passage presupposes oral authoritative structures. By 'speaking' an oath (שבועת אסר), the volunteer reverts to Torah, according to all that God 'commanded' (that is, 'dictated') to Moses (כול אשר צוה). His return to Torah complies with all (לכול) that has been 'revealed' to the priests by virtue of their *darashing* God's will. While דרש indicates various kinds of examination,[88] the priests' *darashing* of God's will is done through an examination of the Torah, which is the immediate context here (תורת מושה ככול אשר צוה). The authority of the Zadokites' public pronouncement upon the meaning of the Torah is paramount throughout *1QSerekh ha-Yaḥad*.[89]

The ancestral literature has authority because God uttered the Torah to Moses and because God revealed the meaning of the Torah to the prophets. Within the community, the ancestral literature has authority principally because God continues to reveal its meaning (primarily) to the priests. Emphasized throughout is the duty of the priests and the *Maskil* to teach the revelation of the meaning of literature to the laity. The priests' authority resides in their status as purveyors of traditional literature. They receive divine insight into the meaning of this literature. A member should follow the commandments in the Torah of Moses 'in compliance with that which has been revealed in the Torah to the sons of Zadok' (5.9). The three priests required in the council of the community are 'perfect in all that is revealed from the whole Torah' (תמימים בכול הנגלה מכול התורה).[90] (IQS 8.1-2) This revelation is primarily the priests' domain. 1QS 8.14-16a reads:

87 See Footnote 21, above.

88 One can *darash*: a person's spirit (e.g. 5.20-21); a misdemeanour (8.26); Torah (e.g. 8.15). Usually, one *darashes* God (e.g. 1.1, 5.11).

89 So, for example, in 1QS 5.2: 'to be a community in Law and possessions according to (על פי) the *authority* (literally: 'mouth') *of the sons of Zadok*'. In 5.20ff. a man's deeds in the Torah will be examined according to the *priests' authority* ('mouth') (על פי בני אהון).

90 'Perfect in the Law' (García Martínez and Tigchelaar 1997). Vermes' (1997) 'perfectly versed'

'Prepare ye the way of the Lord, make straight the paths of our God' (Isa. 40.3). This is the study of the Torah (היאה מדרש תורה) which He commanded by the hand of Moses, that they may do according to all that has been revealed (ככול הנגלה) from age to age, and as the prophets have revealed (נלו) by His holy spirit.

1QS is concerned with priestly matters, presenting the Council of the Community in Aaronic terms. These lines show that the revelation received by Sectarian priests, which is mentioned throughout 1QS and which leads to proper Torah observance, is related to the prophetic revelations recorded in Jewish scripture. Right Torah observance is not only discerned by studying the prophetic revelations concerning the Mosaic codes – the prophetic literature appears here as a set of commentaries *on* Mosaic Law – but also directly through the revelations received by Sectarian priests. These priests engage in the same prophetic project as the ancestral prophets of Hebrew literature.

The *Maskil* is to 'teach' the members of the community to *darash* God and to 'do well' as He commanded in the Torah 'by the hand of Moses and all His servants the prophets' (1.1-3). This involves 'living perfectly before Him according with all that has been revealed (הנגלות) [. . .]' (1.8-9). The *Maskil* is privy to 'that which has been revealed from age to age' (9.13). He should conceal the 'counsel of Torah' from men of injustice, but shall instruct those who have chosen the 'way' (דרך as Isa. 40.3) in the 'mysteries' (רזים) so that the 'men of the Community' will walk perfectly in 'all that has been revealed to them' (9.16-19). 'The interpreter' (הדורש) should likewise not withhold any 'hidden thing' from the Community. If הדורש is a specific person, he may be priestly, since the דורש התורה of CD[A] 7.18 is a priestly figure who searches the ספרי הנביאים (CD[A] 7.17). Or this might designate a role that can be assumed by any member of the *Yahad*.[91] In any case, within the *Yahad*, while it can be said that the Torah has authority in and of itself, the authority of the Torah cannot be imagined separately from the priests who are perpetually privy to its hidden, divine meaning, and who convey this to other members. Within the framework of oral culture, the very notion of the authority of written Torah is only sensible as an element of the immediate personal authority of the tradents who act as conduits of the divine will.

Other rulings involve chirographic elements where an official inscribes certain details. Tov notes that these rules show the presence of chirographs in the 'scribal community' at Qumran.[92] While these passages assume the chirographic skills of

suggests that they are experts by virtue of reading written texts. However, the 'revelation' so often emphasized in 1QS suggests an extra-literary experience that objectifies and illuminates the literary content of Torah.

91 הדורש may mean 'someone who *darashes*', possibly including a lay member on the model of 1QS 6.6f.

92 Tov (2004, 10) mentions administrative recording in 1QS 5.23; 6.22; 4QS[d] 3 ii ₂; CD 13.12; and CD 11.18 (the *mebaqqer* records sins). He also notes the inscription of military slogans on the banners in 1QM.

individual members of the *Yaḥad* (namely, priests, the *Maskil* and the *Mebaqqer*), the practices depicted are limited to the documentary recording (כתב) of: names (1QS 5.23), property (6.20), rank (6.22), insight and deeds (6.14), as well as other biographical details. Such activities indicate only that these chirographs engaged in clerical administrative tasks, tasks subsumed in oral relationships. The duty of lay-men is to submit to the oral authority (על פי) of the priestly sons of Zadok 'in Torah' (בתורה) (1QS 5.2). The laity is to 'respond' with regard to the Torah (as is seen in the parallel use of *Hiphil* of שוב in 6.9).[93] The laity is consulted for its insights on Torah, insights over which the priests have the power of veto (5.3; 9.7). The 'counsel' (עצה) of non-priestly members is consulted in order of members' rank (6.4). In 5.21 the 'man and his neighbour' (that is, their names) will be 'recorded by rank' on the basis of enquiries into their 'understanding' and 'deeds' in Mosaic law (שכלו ומעשיו בתורה). The results of these enquiries that will be written down is the 'rank' of the man and his neighbour, which is determined by oral examination and discourse.

When a man is inscribed in his rank relative to his brothers' (6.22), his position is determined on the basis of his understanding of Torah and judgement. Once he has a rank, his 'counsel' (עצה) can be sought on these matters. This 'counsel' appears to include his exposition of the Torah (6.6f.) because elsewhere members should with-hold the 'counsel of Torah' (עצת התורה) from the 'men of The Pit' (9.17). Moreover, whoever commits a misdemeanour cannot know his fellows' 'counsels'.[94] In the *Yaḥad*, then, writing is subordinate to an individual's perception and exposition of Torah, a perception tested by direct questioning. And the person's rank inscribed in the *mebaqqer*'s ledger determines that individual's authority to express his opinions on Torah and his right to know that of his fellows. In these examples, written word in the *Yaḥad* always presupposes word that is spoken and heard.

Nothing indicates that any exegesis proposed by members of The Many (1QS 6.6f.) was written down in the first instance, but rather that such exegeses were to be sought within the Council according to a person's rank, and that the Zadokite priests wielded the authority to approve or reject these exegeses. Nothing indicates, either, that members of The Many involved in the nightly Torah *darashing* sessions were scribes. Many exegetical comments on traditional 'biblical' verses in the *pesharim* may be the result of such nightly exegesis.

5.7 *Conclusions*

Exegetical use of textual plurality is often conceived in terms of an individual's appeal to distinct text-forms, which are treated as fixed literary objects. On these grounds, Paul's negotiation of textual plurality is often doubted. However, the various authors, copyists, revisionists and transmitters of Jewish literature – who have determined the

---

93 Cf. Wernberg-Møller 1957, 27 [11].
94 1QS 8.17, 25.

form of these literary objects – engaged with the same semantic exercises as 'common' exegetes like Paul. Hence, analysis of ancient exegetes' use of textual plurality cannot be predicated upon a distinction between a transmitter and a user of traditional literature. In important respects, a variety of expert, literate and lay persons partook in a common repertoire of exegetical practice. Much of this shared experience was discursive and oral. Just as we have seen the Dead Sea sectarians draw on a range of traditional text-forms, we can conceive of Paul, their contemporary, as working in similar ways.

6

6.1 *Text and interpretation*

The previous three chapters have shown that exegetes operated within a discursive environment, in which they participated in diverse traditions, not as mute receivers of available textual material, but often as creative arbiters. Ancient Jewish textual traditions have, to a great extent, been defined by ancient interpreters' exegesis. That is, text does not necessarily precede exegesis either historically or logically. Instead, text and exegesis stand in a mutually generative relationship. Therefore, exegesis cannot be viewed as a process peripheral to fixed text, and no traditional work can be considered an autonomous standard that sets the range of interpretive possibilities. Examples of exegetical use of textual plurality, surveyed in previous chapters, show that, despite levels of ancient consensus regarding the literary form of traditional works, these forms remained porous and fluid, and the semantic form of traditional Jewish passages was fixed differently on different occasions.

In the last chapter I have shown that even some of Paul's most expert literary contemporaries were immersed in oral discussion that was deeply constitutive of their exegetical work. This is true both of their engagement with traditional Jewish literature and of their own literary composition. In this chapter I locate Paul's writing and use of traditional works within this oral environment, showing the ways in which his engagement with literature shares a common ethos with the *Yaḥad*.

6.2 *Orality, chirography and authority in Paul's letters*

Like *Serekh ha-Yaḥad*, Paul's thought and communication were orally structured. Paul's letters were surrogate oral performances. His use of traditional scripture within these letters suggests that Israel's scripture was primarily orally performed and publicly elucidated in his ministry. See, for instance, 1 Cor. 15.1-3.

> But *I make known to you* (γνωρίζω), brethren, the good news that *I proclaimed to you*
> (ὃ εὐηγγελισάμην ὑμῖν), which *you received* (παρελάβετε), in which also you stand, [2] through
> which also you are being saved, if you hold to the sort of word that *I proclaimed to you* (τίνι
> λόγῳ εὐηγγελισάμην ὑμῖν) – unless you believed in vain. [3] For *I transmitted* (παρέδωκα) *to*

you first of all what *I also received* (παρέλαβον): that Christ died for our sins in accordance
with the scriptures (κατὰ τὰς γραφάς).

Paul relates his *euangelion* to Jewish scriptures here (κατὰ τὰς γραφάς 15.3, 4) and
elsewhere (e.g. Rom. 1.2; 3.21). This passage consistently elevates the *teaching* and
reception of the *euangelion* above the written copy itself (γνωρίζω, εὐαγγελίζω,
παραλαμβάνω, παραδίδωμι). The Corinthians do not 'stand in' *scripture* nor are they
'saved' because of the words of scripture. They stand in Paul's εὐαγγέλιον, which he
taught them, and they are saved because they *received* and *respond* to it.

Paul 'portrayed' or 'depicted' (προγράφω) Christ crucified in Galatia (Gal. 3.1),
yet it is the ἀκοή that brings faith (Gal. 3.2), not the γραφή. His objection to teachings
circulating in Galatia presupposes the same. The Galatian teachers' 'other gospel' is
received or *taught* (οὐδὲ γὰρ ἐγὼ παρὰ ἀνθρώπου παρέλαβον αὐτὸ οὔτε ἐδιδάχθην,
Gal. 1.12). Traditional literature, such as Genesis 17–21, forms *part* of that teaching[1]
– it is not distinct. Paul further contrasts the revelation of Christ (Gal. 1.12, 16), which
he *received* and *preached* in Galatia, with his former expertise in the 'handed-down
traditions of my ancestors' (ἡ πατρικὴ παράδοσις, 1.14). His bid to assert his authority here places his own oral teaching, and its reception, in competition with the oral
teaching of others, not with written word.[2]

In Romans, the voice of scripture, mute on the page, lives through the performer.
Scripture 'says' (ἡ γραφὴ λέγει, e.g. Rom. 4.3; 10.11; 11.2) and 'speaks' to Pharaoh
(Rom. 9.17). Scripture 'speaks' as the ἐκ πίστεως δικαιοσύνη. Isaiah 'says' (e.g. Rom.
10.16, 20, 21). Moses and David 'say' (Rom. 10.19; 11.9). Isaiah 'cries out' (Rom.
9.27). It 'says in Hosea' (Rom 9.25). The manuscript preserves the voice. Paul's
frequent expression καθὼς γέγραπται pays homage to the written word – but only as
a record of, and a cue to oral performance, an inscribed memory of the voice, and a
prompt to its reiteration.

The written word of scripture is not subordinate to Paul's spoken preaching. For
Paul the written and the spoken are inseparable. Indeed, the written implies the spoken
and stands in antecedent continuation with it. 2 Cor. 3.14-15 highlights the oral role
of the written word:

[14] To this very day, at the reading-aloud of the old covenant (ἐπὶ τῇ ἀναγνώσει τῆς παλαιᾶς
διαθήκης), that same veil is still there, since it is only set aside in Christ. [15] Indeed, to this
very day whenever Moses is read aloud (ἂν ἀναγινώσκηται), a veil lies over their hearts.

1 Cf. Martyn 1997, 7–25 (esp. 20–25), 191–208 (esp. 201–203).
2 Of course, Paul's gospel trumps their teaching because, while theirs is 'transmitted' through a
human lineage, his is 'revealed' to him directly by the Lord (Gal. 1.1, 8, 10-12). Indeed, he previously
ran disastrously astray because he engaged in humanly transmitted tradition (καθ᾽ ὑπερβολὴν ἐδίωκον
τὴν ἐκκλησίαν τοῦ θεοῦ καὶ ἐπόρθουν αὐτήν, [. . .] περισσοτέρως ζηλωτὴς ὑπάρχων τῶν πατρικῶν μου
παραδόσεων, Gal. 1.13-14). But now moved by revelation (1.15; 2.2) none can fault his teaching (2.6-10).
But whether divine or human, the two missions (Paul's and that of the 'others' in Galatia, cf. Martyn 1997,
191ff.) are essentially oral and orthoprax, not literary and orthodox.

LXX uses ἀναγινώσκω chiefly for קרא, which indicates speaking, reading or reciting aloud.[3] Only in very few cases is 'private reading' intended.[4] The 'veil' does not obscure a visual act of private reading. Moses is 'read out loud', himself invoked through the recitation of his words. The hearers enact the moment of covenantal oath; the reader or tradent invokes and represents Moses. Paul claims that the 'veil' prevents hearers in his own day from properly perceiving Moses, now invoked through the recitation of Torah, just as it prevented the Israelites at Sinai from discerning his face. The 'veil' does not hinder a hundred acts of *private* reading. Rather, it obscures their communal perception of Moses and the covenant.

The immediacy of the oral encounter is evident in 1 Cor. 4.14-19.

[14] I do not write this to shame you, but to admonish you as my beloved children . . . [18] Some are arrogant, as though I were not coming to you. [19] But I will come to you soon, if the Lord wills, and I will discern not the talk of the arrogant but their power. [20] For the kingdom of God does not consist in talk but in power.

Paul writes to his audience, but he really speaks, bending his rhetorical skill to make his presence felt. He restricts his written threat to declaring his imminent approach and invokes the subordination of children to father. He distinguishes between 'talk' and 'power', shifting the locus of the engagement away from the page to the immediacy of their anticipated meeting.[5]

The presence of oral patterning within Paul's letters has two important implications. First, it highlights his writings as rhetorical acts of persuasion, whose immediate context is oral. As I argue below, his invocation of Jewish scripture belongs to the exercise of divinely endorsed personal authority, authority sealed by written traditions left by Israel's ancestors, in whose succession Paul stands.[6] Secondly, while Paul's explicit citations are often treated as formal indicators of his authorial appeal to 'foreign literary material', Paul's agenda seems quite different. Explicit citations are rhetorical signifiers of his claim to a succession of personal authority, rather than indicators of the written nature of his sources, and thus not formal cues to text-critical analysis. As Paul does not dichotomize writing and speaking, neither should we.

3   Brown *et al.* 1979, 894f. 'קרא', *ad loc.* Cf. Achtemeier 1990, 15–19 on private and public dictation in the ancient world. See Slusser 1992; Gilliard 1993 for references to private, silent reading in antiquity.
4   See Chapter Five, Footnote 83, above.
5   Compare 1 Cor. 5.3-4, where he proclaims himself threateningly 'present in spirit' (although 'absent in body'), and thus able to judge an offending believer.
6   By this, of course, I do not mean to suggest that Paul thinks that he is in some sense 'writing the Bible'. Rather, he presents himself rhetorically in an authoritative lineage for the sake of his efforts to persuade audiences.

6.3 *Reader-centred and author-centred perspectives*

According to Stanley, a 'reader-centred' approach aids the text-critical study of Paul's written sources by limiting contamination by 'heterogeneous' material.[7] Yet from a text-critical perspective, Stanley's reader-centred approach yields remarkably varied material for study. Paul explicitly introduces:

A.   citations that verbally correspond exactly or closely with known LXX textual traditions
B.   citations deriving from known textual traditions, which Paul has modified for his own purposes
C.   loose paraphrases of recognizable textual traditions
D.   textual units whose linguistic relation to any known Jewish literary tradition remains a matter of perennial uncertainty.

From the text-critical perspective, Paul's explicit citations, in which he alerts the audience to his use of traditional material, form a heterogeneous group. Cases 'A' to 'D' reveal that Paul meant various things by καθὼς γέγραπται and similar explicit citation formulae.[8] 'B' shows that Paul is often less interested in what was inscribed on copies than with what he considers the γεγραμμένον to mean within the context of his own rhetoric. Indeed, the only case where Paul shows explicit concern with the 'exact' wording of a tradition is Gen. 22.18 cited in Gal. 3.16. His insistence that the tradition 'does not say τοῖς σπέρμασιν but τῷ σπέρματι' throws into relief his frequent verbal alteration of his sources ('B' cases). He never explicitly draws attention to such alteration. It follows, then, that in 'A' cases he generally replicates the wording as he finds it because it is easily integrated into his prose. Hence, in 'A' cases he sees no rhetorical need to alter the passage. The loose verbal relation of 'C' and 'D' cases to the traditional material cited shows that formulations like καθὼς γέγραπται indicate that Paul is not interested in alerting his audience to his use of foreign literary material – to its written-ness as such, but rather to the ancestral authority of the traditions to which he appeals.

On the text-critical level, it is instructive to compare reader-centred studies and author-centred studies. Paul often replicates the wording of traditional Jewish scripture with no indication to his audience that he is doing so. These verbal replications are embedded in Paul's text. Ellis and Koch include fourteen of these as 'quotations'/'Zitate' (see Table 6.1, below). They deem these to be subtly marked as citations, either by words such as γάρ, ἀλλά, δέ, ὅτι, or through stylistic variance with the Pauline context.[9] Stanley, adopting a reader-centred approach, counts as

7   Stanley 1992, cf. Chapter 1, above. Elsewhere (1997a, 1997b, 1999) he justly emphasizes socio-historical advantages of reader-centred approaches (see Section 7.1.1, below).
8   See Koch 1986, 11–24 on the various introductory formulae. Further, Fitzmyer 1961.
9   Examples which Ellis, Koch and Stanley count as 'citations' lacking introductory formulae include Rom. 9.7 (Gen. 21.12) and Rom. 9.9 (Gen. 18.10). The personal pronouns in the cited material render

'quotations' only three of the fourteen (see Table 6.1, below). The rest lack explicit indication that Paul is citing foreign literary material.

In the following discussion, 'verbal replication' indicates that an author replicates the wording of a literary passage without alerting the audience. 'Verbal replication' refers to passages that the modern analyst recognizes as reproducing the wording of a known textual tradition. Lacking explicit indication, these replications are embedded in the author's text and should be distinguished from 'explicit citations' and 'allusions'. The latter are by definition intended by an author to be recognized by the audience. By contrast, we may not assume that an author intended his audience to perceive a 'verbal replication'.

'Verbal parallel'[10] is a similar term that indicates that a modern interpreter perceives an ancient author's use of the language of a literary passage, but without close verbal replication. Again, unmarked in the text by an author, it cannot be called 'citation' or 'allusion', both of which are intentional references, flagged to be recognized by the audience.[11]

Table 6.1 displays the material in question (columns 1–2). Column 3 displays the audience-alerts, by which Ellis deems Paul to announce the material as 'quotations' (although two of these lack demarcation). Column 4 displays Koch's inclusion of the same material under the rubric of 'Zitate' (the footnotes give his categorization; he deems the citation of Deut. 19.15 in 2 Cor. 13.1 to be completely unmarked). Column 5 shows the few that Stanley considers 'quotations'. Column 6 indicates when the passage appears in another Pauline letter. The citations are divided into the categories: 'verbatim', 'near verbatim', 'loose', and 'Hebraizing revision'.

---

it incongruous with Paul's context. Rom. 9.7: '. . . not all are children of Abraham because they are his descendants, but "Through Isaac shall *your* descendants be named".' Rom. 9.9: 'For this is what the promise said, "About this time *I will* return and Sarah shall have a son".'

10 Aland *et al.* use the term verbal parallel. See their 'Index of Allusions and Verbal Parallels' (Aland *et al.* 1993, 891–901) following their 'Index of Quotations' (ibid., 887–890).

11 Such definitions were not necessary in the discussion of Josephus or the *Yaḥad* (Chapters 3 and 4). Josephus explicitly states at the outset that he is relaying Judaean history as presented in the ancestral literature (see Section 3.3, above). The Habakkuk Pesher and Genesis Commentary distinguish explicitly between the traditional literary material and the exegetical comment (see Sections 4.2 and 4.4, above). Although CD^A 7.14 gives the impression that the citation from Amos 5.26-27 comes from 'Isaiah the son of Amos' (CD 7.10) and not Amos himself, the traditional material is nevertheless explicitly marked (see Section 4.3, above). In the case of Paul's letters I examine both explicit citations and embedded verbal replications (see Chapter 7).

Table 6.1 Embedded replications listed as 'quotations' in Ellis 1957[12]

Pauline letter	Scripture passage	Explicit indication (Ellis 1957)	'Zitat' (Koch 1986)	'Quotation'[13] (Stanley1992)	Other Pauline letter?
Verbatim					
Rom. 10.13	Joel 2.32	γὰρ	*yes*[14]	–	
Rom. 10.18	Ps. 18.5	μενοῦνγε	*yes*[15]	*yes*	
Rom. 12.20	Prov. 25.21-2	ἀλλὰ	*yes*[16]	–	
1 Cor. 10.26	Ps. 23.1[LXX]	γὰρ	*yes*[16]	–	
1 Cor. 15.32	Isa. 22.13	–	*yes*[16]	–	
Near verbatim					
Rom. 11.34	Isa. 40.13	γὰρ	*yes*[16]	–	1 Cor. 2.16 (not explicit)
1 Cor. 2.16	Isa. 40.13	γὰρ	*yes*[14]	–	Rom. 11.34 (not explicit)
1 Cor. 15.27	Ps. 8.7	γὰρ	*yes*[17]	*yes*	
2 Cor. 13.1	Deut. 19.15	–	*yes*[18]	–	
Gal. 3.6	Gen. 15.6	καθὼς	*yes*[15]	–	Rom. 4.3 (explicit)
Gal. 3.11	Hab. 2.4[19]	ὅτι	*yes*[14]	–	Rom. 1.17 (explicit)
Gal. 3.12	Lev. 18.5	ἀλλὰ	*yes*[15]	*yes*	Rom. 10.5 (explicit)
Loose					
2 Cor. 10.17	Jer. 9.22-23[LXX]/ 1 Kgdms 2.10?	δὲ	*yes*[14]	–	1 Cor. 1.31 (explicit)
Hebraizing revision					
Rom. 11.35	Job 41.3	γὰρ	*yes*[16]	–	–

12 Ellis 1957, appendix II, 155–182.
13 Stanley 1992 limits his study to explicit citations (see Section 1.3.2, above).
14 'Lediglich indireckt markierte Zitate', Koch 1986, 23.
15 'Mit dem Kontext incongruente Zitate', ibid.
16 'Zitate mit stilistischer Differenz zum Kontext', ibid.
17 'Durch nachträglicher Interpretation hervorgehobene Zitate', ibid., 22.
18 'Völlig ungekennzeichnete Zitate', ibid., 23.
19 Koch 1985 argues that Paul's citation of Hab. 2.4 derives from the LXX form of this passage and omits the word μου (rather than deriving from a G[HR] and omitting the word αὐτοῦ).

Notes to Table 6.1

1. 2 Cor. 10.17 is exceptional. It is reminiscent of either Jer. 9.22-23[LXX] or 1 Kgdms 2.10. Paul cited the same syntax to the Corinthians in a previous letter with the formula καθὼς γέγραπται (1 Cor. 1.31), so he may assume that they will recognize the material as authoritative γεγραμμένον in the later letter.[20]
2. The replication of Job 41.3 seems to derive from a non-extant Hebraizing revision, so one cannot say how closely it replicates its source.

Of the fourteen, five are verbatim, and seven near-verbatim replications of the wording of known textual traditions. From a reader-centred or 'rhetorical' perspective, I follow Stanley in suspecting that Paul did not expect his illiterate audiences to perceive the traditional literary contexts of these replications without being alerted to them. That is, Paul did not mean these twelve unmarked, embedded verbal replications to be recognized as literary material distinct from his own text.

Koch includes a further four 'Zitate', which neither Ellis nor Stanley counts as 'citations', three of which are verbatim or near-verbatim replications of textual traditions. Two of these Ellis designates as 'OT allusions'.[21]

Table 6.2 'Völlig ungekennzeichnete Zitate', included by Koch (1986)

Pauline letter	Scripture passage	Ellis 1967	Stanley 1992
Near verbatim			
Rom. 2.6	Ps. 61.13b	*'allusion'*	–
1 Cor. 5.13	Deut. 17.7c	–	–
2 Cor. 13.1	Deut. 19.15c	–	–
Loose			
Rom. 9.20	Isa. 29.16	*'allusion'*	–

Together, Table 6.1 and 6.2 present eighteen embedded verbal replications counted by Koch as 'citations' (twelve of which Ellis also counts as citations, two more as 'allusions'). Fifteen of these are (near-)verbatim.[22] By contrast, 40 per cent of the Pauline 'citations', which Koch designates as *explicit*, are verbatim.[23] Stanley's considerably more conservative list of explicit citations displays a very similar ratio of verbatim to non-verbatim citations.

---

20 Note that Gen. 15.6 is similarly first explicit in Rom. 4.3 and then embedded in Rom. 4.9, 22. Isa. 28.16 is explicit in Rom. 9.33 and then embedded in Rom. 10.11.

21 Ellis 1957, 153–154: 'Appendix I (B) OT Allusions and parallels in Pauline Epistles'.

22 The accuracy of the replication of the Hebraizing revision is unverifiable.

23 Thirty-seven of ninety-three 'explicit' citations are verbatim, according to Koch's reckoning of a) explicit citations and b) the wording of Paul's LXX source in each case (1986, 33 and 186). Of these, twenty-nine of Paul's citations of traditional Jewish scripture ('Schrifttexten') agree entirely with the received wording of the LXX (G[Ed]) (ibid., 101).

While this comparison of reader-centred and author-centred approaches is not objective because scholars disagree on what constitutes explicit and embedded citation, in Ellis' and Koch's very similar lists of embedded citations there is a high proportion of verbatim replication of traditional literary material. On the other hand, in Koch's and Stanley's conservative lists of explicit citations there is a very high level of verbal deviation from known textual traditions. Therefore, the reader-centred restriction of material to explicit citation does not seem to assure that citations represent traditional literary material rather than 'heterogeneous materials'.[24]

Because Paul could not expect the majority of his audiences to detect them, embedded verbal replications of traditional passages must often have a private authorial purpose, not a rhetorical one.[25] But from an author-centred perspective, the wording of Jewish scripture often plays an important role in Paul's authorial process, even though he does not alert his audience to this process. For example, Paul identifies the only three passages in Jewish scripture where cognates of δικαιόω and πιστεύω occur together: Gen. 15.6, Ps. 143.2 (142.2^{LXX}) and Hab. 2.4.[26] He explicitly cites Gen. 15.6 and Hab. 2.4 in Rom. 4.3 and Rom. 1.17, respectively. He replicates the same two passages in Gal. 3.6 and 3.11, respectively, but fails to mark the material clearly.[27] Paul never explicitly cites Ps. 143.2 (142.2^{LXX}), but replicates its literary content in exegetically modified forms in Rom. 3.20 and Gal. 2.16.[28] While Ellis lists Paul's two appeals to Ps. 143.2 as 'allusions', neither Koch nor Stanley treats them. However, it is almost universally accepted that all three passages play important roles in Paul's private exegetical process.[29] Paul often explicitly cites a passage in one place, embedding it elsewhere. This indicates that he does not necessarily choose to invoke the exegetical function of a passage in his public rhetoric.

On the other hand, when Paul alerts his audience to his invocation of traditional material, he often does so in order to invoke its traditional authority rather than literary character. For example, in 1 Cor. 1.31 Paul introduces a passage: καθὼς γέγραπται, Ὁ καυχώμενος ἐν κυρίῳ καυχάσθω. In 2 Cor. 10.17 he embeds the same passage, using no explicit introduction. While this text bears a resemblance to Jer. 9.22-23^{LXX} or 1 Kgdms 2.10, its relationship to known textual traditions is unclear. As far as anyone can discover, Paul (or his secretary) was the first to write the phrase designated with γέγραπται here.[30] On the other hand, Paul reproduces the text of Isa. 40.13a,c

---

24 *Pace* Stanley 1992, 34, 56; cf. Section 1.3.2, above.

25 Not all would agree; for example Hays (1989). Below, I discuss the problems with Hays' approach.

26 Gen. 15.6 (cited in Rom. 4.3, 9, 22; verbally replicated in Gal. 3.6); Hab. 2.4 (cited in Rom. 1.17; verbally replicated in Gal. 3.11); Ps. 143.2 (142.2^{LXX}) (loose verbal parallels in Rom. 3.20 and Gal. 2.16).

27 Paul only offers καθὼς; ὅτι. Therefore, Stanley will not treat them as citations.

28 The combination of Gen. 15.6 and Hab. 2.4 appears in *Shemoth Rabba* (Vollmer 1895, 38). It cannot be known whether Paul and *Shemoth Rabba* share an interpretive tradition, or whether it is Paul's innovation. Romans is the earliest witness to this combination and Paul's letters stand alone among extant ancient literature in combining all three: Gen. 15.6; Hab. 2.4; and Ps. 143.2.

29 e.g. Dunn 1988; Fitzmyer 1993; Hays 1989; Moo 1996; Morgan 1997.

30 Koch (1986, 36) thinks Paul knew the passage in 1 Cor. 1.31/2 Cor. 10.17 through pre-Pauline

in 1 Cor. 2.16 and Isa. 40.13a,b in Rom. 11.34 without any explicit indication. From an author-centred perspective these are 'verbal parallels'. We may not assume that Paul expected or intended his audiences to recognize this Isaian material. The literary material explicitly cited in 1 Cor. 1.31 is a loose approximation to one of two possible traditional passages (Jeremiah or 2 Kingdoms). Text-critically speaking it is 'heterogeneous material'.[31] Conversely, Paul's embedded replications of Isa. 40.13a,b,c seem to be the earliest witnesses to the wording of Isa. 40.13^{LXX} – more or less endorsed by G^{Ed} – but which cannot be treated as citations.[32]

Using the reader-centred approach as a formal text-critical strategy, whose goal is to limit 'textual contamination', is to attribute modern textual concerns to the ancient author. Paul's copious alteration of the wording of scripture reveals a divergence between the interests of Paul and his modern critics. This speaks against taking Paul's citation formulae as formal cues for text-critical analysis. While γέγραπται might be seen as a signifier of text-critical data, within the logic of the argument Paul's use of the γεγραμμένον serves his rhetorical claim to stand in an authoritative lineage. Paul is rarely interested in the 'exact' received wording, but an idea expressed by authoritative ancestors that supports his own. Of course, this idea is transmitted to each generation in written form; and this written form becomes a 'seal' of the authority of the divinely commissioned ancestors who uttered these ideas. But in these instances the cited material is not textually, but rhetorically important for Paul.

Paul's language supports this argument. In Romans, 1 and 2 Corinthians, and Galatians, Paul explicitly introduces thirty-one citations with phrases incorporating perfect forms of γράφω.[33] On the other hand, Paul also explicitly introduces thirty-three citations, by attributing the cited material to authoritative persons. Eleven times the persons are Israelite ancestors (Moses, Isaiah, Hosea, Elijah and David).[34] Nearly all of these thirty-three formulations use λέγω, three use a synonym for speaking[35] and

---

Jewish or early Christian oral tradition. Stanley (1992, 187) suggests, on the basis of 'striking echoes of Jer 9:22' in 1 Cor. 1.27-28, that the formulation is Paul's own coinage. Tuckett (2000, 416–423) believes that it derives from 1 Kgdms 2.10, rather than Jer. 9.22-23^{LXX}.

31 For Koch, it is a pre-Pauline oral tradition – see previous footnote.

32 The lack of formula here (1 Cor. 2.16; Rom. 11.34) militates against the influence of the idiosyncratic Pauline wording influencing later LXX manuscript traditions. An example of the latter is the explicit citation of Hos. 2.25^{LXX} in Rom. 9.25 (introduced: ὡς καὶ ἐν τῷ Ὡσηὲ λέγει). Rom. 9.27 led some Christian LXX copyists to inscribe ἀγαπάω in place of the more common ἐλεέω (cf. Ziegler 1959).

33 He uses καθὼς γέγραπται/καθάπερ γέγραπται sixteen times (1 Cor. 1.31; 2.9; Rom. 1.17, 2.24; 3.4, 10; 4.17; 8.36; 9.13, 33; 10.15; 11.8, 26; 15.3, 9, 21); γέγραπται γάρ six times (Rom. 12.19; 14.11; 1 Cor. 1.19; 3.19; Gal. 3.10; 4.27); ὅτι γέγραπται three times (2 Cor. 8.15; 9.9; Gal. 3.13); other perfect forms of γράφω six times (ἐν γὰρ τῷ Μωϋσέως νόμῳ γέγραπται, 1 Cor. 9.9; ὥσπερ γέγραπται, 1 Cor. 10.7; ἐν τῷ νόμῳ γέγραπται ὅτι, 1 Cor. 14.21; οὕτως καὶ γέγραπται, 1 Cor. 15.45; τότε γενήσεται ὁ λόγος ὁ γεγραμμένος, 1 Cor. 15.54; κατὰ τὸ γεγραμμένον, 2 Cor. 4.13).

34 *Moses*, Rom. 10.5, 19. *Isaiah*, Rom. 9.29; 10.16, 20, 21; 15.12. *Hosea*, Rom. 9.27. *Elijah*, Rom. 11.3. *David*, Rom. 4.6; 11.9.

35 Rom. 9.27 Ἡσαΐας δὲ κράζει; 1 Cor. 6.16 γάρ φησίν; Gal. 3.8 ἡ γραφὴ . . . προευηγγελίσατο.

almost all are in the present tense.[36] God speaks six times,[37] the 'Law' speaks twice,[38] 'scripture' thirteen times,[39] and once the 'Faith-Righteousness', advocated by Paul, speaks words from Deuteronomy.[40] Only Rom. 10.5 uses γράφω, but the citation is still attributed to Moses (Μωϋσῆς γὰρ γράφει).

These thirty-three 'personified' citations are not alternative ways of indicating the literary nature of cited material. Paul is presenting his pursuit of his Gentile mission – to which these letters belong[41] – as his own engagement in an ongoing divinely ordained project and his own place in an authoritative succession. By invoking Israel's traditions, Paul presents himself as leading a conversation in which authoritative figures from Israel's history support his Gentile gospel and his own rhetorical efforts.[42] Paul never presents his letter as a literary successor to a written canon, but *himself* as a legitimate heir of Jewish ancestors.[43] In light of this, the thirty-one γράφω-formulae do not seem to indicate Paul's desire primarily to indicate the literary character of the cited material but rather the authority it conveys. Indeed, thirteen of the thirty-three λέγω-formulae personify *scripture*, which 'speaks'; a voice of authority, not a written canon. In Rom. 15.9-12 Paul combines γράφω- and λέγω-formulae, showing that, for him, they express the same kind of authority.[44]

Of course Paul's καθὼς γέγραπται and similar formulae invoke a general reverence for written works and the technical acumen that accompanies them. It acknowledges the awe that writing inspires in illiterate folk and the various associations of writing with authority, officialdom, education, social standing and divine endorsement. It

36 Exceptions, where past tenses are used, are: Rom. 4.18; 7.7; 9.12, 29; Gal. 3.8; 2 Cor. 6.16-18.
37 Rom. 11.4; 12.19; 14.11; 2 Cor. 6.16, 17, 18.
38 Rom. 7.7; 1 Cor. 9.8.
39 'Scripture says': Rom. 4.3; 9.15, 17; 10.11; 11.2; Gal. 3.8. 'It says': Rom. 9.25; 15.10; 1 Cor. 6.16; 2 Cor. 6.2; Gal. 3.16. Characters within narratives 'are told': Rom. 9.12; 4.18.
40 Rom. 10.6, 8.
41 See Chapter Seven, Footnote 28, below, for discussions of the ethnic composition of the Roman audience. In any case, all of Paul's letters seem written in pursuit of his commission from the Risen Lord to preach to the gentiles (for the gentile character of his assemblies, see, for example: 1 Thess. 1:9; 1 Cor. 8:7; 10:14; 12:3; Gal. 2:2, 7-9; 4:8-10; Rom. 1.5, 13; 6:19; 11.13; 15.15-19, 27-28).
42 Paul presents Rom. 9.25–11.19 as such a conversation. God speaks through Hosea, and Isaiah chimes in (Rom. 9.25, 27, 29). Moses writes, and the Righteousness from Faith speaks (10.5, 6-8). Scripture addresses Paul's audience, and Isaiah joins in again (10.11, 16). Paul joins in, and Moses responds in support (10.18, 19). Isaiah 'grows bolder', drawing Israel into the conversation (10.20-21). Scripture speaks again, through Elijah (11.3), and God responds (11.4). David joins the dialogue (11.9) and Paul responds (11.11). Now Paul addresses the Gentiles, as Isaiah addressed Israel a little while before (11.11, 13). A rhetorical interlocutor joins in (11.19). Λέγω or synonyms for speaking aloud characterize this conversation in the present tense. (The only aorist expresses that Isaiah previously 'predicted' (καὶ καθὼς προείρηκεν Ἡσαΐας), emphasizing the immediacy of *this* conversation in Rom. 9-11.)
43 This is evident in Rom. 4.3, where Paul first cites 'scripture' (τί γὰρ ἡ γραφὴ λέγει, Ἐπίστευσεν δὲ Ἀβραὰμ τῷ θεῷ καὶ ἐλογίσθη αὐτῷ εἰς δικαιοσύνην, Gen. 15.6) and then attributes the citation to himself and his audience (or fellow apostles?) in Rom. 4.9 (λέγομεν γάρ, Ἐλογίσθη τῷ Ἀβραὰμ ἡ πίστις εἰς δικαιοσύνην). 'Scripture says' and '*we* say' are equivalent.
44 Rom. 15.9 καθὼς γέγραπται [Ps. 17.50^LXX]; 15.10 καὶ πάλιν λέγει [Deut. 32.43]; 15.11 καὶ πάλιν [Ps. 116.1^LXX]; 15.12 καὶ πάλιν Ἡσαΐας λέγει [Isa. 11.10].

simultaneously engages the erudite in a gratifying expert dialogue, and the general crowd, which sees the text as a potent, authoritative object. The γεγραμμένον seals the authority of the traditions he cites and the persons traditionally associated with them. His formulae are fundamentally rhetorical and engaged in the conversation with his audience. They are not simply indicators of text-critical data nor of Paul's interest in the literary nature of the material.

6.4 *Conclusions*

To a great extent Paul's thought and communication are orally structured. Much of his writing is characterized by the oral and aural language of transmission and reception. Paul does not separate the written from the spoken, his use of scripture emerging from the same kind of discursive environment as the *Yaḥad* writings (Chapter 5), whose authors make use of textual plurality (Chapter 4). In this chapter I have shown that in text-critical analysis the reader-centred approach produces ambiguous results, when applied to Paul's use of citation. Paul's alerts to citations are more indicative of their rhetorical usage than the literary quality of what follows. His explicit marking of citations is part of demonstrations of personal charisma and authority, characteristic of oral discussions.

7

PAUL AND TEXTUAL PLURALITY

7.1 *Varieties of Citation*

Some of the scholars discussed in previous chapters have taken Paul's occasional failure to cite a passage in a form they consider 'most suitable' to his argument as indicative of his ignorance of alternative forms of that passage (what I call the 'suitability argument' in Sections 1.2.2.3 and 2.2.2, above). From this point, they generalize that he was never aware of textual alternatives. This generalization is based on their idea that Paul's explicit citations are always theologically integral to the logic of his argument.[1] Hence, it is reasoned, were Paul aware of alternatives, he would certainly have chosen among them.

However, Paul's citations play a variety of roles in his writing – some are logically integral to his thought while others are rhetorical flourishes – so that no general inference about his use of citation can be drawn from the available sample of 'less suitable' cases (see Section 7.4, below). I begin with a survey of different rhetorical roles that citation can play in Paul's writing, where the precise wording used – with respect to his literary source – is apparently of no consequence. I argue that, were Paul ever aware of distinct forms of a single passage, in many cases he has no pressing exegetical or rhetorical reasons for choosing among them.

7.1.1 *The role of citations*

I identify two broad positions on the function of citation in Paul's letters. A common 'hermeneutical position' holds that the context in which a passage is cited (its 'citation context') is semantically informed by the traditional context from which it is taken. Both allusions and citations are seen to invoke the traditional context within the new one.[2] In recent decades the hermeneutical position has been framed in terms of 'intertextuality',[3] which concerns 'das, was *zwischen* Texten abspielt'.[4] The

---

1 For Koch, Paul's citations are 'ein konstitutiver Bestandteil der Argumentation des Paulus, die gar nicht unter Absehung von den Zitaten erfaßt werden kann' (1986, 284). In his 1992 study Stanley endorses 'exactly [this] position' (78 [47]).

2 Dodd's *According to the Scriptures* (1965) is representative.

3 For useful discussions, see Broich and Pfister 1985; Rese 1997.

4 Rese 1997, 433.

interaction between different passages of scripture used in Paul's letters is considered to provide the key to understanding Paul's arguments. Thus Hays, for example, argues that attention to textual interaction of citations and allusions in Paul's writing prevents his original and modern audiences alike from 'slip[ping] into the error' of misreading Paul's argument.[5] For those with 'ears to hear', fainter echoes produce literary effects of greater potency than explicit citations.[6]

However, such a conception tends to frame Paul's work within a rarefied and closed literary paradigm that disregards the urgent and vivacious rhetorical contexts within which he wrote. Paul is hereby portrayed concealing his message within complex exegetical encryption, subordinating his own explicit rhetoric to a subtle literary game. This is dubious. First, the general ability of Paul's audiences to detect such 'echoes' is a matter of uncertainty (see below). Second, Paul earnestly and anxiously sought to persuade audiences, who were often doubtful or even hostile to his position. Under such circumstances it would surely be expedient for Paul to attempt arguments whose rhetoric was clear and compelling enough to sway those disinclined to agree, without expecting them willingly to engage in intricate literary excavation of his letters.[7] Intertextual readings of a modern scholar studying Paul's edited letters, concordance in hand, must not be confused with an ancient audience's perception of authorial intent under politically trying circumstances. While some of his more erudite associates may indeed have engaged in exegetical subtlety, it is fair to assume that Paul intends his *explicit* rhetoric to convey his message, however successful or confused we might deem that rhetoric to be.

A 'rhetorical position' represents an effort to address these concerns.[8] Advocates argue that citation must be treated as a rhetorical act that takes place in a live communicative context, within which citation exists as 'part of a broader argument designed to convince others to believe or act in a certain way'.[9] An argument's general efficacy must be congruous with an audience's ability to perceive it. Thus, a citation's rhetorical efficacy within an argument should not be taken to depend on an audience's supposed familiarity with its traditional literary context. Since early urban Christian congregations were at least 80 per cent illiterate,[10] the majority of Paul's audiences

---

5   Hays 1989, 66. For Hays a 'common sense hermeneutics' unites attentive ancient and modern audiences in correctly understanding Paul's arguments (ibid., 28).

6   e.g. ibid., 64, 65 and 77ff.

7   The Corinthian, Galatian and Roman correspondences – the letters in which Paul explicitly cites scripture – are the most diplomatically precarious of Paul's extant letters. Sections of the audience of 1 Corinthians are dubious about him and his message (see Footnote 123, below). 2 Corinthians and Galatians reflect direct confrontation involving both the audience and third-parties, apparently rival missionaries. Paul's diplomatic caution in Romans (e.g. Rom. 3.1-8, 31; 6.1, 15-17; 12.3; 14.14; 15.15-20, 30-32) betrays his awareness of potential doubts within the audience.

8   For example, Stanley 1997a, 1997b, 1999; Tuckett 2000. Both respond, in part, to Hays 1989.

9   Stanley 1997b, 44.

10 Bar-Ilan (1988, 164 [8]); Harris 1989; Gamble 1995, 165 [13]; Jaffee 2001, 164 [7].

would be unfamiliar with the written text of the passages cited by Paul.[11] Most were presumably unable to recognize even verbatim replications of scripture embedded in his letters, at least from personal literary experience. Indeed, an explicit citation was often the only version of a passage known to a hearer.[12] Paul may not overestimate his audience's literary competence. Rather, he assumes their reverence for Jewish scripture and the place in an authoritative ancestral lineage that citation affords him (see Chapter 6, above).

To be effective, Paul's rhetorical appeals to literature must correspond with a literary experience, which the author assumes he shares with his audience. One aspect of such 'shared experience' is a thematic reading of scripture. Ancient Jews took a thematic approach to their generically diverse and often textually fluid ancestral literature,[13] a practice apparently adopted by early Christian groups, as the *florilegia* of the second century suggest. Thematic approaches to literature are evident among non-Jews (cf. Section 1.8.2.1, above) and, furthermore, Paul's assemblies witnessed this approach to Jewish scripture in Paul's own letters. Many of Paul's citations evoke certain traditional themes. The wording of these 'evocative' citations can be interchangeable because Paul is fundamentally interested in appealing to a broader theme, rather than a particular passage, in support of his argument.

Examples of Paul's thematic collection and citation of passages abound. Isaiah[14] and the Psalms,[15] for example, while often vitriolic towards 'the nations', also present a hopeful image of Gentiles' peaceful submission to Yahweh and Israel. In Rom. 15.9-12 Paul assembles passages – one from Moses (Deut. 32.43), two from David (Pss. 17.50^{LXX}; 116.1^{LXX}) and one from Isaiah (11.10) – narrating the Gentiles' glorious reconciliation with God and Israel. The Abraham story forms the archetype for

---

11 See Stanley 1997a, 1997b, 1998, 1999, 2004; Tuckett 2000, 411–416.

12 Cf. Campbell 1995. Similarly Jaffee 2001, 8, 18–19.

13 For example, 4Q158 (*Reworked Pentateuch*); 4Q175 (*Testimonia*); 4Q176 (*Tanhumim*); 4Q339 (*List of False Prophets*, Aramaic); 4Q340 (*List of Netinim*); and 4Q559 (*Biblical Chronology*) are all thematic collections of passages (cf. Section 1.8.2.1, above). Psalms 1–89 appear to be organized by author- and genre-distinctions, while Psalms 90–150 consist of smaller collections organized by common themes or catchwords (Wilson 1985). Stanley (1993, 126–127, 136 [48]) cites other studies of thematic reading in various Jewish literature: Hanson 1979 and Collins 1984 on 'apocalyptic' literature; Perrin 1976 on 'Kingdom of God' in the Jesus narratives.

14 Stanley (1993, 126–127) traces throughout Isaiah a narrative strand that depicts the nations peacefully submitting to Israel's rule, worshipping Yahweh and obeying the law (Isa. 2.2-4; 14.1-3; 25.6-9; 49.1-13; 51.4-11; 54.1–55.5; 56.3-8). The OG translation increases the thematic unity of these sections, already present in the Hebrew, improving narrative continuity: i.e., Isa. 10.20-23, 26-28; 26.18; 27.2-6 (Stanley 1993, 127 [31]). The same preoccupations also appear in 1 Enoch, Baruch, Sirach, Psalms of Solomon, Testaments of the Twelve, or 1QMilhamah (ibid., 131), reflecting the preoccupations of Diaspora Jews at the time of translation. (Seeligmann (1984, 76–94; Seeligmann *et al.* 2004) dates LXX Isaiah to 170–150 BCE; cf. Seeligman *et al.* 2004, 222–250.)

15 Similarly in the Psalms, for example: 18.43-48; 22.27-31; 45.9-17; 47.1; 49.1; 57.9; 67.1-5; 72.8-11, 17; 86.9; 96.3, 10, 13; 97.6; 98.2, 9. The Psalms were prevalent in Second Temple Jewish liturgy. Cf. Marcos 2000, 267–268 on the preference for the Psalms in inscriptions in Palestine, Syria, Asia Minor, Egypt, and Greece; ibid., 295 on the *catena* to the Psalms.

this narrative, exemplified by passages such as Gen. 17.24 (invoked in Rom. 4.10) or Gen. 18.18 (cited in Gal. 3.8). At other times the Gentiles function as a 'foil' against which God rebukes Israel through a prophet. Paul collects several such passages: Deut. 32.21[16] (Rom. 10.19); Isa. 56.1 (Rom. 10.20); Isa. 52.5[LXX] (Rom. 2.24). He also collates passages in which God leaves a remnant of Israel: Isa. 10.22-23 and 1.9 in Rom. 9.27-29; 1 Kgs 19.10 and 14 (3 Kgdms 19.10, 14) in Rom. 11.3. The language of righteousness in Romans is infused with the righteousness language found in Psalms. The Psalter and Isaiah consistently associate δικαιοσύνη with 'salvation' and 'the nations'. Psalms 96–98 appear to influence Paul's statement in Rom. 1.16-17, in which God extends righteousness and salvation to the Gentiles.[17] These examples show that through thematic citation an author can appeal to ideas he considers to belong to the audience's general encounter with the literature.

7.2 *The rhetorical impact of citations*

7.2.1 *Distinction between supportive and logically structural roles*
Many of Paul's citations play purely supportive rhetorical roles in his writing. While a supportive citation can have a high rhetorical impact, it could be removed from Paul's letter without damaging the logical structure of the argument. Such citations can work in a variety of ways in the author's text. Some supportive citations are rhetorical flourishes. Examples include: Ps. 44.22 in Rom. 8.36; Prov. 25.21-22 in Rom. 12.20; Isa. 52.15 in Rom. 15.21; Ps. 24.1 in 1 Cor. 10.26; Isa. 28.11 in 1 Cor. 14.21. As Morgan puts it, in Romans 3 '[t]he seven or so confirmatory quotations at 3:10-18 say much less than the five in ch. 4 which constitute an elaborate argument'.[18] Not that citations with supportive roles are 'mere' flourishes; many are rhetorically significant in Paul's arguments. However, supportive citations do not logically structure Paul's argument. That is, they are not semantically integral to his reasoning.

In contrast to supportive citations, some passages structure Paul's logic. A passage playing a structural role need not be cited explicitly. For example, Lev. 18.8 plays no rhetorical role in Paul's attitude to the incestuous man's co-habitation with his father's wife in 1 Cor. 5.1f. Instead, it is logically integral to his thought. He reproduces the words of Lev. 18.8 (γυναικὸς πατρός σου) in his letter (γυναῖκά τινα τοῦ πατρὸς ἔχειν – 1 Cor. 5.1), but with no indication that he has done so. Nevertheless, Paul's conviction that the man's practice is unacceptable reflects Paul's implicit acceptance of the ruling in Leviticus 18. Paul echoes Deut. 17.7 in 1 Cor. 5.2 (again, in relation to the incestuous man) and verbally replicates the OG-form[19] in 1 Cor. 5.13 (in relation

---

16 The passage is critical of Jeshurun [= Israel in MT], Jacob [= Israel in LXX] who 'Scoffed at the Rock of his Salvation [i.e. God]' in Deut. 32.15.

17 Morgan 1997, 20, 26, 28. Hays (1989, 36–37) proposes that, for example, Ps. 51.14 (50.16 LXX), 97.2 (96.2 LXX), 98.2 (97.2 LXX) and Isa. 46.13; 60.21; 61.8; 62.2 inform Paul's righteousness language.

18 Morgan 1997, 79.

19 The echo in 5.2 is verbally closer to 𝔐 while remoter from the LXX-form he replicates in 5.13.

to the lawsuit).[20] Deut. 17.7 does not form part of his rhetoric because he does not cite it explicitly. However, it is constitutive of his thought. Similarly, 1 Corinthians 10 belongs to an argument against believers' participation in idolatry (1 Cor. 8-10). Two passages in particular (Exod. 20.4 and Num. 25.1-5) logically structure his argument that those baptized into Christ are subject to divine punishment for idolatry, as Israel was. Yet the only passage he cites explicitly is Exod. 32.6: 'and they rose up to play' (1 Cor. 10.7),[21] which rhetorically corresponds to his frequent reproaches of the Corinthians' childishness.[22] Passages that structure Paul's logic, then, are distinct from many explicit citations that play purely rhetorical roles.

7.2.2 Verbal congruence

The verbal congruence between Paul's argument and a cited passage is rhetorically significant. Yet, however rhetorically effective the congruence, the audience need recognize neither the literary source of the citation nor the possible semantic correspondence between the source and destination contexts.

Syntactical congruence is achieved through replication of key vocabulary in order to increase the audience's sense that Paul's citation of traditional material is congruous with his argument. For example, the words δικαιωθῇς and κρίνεσθαι in the citation of Ps. 51.4 (50.6^{LXX}) in Rom. 3.4 are echoed by Paul's words θεοῦ δικαιοσύνην (3.5), ἔνδικον (3.8), κρινεῖ (3.6), κρίνομαι (3.7) and τὸ κρίμα (3.8). Here the citation of Psalm 51 plays a supportive role. The citation is a rhetorical flourish – not an exegetical argument, and an indication that Paul sees his answer to be self-evident.[23] A supportive citation can be verbally integrated into the language of Paul's argument, as Vollmer and Michel amply show.[24] For hearers of Paul's letters who do not have an intimate knowledge of the traditional literature, such recurrence of vocabulary does not produce a closer logical link between traditional and Pauline context, but rather creates a sense of congruence between Paul's argument and the citation.

Deut. 17.7^{LXX} reads: καὶ ἐξαρεῖς τὸν πονηρὸν ἐξ ὑμῶν αὐτῶν, 'and you will put this evil (one) out from you' (1 Cor. 5.13 ἐξάρατε τὸν πονηρὸν ἐξ ὑμῶν αὐτῶν). 𝔐 reads: וּבִעַרְתָּ הָרָע מִקִּרְבֶּךָ, 'and you shall purge/incinerate the evil from in your midst'(1 Cor. 5.2 ἵνα ἀρθῇ ἐκ μέσου ὑμῶν ὁ τὸ ἔργον τοῦτο πράξας). Paul uses a form of αἴρω in each case (LXX ἐξαίρω), but in 5.2 he has ἐκ μέσου ὑμῶν (cf. מִקִּרְבֶּךָ).

20 Was the law suit to do with this man, then? Such relations were also banned in Roman law, as Paul mentions. βιωτικά may mean 'property', or more generally 'affairs'.

21 See Meeks 1982, 64–78; Fee 1987, 453–455.

22 1 Cor. 1.12 ('I am of *x*' exemplifying the relation of a child or a slave to a master; Mitchell 1991, 83–86); 3.1; 4.15f.; 13.11-12; the pedagogical style of 1 Cor. 15, cf. Asher 2000; the contrast of 'children' and τέλειοι (13.10; 14.20; cf. 2.6). 'Playing' is also associated with idolatry in the LXX (Fee, 453–455). This may have been widely known in the Corinthian audience, especially if some associated with synagogues (Paul names Jews in the Corinthian assembly). However, most of the Corinthians are non-Jews (e.g. 12.2; cf. 1 Cor. 8-10, esp. 8.7; further 6.11) and the intertextual intricacy of tracing the relation of 'playing' to idolatry must surely exceed their Jewish literary competence.

23 Cf. Morgan (1997, 28).

24 Vollmer 1895 (see Section 1.1.2, Footnote 25, above) and Michel 1929 (see Section 1.3.1, Footnote 96).

Paul often connects two cited passages through 'key-word linkage',[25] memorably connecting Gen. 15.6, Hab. 2.4 and Psalm 143 (142^{LXX}) by means of δικαιόω, πιστεύω and their cognates.[26] He connects Isa. 8.14 and 28.16 through 'stone' language (Rom. 9.33); and Gen. 15.6 and Ps. 32.1-2 (31.1-2^{LXX}) with λογίζομαι (Rom. 4.3, 7). A technique belonging to the common exegetical heritage (see Section 5.3, above), key-word linkage had a technical status in exegetical circles. Those with exegetical aptitude may have acknowledged his use of this technique. However, his use of key-words can also have a purely rhetorical effect on uninitiated audiences. In an environment in which most people encountered literature, teaching and argument as public oral address, the strategic repetition of words gave 'rhythm and rhyme' to the argument for the non-erudite hearer.

7.2.3 *Changing wording*

Paul changes the wording of more than half of his citations for stylistic and rhetorical reasons.[27] At times, Paul's treatment of a passage seems cavalier. For example, in Deut. 30.10-14, cited in Rom. 10.6-8, Paul replaces all references to 'doing' the law with references to Jesus' death and resurrection (encapsulating his 'gospel', cf. Rom. 1.4; 1 Cor. 15.4f; 1 Thess. 4.14f.). Paul derives meaning foreign to the traditional understanding of this passage and imports his innovative understanding into the text itself. Perhaps this innovation is not as drastic as it appears. Romans presupposes – more than any other indisputably Pauline letter – the audience's familiarity with traditional Jewish literature.[28] His discussion predicates the question of how a person is to 'attain Law' (Rom. 9.31) and thereby find 'righteousness' (δικαιοσύνην, Rom. 9.30). He inserts Christ into Deuteronomy 30 in order to persuade his audience that Christ is τέλος νόμου εἰς δικαιοσύνην (Rom. 10.4). In terms of his rhetoric, Paul has not so much excised the Torah observance from the passage as proposed a continuity between Torah observance and faith in Christ. This is broadly congruent with his efforts to trace continuities between Torah and Christ in Romans.[29] Note that he thereby appeals to a Jewish tradition of identifying personified Wisdom with Torah by reference to Deut. 30.11-14.[30]

While the language of Paul's own argument is verbally integrated into the citation,

---

25 Commonly identified with the later Rabbinic term *gezera shawa*, for which see, for example, Daube 1973; Fishbane 1985, 1988; Kasher 1988; Hays 1989.

26 Gen. 15.6 (cited in Rom. 4.3, 9, 22; verbally replicated in Gal. 3.6); Hab. 2.4 (cited in Rom. 1.17; verbally replicated in Gal. 3.11); Ps. 143.2 (142.2^{LXX}) (loose verbal parallels in Rom. 3.20 and Gal. 2.16).

27 See Chapter One, Footnote 80, above.

28 It is much discussed whether the Roman audience was entirely gentile (e.g. Kümmel 1975; Sanders 1991; Gager 1983; Stowers 1994; Das 2007), Jewish (e.g. Baur 1876; Schmithals 1975; Wiefel 1991; Mason 1994) or mixed (e.g. Dunn 1988; Watson 1991; Nanos 1996; Morgan 1997). The last is the most common position.

29 See Wedderburn 1988, 35–37.

30 So Job 11.5-9 and Bar. 3.29-31, which substitute 'seeking Wisdom' (personified) for 'doing Torah'. Cf. Targum Pseudo Jonathan Deut. 30.

the citation remains supportive. Paul argues that believing in Christ leads to righteousness and that this is indeed what the law requires; however, 'keeping the law' (ἔργα
τοῦ νόμου) without faith in Christ does not lead to righteousness. Deut. 30.10-14
is rhetorically important for the argument because it is concerned with 'searching
high and low for the law' (cf. Rom. 9.31 Ἰσραὴλ δὲ διώκων νόμον δικαιοσύνης), a
quest whose 'goal' Paul identifies as Christ (Rom. 10.4). Nevertheless, no claim of
Deuteronomy 30 can be said to structure the logic of Paul's argument here. That is,
Paul's use of Deut. 30.10-14 has a high rhetorical impact, yet its role remains logically subordinate to the argument it supports. Were this appeal to Deuteronomy 30
removed, Paul's argument – that Christ is continuous with the Torah – would remain
cogent, as it did in Romans 5–8, where virtually no scripture is cited.

7.3 *Structurally indispensable citations*

The previous section has shown that a supportive citation does not structure Paul's
argument and could in fact be removed without interfering with the argument's logical
coherence. By contrast, some appeals to scripture are indispensable for the coherence
of Paul's argument. That is, the cited material semantically structures his case. A citation of this kind may have rhetorical weight (on account of factors discussed above
in relation to supportive citations). However, unlike supportive citations, structurally
indispensable citations are essential to Paul's logic.

7.3.1 *The structural substance of Genesis 15.6 and 17.10-14 in Romans*
Gen. 15.6 structures Paul's argument in Romans 4. It is not adduced as a supportive
'proof-text'. Abraham is the prototype of the believer in Christ. Paul applies the narrative of Genesis – God's righting Abraham 'on account of his faith' – to the righting
of all believers in Christ. Paul apparently expects his audience to know the story, but
there is no indication that he considers any detailed lexical familiarity with the passage to be necessary for their understanding of his argument.[31] Paul explicitly cites
Gen. 15.6 only once in Rom. 4.3, but it structures the chapter. Paul also allows Gen.
15.6 to work alongside Gen. 17.10-14, 24. This passage, too, logically structures
Paul's argument because the narrative chronology of Gen. 17.10-14 – Abraham was
circumcised only *after* he was reckoned righteous – is crucial to Paul's argument
(Rom. 4.10-11).[32]
    In Paul's appeal to Gen. 15.6, the lexical is subordinate to the semantic. In Rom. 4.3
Paul explicitly cites the passage: 'For what does the scripture say? Abraham believed
God, and it was reckoned to him as righteousness.' Paul's citation (ἐπίστευσεν [δὲ]

---

31 Paul generally assumes the Romans' familiarity with Jewish scripture. They know the law
(γινώσκουσιν γὰρ νόμον λαλῶ, 7.1). Terse references to David (Rom. 4.6-8), Moses (Rom. 9.14), Pharaoh
(Rom. 9.16), and Elijah (Rom. 11.2-4) presuppose narrative familiarity.
    32 Note that Paul *cannot* make this chronological argument in Galatians because it would endorse
what the Galatians seek to do: *first* to be righted by faith and *then* to receive circumcision as a seal.

'Αβραὰμ τῷ θεῷ καὶ ἐλογίσθη αὐτῷ εἰς δικαιοσύνην) replicates the traditional wording (ἐπίστευσεν Αβραμ τῷ θεῷ καὶ ἐλογίσθη αὐτῷ εἰς δικαιοσύνην). Yet his reiteration of the passage a few verses later (Rom. 4.9) alters the wording (λέγομεν γάρ, ἐλογίσθη τῷ 'Αβραὰμ ἡ πίστις εἰς δικαιοσύνην). While the sense in which he is interested remains unchanged, the syntax is altered. The peripheral importance of lexical fidelity to Paul's semantic concerns is also evident in his reference to Genesis 17. Here he refers to temporal narrative elements of Genesis 17.10-14, 24 – Abraham was circumcised after he was reckoned righteous – without replicating the wording at all.

Along with the structural importance of these passages, the citation of Genesis 15 and 17 also plays rhetorical roles, of the types discussed above (Section 7.2.2-3). Paul's linkage of Gen. 15.6 to Ps. 32.1-2 (31.1-2^LXX) by λογίζομαι (Rom. 4.3, 7) can affect his audience rhetorically, regardless of scriptural expertise. Key words recur throughout Paul's text and within each cited passage, repetition that impresses upon the listener both a sense of cogency of his argument and of the unanimous agreement between Paul and authoritative scripture, which demonstrates that important Jewish ancestors – Moses and the Prophets – support Paul.[33] A single citation, then, can exhibit both rhetorical and logically structural characteristics. Nevertheless, Paul's interest in passages that structure his logic is primarily a semantic interest, to which lexical considerations are subordinate.

7.3.2 *The structural substance of Genesis 21.12; 18.10, 14; and 25.23 in Romans 9*

The patriarchal narratives to which Paul appeals in Romans 9 similarly exhibit a structural integrity with Paul's argument. Paul modifies the traditional understanding of Gen. 21.12 (ἐν Ισαακ κληθήσεταί σοι σπέρμα). Referring to the narrative extending from God's promise of a son to Sarah (Genesis 18) to the birth of Jacob and Esau by Rebecca (Genesis 25), Paul employs three citations of this narrative, and one from Malachi, which itself comments on the Genesis narrative:

Rom. 9.7 Ἐν Ἰσαὰκ κληθήσεταί σοι σπέρμα (Gen. 21.12)

Rom. 9.9 Κατὰ τὸν καιρὸν τοῦτον ἐλεύσομαι καὶ ἔσται τῇ Σάρρᾳ υἱός (Gen. 18.10, 14)

Rom. 9.12 Ὁ μείζων δουλεύσει τῷ ἐλάσσονι (Gen. 25.23)

Rom. 9.13 Τὸν Ἰακὼβ ἠγάπησα, τὸν δὲ Ἠσαῦ ἐμίσησα (Mal. 1.2)

Gen. 21.12 is traditionally understood to designate Abraham's heirs through Jacob's bloodline. Capitalizing on the dative construction ἐν Ἰσαὰκ, Paul shifts the criterion of descent from 'progeny' to 'promise'. Paul's logic may be summarized as follows:

---

33 4QMMT (4Q398 C 10-11) counts Moses, the prophets and David together. So too Lk. 24.44. In 11QPs. David is said to prophecy.

> Born according to God's promise, Isaac is the child of the promise (Gen. 21.12, ἐν Ισαακ κληθήσεταί σοι σπέρμα). Like Isaac, then, Abraham's descendents are children of promise (Gen. 18.10, 14). Look! Although both sons share Isaac's bloodline, the promise passed only to *one* of them, Jacob. Neither deserved it more than the other (Gen. 25.23; Mal. 1.2). So the statement, ἐν Ισαακ κληθήσεταί σοι σπέρμα, indicates that the criterion of decent from Abraham is 'promise'.

Two elements of the passage logically structure Paul's argument: first, God's promise to Abraham concerning Isaac (Gen. 18.10, 14); second, God's acceptance of one of Isaac's sons and His rejection of the other (Gen. 25.23; Mal. 1.2). The argument depends not only on Gen. 25.23, which Paul cites explicitly (ὁ μείζων δουλεύσει τῷ ἐλάσσονι), but also upon the narrative of Rebecca's exclusive coital relations with Isaac (Ῥεβέκκα ἐξ ἑνὸς κοίτην ἔχουσα, Ἰσαὰκ τοῦ πατρὸς ἡμῶν) (Rom. 9.10), which Paul adduces without citation. That is, the Genesis narrative structures the argument of Romans 9 just as Gen. 17.10-14 structured Romans 4 (Abraham was circumcised only after the reckoning of his righteousness by faith). These passages underlie Paul's thought.

The OG and pM-forms of Gen. 18.10 and 14; Gen. 21.12 and Gen. 25.23 are in semantic agreement. Paul prioritizes the sense of God's promise to Abraham over lexical particularity; citing the promise (ἐπαγγελίας γὰρ ὁ λόγος οὗτος) (Rom. 9.9), Paul conflates Gen. 18.10 with Gen. 18.14 (both of which express the same sense in slightly different ways). He introduces some syntactical alterations, but these make no changes to the sense of the narrative that structures his argument.

Table 7.1 Genesis 18 and Romans 9

Gen. 18.10	Rom. 9.9	Gen. 18.14
a ἐπαναστρέφων ἥξω πρὸς σὲ		
b κατὰ τὸν καιρὸν τοῦτον	κατὰ τὸν καιρὸν τοῦτον ἐλεύσομαι	εἰς τὸν καιρὸν τοῦτον ἀναστρέψω πρὸς σὲ
c εἰς ὥρας		εἰς ὥρας
d καὶ ἕξει υἱὸν Σαρρα ἡ γυνή σου	καὶ ἔσται τῇ Σάρρᾳ υἱός	καὶ ἔσται τῇ Σαρρα υἱός
a *I will return and be present to you*		
b *according to* the time	*According to* the time I will come	at the appointed time I will return to you
c seasonably,		seasonably,
d and Sarah your wife shall have a son	<u>and a son will be to Sarah</u>	<u>and a son will be to Sarah</u>

Paul removes the phrases πρὸς σὲ and εἰς ὥρας from both verses; agrees with 18.14

by omitting ἡ γυνή σου of 18.10e; agrees with the order of 18.14 against that of 18.10; agrees with 18.14 (κατά) against 18.10 (εἰς); agrees with 18.14, putting the verb (ἐλεύσομαι) after the time clause.

7.3.2.1 *Implications of structural citations*

I have proposed logical structure as a criterion for distinguishing two kinds of appeal to scripture. A *structural citation* is logically integral to the argument it structures. By contrast, *supportive citations*, which can create a variety of rhetorical effects, do not structure Paul's internal logic. Explicit supportive citations often invoke a traditional theme or produce a sense of unanimity between the author and tradition. Frequently, neither the passage chosen nor the syntactical form in which it is cited is uniquely significant, either for achieving these rhetorical effects or for the constitution of Paul's argument. Thus, in many such cases, the question of Paul's preference for a particular available form of a passage is irrelevant.

This observation undermines the 'suitability argument' – namely, that there is always a 'most suitable' form of a passage for Paul's argument and that Paul would always choose that form, if he knew it. In the case of many rhetorical citations Paul has no pressing need to prefer a particular lexical form of a passage. Moreover, Paul changes the wording of more than half of his citations for stylistic and rhetorical reasons.[34] So, in the majority of cases, preservation of the syntax of the written source is not his concern. Therefore, it cannot be assumed that Paul would always prefer the most 'suitable' form as judged by commentators. However, in the case of a logically structural passage, which *uniquely* structures an argument, the question of Paul's preference for a particular form of a passage, characterized by a distinct sense contour, becomes significant.

We have also seen that, while *some* structural appeals to scripture are explicit citations, others are not cited at all. Here is an important distinction. As rhetorical devices, supportive citations *must* be explicitly cited. Conversely, a passage that logically structures Paul's argument need not be 'cited' (cf. Sections 7.2.1, 7.3.1, above). Attention, therefore, must be paid to the distinction between rhetorical and exegetical context and to the function of a given reference.

Textual variation in first-century Jewish scripture ranged well beyond the limits of our categories, OG and proto-Masoretic. However, the OG and pM-forms are invaluable heuristic means of observing an exegete's use of discrete variations. In the above examples of logically structural Genesis citations, the OG and pM-forms present a single sense contour, so the question of whether Paul 'chose' the cited form does not arise. In contrast, Isa. 8.14 and 25.8 each exists in markedly different traditional forms, presenting contradictory sense contours. Moreover, Paul's citations of these Isaiah passages (in Rom. 9.33; 1 Cor. 15.54) structure the surrounding argument. In

---

34 See Chapter One, Footnote 80, above. Paul modifies fifty-two of ninety-three: twelve 'intensively' (three times or more), and fifteen for stylistic reasons (Koch 1986, 186).

each case the cited form plays an indispensable structural role in Paul's logic and alternative forms of each verse are unusable.

Isa. 8.14 and 25.8 are two of only four instances in which Paul cites Isaiah in a pM-form (see also Isa. 28.11; 52.7),[35] in contrast to his numerous citations reflecting OG Isaiah. While his citations of Isa. 8.14 and 25.8 cannot prove that Paul preferred these pM-forms, I argue that Paul has *reason* to prefer a distinct semantic form of a passage when the passage is *both* structurally indispensable to Paul's argument *and* only one semantic form of the passage suits his argument. This convergence of conditions would make preference imperative, were he to know alternatives.

7.3.3 *The structural substance of Isaiah 8.14ᵖᴹ in Romans 9.33*

Table 7.2 Isaiah 8.13-14 (Romans 9.33)[36]

Isa. 8¹³⁻¹⁴ LXX	Isa. 8¹³⁻¹⁴ MT	1QIsa.ᵃ	Rom. 9³³ = 1 Pet. 2⁸	σ' (= θ' when extant)	α'
κύριον	אֶת־יְהוָה	את־יהוה		κύριον[37]	τὸν [κύριον]
	צְבָאוֹת	צבאות *vacat*		τῶν δυνάμεων	τῶν δυνάμεων
αὐτὸν ἁγιάσατε	אֹתוֹ תַקְדִּישׁוּ	אתו תקדישו		αὐτὸν ἁγιάσατε	[. . . . .
καὶ αὐτὸς ἔσται	אֲכֶם וְהוּא מוֹרַ	והוא מוראכם		καὶ αὐτὸς ἔσται	. . . .]
σου φόβος				φόβος ὑμῶν	
καὶ ἐὰν ἐπ' αὐτῷ πεποιθὼς ἦς	צְכֶם וְהוּא מַעֲרַ	והוא מערצכם		καὶ κραταίωμα ὑμῶν	καὶ αὐτὸς θρόσησις ὑμῶν
ἔσται σοι	וְהָיָה	והוא		καὶ ἔσται	καὶ ἔσται
εἰς ἁγίασμα	לְמִקְדָּשׁ	למקדש		εἰς ἁγίασμα	εἰς ἁγίασμα
καὶ οὐχ ὡς					
λίθου	וּלְאֶבֶן	ולאבן	λίθον	εἰς δὲ λίθον	καὶ εἰς λίθον
προσκόμματι	נֶגֶף	נגף	προσκόμματος	προσκόμματος[38]	προσκόμματος
συναντήσεσθε αὐτῷ οὐδὲ ὡς					
πέτρας	וּלְצוּר	ולצר	καὶ πέτραν	καὶ εἰς πέτραν	καὶ εἰς στερεὸν
πτώματι	מִכְשׁוֹל	מכשול	σκανδάλου	πτώματος	σκανδάλου

---

35 Deriving from a Hebraizing revision of OG Isaiah (Koch 1986, 78–81; Wilk 1998, 41–42).
36 Cf. Koch 1986, 58.

Isa. 8[13-14 LXX]	Isa. 8[13-14 MT]	1QIsa.ᵃ	Rom. 9³³ = 1 Pet. 2⁸	σ' (= θ' when extant)	α'
ὁ δὲ οἶκος	לִשְׁנֵי בָתֵי	לשני בתי		τοῖς δυσὶν οἴκοις	τοῖς δυσὶν οἴκοις
Ἰακώβ	יִשְׂרָאֵל	ישראל		Ἰσραήλ	Ἰσραήλ
ἐν παγίδι	לְפַּח	לפח		εἰς παγίδα	[. . . . .
καὶ ἐν κοιλάσματι	וּלְמוֹקֵשׁ	ולמוקש		καὶ εἰς σκάνδαλον	. . .] εἰς σκῶλον
ἐγκαθήμενοι	לְיוֹשֵׁב	ליושב		τῷ οἰκοῦντι	[. . . . .]
ἐν' Ἰεπουσαλήμ	יְרוּשָׁלָם	ירושלם		ἐν' Ἰερουσαλήμ	

Isa. 8.14ᴾᴹ expresses a striking idea: God can be both a sanctuary and a stumbling stone to Israel.

> But the LORD of hosts, him you shall regard as holy; let him be your fear, and let him be your dread. ¹⁴ And he will become a *sanctuary*, and a *stone of offence*, and a *rock of stumbling* to both houses of Israel, *a trap and a snare* to the inhabitants of Jerusalem. ¹⁵ And many shall stumble thereon; they shall fall and be broken; they shall be snared and taken.

The idea is abrupt and perplexing. Perhaps מִקְדָּשׁ ('sanctuary') may be a 'dogmatic corrective'³⁹ for a difficult original reading. Some suggest an original מוקש ('lure, snare'), and others מקשר ('conspiracy'). Despite the corrective מקדש, the pM-stream (1QIsa.ᵃ α' θ' σ' 𝔐) maintains the harsh tone against Israel by maintaining the idea of stumbling.

The OG entirely suppresses this harshness by adding an *if*-clause and 'not': 'Sanctify the Lord; and he shall be your fear. *And if you trust in him*, he shall be to you as a sanctuary; and you shall *not* come against *him* as against a stumbling stone, neither as against a rock of falling.'⁴⁰ The Targum of Isaiah maintains the sense of proto-𝔐, but also resolves the abruptness by the addition of an *if*-clause, which explains that the addressees' disobedience will render God's *word* a stumbling stone:

> 8¹³ The Lord of Hosts, him shall you call holy; and let him be your fear and let him be your strength.¹⁴ *And if you will not hearken, his Memra shall be amongst you for vengeance* and for a stone of smiting, and for a rock of offence to the two houses of the princes of Israel, for a breaking, and for a stumbling, because the house of Israel has been separated.

---

37 θ' reads: τὸν [κύριον] τῶν δυνάμεων (with σ'), cf. Koch 1986, 58.

38 θ' reads: καὶ εἰς λίθον προσκόμματος (with σ'), cf. Koch 1986, 58.

39 Wildberger 1991, 356.

40 The Hebrew reads, לָאבֶן, 'as a stone'. The OG reads οὐχ ὡς λίθο[ς] ('not as a stone'). The scribe of the Hebrew text presupposed by the OG, or the Greek translator of OG, duplicated the letters לא, producing לא לאבן ('not as a stone'). This was either an intentional exegetical change or a scribal error.

Wildberger[41] notes how Isa. 8.14 contrasts starkly with a common traditional theme, where 'rock' designates God as protector of Israel: the pious are protected from striking their foot on the stone (אֶבֶן, Ps. 91.12) and Yahweh is praised as a rock (צוּר, 1 Sam. 2.2; Pss. 18.3, 32, 47; 19.15; 62.8; 89.27; Isa. 30.29).[42] From the 'snare', too, God rescues the pious (Pss. 91.3; 124.7; 141.9; 69.23).

Proto-𝔐 of Isa. 8.14, then, presents a puzzle: God as both holy *and* a stumbling stone to Israel. This 'unprecedented tension within Isaiah's thinking about God'[43] resonates curiously closely with Paul's anxieties about the fate of Israel in Romans (cf. Rom. 3.5; 9.6; 10.1; 11.1, 15). Paul approaches the passage with a similar puzzle; many of his kin had not accepted God's Christ. In Isa. 8.14 Paul finds this stated in suitably stark terms: God represents both sanctuary and stumbling stone. But Isaiah also provides a solution. Together Isa. 28.16 and 8.14 present two alternatives – a 'precious cornerstone' or a 'stumbling stone'. This encapsulates Paul's conundrum. The encounter with Christ leaves only two options for Israel: to believe, or to stumble over that in which Israel fails to believe; to step or to stumble; to recognize or to mistake.[44] Together, Isa. 8.14 and 28.16 offer an answer: God himself provides the means by which some attain righteousness and others not, depending on their πίστις or ἀπιστία.[45]

When a passage which structures Paul's logic is characterized by distinct traditional sense contours, the question of his preference arises. As we have seen in Sections 7.3.1–7.3.2, Paul can construct substantial arguments from combinations of logically structural passages. For instance, Gen. 15.6 *plus* Gen. 17.10-14; Gen. 18.10, 14 *plus* Gen. 21.12 *plus* Gen. 25.23. By means of this *Mischzitat*, Isa. 8.14 and 28.16, he associates verbal features common to both passages. 'Stone' occurs in both passages (λίθος, πέτρας, Isa. 8.14; λίθος, Isa. 28.16). Both concern the Temple sanctuary (ἁγίασμα/מִקְדָּשׁ Isa. 8.14; Σιων/צִיוֹן Isa. 28.16) and both relate to Jerusalemites' transgressions: Isa. 8.14 refers to the stumbling of 'both houses of Israel' and 'the inhabitants of Jerusalem', while Isa. 28.14-16 addresses the 'scoffers who rule this people in Jerusalem' (Isa. 28.14); that is, the 'drunkards of Ephraim' (vv. 1-2). However, both offer hope: Isa. 8.14 concerns God's redemption and Isa. 28.16

41 Wildberger 1991, 356.

42 Note, however, how the LXX Psalms persistently suppresses the rock image for God, simply using θεός (so Olofsson 1990, 35–45). The OG of Deuteronomy 32 does likewise: 𝔐 of Deuteronomy 32 refers to Israel's God as a צוּר six times (Deut. 32.4, 13, 15, 18, 30, 31). OG Deut. 32 renders all six occurrences with θεός. Even in 32.37 where 𝔐 designates the foreign gods to which Israel turned (v. 16 f.) as צוּר, the OG renders οἱ θεοί. Only in Deut. 32.13 does OG offer πέτρας, that is: ἐθήλασαν μέλι ἐκ πέτρας καὶ ἔλαιον ἐκ στερεᾶς πέτρας. Here πέτρας respectively parallels סֶלַע and צוּר of 𝔐, but in neither case is a metaphor for God intended in Hebrew or Greek.

43 Wildberger 1991, 361.

44 So also 1 Cor. 1.22-23: 'to the Jews a σκάνδαλον, and to the Greeks foolishness', but to believers 'Christ the power of God, and the wisdom of God', suggesting Paul's reflection on Isa. 8.14^PM (σκάνδαλον) prior to the writing of Romans.

45 Paul considers that some, while presently excluded, will be included in the end, cf. Rom. 11.25-32.

promises God's vindication of the faithful one ('he will not be ashamed'). Paul combines Isaiah's uniquely harsh statement of Isa. 8.14 with the positive declaration that 'the one who believes' in the stone of Isa. 28.16 'will not be ashamed'. He mitigates the severity of Isa. 8.14 in light of the more usual image of God as a 'protective rock'. Isa. 8.14[OG], which offers none of these interpretive possibilities, simply does not resonate with Paul's concerns in Romans 9–11.

Isa. 8.14 speaks to Paul's concerns for Israel regarding many of his kinfolk's rejection of his gospel. While we cannot assume that Paul expected the audience (except, perhaps, the most erudite) to detect the exegetical process outlined above, Paul does *explicitly* express his concerns about his kin throughout the letter (Rom. 3.1-4; 9.1-6; 10.1-5; 11.1-36) in a manner easily followed by an audience of literary non-experts. To the uninitiated the citation provides a rhetorically cogent endorsement of his argument from ancestral scripture.

While the majority of Paul's Isaiah citations broadly reflecting the OG-form are supportive, the form of Isa. 8.14[PM] Paul cites semantically structures his thought, and *only* this form is useful. Therefore, were Paul aware of the OG-form, he would prefer Isa. 8.14[PM] here. However, it is impossible to prove that he preferred one of these known alternatives because we should *expect* to find no trace of the semantically unserviceable OG-form in his text, as is indeed the case. Nevertheless, as a contemporary exegetical practice, the possibility of Paul's preference here is less remarkable than commonly claimed. This would not amount to attributing to him anachronistically a text-critical interest in lexical variation. Rather, the examples of 'supportive' citations (see Sections 7.2.1–7.2.3, above) show that lexical fidelity to sources is rarely his primary concern. Indeed, in his citation Paul makes lexical changes to Isa. 8.14[PM]: he integrates a single phrase from Isa. 8.14[PM] – λίθον προσκόμματος καὶ πέτραν σκανδάλου – into the syntax of Isa. 28.16 in order to increase rhetorical congruence between his source and his argument. Notably, the sense contour that structures Pauline logic, which appears to be of primary concern to him, remains unaffected by his lexical intervention.

7.3.4 *The structural substance of Isaiah 25.8[PM] in 1 Corinthians 15*

Table 7.3 Isaiah 25.8

Isa. 25.8[LXX]	1 Cor. 15.54	Isa. 25.8[MT]	1QIsa.[a]	1QIsa.[b]
κατέπιεν ὁ θάνατος	κατεπόθη ὁ θάνατος	בִּלַּע הַמָּוֶת	בלע המות	
ἰσχύσας	εἰς νῖκος.	לָנֶצַח	לנצח	
καὶ πάλιν ἀφεῖλεν		וּמָחָה אֲדֹנָי	ומחה אדוני	
ὁ θεὸς		יְהוָה	יהוה	
πᾶν δάκρυον ἀπὸ		דִּמְעָה מֵעַל	דמעה מעל	
παντὸς προσώπου		כָּל־פָּנִים	כל פנים	

(continued)

Isa. 25.8[LXX]	1 Cor. 15.54	Isa. 25.8𝔐	1QIsa.ᵃ	1QIsa.ᵇ
τὸ ὄνειδος τοῦ λαοῦ		וְחֶרְפַּת עַמּוֹ	וחרפת עמו	וחרפת עמו
ἀφεῖλεν		יָסִיר	יסיר	יסיר
ἀπὸ πάσης τῆς γῆς		מֵעַל כָּל־הָאָרֶץ	מעל כל הארץ	
τὸ γὰρ στόμα		כִּי	כי	
κυρίου ἐλάλησεν		יְהוָה דִּבֵּר:	יהוה דבר	

Isa. 25⁸ LXX	Isa. 25⁸ MT
Death has prevailed[46]	He will[47] swallow up death
and swallowed up;	in victory;
but again	and
the Lord God has taken away every tear	the Lord God will wipe away tears
from every face.	from off all faces;
He has taken away	and the rebuke of his people
the reproach of the people	shall he take away
from all the earth:	from off all the earth:
for the mouth	for
of the Lord has spoken	the Lord hath spoken

The Hebrew verb נצח means 'be pre-eminent, enduring'. The noun נֵצַח signifies 'eminence, enduring, prevalence'.[48] The OG generally translates 'forever' (εἰς τέλος, εἰς τὸν αἰῶνα).[49] In Aramaic, נצח assumes the meaning 'exceed', 'succeed' or 'be victorious'.[50] The Hebrew meaning of נצח was influenced by the Aramaic 'victory', as the use of (κατ)ἰσχύω for נצח (OG Jer. 15.18 and Isa. 25.8) shows. In the LXX, the nouns νίκη and νῖκος always parallel נֶצַח and נֵצַח of proto-𝔐.[51]

Isa. 25.8a^OG and proto-𝔐 represent distinct sense contours. From v. 5, proto-𝔐 predicts that death 'will be swallowed' (*Pu'al* imperfect, בלע) by God, who will comfort his people. By contrast, the OG reads בלע as *Pi'el* perfect, whereby death, as usual, has 'swallowed up' (κατέπιεν) 'mightily' (ἰσχύσας). In the OG, death's initial virulent gulping, followed by God's comforting His people (v. 8), corresponds with

46 ἰσχύσας, aorist adverbial participle (from ἰσχύω) relating to κατέπιεν. Koch (1986, 61 [16]): 'Mächtig geworden, verschlang der Tod'.

47 *Pi'el* perfect בלע appears within a chain of *waw*-consecutive perfects. The passage narrates the future.

48 Brown *et al.* 1979, 663. Hence, in *Pi'el* 'lead'; 'oversee'; 'supervise'.

49 So too OG Isa. 13.20; 28.28; 33.20.

50 Levy 1924 vol. II 'נצח'; 'hervorragen, übertreffen', '(be)siegen'.

51 Hatch *et al.* 1998, 945. In the LXX, νικάω corresponds with זָכָה (Ps. 50.6[LXX] [51.4]), חָמַד (Prov. 6.25), and נֶצַח (Hab. 3.19).

the violence and injustice of 'wicked men' (ἀνθρώπων πονηρῶν, v. 4) and 'ungodly men' (ἀνθρώπων ἀσεβῶν, v. 5), from whom God then delivers His people.[52]

Paul's citation is close to known G^{HR} forms of the verse, especially θ'.

Table 7.4 Isaiah 25.8 α' θ' σ'

LXX	α'	θ'	σ'	𝔐
κατέπιεν	καταποντίσει	κατεπόθη	καταποθῆναι ποιήσει	בִּלַּע
ὁ θάνατος	τόν θάνατον	ὁ θάνατος	τόν θάνατον	הַמָּוֶת
ἰσχύσας	εἰς νῖκος	εἰς νῖκος	εἰς τέλος	לָנֶצַח
	He will sink	Death has been	['God's anointing', v. 7]	
	death	swallowed up	will cause death to be	
	in victory	in victory	swallowed up at the end[53]	

Paul's reading εἰς νῖκος agrees syntactically with G^{HR}, against OG's ἰσχύσας. The reading καταποντίσει accords with Aquila's usual rendering of בלע with καταποντίζειν. In α' God is subject of the verb (καταποντίσει). In σ' God's *anointing* (v. 7) is the subject of the verb (ποιήσει [κατεποθῆναι]), implying 𝔐's *Pi'el* pointing (בִּלַּע). 1 Corinthians 15 and θ' stand between the OG and 𝔐. As in the OG, ὁ θάνατος is the subject of the verb (LXX κατέπιεν; 1 Cor. 15.54, θ' κατεπόθη). However, because in 1 Corinthians and θ' the verb is now passive, ὁ θάνατος is 'swallowed up' (by God in 𝔐, α'; by God's anointing in σ'). Thus, despite lexical and grammatical variation among all witnesses, the OG sense contour, in which death 'swallows', stands in conspicuous opposition to the sense contour of the entire pM group (α' σ' θ' 1 Cor. 15.54), in which God swallows death.

While in 𝔐 God is the subject of בִּלַּע (*Pi'el*), OG translator reads 'death' (הַמָּוֶת) as the subject, since the Hebrew accusative marker is lacking.[54] 𝔐 and 1QIsa.ᵃ agree consonantally (בלע). However, in the *plene* orthography of a number of Judaean manuscripts, '*Yod* as mater lectionis' represents *sérê* or *hîreq*.[55] Thus, the *Pi'el* of

---

52 OG Isaiah 25 differs consistently from 𝔐 in that the 'strong peoples', 'ruthless nations', 'noisy aliens' and 'ruthless nations' (25.3-4 𝔐) become the 'poor', 'needy', 'thirsty' and 'injured' in Isa. 25.3-4ᴼᴳ. In the OG these suffering parties are God's people, whom He saves. This element is either absent or very unclear in 𝔐. Thus Isa. 25.8ᴼᴳ, where 'death' prevails but God 'once again' comforts his people, fits into OG's idiosyncratic narrative. This suggests that Paul's source for Isa. 25.8 cannot have represented a discrete Hebraizing revision of this verse only (as Koch suggests, cf. Section 1.2.1, above) because a single harmonization of this verse alone with the pM-form of Isaiah 25 would be incongruous with the remaining OG context. Thus all of Isaiah 25 in this copy must have represented the pM-form, not just v. 8.

53 Over fifty LXX Psalms parallel למנצח (לָנֶצַח) with εἰς τὸ τέλος (Williams 2001, 259). Van der Kooij finds hermeneutical and translation-technical similarities between καιγε and Psalmsᴸˣˣ (Williams 2001, 251).

54 𝔐 and 1QIsa.ᵃ agree in reading בִּלַּע הַמָּוֶת, not בִּלַּע אֶת הַמָּוֶת.

55 Numerous examples from 1QIsa.ᵃ (Kutscher 1974, 149–153). Cases where *yod* represents a medial Sérê (Qimron 1986, 19–20).

בלע (בְּלַע) spelled בילע could be read as *Pu'al* perfect (בֻּלַּע) because *yod* and *waw* are frequently indistinguishable in Hasmonaean hands. (The reverse is also possible, where an original בֻּלַּע became בילע and finally בְּלַע.) Thus, κατεπόθη, attested by Paul and θ', might derive not from an innovative rationalizing of the proto-Masoretic בְּלַע, but from a tradition of reading בֻּלַּע in place of בילע.

7.3.4.1 *Isaiah 25.8ᵖᴹ in 1 Corinthians 15.54*

Of the occurrences of the noun θάνατος in the Septuagint, none speak of God's destruction of death.[56] Only Isa. 25.8ᵖᴹ refers to death's final destruction. The pM sense contour of Isa. 25.8 cited in 1 Cor. 15.54 uniquely structures Paul's logic. In contrast, the OG is unusable.

The explicit argument

According to commentators, Corinthian doubts about the resurrection of the dead (15.12) presuppose a physical or metaphysical position.[57] Whatever the precise nature of their objection, Paul's response is primarily Christological. His argument is not a straightforward assertion of the resurrection of the dead. Rather, he identifies Christ's erasure of Sin *as* Christ's defeat of Death. His assumption that *they* believe that they are already saved from Sin through Christ's resurrection pervades the chapter (vv. 2-3, 14, 17, 34, 56, 58), a belief that serves as his rhetorical lever and lends teeth to the threat that their faith might be futile (15.2, 14, 58). His strategy in this chapter, then, is to argue that the premise they accept (Christ saves from Sin) entails the position they currently deny (resurrection of the dead).

In vv. 1-11 he calls the Corinthians as chief witnesses in an auspicious list of witnesses to the veracity of his gospel: that Christ's resurrection saves from sins (15.1-3). The syllogism that follows in vv. 12-19 is no more than a blunt assertion that Christ's resurrection precipitates believers' resurrection.[58] But the rhetorical

---

56 Using Hatch *et al.* 1998 (*ad loc.*), I have surveyed the occurrences of θάνατος in the Septuagint. A number of common ideas regarding God's power over death emerge, but none implies an ultimate defeat of death. *Human death displeases God* (e.g. Ps. 116.15 [115.6]; Ezek. 18.32; 33.11; Wis. 1.12; 2.24). *Humans call on God to protect them from death* (e.g. Ps. 13.3 [12.4]; Prov. 24.11; Ps. 9.13 [9.14]; 33.19 [32.18]; 89.48 [88.49]). *Some virtues deliver from* (ῥύομαι) *death* (e.g. Tob. 4.10 [charity]; 12.9 [almsgiving]; Prov. 10.2 [righteousness]). *God has power to save particular humans from death* (e.g. Job 7.15; 33.19; Ps. 118.18 [117.18]; Wis. 16.13; Sir. 48.5 [God can raise a corpse by Elijah's hand]; Hos. 13.14).

57 Some propose a radical Hellenistic body/spirit dualism, e.g. Fee 1987, 11, 715. But according to Adams (2000, 102), this radical dualism constituted an extreme interpretation of Plato that is uncharacteristic prior to the second–third century CE (ibid., 41–81). The Corinthians' view of spirit and body was more hierarchical than dualistic, tracking their notion of social relations as a microcosm of the universe (cf. Barclay 1992, 69–70). Asher (2000) has persuasively argued that theirs is a Greek-philosophical denial that terrestrial materials can occupy celestial space. See further Sider 1977; Wedderburn 1987; Tuckett 1996.

58 Contrary to many commentators, the syllogism is far from logically compelling. The Corinthians could accept that Christ rose from the dead without believing they would do the same. Other resurrection accounts in antiquity were not considered to result in a general resurrection of others. For Graeco-Roman

force of this assertion is to engender anxiety: their denial of resurrection is really an admission that they are not saved. The futility of believing in vain (15.14; cf. 15.2) and the hopelessness of remaining in their sins (15.17) belongs to the mortal state of Adam (15.21a, 22a). Paul claims that Christ reverses this state of human mortality (15.21b, 22b) because His resurrection has a universal effect: the quality of the 'first fruits' determines the quality of the whole harvest (15.20, 23). But the logic of this claim resides in the following six verses (15.23-28). That is, Christ's resurrection inevitably begins a process of conquests in which cosmic powers are subordinated. Paul locates humans' present subjugation to Adam's mortality (δι' ἀνθρώπου θάνατος, 15.21a) within a wider narrative of cosmic restoration. Christ's reversal of mortal-ity, introduced in 15.21b (δι' ἀνθρώπου ἀνάστασις νεκρῶν), belongs to a process of 'subjugation' of 'enemies' that culminates in Christ's defeat of Death (15.26). He warns them (15.29-34) that their present behaviour during this interim is inconsistent with their denial of resurrection (15.29-34).[59] He now directly broaches the grounds of their denial (15.35-54b; 'someone might say . . .', v .35), accommodating worries about the incompatibility of terrestrial and celestial materials, which resurrection implies to them, and correcting by appeal to the philosophical principle of change.[60] To the process of cosmic restoration initiated by Christ's resurrection (15.20-28), then, belongs the sequential transformation of terrestrial mortals, like Adam, into celestial immortals in Christ (15.35-54a). Paul thereby identifies this physical 'change' as part of the process of cosmic restoration (15.20-28, 54b-57) that forms the centre of his argument.

And with this resolution of their cosmological concerns, he presents in 15.54b-58 an interpretation of ὁ λόγος ὁ γεγραμμένος that encapsulates the entire argument of the chapter: the eradication of Sin is the defeat of Death. The victory which God gives 'us' (15.57) is the salvation from Sin that Christ's resurrection affords believers (15.56), the premise established at the outset (15.1-3). The final assurance in 15.58, that their 'labour in the Lord is not in vain' (οὐκ ἔστιν κενός), resolves the initial threat that they trusted in this salvation in vain (ἐκτὸς εἰ μὴ εἰκῇ ἐπιστεύσατε, 15.2; κενὴ καὶ ἡ πίστις ὑμῶν, 15.14).

Sin is Death's sting; that is, Sin is what makes Death fatal (15.56). Human mortal-ity (cf. v. 21), Death's victory, has been swallowed in Christ's victory (15.54b, cf. vv. 26, 57). Whatever the relevance for the Corinthians of Paul's reference to the law here, by 'disempowering' Sin (ἡ δύναμις τῆς ἁμαρτίας, 15.56) Christ removes Death's fatal

---

resurrections see Smith 1978, 118f.; Apollonius' resurrection of a dead girl; Lucan's *Pharsalia* VI 624-830 and *Philopseudes* 26f.; *Papyri Graecae Magicae* XIII 277ff. and XIXb. Also Elisha's raising of the Shunammite's son (2 Kgs 4.32-35).

59 Whether v. 29 refers to a practice of vicarious baptism 'on behalf of' the dead (as often proposed), or 'in the name of' apostles who are – according to the Corinthian denial of resurrection – truly dead (cf. White 1997; Hull 2005), Paul is arguing from experience that the Corinthians' views are inconsistent with their behaviour.

60 Asher 2000.

sting. If Sin is disempowered, Death is disarmed. Thus, Christ's victory over Sin is the defeat of Death introduced explicitly into the argument at 15.26 (ἔσχατος ἐχθρὸς καταργεῖται ὁ θάνατος). There the language of subjugation (ὑποτάσσω, vv. 27-28) and destruction (καταργέω, vv. 24, 26) of 'enemies' already invoked the semantic field of victory. So in these final five verses of ch. 15, Paul identifies Christ's reversal of human mortality (15.21-22) as Christ's victory over Sin.

In declaring Death the 'final enemy' in 15.26, Paul shifts the perspective from many individual deaths (οἱ νεκροί, vv. 12, 13, 20; πάντες ἀποθνῄσκουσιν v. 22; οἱ κοιμηθέντες v. 18) to Death personified. Likewise the individual sins of vv. 3 (ἁμαρτία ἡμῶν), 17 (ἁμαρτία ὑμῶν), and 34 (μὴ ἁμαρτάνετε) become Sin in v. 56, now identified as the source of human mortality, Death's fatal barb (κέντρον).[61] Thus, at the conclusion of the argument Sin and Death emerge as two of the cosmic powers that Christ is said to subjugate in 15.23-28. The announcement of the defeat of Death in 15.26, then, is a rhetorical crux. Moving from individual deaths and sins to the personified agents of 15.54b-57, Paul is able to explain how Christ's resurrection engenders that of all believers (15.21-22) by conquering the fatality of Death, conceived as the culmination in a sequence of victories over various cosmic enemies (15.24) that have so far prevented God from being 'all in all' (15.28). In 15.54b-57 Sin emerges as that cosmic power whose destruction is Death's undoing.

Paul's private exegetical process

If 1 Cor. 15.26 is a rhetorical crux, it is also an exegetical crux founded on Paul's interpretation of Isa. 25.8[PM], which he reads as a commentary on Genesis 2–3. This interpretation logically structures the argument of 1 Corinthians 15. However, Paul did not intend his audience to follow this exegetical process, which is never presented explicitly and surfaces only obscurely throughout the chapter.

It is apparent from 1 Cor. 15.21a (δι' ἀνθρώπου θάνατος) and 22a (ἐν τῷ Ἀδὰμ πάντες ἀποθνῄσκουσιν) that Paul finds in Genesis 2–3 the origin of human mortality.[62] Paul first invokes Adam as representative of a universal mortal state in order to highlight the universal effect of Christ's resurrection for believers (15.21b, 22b). Paul then attributes this mortality to humans' subjugation to a cosmic enemy, Death (15.26). He apportions no blame to Adam for human mortality, indeed according to 15.44-49 Adam and humans in general are mortal simply because they are terrestrial creatures, who must be physically changed in order to inhabit eternal celestial space.

While Genesis can be understood to narrate the origin of Death, it offers no hint

---

61 Outside ch. 15 ἁμάρτημα appears once (1 Cor. 6.18) and ἁμαρτάνω three times (1 Cor. 6.18, 7.36, 8.12). These relate to the subversion of proper social relations (1 Cor. 7.36, 8.12) or corporate group membership (1 Cor. 6.18). In ch. 15 sin has a different quality.

62 Gen. 2.17 and 3.3, in conjunction with the narrative evidence that the humans did not die immediately, could be taken to indicate that they were immortal in Eden prior to their disobedience (and Romans 5 can be understood this way). But this is certainly not a self-evident reading; other verses, like Gen. 3.17 and 22, suggest that the humans were never immortal. However Paul resolved this is immaterial here.

of Death's annulment. Paul finds this annulment in Isa. 25.8ᴾᴹ, which he now uses to structure the argument. Isa. 25.8ᴾᴹ lies at the logical heart of 1 Cor. 15.20-28, determining both the argument that Christ reverses human mortality (15.21b, 22b) through a process of conquests initiated by His resurrection, and the key assertion that Death is the arch-enemy whose defeat consummates this process of cosmic restoration (15.26). Paul's subtle appeal to two Psalms,⁶³ whose language of 'subjugation' (Pss. 8.6 and 110.1) and 'enemies' (Ps. 110.1; cf. Ps. 8.2) reflects the victory over death referred to in Isa. 25.8ᴾᴹ, prepares the way for Paul's presentation of Death and Sin as personified cosmic agents in 15.54b-57. Paul's appeal to these Psalms is exegetically determined by the guiding sense contour of Isa. 25.8ᴾᴹ.

When Paul concludes that Sin is Death's fatal property (15.54b-57), Sin and Death are now personified agents belonging to the powerful enemies of 15.23-28. The unique sense contour of Isa. 25.8ᴾᴹ asserts that Death is swallowed in 'victory'; that is, Christ's victory (cf. 15.26, 57). Paul's modifications of Hosea 13.14ᴸˣˣ allow him to present Sin as Death's erstwhile victory.⁶⁴ Death now is disarmed, its sting disempowered. Paul's changes to Hos. 13.14ᴸˣˣ are themselves determined by the sense contour of Isa. 25.8ᴾᴹ.

Isa. 25.8ᴾᴹ stands at the exegetical epicentre of the argument. Its sense contour presents conquest as the logical basis for the narrative of cosmic restoration (15.20-28), a narrative which itself gives logical substance to the blunt assertion in the previous section, that Christ's resurrection entails a general resurrection (15.12-19). Isa. 25.8ᴾᴹ formally structures the argument from 15.26 onward, finally appearing as a citation in 15.54b, where Hos. 13.14ᴸˣˣ is modified so that Death's erstwhile victory can be identified as Sin (1 Cor. 15.55-56).

Comparison of Romans 5–8 with 1 Corinthians 15 is instructive. In both passages: Paul closely relates Sin and Death, personified agents, as factors determining the state from which Christ saves humans;⁶⁵ Paul traces the origin of a present human state to Adam;⁶⁶ Christ's erasure of Sin is related to the resurrection of dead believers,⁶⁷ a resurrection which is part of a wider narrative of cosmic restoration.⁶⁸ However,

---

63 There is no explicit indication to a listening audience that Paul refers to Ps. 110.1. Koch (1986, 22) counts Ps. 8.6 as a citation 'emphasised through subsequent interpretation' in Paul's text, but not formally introduced (γὰρ ... ὅταν δὲ εἴπῃ ὅτι, 1 Cor. 15.27).

64 Hos 13.14ᴸˣˣ ποῦ ἡ δίκη σου θάνατε ποῦ τὸ κέντρον σου ᾅδη; 1 Cor. 15.55 ποῦ σου, θάνατε, τὸ νῖκος; ποῦ σου, θάνατε, τὸ κέντρον; In Paul's citation Death's δίκη (Hos. 13.14ᴸˣˣ) becomes Death's νῖκος to correspond with Christ's νῖκος, which Paul finds in his citation of Isa. 25.8ᴾᴹ in 1 Cor. 15.54b. Perhaps Paul derives νῖκος from νίκη, which is visually and aurally close to δίκη. Indeed, Paul apparently sees 'punitive justice' (δίκη) and 'victory' as morally cognate. Paul dispenses with 'Hades', the synonym for 'Death' (Hos. 13.14), repeating θάνατος to produce emphatic consistency in Paul's exegesis.

65 Rom. 5.12-21; 1 Cor. 15.54b-56.

66 Rom. 5.12-21; 1 Cor. 15.21-22, 45-49.

67 e.g. Rom. 6.4-5, 9; 7.4; 8.11, 23. Cf. 4.17; 11.15; 14.9.

68 Cosmic restoration (Rom. 8.18-39) is connected with resurrection, esp. 8.23. Paul invokes a similar exalted image of cosmic restoration in 11.36, once the full number of the Gentiles has come in (11.25) and

these commonalities belie differences, which highlight the distinct argument of 1 Corinthians 15 and the way in which Isa. 25.8ᴾᴹ uniquely structures its logic.

In 1 Corinthians 15 resurrection is the contentious issue. Thus, while Paul establishes that resurrection inevitably follows Christ's eradication of Sin, he does not dwell on arguments demonstrating this eradication of Sin because it is not only assumed but forms his principal rhetorical lever. Romans 5–8 shows that when his purpose is to *argue* that faith in Christ frees from Sin, the eradication of Death receives less emphasis. Indeed, the resurrection of the believers' bodies as part of Christ's cosmic restoration is mentioned throughout as though assumed by the Roman audience.[69] By contrast, in 1 Corinthians 15 the narrative of cosmic restoration constitutes the logical framework for Paul's assertion that resurrection follows Christ's erasure of Sin. This is why Paul does not apportion blame to Adam for the origin of Sin in this argument,[70] because Christ's erasure of *believers'* sins (including the Corinthians') founds Paul's argument that resurrection is inevitable for believers. In 1 Corinthians 15 the audience's *experience* of Christ's erasure of sins, and ultimately of Sin as an agent, gives the argument persuasive force.

Whereas in 1 Corinthians 15 Christ's erasure of Sin is the rhetorical solution in Paul's argument, in Romans 5–8 Sin is the problem. Romans 5–8 concerns the question of how to escape Sin within a discussion of two competing alternatives: law observance and faith. Here Paul argues that Sin itself sabotages any human effort to be sinless through law observance, while faith in Christ breaks this deadlock by liberating the believer from Sin, reversing mortality and allowing the believer to fulfil the δικαίωμα of the law (Rom. 8.4). For this reason Paul seeks explicitly to establish: the origin of Sin's universal effect (Adam's disobedience); the reversal of this effect (Christ's obedience); and the solution for believers (faith in Christ). Exegetically deriving the origin of Sin as a human state from Genesis 2–3 (which he takes to narrate Adam's disobedience), Paul finds Christ's reversal of this state in Isa. 53.11ᴾᴹ (which he takes to narrate Christ's obedience). These interpretations of Genesis 2–3 and Isa. 53.11ᴾᴹ are represented respectively in Rom. 5.19a (ὥσπερ γὰρ διὰ τῆς παρακοῆς τοῦ ἑνὸς ἀνθρώπου ἁμαρτωλοὶ κατεστάθησαν οἱ πολλοί) and 19b (οὕτως καὶ διὰ τῆς ὑπακοῆς τοῦ ἑνὸς δίκαιοι κατασταθήσονται οἱ πολλοί). Interestingly, only the distinct sense contour of Isa. 53.11ᴾᴹ serves this purpose.[71]

Paul broadly attributes Death's influence to Sin in both arguments (1 Cor. 15.56 τὸ

---

after 'all Israel' (11.26) then 'everyone' (11.32) is saved. Phil. 3.20-21 also relates the resurrection of the dead (cf. 3.9-11) with cosmic restoration through Christ's subjugation of powers.

69 See the previous two footnotes.

70 As noted above, Adam is merely a paradigm for the universal mortality that Christ's resurrection reverses (15.21-22, 45-49).

71 The sense contour of Isa. 53.11ᴾᴹ structures Rom. 5.19b, which encapsulates Paul's argument that Christ makes many righteous. Isa. 53.11ᴾᴹ reads: 'The righteous one, my servant, shall make many righteous . . .' (בְּדַעְתּוֹ יַצְדִּיק צַדִּיק עַבְדִּי לָרַבִּים). By contrast, in Isa. 53.11ᴼᴳ God is pleased 'to justify the just one who serves many well'. In the latter case only one favoured individual is made righteous, a sense contour unusable for Paul in Romans 5.

κέντρον τοῦ θανάτου ἡ ἁμαρτία; Rom. 5.12 διὰ τῆς ἁμαρτίας ὁ θάνατος [εἰσῆλθεν])
and Paul's obscure reference to the law in 1 Cor. 15.56 suggests that ideas similar to
those in Romans 5 lurk in his mind. However, if such ideas lurk, they play no part in
the argument of 1 Corinthians 15, because Sin serves a distinct rhetorical function
in each case. The Corinthians already accept that faith in Christ saves from Sin (1
Cor. 15.1-3), whereas in Romans Paul must show that Sin is a congenital condition,
which can only be escaped through faith. Thus the Adamic origin of Sin is important
in Romans, while not at all in 1 Corinthians 15. While a process of cosmic restoration is seen elsewhere in Paul's thought,[72] the unique sense contour of Isa. 25.8ᵖᴹ
determines the special role of Death as final enemy in 1 Corinthians 15, which serves
his wider aim in the chapter.

Isa. 25.8ᵖᴹ structures the argument of 1 Corinthians 15. Since Paul only cites
Isa. 25.8 in the pM-form (and since nothing in his writing indicates that he knew
its OG-form), there is no certainty that he *preferred* the pM-form of this passage.
However, selection of a particular form of a passage belongs to the exegetical repertoire current in Paul's day. Since Isa. 25.8ᵖᴹ is integral to Paul's logic, in a way that
the alternative sense contour is not (a type B case; see Section 2.2.2), the choice of
this form would be imperative, were Paul aware of both. Moreover, Isa. 25.8 does
not structure Paul's thought in isolation. Rather, Paul interprets Genesis 2–3 through
Isa. 25.8, and this interpretation underlies his argument in 1 Corinthians 15. Thus,
his preference for the pM-form of Isa. 25.8 would not amount to an arbitrary and
isolated item of residual lexical detail in Paul's memory, but to his engagement with
the exegetical discussion reflected in his literary sources.

7.4 *The suitability argument*

Michel, Koch and Stanley all appeal to what I have called the 'suitability argument'.[73]
That is, because Paul occasionally cites a passage in a form apparently less suitable to
the logic of his argument than another available form, it is inferred that he is *generally*
ignorant of available alternative.[74] Koch presents five cases, Job 5.13; Isa. 25.8; 28.11;
59.20; Hos. 2.1ᴸˣˣ,[75] which I examine in the following sections.

The cumulative force of the suitability argument dissipates under closer inspection.
First, the form of each of the passages that Paul cites can be seen to suit his context
perfectly well. Second, my survey of the varied roles played by citations in Paul's

72 See Footnote 68, above.

73 Michel 1929; Stanley 1992; Koch 1986. See Sections 1.2.2.3 and 2.2.2, above.

74 Michel (1929, 68) thinks the form of Isa. 40.13ᴼᴳ and Exod.12.40ᴼᴳ, cited respectively in 1 Cor.
2.16 and Gal. 3.17, less suitable than 𝔐 in each case. Stanley 1992 cites Michel 1929, 68 (cf. Section
1.3.2, above). I gather together Koch's examples immediately below.

75 Isa. 25.8 (1 Cor. 15.54), Isa. 28.11 (1 Cor. 14.21) and Job 5.13 (1 Cor. 3.19) (Koch 1986, 80 [113]
contra Ellis 1957, 139); Hos. 2.1ᴸˣˣ (Rom. 9.25) (Koch 1986, 55 [34]); Isa. 59.20 (Rom. 11.26) (ibid.
1986, 177 [34]).

letters (Sections 7.2–7.2.3) undermines the founding assumption of the suitability argument: that there is always an identifiable 'most suitable' form of a passage for Paul's text and that, were he aware of alternatives, he would always prefer that form. I do not suggest that Paul preferred each of these forms because I consider none to be logically intrinsic to his argument. Rather, I argue that his appeal to each of these forms can demonstrate neither his ignorance of an alternative form in each case nor a general lack of awareness of textual plurality.

7.4.1 *Isaiah 25.8 (1 Corinthians 15.54)*

Paul cites Isa. 25.8 in a form identical to that of Theodotion. Koch argues that the aorist of θ' (κατεπόθη) is less suitable for Paul's argument than the future tense of α' (καταποντίσει) and σ' (κατεποθῆναι ποιήσει), which would better fit with Paul's future γενήσεται (1 Cor. 15.54). However, this case fails on two counts. First, Koch raises the syntactical issue of the temporal congruence between the citation and Paul's narration. But, as I have already observed, the general preoccupation with lexical differences between available forms obscures the relation of a particular sense contour to Paul's own citation context (see Sections 2.2.2–2.2.3, above).

Furthermore, Koch's argument that Theodotion's aorist is less suited to Paul's argument than Aquila and Symmachus' future is not compelling. The future γενήσεται in 1 Cor. 15.54 does not apply to the temporal aspects of Paul's narration of the future resurrection: that which 'will come about' is the '*word* which has been written' (γενήσεται ὁ λόγος ὁ γεγραμμένος). The aspects of Paul's description in 1 Cor. 15.50-54 are couched in the aorist infinitive[76] and the aorist subjunctive[77] in order to describe the necessary relation of discrete events on a particular occasion (when condition *x* pertains, then event *y* occurs).

Of course, Paul's narration of the resurrection in ch. 15 envisages a future moment in which the believers' transformation of state (already begun 'in Christ') will be completed. Yet, while the future tense is used eight times,[78] the chapter is generally characterized by the use of present tense.[79] Significantly, the destruction of Death is framed in the present tense: ἔσχατος ἐχθρὸς καταργεῖται ὁ θάνατος (1 Cor. 15.26). And essential aspects of Paul's narrative are expressed in the aorist.[80] Although for

---

76 15.50 κληρονομῆσαι οὐ δύναται; 15.53 δεῖ [. . .] ἐνδύσασθαι [. . .] ἐνδύσασθαι . . .

77 15.54 ὅταν [. . .] ἐνδύσηται [. . .] ἐνδύσηται . . .

78 Future: ζῳοποιηθήσονται 15.22; ὁ υἱὸς ὑποταγήσεται 15.28; φορέσομεν καὶ τὴν εἰκόνα τοῦ ἐπουρανίου 15.49; πάντες οὐ κοιμηθησόμεθα, πάντες δὲ ἀλλαγησόμεθα 15.51; σαλπίσει [. . .] ἐγερθήσονται [. . .] ἀλλαγησόμεθα 15.52.

79 Present: εἰ δὲ ἀνάστασις νεκρῶν οὐκ ἔστιν . . . 15.13; . . . εἴπερ ἄρα νεκροὶ οὐκ ἐγείρονται 15.15; εἰ γὰρ νεκροὶ οὐκ ἐγείρονται 15.16; ὅταν παραδιδῷ (subjunctive) 15.24; δεῖ γὰρ αὐτὸν βασιλεύειν (infinitive) 15.25; καταργεῖται ὁ θάνατος 15.26; εἰ ὅλως νεκροὶ οὐκ ἐγείρονται 15.29; εἰ νεκροὶ οὐκ ἐγείρονται 15.32; Πῶς ἐγείρονται οἱ νεκροί, ποίῳ δὲ σώματι ἔρχονται 15.35; σπείρεται ἐν φθορᾷ, ἐγείρεται ἐν ἀφθαρσίᾳ 15.42, ἐγείρεται ἐν δόξῃ [. . .] ἐγείρεται ἐν δυνάμει 15.43; ἐγείρεται σῶμα πνευματικόν 15.44; οὐδὲ [δύναται] [. . .] κληρονομεῖ 15.50.

80 The aorist subjunctive is used for grammatical reasons with ὅταν (ὅταν καταργήσῃ 15.24; θῇ

him the 'subjugation' lies in the future, Paul cites Ps. 8.6 in the aorist (πάντα γὰρ ὑπέταξεν ὑπὸ τοὺς πόδας αὐτοῦ, 1 Cor. 15.27). This rhetorically parallels the citation of the aorist construction of Isa. 25.8, which is in question. In fact, the entire discourse predicates a past event (νυνὶ δὲ Χριστὸς ἐγήγερται ἐκ νεκρῶν, 1 Cor. 15.20) that affects believers' present and future. Here the aorist of θ' (and 1 Cor. 15.54) is argu-ably well suited to the 'already/not yet' framework of Paul's thought. That is, Christ's resurrection has already changed the cosmos, and yet this change has still to reach completion (compare the like thought in Romans 8). Believers have been saved (they are 'in Christ'), yet Paul still requires them to behave *as though* they were saved (as though they were 'in Christ'). They *have been* sanctified, and so they must behave as ones who *are* sanctified (cf. 1 Cor. 6.9-11). 1 Corinthians 15 dwells on the present result of a past event (Christ's resurrection), a process unfolding now (15.23-28), only whose completion lies in the future (15.50f.). Paul is content for Isa. 25.8 to proclaim that death 'was swallowed' already, and sees no need to alter the present tense of the adjoining Hos. 13.14 (1 Cor. 15.45b-55), which asks 'Oh Death, where is thy sting?'. Here Paul is primarily interested in the defeat of Death – the sense contour shared by Aquila, Symmachus and Theodotion – rather than tense coherence, which he fre-quently changes at will in any case, in order to ease citation into his prose. Therefore, Koch's idea that the future tense of Aquila and Symmachus would be more suitable reflects more the commentator's grammatical focus regarding Paul's use of future tenses in this argument than Paul's ignorance of alternatives to Theodotion's form.

The second problem with Koch's suitability argument is his anachronistic assessment of the sources that could have been available to Paul. The close verbal cor-respondence between Paul's Isa. 25.8 citation and the second-century CE Theodotion revision (known from Patristic citations) suggests the existence of proto-Theodotion in the early first century, an inference supported by the Greek Minor Prophets Scroll (καιγε, also known as proto-Theodotion) and other first-century manuscript evidence (see Chapter 2). However, the late second to early third centuries CE forms of Aquila and Symmachus are generally considered reworkings of the earlier Theodotion revi-sion. Since Paul's citation of Isa. 25.8 is the earliest known witness to Theodotion's reading, it is anachronistic to consider Paul's 'failure' to choose the form offered by the apparently later α' or σ' as indicative of his ignorance of various forms of the verse.

7.4.2 *Isaiah 28.11ᴾᴹ (1 Corinthians 14.21)*

Paul cites Isa. 28.11ᴾᴹ in an otherwise unknown form. Koch considers that the minor-ity NT manuscript reading,[81] καὶ ἐν χειλέσιν ἑτέροις, 'weit besser zur [paulinischen]

15.25; ὅταν δὲ ὑποταγῇ 15.28; ὅταν ἐνδύσηται [. . .] ἐνδύσηται 15.54). I do not count the perfect (πάντα ὑποτέτακται) and aorist (ἐκτὸς τοῦ ὑποτάξαντος) of 15.27b because these bear internal temporal relations – corresponding with ὅταν δὲ εἴπῃ ὅτι [. . .] – that are independent of the rest of the narration.

81 Witnesses: P⁴⁶ Dˢ K L P 365 630 1175 1881 2495 𝔐 lat syr co (Koch 1986, 65 [31]); cf. Nestle *et al.* 1994, 465, who list: P⁴⁶ Dˢ F G 1881 𝔐 lat sy⁽ᵖ⁾ co; Mcionᴱ. Cf. Aland *et al.* 1994, 5f.

Verwendung passen würde'[82] than the majority reading of 1 Cor. 14.21, καὶ ἐν χείλεσιν ἑτέρων,[83] presumably because in the former the *language* is strange – as in 1 Corinthians 14 – rather than the 'strangers' (ἑτέρων) who speak it, in the latter.

However, significant for Paul's purpose is the sense contour that he cites. Only the pM-form[84] refers to God's efforts to communicate with people, which is precisely Paul's concern here. Paul continually stresses the indispensable and sole agency of the 'same spirit' as God's medium of prophetic communication, revelation of mysteries and transmission of knowledge (1 Cor. 2.10-13, 16; 12.4-6, 8-11, 13). The same spirit mediates various gifts (12.8-11, 27-30) which, used co-operatively, constitute community ('body', 12.12-27). In presenting the socially unifying 'love' (12.31–14.1) as the modus for the pursuit of 'prophecy' (14.1), Paul seeks to establish a cohesive communal behaviour by which God's communication with spiritually gifted believers is disseminated throughout the whole church.

Paul approves tongues (14.5, 9-10, 13-14, 16-17) but complains that the cacophony disrupts cohesion and edification. Thus, in 14.18 he renounces his own right to glossolalia for the greater communal good, favouring prophecy, by which God communicates with the whole assembly through direct revelation and its communal dissemination (14.3-4, 5, 12, 23, 26). In 14.10-19 Paul warns that the Corinthian babbling estranges brethren *within* the assembly: they become βάρβαρος to one another (v. 11). The ἕτερος (v. 17), ἄλλοι (vv. 19, 29) and the ἄλλος (v. 30) are brethren estranged by incomprehensible babbling. 'He who occupies *the position of* a non-initiate' (ὁ ἀναπληρῶν τὸν τόπον τοῦ ἰδιώτου, v. 16) is also a believer. Prevented by the obscure babbling from uttering 'the Amen', he is placed '*in the position of*' an ἰδιώτης.

Paul now moves from internal alienation (14.10-19) of brothers to uninitiated and unbelieving *outsiders* (ἰδιῶται ἢ ἄπιστοι, 14.22-24). Calling on the audience not to be 'children' or 'babes', but 'mature' (τέλειοι, 14.20; cf. 2.6; 13.10),[85] Paul distinguishes tongues, a 'signal' to unbelievers that believers are different ('mad'), from prophecy, an edifying sign for believers. However, while glossolalia estranges those who are already brothers and excludes outsiders, prophecy transforms the

---

82 Koch 1986, 65 appeals to this verse, among others, to demonstrate Paul's ignorance of more suitable forms; cf. ibid., 80 [113].

83 For וּבְלָשׁוֹן אַחֶרֶת 𝔐; cf. διὰ γλώσσης ἑτέρας LXX.

84 The form of Isa. 28.11 cited by Paul diverges from both 𝔐 and OG (cf. Koch 1986, 64–65; Stanley 1992, 199–200). There seems to be no direct evidence this reading prior to 1 Corinthians. However, Origen notes that he found an equivalent expression in Aquila's translation (ευρον γαρ τα ισοδυναμουντα τη λεξει ταυτη εν τη του α' ερμηνεια κειμενα, *Philocalia* 9.2; cf. Ziegler 1939, 217). Aquila uses the rare ἑτερογλώσσος for לָעֵז ('speak unintelligibly') in Ps. 113.1 (cf. Stanley 1992, 199; Koch 1986, 64 [29]). The Greek translator of Paul's source may have read לָעֵז instead of לָעֵג (note that if the left hand leg of a *gimel* in the Hasmonaean script of 1QIsaᵃ, for instance, were indistinct, the resulting letter would appear like *zayin*).

85 Paul accuses them of childishness throughout: 1.10 'ἐγώ + *genitive*' (Mitchell 1991); 3.1; 4.15f.; 13.8-13. The designation 'child/babe' seems to mean 'uninitiated' in 3.1 (contrasted with τέλειοι, 2.6); 13.11 (contrasted with τέλειον, 3.10); and 14.20 (contrasted with τέλειοι).

unbeliever *into* a believer (14.24-25). Thus, glossolalia alienates all while prophecy edifies brothers and *includes* outsiders.

Thus, Paul rhetorically constructs two kinds of 'foreigner': the estranged fraternal believer and the uninitiated Corinthian neighbour, a potential convert.[86] Both kinds are alienated because God's communication is not disseminated for edification, as it should be, so they are unable to grasp it. The rhetorical impact of this citation of Isa. 28.11ᵖᴹ, and Paul's own modifications of it in 1 Cor. 14.21,[87] lies in God's unsettling lament that 'this people' fails to heed *His* message. In Isaiah 28ᵐ 'this people's' failure to hear God's message resides in the nightmarish disarray of those responsible for its orderly dissemination.[88] Thus, His communication with the people amounts to the incomprehensible talk of 'men of strange tongues and with the lips of foreigners' (1 Cor. 14.21), which has the same semantic value as an attempt to speak to 'suckling' infants (28.9ᵐ; cf. 1 Cor. 14.20).

Paul and Isaiahᵐ share an interest in God's communication through intermediaries, which is not found in the OG. In the OG it is not *God* who attempts to speak to 'this people' but the wickedly drunken ἱερεὺς καὶ προφήτης of Isa. 28.7ᴼᴳ who are those who speak falsehood 'through contempt of the lips and through a strange tongue' in Isa. 28.11ᴼᴳ.[89] The OG-form is irrelevant to Paul, who in 1 Corinthians 14 is concerned with how *God's* communication with certain believers should edify the congregation. In the rhetorical context of Paul's citation of Isa. 28.11ᵖᴹ, the inability of 'this people' to grasp the strange talk of 'foreigners' becomes a warning against alienating babbling in the ἐκκλησία. Paul's addition of λέγει κύριος fits the prophetic context of 1 Corinthians 14, which concerns God's direct utterances to humans.[90]

86 Since Paul is arguing that the Corinthians become foreigners to each other and to unbelievers, the wording of Paul's citation, ἐν χειλέσιν ἑτέρων ('by the lips of strangers'), is suitable to the context, *pace* Koch, 1986, 65, 80 [13]; see Footnote 82, above.

87 Paul used a Gᴴᴿ but altered his source: adopting the first person λαλήσω; omitting λέγοντες [. . .] σύντριμμα; substituting οὐδ' οὕτως for οὐκ; conflating 28.11 and 12b καὶ οὐδ' οὕτως εἰσακούσονταί μου; adopting future tense εἰσακούιεν; adding λέγει κύριος (Koch 1986, 64–66, 112, 123, 151; Stanley 1992, 197–207).

88 The safety of 'this people' (28.11, 13) is jeopardized by corrupt leadership, represented by 'drunkards of Ephraim' (28.1, 3ᵐ), the drunken and confused 'priest and prophet' – who 'erring in vision and stumbling in judgement' fail to convey God's message (28.7-8ᵐ), and the 'scoffers who rule this people in Jerusalem' (28.14ᵐ), whose refuge is in lies and whose covenant is with death (28.15-18ᵐ). The failure of leaders, upon whose vicarious role the people's relationship with God depends, constitutes the worst imaginable breakdown of social order. Nevertheless, God hopes to reach a 'remnant of his people' (28.5ᵐ), restoring their 'crown' (in contrast to the trampled crown of the 'drunkards', 28.3), a remnant which might heed Him (28.13-14ᵐ) and which is represented by him 'who trusts' God's stone in Zion (28.16ᵐ).

89 Where in Isa. 28.7-11ᵐ 'He (God) will speak', in the OG 'they (priest and prophet) will speak' (compare 'they speak', 1QH 4.14). In ᵐ the phrase, 'This is rest: give rest to the weary and this is repose' (28.12aᵐ), is God's message, which 'this people' will not hear. By contrast, in the OG the phrase 'This is the rest to him that is hungry, and this is the calamity' is a drunken lie of the priests and prophets.

90 Ellis (1957, 107–112) grouped 1 Cor. 14.21 with the 'λέγει-Κύριος quotations', which diverge from LXX and ᵐ according to a pattern he attributes to the collection of prophetic *logia* in early Christian *testimonia*. Koch (1986, 65, cf. 139) suggests that Paul added λέγει-Κύριος himself in this and other cases.

I do not claim that Paul 'preferred' this form, because the citation does not seem logically to structure Paul's argument. However, I emphasize that, because the form of Isa. 28.11 that Paul cites is broadly suitable for Paul's argument, his use of this form does not evince his ignorance of other forms.

7.4.3 *Isaiah 59.20-21 (Romans 11.26)*

Scholars often observe that the unique variant ἥξει ἐκ Σιὼν does not fit Paul's purpose in Rom. 11.26 as well as would the OG-form of Isa. 59.20-21.[91] Since Paul is apparently worried about Israel's failure to accept Christ, they reason, OG's ἥξει ἕνεκεν Σιων (compare 𝔐's וּבָא לְצִיּוֹן) would be more suitable. However, the case can be seen quite differently. Throughout the letter, Paul argues that the righteousness of God is revealed for both Jews and Greeks. However, since Rom. 3.3 he has hinted that some Israelites might be 'unfaithful' (εἰ ἠπίστησάν τινες). Thus, ἀπιστέω in ch. 11 is best understood within the context of Deuteronomic and prophetic covenant language. That is, it is not that some of Israel do not 'believe',[92] but that they are 'unfaithful', *reneging* on fidelity to God's will. This argument reflects a recurrent pattern in Jewish scripture: Israel forgets the covenant with God, God punishes them, but God retains his fidelity to the covenant. God is faithful (μὴ ἡ ἀπιστία αὐτῶν τὴν πίστιν τοῦ θεοῦ καταργήσει; μὴ γένοιτο – 3.3-4) and he always leaves a remnant for himself with which to renew his covenant. Paul maintains precisely this idea at the end of Romans 9. To his supposedly radical interpretation of Hos. 2.25[LXX] [2.23] and 2.10[LXX] (that the 'not-my-people', which God favours, should be Gentiles) he gives an answer familiar to the Hebrew prophets: 'remnant theology' (in Rom. 9.27-29 via Isa. 10.22-23 and 1.9; and in Rom. 11.3 appealing to 'Elijah'). Therefore, his warning to Gentile believers in Rom. 11.13-24 is predicated on a traditional tendency for Israel to introspect on her own faithlessness. When Paul reaches Rom. 11.25, then, he is not trying to argue that God sent Christ for Israel's sake as such. Rather, he is still involved with appealing to a covenantal 'remnant tradition' in order to account for the 'hardening' that has 'come upon part of Israel' (11.25), arguing that *Gentile believers* are the means for God's salvation of Israel. This is part of his broader concerns for his kin, expressed throughout the letter; 'hardening' is identical with

---

Stanley suggests that this, and all of the occurrences of λέγει κύριος in Paul's 'orally dictated letters' (and in the speech of Stephen in Acts 7.49, cf. Peter's speech in Acts 2.17), 'might reflect the influence of biblical language on the oral reproduction of Scripture in the synagogue' (1992, 177).

91 For example, Schaller 1984, 203. Ellis (1957, 294) attributes to Paul both this variant and the combination of Isa. 59.20-21 with 27.9. Koch (1980, 188–189; 1986, 175–177) attributes the variant to a pre-Pauline Christological tradition (1986, 95, 241), attributing only the combination of 59.20-21 and 27.9 to Paul (1980, 187 [54]; 1986, 113 [3], 177). Stanley (1993, 123 [20]) argues that the variant (ἐκ Σιὼν) and the combination (Isa. 26.7-27.13 + 59.12-63.7) reflect a Jewish Diaspora perception of a militant Isaian narrative of political hope (Stanley 1993, 128–142, esp. 136ff.; cf. Footnote 14, above).

92 The translation 'believe', reminiscent of nineteenth- and twentieth-century empiricism, is inappropriate for the context of Romans 11.

the 'stumbling' of some, mentioned in 9.32-33 and 11.11,[93] precipitating his worries about their salvation (10.1; 11.14, 26). The difference between ἔνεκεν and ἐκ would not move him much at this point. If anything, the drift of his argument – that Gentile 'faithfulness' will ultimately save 'all Israel' (11.26) – leaves little need for a redeemer 'for the sake of' Israel. In this argument the redeemer has saved *Gentiles*, who, in turn, will save Israel through provoking jealousy. Indeed, Zion in Rom. 11.26 is not synonymous with Israel. At this stage in his argument, Paul is concerned with Israel's estrangement from God brought about by the faithlessness of some. The redeemer comes 'from Zion', the abode of God, to reach out to his estranged people, and in ch. 11 Paul presents his Gentile mission as playing an integral role in that process of reaching out. The idea four chapters later – that 'Christ became a servant to the circumcised to show God's truthfulness, in order to confirm the promises given to the patriarchs, and in order that the Gentiles might glorify God for his mercy' (Rom. 15.8-9) – maintains the intimate connection between the salvation of Israel and Paul's Gentile mission; so too the following string of citations depicting Israel and the Gentiles united in praise for God (Rom. 15.10-12). Since Romans 4, 'the promises to the Patriarchs' have been identified with the promise to the Gentiles through Abraham, archetype of Paul's faithful Gentiles. And in 15.19 Paul depicts his own Gentile mission – which, according to ch. 11 will save Israel in the end – proceeding in a wide arc *from Jerusalem* round to Illyricum, culminating in Rome, then Spain in the West. Paul confidently (τὴν διακονίαν μου δοξάζω, 11.13) sees the redeemer's trajectory from Zion into the Diaspora (11.26) described in his own mission. He certainly sees the fruits of his Gentile mission flowing *back* to Jerusalem as a kind of Gentile Temple offering (15.25-32), and asks for the Romans' support. The intimate connection between the salvation of Gentiles and Israel can be expressed the other way round, too: Israel's 'acceptance means *life from the dead*' (τίς ἡ πρόσλημψις [αὐτῶν] εἰ μὴ ζωὴ ἐκ νεκρῶν;). The resurrection of believers, at the heart of Paul's Gentile gospel, is contingent on Israel's acceptance in Rom. 11.15.

The form of this combined *logion* (Isa. 59.20-21 and 27.9) apparently originates in the Diaspora synagogue.[94] This citation in Rom. 11.26 does not logically structure Romans 11. Rather, it illustrates the assertion, expressed in 11.28-29, that God's 'gifts' to and 'call' of Israel 'are irrevocable' (11.29) because of the promises to the 'Patriarchs' (Rom. 11.28; 15.8; cf. 9.1-3). Paul wanted to end on a 'high note' by concluding that 'all' will be saved. Although rhetorically dramatic, neither this *logion*, nor Isa. 40.13 in the doxology of Rom. 11.33-34, structures the logic of his argument here. So, the context does not urge him to choose another form.

---

93 Note the correspondence of ideas in Rom. 9.31-32 (cf. Isa. 8.14) and 11.6-7 (cf. Ps. 68.23[LXX]). Failure to 'attain' (φθάνω εἰς; ἐπιτυγχάνω) what was 'sought' (διώκω; ἐπιζητέω). 'Stumbling' in 9.32-33 (προσκόπτω) (cf. 11.11, πταίω) is equivalent to 'hardening' in 11.7. Compare also παγίς and σκάνδαλον in 9.33 and 11.9 (Isa. 8.14; Ps. 68.23[LXX]).

94 Stanley 1993, see Footnote 91, above.

7.4.4 *Job 5.13ᵖᴹ (1 Corinthians 3.19)*

The claim that Paul's citation of Job 5.13ᵖᴹ (1 Cor. 3.19) is unsuitable[95] cannot carry weight because Paul only ever cites Job Gᴴᴿ. Therefore, no case can be made either way for Paul's preference for (or ignorance of) various forms of Job.

7.4.5 *Hosea 2.1ᴸˣˣ (Romans 9.25)*

The case of Hos 2.1ᴸˣˣ [1.10] (Rom. 9.25)[96] is similar because the reading τὴν ἠγαπημένην is a minority LXX manuscript reading.[97] Ziegler considers the reading τὴν ἠγαπημένην in Hos. 2.25bᴸˣˣ to be secondary in the LXX text tradition.[98] Although the appearance of this reading in Rom. 9.25 may have lent it currency in the later copying traditions,[99] Koch notes that the reading τὴν ἠγαπημένην can hardly derive from Paul, since ἀγαπάω does not figure in Romans 9, 'apart from the citation in Rom 9:13'.[100] In contrast, Koch notes that ἐλεέω (of A Q O L, etc.) recurs in Rom. 9.15, 18 and 23. Neither could Paul, for the same reason, have *preferred* the reading ἀγαπάω (found in some manuscripts[101]) to ἐλεέω. Hence, according to Koch, Paul's *Vorlage* must have supplied Paul with the reading τὴν ἠγαπημένην in Hos. 2.25bᴸˣˣ.

Yet, the form of Hos. 2.1ᴸˣˣ cited by Paul fits well into the context of Romans 9. With Mal. 1.2-3, it is one of two *explicit* citations in Romans 9 (vv. 13 and 25) that include the *only* two occurrences of ἀγαπάω in this chapter.[102] These form rhetorical parentheses in the argument, which will have had an impact on hearers, regardless of their familiarity with traditional Jewish literature. Hence, this form cannot be declared 'unsuitable' for Romans 9.

7.4.6 *Jeremiah 9.22-23ᴸˣˣ/1 Kingdoms 2.10 (1 Corinthians 1.31)*

Koch thinks that the passage that Paul explicitly cites in 1 Cor. 1.31 is an 'oral' form of Jer. 9.22-23ᴸˣˣ, known to Paul through pre-Pauline Jewish or early Christian tradition.[103] Koch considers this form less suitable than the traditional form. Others, however, see Paul's argument from 1 Cor. 1.17-30 as substantially structured around the traditional form of Jer. 9.22-23ᴸˣˣ, the explicit 'citation' of 1 Cor. 1.31 forming

---

95 Koch 1986, 80 [113], 72.

96 Koch 1986, 55 [34].

97 Witnessed only by B V 407 Laˢʷ against A Q O L, etc. Koch 1986, 55.

98 Deriving from the secondary B V 407 Laˢʷ reading τὴν ἠγαπημένην in Hos. 1.6, 8: 2.3 (Ziegler 1942; cf. Koch 1986, 55 [34]).

99 Koch 1986, 55 [34].

100 Ibid.

101 Ibid. A Q O L, etc.

102 'Love' is rhetorically significant. Ἀγαπάω only occurs three times in Romans 9–11; that is, in 9.13, 25 and 11.28, where it indicates God's love for Israel. In 9.25 God's love is associated with God calling believers from among the Jews and the Gentiles. Chapter 11 ends with Gentiles (v. 25) and Israel (v. 26) *all* being saved (v. 32). Paul's talk of God's (or Christ's) love for believers at the end of ch. 8 (vv. 35, 37, 39) prefigures this triumphant note of pan-ethnic reconciliation in ch. 11.

103 Koch 1986, 36. Stanley suggests, on the basis of 'striking echoes of Jer. 9:22' in 1 Cor. 1.27-28, that the formulation is Paul's own coinage (1992, 187).

a terse paraphrastic summary of this argument.[104] On this view, the traditional form that Koch feels would have been more suitable is already woven into Paul's prose.

7.4.7 *Concluding remarks*

Paul probably consulted various scrolls of Isaiah over the period of his letter writing. Wilk's analysis suggests that during the composition of Galatians, 1 and 2 Corinthians and Romans, Paul used several scrolls representing Isaiah[OG], *one* partial Hebraizing revision of Isaiah[OG], and *one* thorough Hebraizing revision of Isaiah[OG] (see Section 1.8.2, above).[105] The pM-forms of Isa. 8.14 and 25.8 examined above belong to this last source.

Exegetical use of textual plurality was current among ancient Jewish exegetes. Therefore, common objections to the notion of Paul's preference for pM-forms of some Isaiah passages are based on a misplaced vision of his historical context. Moreover, scholars often invoke some form of the 'suitability argument' to make a case against the general possibility of Paul's awareness and choice of alternatives. My distinction between various kinds of supportive citation (Sections 7.2–7.2.3) and structurally indispensable citations (Sections 7.3–7.3.4.1) undermines the assumption that there is always an identifiable most suitable form of a passage for Paul's logic. My analysis of the individual cases comprising the suitability argument dispels the claim to a cumulative case (Section 7.4). I point out that the commentators' preoccupation with assumed lexical suitability of available forms of a given passage obscures the role of sense contours in Paul's logic (Sections 2.2.2–2.2.3). I have shown that Paul's preference for a particular sense contour is possible within his socio-historical and exegetical context. I now turn to a case in which Paul's writing reveals his knowledge of two forms of the same passage.

7.5 *Two semantic forms of Isaiah 40.13 in 1 Corinthians 2.16*

Paul's verbal replication[106] of Isa. 40.13[OG] in 1 Cor. 2.16 is anticipated by his language a few verses earlier, language that presupposes Isa. 40.13[pM].[107] This suggests that he makes exegetical use of both forms.

Many consider this verbal replication of Isa. 40.13 a 'citation'. Verdicts vary regarding Paul's awareness of two available forms of this passage. For Michel, Paul did not know the 'Hebrew' version of the verse because רוּחַ ('spirit') 'would have

---

104   So, for example, Hooker 1990a, 106–112; 1990b, 139–154. Contrast Tuckett (2000, 416–423), who believes that the citation in 1 Cor. 1.31 derives from 1 Kgdms 2.10. Stanley (*ad loc.*) thinks that 1 Cor. 1.27-28 testifies to Paul's own loose rendering of 'biblical' Jer. 9.22-23[LXX].

105   Wilk 1998.

106   'Verbal replication' and 'verbal parallel'; see Section 6.3, above.

107   Verbal anticipation of a following citation is frequently observed in Paul's writing, cf. Chapter One, Footnotes 25 (Vollmer) and 96 (Michel), above.

suited' Paul's πνεῦμα-language in 1 Cor. 2.10-15 better than νοῦς ('mind').[108] By contrast, Scroggs suggests that Paul has both the Hebrew and Greek forms 'in mind' and Hanson asserts that Paul 'clearly knows' both.[109] While all agree on the suitability of 'spirit' for Paul's argument here, none offers any argument for his judgement.

I do not consider the verbal replication of Isa. 40.13 in 1 Cor. 2.16 an explicit citation.[110] Paul has private exegetical reasons for appealing to Isaiah 40 in 1 Corinthians 2 that relate to his wider rhetorical agenda in 1 Corinthians 1–4, within which πνεῦμα and νοῦς play distinct rhetorical roles.[111]

7.5.1 *Problems relating to 1 Corinthians 2.6-16*

The issue is complicated because many, considering 1 Cor. 2.6-16 peculiar within Paul's letters, observe differences between this passage and the preceding material in 1.18-2.5. These differences manifest in shifts: from singular to plural first-person pronouns; from aorist to present tense; from autobiographical material to 'a timeless panegyric to Wisdom'[112]; from an opposition of mundane and divine wisdom to the peculiar ψυχικός-πνευματικός dichotomy; from an inclusive to an elitist outlook.

Most commentators ascribe authorship of the passage to Paul, some proposing that Paul makes use of traditional material or generic forms,[113] most seeing Paul in some way reflecting the language of his Corinthian interlocutors.[114] Acknowledging these positions, influential studies consider 1 Cor. 2.6-16 to be Paul's own authentic literary composition and entirely congruous with Paul's argument.[115]

---

108   Michel 1929, 68.
109   Scroggs 1967–1968, 53; ibid., 54 [1]; Hanson 1974, 197.
110   Following Stanley 1992 (cf. Tables 6.1 and 6.2, above) and Wilk 1998, 288f.; *pace* Ellis 1957 and Koch 1986 (see Section 6.3, above).
111   In question is Paul's awareness and use of variant Greek forms, not his possible knowledge of Hebrew (see Section 1.8.3, above).
112   See Walker 1992, 86–87) for a detailed survey of peculiarities in 1 Cor. 2.6-16.
113   Wuellner (1970) considers 1 Corinthians 1–4 Paul's own composition (e.g. ibid., 201), based on a traditional haggadic wisdom homily. Similarly Branick (1982) deems 1 Corinthians 1–3 a 'homiletic-midrash', highlighting poetic parallelism between chs 1 and 2 (ibid., 261, 264–266). For Lührmann (1965, 113–140) Paul employs a traditional 'threefold revelation pattern'. Conzelmann (1969, 75) detects a model developed in the school activity surrounding Paul. For Scroggs (1967–1968) Paul authored 1 Cor. 2.6-16, influenced by Wis. 9.9-18 (ibid., 49), drawing on an 'esoteric wisdom teaching [. . .] consistent with his theology as a whole' (ibid., 35, 54). Theissen (1987, 347–350) sees 2.6-16 as a 'literary deposit' of oral discourse arising within Paul's inner circle, now imparting new information to the larger assembly as a public letter; 1 Corinthians 1 and 2 exhibit close parallelism (ibid., 345–350); the peculiarities of the passage derive from Paul's use of Jewish wisdom traditions (ibid., 353–367). Gillespie (1990) labels the passage 'early Christian prophecy', assuming Paul's authorship.
114   Accommodating his interlocutors' 'Gnostic' position, Paul undermines his own argument in 1.17-2.5 (variously Goudge 1903, 16; Wilkens 1959, 52–96; Bultmann, 1969, 70–72; Conzelmann 1975, 57). Alternatively, Paul employs the interlocutors' terms in order to correct their position (Funk 1966, 275–305; Gärtner 1967–1968, 215–221; Pearson 1973, 27–37; Horsley 1976; Francis, 1980, 41–61; Murphy-O'Connor 1986, 81–94; Fee 1987, 98–120, esp. 100; Thiselton 1978, 510–526; 2000, 232, 252; Barclay 1992, 68; Adams 2000, 91–92).
115   Especially Mitchell 1991; cf. Dahl 1967, 317, 237; Theissen 1987, 345–350; Fee 1987, 4–15;

A minority proposes that Paul did not write 1 Cor. 2.6-16. Ellis suggests that the passage represents a 'midrash' developed within a group of 'Pauline pneumatics' prior to the writing of 1 Corinthians, and not 'necessarily' by Paul himself.[116] This view has not found support.[117] Both Widmann and Walker deem the passage an interpolation by Corinthian 'pneumatics' seeking to correct Paul's 'distortion' of their position.[118] Walker seeks to exonerate Paul of an elitist 'Gnosticism' reminiscent of a type branded 'heretical' in later centuries.[119] However, the majority finds that 1 Cor. 2.6-16 represents neither spiritual elitism nor 'Gnostic' ideology.[120] Moreover, widespread affirmation of the congruence of the passage with its literary context counts against interpolation,[121] the principal criterion for which is a claimed incoherence between the passage and its context.[122]

Accepting Paul as the author, I argue that Paul's πνεῦμα-language in 1 Cor. 2.10-12 indicates his use of the πνεῦμα-form of Isa. 40.13[PM]. Πνευματικός-language is apparently common to Paul and his interlocutors, but Paul's distinctive emphasis on 'unity through participation in the *same* πνεῦμα' in 1 Corinthians 2 is distinctively his own. Even if they have invoked πνευματικός-language, he has reason to employ the πνεῦμα-form of Isa. 40.13[PM] while verbally replicating the νοῦς-form of Isa. 40.13[OG].

The various judgements on the origins of this pneumatic language, which belong to diverse historical reconstructions of 1 Corinthians, fall broadly into two categories. One position, represented by Fee, holds that Paul's reaction to what he calls 'factions' within his audience is integrally entwined with Paul's self-defence against criticism arising within some of these factions.[123] Conversely Mitchell finds that no actual

Thiselton 2000, 38–41.

116   Ellis 1978, 25–28, 154f., 213f.; cf. 1986, 490.

117   Conzelmann (1969) and Theissen (1987) see a Pauline 'inner circle' as the *life-setting* for this passage, but the latter two consider Paul the author. Refuting Ellis, see, for example: Fee 1987, 100 [10]; Gillespie 1990.

118   Widmann 1979; Walker 1992.

119   e.g. Walker 1992, 89, 92, following Conzelmann 1975, 57–58.

120   Generally refuting Wilkens (1959), for example: Funk 1966, 300 [107]; Scroggs 1967–1968, 33–37; Theissen 1987, 350–353; Fee 1987, 99f.; Mitchell 1991.

121   For the congruence of the passage with its context, see scholars cited in Footnotes 113-115. For explicit rejection of 'interpolation, see, for example: Gärtner 1967–1968, 216; Murphy-O'Connor 1986, 81–94; Theissen 1987, 349 [7]; Fee 1987, 99–100; Mitchell 1991; Thiselton 2000, 38–41.

122   Walker's failure to acknowledge the pneumatic 'thread' throughout major sections of the letter (chs 2; 10; 12–14; 15) leads Walker to propose a cascade of interpolations – 1 Cor. 15.44b-48 (1992, 87 [56]) and Rom. 16.25-27 (Walker 1987, 92) – in order to maintain his argument, despite the absence of textual warrant for such excisions.

123   Fee's position, indebted to Munck 1959 and Dahl 1967 (Fee 1987, 47–48), is broadly compatible with other studies. While division in Corinth is a 'real' problem (with social causes, cf. Theissen 1982, 124f.; Fee 1987, 5; Clarke 1993; Pogoloff 1992; Horrell 1996, 155f.; Adams 2000, 89), Paul also defends himself against challenges from sections of his audience (Fee 1987, 79–82), possibly from patrons, each affiliated to the baptism of that apostle on the household payroll (Fee 1987, 399–400; Theissen 1982, 50–56; Hock, 1980, 52–59; Marshall 1987, 245–247; Witherington 1995, 209f, Adams 2000, 91–93). Presupposing conventional Graeco-Roman standards, and perhaps treating the 'assembly' as a 'club' (Barclay 1992, 71; Adams 2000, 100; Horrell 1996, 109, 234), their criticism laments Paul's poor oratory

criticism of Paul has arisen, but instead Paul constructs a 'mock defence' as part of a deliberative rhetorical effort to reconcile factious Corinthian parties.[124] Dependence here on any historical reconstruction of the Corinthian situation is unnecessary. It suffices to show that Paul's rhetoric in 1 Corinthians 1–4 – particularly 1.10–2.16 – is internally coherent and that appeals to the πνεῦμα- and νοῦς-forms of Isa. 40.13 relate to distinct rhetorical strands within this argument and throughout the letter.

7.5.2 *Opposition of 'spirit' and 'conventional intellect' (1 Corinthians 1–4)*

In 1 Corinthians 1–2 νοῦς and πνεῦμα emerge as distinct categories of Paul's argument. While Paul's invocation of both νοῦς and πνεῦμα may reflect Corinthian usage,[125] his use of these terms is his own and plays a distinct and deliberate role in his argument. The appearance of πνεῦμα in this passage indicates his appeal to the πνεῦμα-form of Isa. 40.13 (see below).

The themes of unity and disunity run through the letter. At the outset, Paul identifies 'disunity' within his audience as his primary concern (1 Cor. 1.1-12). Consequently, his appeal for unity is characterized by two motifs in particular: believers' corporate participation in Christ and their united participation in the spirit.[126] More specifically, his complaint in 1.10 – that Corinthian factions are affiliating with various apostles – leads him consistently to present himself and the other apostles as the model of unity in the spirit, which the audience must emulate.[127]

In ch. 1, constructing a rhetorically persuasive threat, Paul distinguishes two

(hence emphasis on σοφία, λόγος, γνῶσις, Fee 1987, 11, 48, 64–96) and his flouting of patron-client etiquette (Fee 1987, 9, 399f.; cf. Theissen 1982, 50f.; Marshall 1987, 245–247; Chow 1992, 188–190; Adams 2000, 91–93). Disunity is problematic for Paul precisely because it entails opposition to him from some quarters (Fee 1987, 6–10, 49, 56; cf. Barrett 1968, 43). The critics deem themselves πνευματικοί (who exhibit πνευματικά, particularly glossolalia), but Paul merely ψυχικός (for example, Horsley 1976; Fee 1987, 10–11; Barclay 1992, 66–72; Martin 1995, 88–92; Adams 2000, 92).

124   Mitchell demonstrates the literary and rhetorical unity of 1 Corinthians (1991, 2 [4]; cf. 186–192 esp. 182). Paul's deliberative rhetoric constitutes a sustained effort to reconcile factious parties. Mitchell takes his rhetoric of disunity to indicate 'actual' disunity among Corinthian believers (cf. ibid., 67 [7]). Conversely, she considers Paul's rhetoric of defence to be a heuristic fabrication, finding no evidence of 'actual' criticism of Paul in Corinth (*pace* Munck 1959; Fee 1987), Mitchell 1991, 2, 70 [30], 243 [327], 302.

125   See Footnotes 114 and 123.

126   Participation in the same body: 6.12-20; 10.14-22; ch. 12. Participation 'in the same spirit' reiterated six times: 12.4, 8, 9, 11, 13). He also calls for common participation in the same: assembly (1.2-3); body, spirit (6.12-20); meal, body (10.14-22); meal (11.17ff.); body, spirit, baptism (ch. 12); love (ch. 13); spirit (ch. 14); resurrection (ch. 15).

127   The apostles are united in: 'work' (ch. 3), 'rights' (ch. 9), and 'tradition' (15.1-11). Paul reveals no antagonism towards Cephas (1.12; 3.22; 9.5; 15.5) or 'others' (9.5, 12; 15.5-7). Paul's substantive arguments refer only to himself and Apollos (chs 1–4), Paul's relationship with whom is consistently presented as harmonious (e.g. 3.6; 16.12), even if it is possible to read the barbed warnings of 3.12-15 as obliquely directed at Apollos. The apostles, whose unity exemplifies the unity represented by Christ (1 Cor. 1.13; 3.21b-23), emerge as the πνευματικοί of 1 Cor. 2.6-16 (see Footnote 131).

spheres: that of 'the perishing', characterized by disunity and individualism, and that of 'the saved', characterized by unity in Christ. Associating his audience's disunity with the 'perishing' κόσμος, he edges his appeal for unity with the threat of their exclusion from 'the saved'. These two spheres are founded on a stark dichotomization of intellect. Conventional intellect belongs to the 'perishing' – those individuals disunited by their various futile forms of conventional 'wisdom' and 'reason' (σοφία and λόγος).[128] Opposed to this is potent divine intellect, unfathomable by worldly standards, marked by God's 'wisdom' and 'power' (σοφία θεοῦ and δύναμις θεοῦ).[129] While the perishing sphere of the mundane intellect is the realm of human agents, the divine is mediated through special non-human agency.

Paul maintains this dichotomy in ch. 2, now explaining *how* a person can partake in the divine intellect. Πνεῦμα – replacing 'power' (δύναμις) in 1 Cor. 2.4 – is the *divine agent by which a 'spiritual person' (πνευματικός) perceives God's thought*. The 'conventional intellectual' (ψυχικὸς ἄνθρωπος), representing the disunited inhabitants of the 'perishing' κόσμος, receives neither the spirit nor (consequently) its tuition. Using various terms, Paul consistently emphasizes that *no one* except the spirit 'knows' God's mind.[130] Isaiah's rhetorical question, 'Who has known the mind of the Lord?', in 2.16a expects the same negative answer, 'no one'. The chapter culminates in Paul's claim that 'we', the united apostles, whom the Corinthians are to emulate, 'have the mind of Christ'.[131] Having the mind

---

128 'Those perishing' (1.18) belong to the κόσμος. Those 'called' (1.24), 'who believe' (1.21), and 'who are being saved' (1.18) belong to Christ. Unity and intellect epitomize this cosmic dichotomy. The 'wise man', the 'scribe', the 'debater of this age', 'Jews and Greeks' represent the disunited κόσμος. All are consigned to the 'perishing' sphere by their various mundane intellectual standards, which are incommensurate with God's wisdom (1.23). These mistaken and disunified outsiders are distinct from 'those who are called' (1.24). Paul's accusation of Corinthian division rhetorically associates his audience (1.11-12) with the divided, perishing κόσμος, invoking the threat of their exclusion from the grace and salvation to which they aspire (an aspiration the letter presupposes, e.g. 1.1-8; 6.19-20; 15.2, 17).

129 Potent, divine intellect is antithetical to impotent, conventional intellect. From 1.17–2.4 human σοφία and λόγος consistently stand opposed to δύναμις and σοφία θεοῦ. Inadequate, human σοφία λόγου is opposed to the 'potency' of the cross (ἵνα μὴ κενωθῇ ὁ σταυρὸς – 'potency' is implied by κενόω – 1.17). What is 'folly to those perishing' is λόγος τοῦ σταυροῦ and δύναμις θεοῦ to 'those being saved' (1.18). What is 'scandal' and 'folly' to unbelieving Jews and Greeks is θεοῦ δύναμις καὶ θεοῦ σοφία to 'those called' (1.23-24). Preaching the cross 'according to lofty *words or wisdom*' (λόγου ἢ σοφίας, 2.1) or 'in plausible *words of wisdom*' (σοφίας λόγοις, 2.4) is antithetical to ἀπόδειξες πνεύματος καὶ δυνάμεως (2.4). Σοφία ἀνθρώπων opposes δύναμις θεοῦ (2.5).

130 Τὰ βάθη τοῦ θεοῦ (1 Cor. 2.10), which can mean 'innermost thoughts' (see the use in Jdt. 8.13-14, cf. Footnote 147, below); τὰ τοῦ θεοῦ 1 Cor. 2.11; νοῦν κυρίου 1 Cor. 2.16.

131 Paul distinguishes the audience from the apostles. The apostles are *we* who 'preach' (1.21, 23), 'speak among the mature' (2.6), receive revelation 'through the spirit' (2.10), have 'received the spirit from God' (2.12), and 'have the mind of Christ' (2.16). Paul's audience ('you') is distinct from 'us who preach': in 1.23-24 'we' preach to 'those called', 'you' (1.26); in 2.1-5 and 3.1f. 'you' are distinct from 'I', who 'preaches'. (Compare Schlier 1956, 214f.; Dahl 1967, 327; Scroggs 1967–1968, 52; Fee 1987, 101 [13], 118–120; Wilk 1998, 288. *Pace* Collins 1999, 122, who – without argument – takes 'we' (2.6) to indicate the whole community.) 'Those who believe', 'those called', 'the mature' (1.21, 23-24; 2.6-7) are never said to include the audience. But Paul remains ambiguous as to which sphere – perishing or divine – the

of Christ therefore represents the special situation of the πνευματικός, tutored by the spirit concerning God's mind.[132]

In these two chapters νοῦς appears three times in key rhetorical positions, once in Paul's opening appeal for unity (1.10), twice in 2.16. In the latter verse, νοῦς is used once to reiterate – in Isaiah's words – that *no one* knows 'the mind of the Lord' (that is, God); and once in the climactic claim that 'we (apostles) have the mind of Christ' (which according to 2.6-16 means to 'receive tuition from the spirit').[133] The rhetorical structure of the argument shows that 'unity in the same νοῦς', for which Paul calls in 1.10, is identical to 'having νοῦν Χριστοῦ' (2.16). Because it is the apostles who 'have the mind of Christ', and because the audience's factious, worldly behaviour potentially excludes them from sharing in this united apostolic state, these occurrences of νοῦς at rhetorically crucial moments mark an appeal for the audience to imitate the apostles' spiritual unity in Christ. While νοῦς was initially undifferentiated in 1.10, in light of the cosmic/intellectual dichotomy of chs 1.18–2.16, 'unity in the same mind' can only mean participation with the apostles in the mind of Christ.

Thus, νοῦς and πνεῦμα play distinct rhetorical roles in the argument. Νοῦς represents the 'mind of God', unfathomable to all but the πνεῦμα, and πνεῦμα is the agent which tutors 'spiritual ones' concerning God's mind. Paul expresses the spiritual ones' perception, a unified participation in the πνεῦμα, as 'having the νοῦς of Christ'. These ideas are informed by elements within Isaiah 40. In 1 Corinthians 2 Paul verbally replicates and parallels elements of Isaiah 40, including the OG νοῦς-form and the pM πνεῦμα-form of Isa. 40.13.

7.5.3 *The function of Isaiah 40 in 1 Corinthians 2*

Paul appeals to the dual idea of 'the unfathomability of creation and the divine intellect', which pervades Isaiah 40, through a number of verbal and ideological parallels to Isaiah 40 in 1 Corinthians 2. He appeals to the πνεῦμα- and νοῦς-forms of Isa. 40.13 as distinct sense contours that characterize the notion of the 'unfathomability of creation and the divine intellect'.

7.5.3.1 *The unfathomability of creation and the divine intellect in Isaiah 40*

Isa. 40.12-14 presents God's material creation and His intellect as equally unfathomable. Verse 12 expresses the extent of creation in metric terms: מָדַד, תִּכֵּן/μετρέω

---

132   *Only* because the πνεῦμα, which 'searches all things (even the depths of God', 1 Cor. 2.10), tutors the πνευματικός (2.12-14), is the latter able to 'judge all' (2.15).

133   While 'we' πνευματικοί 'have the mind of Christ' (2.16), the audience are not yet πνευματικοί (3.1).

('measure'); שָׁקַל בַּפֶּלֶס/ἔστησεν τὰ ὄρη σταθμῷ ('weigh in scales'). Verses 13-14 express the extent of the God's creative 'spirit' or 'mind' in intellectual terms: v. 13 תִּכֵּן ('assess')/γινώσκω ('know'); v. 14 בִּינָה /σύνεσις ('understanding'). Greek cannot express the range of תִּכֵּן, which can mean either 'measure' (quantitatively) or 'assess' (qualitatively). Thus, where תִּכֵּן appears in vv. 12 and 13, LXX has μετρέω ('measure') and γινώσκω ('know'), respectively.

Table 7.5 Isaiah 40.12-14

Isa. 40.12^{LXX}	Isa. 40.12^𝔐
τίς ἐμέτρησεν τῇ χειρὶ τὸ ὕδωρ	מִי־מָדַד בְּשָׁעֳלוֹ מַיִם
καὶ τὸν οὐρανὸν σπιθαμῇ	וְשָׁמַיִם בַּזֶּרֶת תִּכֵּן
καὶ πᾶσαν τὴν γῆν δρακί	וְכָל בַּשָּׁלִשׁ עֲפַר הָאָרֶץ
τίς ἔστησεν τὰ ὄρη σταθμῷ	וְשָׁקַל בַּפֶּלֶס הָרִים
καὶ τὰς νάπας ζυγῷ	וּגְבָעוֹת בְּמֹאזְנָיִם:
13 τίς ἔγνω νοῦν κυρίου	13 מִי־תִכֵּן אֶת־רוּחַ יְהוָה
καὶ τίς αὐτοῦ σύμβουλος ἐγένετο	וְאִישׁ עֲצָתוֹ
ὃς συμβιβᾷ αὐτόν	יוֹדִיעֶנּוּ:
14 ἢ πρὸς τίνα συνεβουλεύσατο	14 אֶת־מִי נוֹעָץ
καὶ συνεβίβασεν αὐτόν	וַיְבִינֵהוּ
ἢ τίς ἔδειξεν αὐτῷ κρίσιν	וַיְלַמְּדֵהוּ בְּאֹרַח מִשְׁפָּט
	וַיְלַמְּדֵהוּ דַעַת
ἢ ὁδὸν συνέσεως τίς ἔδειξεν αὐτῷ	וְדֶרֶךְ תְּבוּנוֹת יוֹדִיעֶנּוּ:

12a.	Who has measured in a hand the water	Who has measured in his palm the *mayim*
b.	and the heaven in a span,	*and shamayim* marked-off in the span,
c.	and all the [. . .] earth in a handful?	and all the dust of the earth in a measure
d.	Who has weighed the mountains in scales,	and weighed the mountains in scales
e.	and the (wooded) vales in a balance?	and the hills (hollows, vales) in a balance?
13a.	Who has known the mind of the Lord,	Who has measured the spirit of the Lord,
b.	and who has been His counsellor, to instruct Him?	or as His counsellor has made Him to know?
14a.	Or whom did He consult,	Whom did He consult
b.	one who instructed Him?	that he enlightened Him,
c.	or who has shown Him [. . .] judgement,	that he tutored Him in the path of judgement,
d.	[. . . . .]	and tutored Him knowledge,
e.	or who has shown Him	and made Him to know
f.	the way of understanding?	the way of understanding?

Νοῦς ('mind') standing for רוּחַ ('spirit') in Isa. 40.13 is remarkable. Νοῦς is a unique translation for רוּחַ in the entire LXX.[134] It is, moreover, highly unusual for the LXX to offer anything other than πνεῦμα when רוּחַ applies to God, as it does in this verse.[135] Isaiah[OG] renders the creative term רוּחַ with the intellectual term νοῦς in accordance with its choice of γινώσκω to express the intellectual sense of תִּכֵּן ('assess') in v. 13 (whereas μετρέω expressed the metric sense of תִּכֵּן in v. 12). Moreover, πνεῦμα and νοῦς convey distinct meanings in Jewish scripture. In the Hebrew Bible, when רוּחַ means 'wind' or 'breath', the LXX renders רוּחַ predominantly with πνεῦμα. When רוּחַ indicates human intellect or emotion, the LXX tends to avoid rendering it with πνεῦμα, often supplying ψυχή or θυμός, or some other intellectual term. By contrast, aside from Isa. 40.13, the LXX translators always attribute πνεῦμα to God, rendering רוּחַ יְהֹוָה, רוּחַ אֱלֹהִים (or any other nomenclature for divine רוּחַ) with πνεῦμα.[136] Offering νοῦς ('mind') for רוּחַ ('spirit') as divine attribute in Isa. 40.13, then, contravenes a consistent LXX translation practice. Paul's appeal to both the νοῦς- and πνεῦμα-forms of Isa. 40.13 in 1 Corinthians 2 reflects this unique usage in the OG.

In 𝔐, Isa. 40.12 refers to material creation. Since 'spirit of God' is associated with the Creation in Gen. 1.2, the reference to creation in Isa. 40.12 emphasizes the creative connotation of 'spirit of the Lord' in 40.13a𝔐. The rhetorical question – 'Who has been His counselor, to instruct Him? Whom did He consult for his enlightenment, and who taught Him the path of justice, and taught Him knowledge, and showed Him the way of understanding?' (40.13b-14), then, expresses God's intellectual unfathomability. In the context of the creation references in 40.12, Isaiah 40𝔐 refers to the humans' futile search for knowledge in Genesis 2–3. Isaiah 40 generally identifies this vain human search for knowledge with pagan idolatry, which it presents as a perverse failure to acknowledge the creator.

The title 'spirit of the Lord' (רוּחַ יְהֹוָה [πνεῦμα κυρίου]) of Isa. 40.13a𝔐 recalls both '*spirit* of God' (רוּחַ אֱלֹהִים [πνεῦμα τοῦ θεοῦ]), the aloof creative agent (Gen. 1.2), and '*Lord* God' (יְהֹוָה/אֱלֹהִים/θεός κύριος), the personal 'Lord' of the human creature (Gen. 2.4ff.). 'Spirit of the Lord' (Isa. 40.13𝔐) thus integrates two distinct narratives: the austere creation narrative in Genesis 1 and the story of the humans' futile search for knowledge in Genesis 2–3. In the OG, the term 'mind of the Lord' (νοῦς κυρίου) obscures the combination of these distinct narratives because creative 'spirit' (πνεῦμα)

---

134   Hatch-Redpath 1998, *ad loc.*
135   See Footnote 136, below.
136   Isaacs 1976, 10–13. Of 378 occurrences of רוּחַ in the Hebrew Bible, 277 appear in the LXX as πνεῦμα. When רוּחַ means 'wind' the LXX primarily offers πνεῦμα, less frequently ἄνεμος. When רוּחַ means 'breath' LXX predominantly offers πνεῦμα, occasionally ἄνεμος, rarely πνοή. LXX also offers πνεῦμα for נְשָׁמָה, 'breath'. When Hebrew scripture uses רוּחַ to indicate human 'intellect', 'thought', 'inclination' or 'emotion', LXX generally avoids πνεῦμα, using an alternative Greek term for intellect or emotion: ψυχή or compounds of ψυχή; θυμός or compounds of θυμός; once ὀργή (Prov. 16.32). Josh. 5.1 has φρόνησις. Ezek. 13.3 has καρδία.

is absent. OG's νοῦς κυρίου does, however, invoke a notion of God's great intellect that is common throughout Jewish scripture.[137]

Isa. 40.12-14 and 40.28 expresses the same idea of 'God's unfathomable creation and intellect' in equivalent terms.

> Have you not known, except that you heard? (הֲלוֹא יָדַעְתָּ אִם־לֹא שָׁמַעְתָּ/καὶ νῦν οὐκ ἔγνως εἰ μὴ ἤκουσας) The Lord is the everlasting God, the Creator of the ends of the earth. He does not faint or grow weary, his understanding is unsearchable (Isa. 40.28).[138]

Where Isa. 40.12-14 insisted that *no one has assessed God*, His creation, His creative spirit (𝔐) or His intellect, Isa. 40.28 asserts that no one has known anything *except* that God has made it known to him. That is, God and his creative intellect are 'unsearchable', but he imparts knowledge to those who heed him. In the context of Isaiah 40, pagans who do not heed Him are in mind. As in 40.12-14, His omnipotent role as creator of the unfathomable universe is invoked as proof of His intellectual unfathomability. Both passages, Isa. 40.12-14[𝔐] and 40.28, then, express the equal unfathomability of God's creation and His creative intellect. While the OG broadly expresses the same notion, the association of creation and God's creative 'spirit' is lost by the suppression of 'spirit' (רוּחַ/πνεῦμα) with 'mind' (νοῦς).

7.5.3.2 *Verbal replication Isaiah 40.13^{OG} in 1 Corinthians 2.16*

Table 7.6 Isaiah 40.13 and 1 Corinthians 2.16[139]

G^{Ed} Isa. 40.13	1 Cor. 2.16	Isa. 40.13^{MT}	1QIsa.^a	α' θ'	σ'
τίς ἔγνω	τίς γὰρ ἔγνω	מִי־תִכֵּן	מיא תכן	α' τίς εσταθμήσατο	*quis paravit*
νοῦν κυρίου	νοῦν κυρίου	אֶת־רוּחַ יְהוָה	את רוח יהוה	πνεῦμα κυρίου	*spiritum domini*
καὶ τίς		וְאִישׁ		θ' καὶ ἀνὴρ	*et virum*

(continued)

<hr />

137   As far as I can tell from Hatch-Redpath 1998, *ad loc.*, LXX otherwise twice refers to God's νοῦς: Jdt. 8.14; Job 7.17 (לְבֶּךָ 'Your [i.e. God's] mind'). Other terms for God's intellect include, for example: Job 11.6^𝔐 ('for He is manifold in understanding', כִּי־כִפְלַיִם לְתוּשִׁיָּה); Job 12.13 (σοφία, βουλή, σύνεσις/ תְּבוּנָה, עֵצָה, חָכְמָה); Prov. 3.19 (σοφία/חָכְמָה); Jer. 10.12 (φρόνησις/תְּבוּנָה); 1 Kgs 3.28 (φρόνησις θεοῦ/חָכְמַת אֱלֹהִים); Isa. 40.28 (φρόνησις αὐτοῦ/תְּבוּנָתוֹ); Isa. 55.7-9 (τὰς βουλὰς αὐτοῦ/מַחְשְׁבֹתָיו; διανοία μου/מַחְשְׁבֹתַי); Ps. 146.5 [145.5^{LXX}] (σύνεσις αὐτοῦ/תְּבוּנָתוֹ); Amos 4.13 'His thought' (שֵׂחוֹ); Jdt. 8.14 'His thought' (λογισμὸς); 'words of His thought' (λόγους τῆς διανοίας αὐτοῦ).

138   Within a polemic against idolatry, God's 'neither hungering nor tiring' apparently refers to pagan stories of God's tiring and needing sustenance. There may be a hint of sensitivity at the implication in Gen. 2.3 that God rested on the Sabbath because he tired.

139   For Paul's minor changes, see Koch 1986, 49; Wilk 1998, 288.

G^Ed Isa. 40.13	1 Cor. 2.16	Isa. 40.13^MT	1QIsa.^a	α' θ'	σ'
σύμβουλος αὐτοῦ ἐγένετο		עֲצָתוֹ	<איש> ועצתו	βουλὴν αὐτοῦ	*consilii eius*
ὃς συμβιβᾷ αὐτόν	ὃς συμβιβάσει αὐτόν	יוֹדִיעֶנּוּ	יודיענה	καὶ ἐγνώρισεν αὐτὸν	*quis ostendit*
who has known	who has known	who has measured	who has measured	α' who has estimated[140]	who has prepared[141]
the mind of the Lord	the mind of the Lord	the Spirit of the Lord	the Spirit of the Lord	the Spirit of the Lord	the Spirit of the Lord
and who has become	and *as*	and *as*	[and will make known	θ' and a man	and a man of
his counsellor		His advisor	His counsel?]	of his counsel	his council[143]
who will instruct Him?	who will instruct Him?	will instruct Him?	[or: <a counsellor> who instructs her]	has made him known	who has made known

Aquila and Theodotion witness a second-century CE Hebraizing revision of Isa. 40.13^OG that read πνεῦμα κυρίου.[143] While 1QIsa.^a witnesses to the Hebrew reading 'spirit of the Lord' prior to Paul, direct first-century manuscript evidence for the Greek reading πνεῦμα κυρίου is lacking. The Naḥal Ḥever Minor Prophets Scroll (cf. Chapter 2, above) nevertheless testifies to such revisions in Paul's time. Some of Paul's own citations of a G^HR of Isaiah support this assumption (1 Cor. 15.54 is the earliest witness to Theodotion's form of Isa. 25.8; Rom. 9.33 is the earliest witness to Aquila and Symmachus' forms of Isa. 8.14).[144] While no first-century Greek form of Isa. 40.13 (πνεῦμα κυρίου) is extant, appeal to Aquila, Symmachus and Theodotion for supposedly first-century forms of a passage is analogous to our common appeal to Christian LXX manuscripts, which generally date several centuries after Paul, as witnesses of the OG supposed to have circulated in the first century.

140   σταθμόω – estimate, assess – reflecting תכן.
141   *Parare*, 'prepare', 'make ready'. Often for ἑτοιμάζω, cf. Isa. 40.3^LXX.
142   The phrase 'man of his council' (*virum consilii eius*) is apparently the direct object of the verb *ostendere* – '*virum*' is in the accusative. *Ostendere* agrees in sense with γνωρίζω and *Hiphil* ידע meaning 'to make known (rather than *Hiphil* ידע here meaning 'teach [someone]').
143   The Σ' form is known only in a Latin citation (cf. Ziegler 1939, *ad loc.*).
144   Although Paul's citation partially parallels aspects of α' and σ', where they mutually diverge (Table 7.2, Section 7.3.3). Paul's citations of Isa. 8.14 and 25.8 are not thought themselves to have influenced the later Aquila, Symmachus and Theodotion forms. Although Kautzsch 1869 suspected that some Pauline citations influenced later Hexaplaric readings (cf. Chapter One, Footnote 11, above), Paul's Hebraizing Isaiah citations are thought to reflect his sources, cf. Ziegler 1939, 'Einleitung'; Koch 1986, 58–59.

7.5.3.3 *Ideological parallels of Isaiah 40 in 1 Corinthians 2*

The verbal replication of the νοῦς-form of Isa. 40.13ᴼᴳ in 1 Cor. 2.16 is anticipated by several verbal parallels of Isaiah 40 a few lines earlier (1 Cor. 2.10-12), which include the πνεῦμα-form of Isa. 40.13ᴾᴹ. In 1 Cor. 2.11 Paul mingles both forms of Isa. 40.13. Isaiah's 'rhetorical' question, 'Who has known?' (τίς ἔγνω;) expects the answer 'No one has known!' (οὐδεὶς ἔγνωκεν). Paul provides precisely this answer in 1 Cor. 2.11a, οὐδεὶς ἔγνωκεν. His use of γινώσκω reflects OG (τίς ἔγνω;), while his use of πνεῦμα reflects the pM-form.

Table 7.7 Isaiah 40.13a

OG	pM-stream	1 Cor. 2.11
τίς ἔγνω	τίς ἐσταθμήσατο [α']	τὰ τοῦ θεοῦ <u>οὐδεὶς ἔγνωκεν</u>
νοῦν κυρίου;	πνεῦμα κυρίου; [α' (σ')]	εἰ μὴ <u>τὸ πνεῦμα</u> τοῦ θεοῦ

Paul's mingled form makes two changes. Firstly, the object of the verb ('to know'/'measure'/'assess')¹⁴⁵ becomes τὰ (τοῦ θεοῦ), rather than πνεῦμα (κυρίου), because Paul's discussion with his audience concerns τὰ πνευματικὰ and the implications of receiving them. Throughout 1 Corinthians Paul consistently emphasizes πνεῦμα τοῦ θεοῦ as the sole source of πνευματικὰ and believers' united participation in τὸ πνεῦμα as the sole means of being πνευματικός.

Secondly, Isaiah's 'Lord'¹⁴⁶ becomes θεός in 1 Cor. 2.11b, apparently influenced by Isa. 40.28. 1 Cor. 2.10 reflects ideas reminiscent of Isa. 40.28. Humans cannot 'search out' God's intellect, but can only 'know' what God makes known to them.

Table 7.8 Isaiah 40.28

Isa. 40.28	1 Corinthians 2
καὶ νῦν	
a. <u>οὐκ ἔγνως εἰ μὴ</u>	[11b <u>οὐδεὶς ἔγνωκεν εἰ μὴ</u> . . .]
b. ἤκουσας	10a ἡμῖν δὲ ἀπεκάλυψεν ὁ θεὸς
c. θεὸς αἰώνιος ὁ θεὸς ὁ κατασκευάσας	
d. τὰ ἄκρα τῆς γῆς	
e. οὐ πεινάσει οὐδὲ κοπιάσει	
f. οὐδὲ ἔστιν <u>ἐξεύρεσις</u>	10b τὸ γὰρ πνεῦμα πάντα ἐραυνᾷ,
<u>τῆς φρονήσεως αὐτοῦ</u>	καὶ <u>τὰ βάθη τοῦ θεοῦ</u>
	11b τὰ τοῦ θεοῦ οὐδεὶς ἔγνωκεν
	εἰ μὴ τὸ πνεῦμα τοῦ θεοῦ

(continued)

---

145   OG, γινώσκω; pM, σταθμόω; תכן.
146   All available versions of Isa. 40.13 read 'Lord'. The pM stream: רוח יהוה; πνευμα κυριου; *spiritum domini*. The OG: νοῦν κυρίου.

Isa. 40.28	1 Corinthians 2
And now,	
a. *you have not known (anything), except*	[11b . . . *no one has known except . . .*]
b. *that you heard.*	10a . . . *God has revealed to us*
c. God is everlasting; God, who formed	
d. the ends of the earth.	
e. He shall not hunger, nor be weary,	
f. *and there is no searching*	10b *for the spirit searches everything*
of his understanding.	(πάντα), *even the depths of God. . . .*
	11b *No one has known the things of God*
	except the spirit of God

Paul's οὐδεὶς ἔγνωκεν εἰ μὴ . . . (1 Cor. 2.11b) resembles Isaiah's οὐκ ἔγνως εἰ μὴ . . . (Isa. 40.28*a*.). The claim of Isa. 40.28f. that there is no (human) 'searching' (ἐξεύρεσις) of God's φρόνησις, is echoed in Paul's statement that *only* the πνεῦμα can 'search' (ἐραυνᾷ) the 'deep things/innermost thoughts of God'. The terms φρόνησις θεοῦ and βάθη τοῦ θεοῦ can both indicate God's intellect.[147] Isa. 40.12-14 and 40.28 correspond particularly closely with α' σ' θ': φρονήσεως αὐτοῦ (v. 28) picks up ὁδόν φρονήσεως (v. 14 α' σ' θ'). This verbal correspondence is absent in OG, where 40.14 reads ὁδὸν συνέσεως.

Isa. 40.12-14 and 40.28 both equate the unfathomable extent of material creation, with the unsearchability of the divine intellect that conceived and ordered creation: no one can 'estimate' either God's creation (v. 12) or his intellect (vv. 13-14); no one can 'search out' the 'understanding' of him who 'formed the ends of the earth' (v. 28). Both passages logically structure important aspects of Paul's argument. Paul's claim that the πνεῦμα 'searches out' both πάντα and God's 'depths/innermost thoughts' (1 Cor. 2.10), presupposes the same analogy.[148] God's φρόνησις is manifest in creation.[149] Isaiah 40 asserts that (a) any human effort to comprehend God's intellect

---

147   Τὰ βάθη τοῦ θεοῦ can mean 'innermost thoughts'. In Jdt. 8.13-14 the 'depth' of the human heart (βάθος καρδίας ἀνθρώπου) is synonymous with 'a human thought' (λόγος τῆς διανοίας [ἀνθρώπου]). Like 1 Cor. 2.10-11, Judith compares the impossibility of 'finding out' (εὑρίσκω) or 'grasping' (διαλαμβάνω) another person's thoughts with the *greater* impossibility of 'searching out' (ἐρευνάω; compare Prov. 20.27), 'perceiving' (ἐπιγινώσκω) or 'comprehending' (κατανοέω) God (the Creator of πάντα), His mind (νοῦς), or His thought (λογισμός). Jdt. 8.14 has affinities with Isa 40.12-14; Job 28.20-28; Wisdom 9; and particularly 1 Cor. 2.10-11 (see below).

148   The same is true of Paul's comment on Isa. 40.13 in Romans 11, where τὰ πάντα indicates 'the created universe' more clearly than in 1 Cor. 2.10. However, the continuation of Paul's argument in 1 Cor. 3.21b-23 emphasizes πάντα as 'all creation'.

149   Similar sentiments appear in Wisdom 9–15 and Rom. 1.18-32, both of which, like Isaiah 40, depict idolatry as an ironically ignorant mockery of God's creative act.

is futile, but (b) God chooses to make Himself known to those who are receptive. 1 Cor. 2.10-12 asserts the same.

A. 10a ἡμῖν δὲ ἀπεκάλυψεν ὁ θεὸς (διὰ τοῦ πνεύματος)

B. 10b τὸ γὰρ πνεῦμα πάντα ἐραυνᾷ, καὶ τὰ βάθη τοῦ θεοῦ

B. 11b τὰ τοῦ θεοῦ οὐδεὶς ἔγνωκεν (εἰ μὴ τὸ πνεῦμα τοῦ θεοῦ)

A. 12 ἡμεῖς [. . .] ἐλάβομεν [. . .] τὸ πνεῦμα τὸ ἐκ τοῦ θεοῦ, ἵνα εἰδῶμεν τὰ ὑπὸ τοῦ θεοῦ

While Isa. 40.28 acknowledges that God makes Himself known (οὐκ ἔγνως εἰ μη ἤκουσας), 1 Corinthians 2 exceeds Isaiah in identifying the 'spirit' as the medium by which humans perceive God. Paul replaces pM Isaiah's πνεῦμα κυρίου – the object of the verb in Isa. 40.13a (variously 'know', 'estimate', 'measure'), the thing unknowable to humans – with τὰ τοῦ θεοῦ, assigning πνεῦμα as the *agent by which* believers can 'know' τὰ τοῦ θεοῦ. Paul designates 'receiving' the πνεῦμα as the sole means of perceiving divine intellect (1 Cor. 2.12). No one except the spirit has known God's 'thoughts' (1 Cor. 2.10); God reveals them to believers through the spirit.

The πνευματικός does not *preside* over 'the things of God' (τὰ τοῦ θεοῦ) nor over πνεῦμα τοῦ θεοῦ, which 'knows' them. The πνευματικός merely perceives τὰ ὑπὸ τοῦ θεοῦ χαρισθέντα ἡμῖν (1 Cor. 2.12). This emphasis on a passive receipt of what is freely dispensed explains the phrase τὸ πνεῦμα τὸ ἐκ τοῦ θεοῦ in 2.12. Some have taken this locution, unique in Paul's extant writings, to indicate interpolation.[150] But τὸ ἐκ here emphasizes that πνευματικοί *passively* receive the spirit, just as the phrases τὰ ὑπὸ τοῦ θεοῦ (v. 12) and τὰ τοῦ πνεύματος τοῦ θεοῦ (v. 14) indicate that πνευματικοί receive insight into God's intellect but do not preside over it.

The parallelism between 1 Cor. 2.10-12 and 15-16 reveals the distinction between God's intellect and πνεῦμα τοῦ θεοῦ as mediator of that intellect to humans.

Table 7.9 Parallelism of 1 Corinthians 2.10-11 and 15-16

10	τὸ πνεῦμα πάντα ἐραυνᾷ καὶ τὰ βάθη τοῦ θεοῦ	15a	ὁ δὲ πνευματικὸς ἀνακρίνει πάντα
11a	τίς γὰρ οἶδεν ἀνθρώπων τὰ τοῦ ἀνθρώπου εἰ μὴ τὸ πνεῦμα τοῦ ἀνθρώπου τὸ ἐν αὐτῷ;	15b	αὐτὸς δὲ ὑπ' οὐδενὸς ἀνακρίνεται
11b	οὕτως καὶ τὰ τοῦ θεοῦ οὐδεὶς ἔγνωκεν εἰ μὴ τὸ πνεῦμα τοῦ θεοῦ	16a	τίς γὰρ ἔγνω νοῦν κυρίου;
12	ἐλάβομεν [. . .] τὸ πνεῦμα τὸ ἐκ τοῦ θεοῦ	16b	ἡμεῖς δὲ νοῦν Χριστοῦ ἔχομεν

150   Ellis 1957; Widmann 1979; Walker 1992; cf. Section 7.5.1, above.

In vv. 10 and 15a the πνεῦμα τοῦ θεοῦ and πνευματικός are said respectively to 'search' or 'judge' πάντα. But the πνεῦμα and the πνευματικός are not equally able to 'search'/'know'. The intervening argument (2.13-14) shows that the πνευματικός judges πάντα *only because* the spirit searches πάντα and mediates knowledge to him. The principal 'like is only known by like', stated in 2.11a,[151] is applied in 2.15b to show that the ψυχικὸς ἄνθρωπος (of v. 14) cannot 'judge' the πνευματικός. Isaiah's rhetorical question, 'Who has known the mind of the Lord?', which Paul poses in 2.16a, has already been answered in 2.11b, 'No one, except the spirit of God'. The answer has not changed by the time Paul writes 2.16a. Rather, in light of the argument in 2.10-16, the participation of πνευματικοί in 'the mind of Christ' (2.16b) is a result of their having received the spirit, which searches all things, including God's intellect. 'Everything' (πάντα), 'the depths of God' (τὰ βάθη τοῦ θεοῦ), 'the things of God' (τὰ τοῦ θεοῦ) and the 'mind of the Lord' (νοῦν κυρίου) are all equally unfathomable to any human. Πνευματικοί are never said to preside over these aspects of the divine creative intellect. Rather, they participate in a medium by which they perceive God's thought as He bestows it. This medium is represented by τὸ πνεῦμα (vv. 10, 11, 12) and νοῦν Χριστοῦ (v. 15). According to the structure of the argument, then, νοῦν κυρίου and νοῦν Χριστοῦ (v. 16) are not identical. The answer to Isaiah's rhetorical question continues to be, 'No one' has known God's thought. The δέ of v. 16 has an adversative force: 'no one knows God's intellect, *but* we participate in a medium by which God dispenses insight into his thought.' Πνεῦμα and νοῦς are therefore not synonyms in this argument.[152] This section has shown that Paul draws on both the πνεῦμα- and νοῦς-forms of Isa. 40.13 in 1 Cor. 2.10-16. This reference to the two forms of Isa. 40.13 forms part of his wider argument in 1 Corinthians 1–2, that participation in the spirit is the sole means by which the Corinthian audience can be united in the mind of Christ.

7.5.3.4 *A shared exegetical tradition: Wisdom 9 and 1 Corinthians*

Paul's appeal to Isaiah 40 in 1 Corinthians 2 is distinctively his own. However, his appeal participates in a traditional interpretation of Isaiah 40. Like 1 Corinthians 2.6-16, Wisdom of Solomon 9, appealing to Isa. 40.12-14, presents πνεῦμα τοῦ θεοῦ as mediator of God's intellect to (certain) humans. Wisdom 9 also makes use of the OG- and pM-forms of Isa. 40.13. Paul's interpretation of Isa. 40.13 participates in a traditional understanding of this verse, an understanding that accepts both πνεῦμα- and νοῦς-forms of Isa. 40.13. Yet, while Paul is probably aware of Wisdom 9,[153] his

151   Gärtner 1967–1968, 210f.
152   *Pace* Fee (1987, 112 [60]), for whom πνεῦμα (1 Cor. 2.10-12) 'is another expression for νοῦς' (2.16). *Pace* also Scroggs (1967–1968, 54) who, mistakenly deeming πνεῦμα and νοῦς to be synonymous here, still correctly observes that they are otherwise never synonymous in Paul.
153   For example, Wis. 9.8 in 2 Cor. 5.1-5. Rom 1.18ff. is generally reminiscent of Wisdom 12–16; cf. Dunn 1988, 53–70 on Rom 1.18-32.

construction of 1 Corinthians 2 does not depend upon it. His appeal to both sense contours is his own, carefully tailored to his rhetorical context.

Solomon's praise of Wisdom (Wisdom 7–9) emphasizes the unfathomability of God's creative spirit or intellect. Equally, God's creation cannot be estimated by humans, who cannot 'guess' (εἰκάζω) at what is in the earth' nor 'search out (ἐξιχνιάζω) what is in the heavens' (9.16; for 'searching out', cf. Isa. 40.28ᴼᴳ οὐδὲ ἔστιν ἐξεύρεσις τῆς φρονήσεως αὐτοῦα' οὐκ ἔστιν ἐξιχνιασμός). Like 'the spirit of God' (Gen. 1.2), Wisdom was active in creation (Wis. 9.9). God is addressed as: ὁ ποιήσας τὰ πάντα ἐν λόγῳ σου καὶ τῇ σοφίᾳ σου κατασκευάσας ἄνθρωπον (9.1-2). Humans know nothing without the wisdom that comes from God (9.6). Solomon's epigrapher asks: 'For what man can know the counsel of God (τίς γὰρ ἄνθρωπος γνώσεται βουλὴν θεοῦ)? Or who can discern what the Lord wills?' (9.13); 'Who has known Your counsel?' (βουλὴν δέ σου τίς ἔγνω;), except that You have given wisdom (σοφίαν) and sent Your holy Spirit (τὸ ἅγιόν σου πνεῦμα) from on high? (9.17a).[154] Responding to Isaiah's 'Who has known . . .?', the epigrapher answers 'no one, except that God gave wisdom and sent the spirit' (βουλὴν δέ σου τίς ἔγνω εἰ μὴ σὺ ἔδωκας σοφίαν καὶ ἔπεμψας τὸ ἅγιόν σου πνεῦμα ἀπὸ ὑψίστων;, 9.17). 1 Cor. 2.11 is close in sense: τὰ τοῦ θεοῦ οὐδεὶς ἔγνωκεν εἰ μὴ τὸ πνεῦμα τοῦ θεοῦ, which searches all (v. 10), which 'we' have received (v. 12), and through which God has revealed 'to us' (v. 10). Wisdom 11 again paraphrases Isa. 40.12-14, replicating the metric language of 40.12.[155]

Like Paul, the epigrapher reiterates the claim of Isaiah 40 that neither creation, nor the creative intellect is fathomable to humans. Both exceed Isaiah in presenting the 'spirit' as the mediator of God's intellect to humans. Yet their respective treatments of Isaiah 40 are quite independent. Not only is there no verbal correspondence between 1 Corinthians 2 and Wisdom 9, each independently replicates different clauses of Isa. 40.13, Paul presenting Isa. 40.13a,c (see Table 7.6, above), the epigrapher Isa. 40.13a-b.[156] Wisdom 9 highlights that Paul's appeal to the πνεῦμα- and νοῦς-forms of Isa. 40.13 belongs to a wider exegetical tradition of interpretation of Isaiah 40. However, Paul's particular treatment of Isaiah 40 in 1 Corinthians 2 is independent of Wisdom 9.

---

154   For βουλὴν compare the variant of 1QIsa.ᵃ 40.13, which omits איש and can be read, 'and (who will) make His counsel known?' (ועצתו יודיענה). Wilkens (1959, 160–174) argues that Wisdom of God and spirit of God are identical, here as well as in 1 Enoch 42 and Sirach 24.

155   Wis. 11.20 'you have arranged all things by measure and number and weight (πάντα μέτρῳ καὶ ἀριθμῷ καὶ σταθμῷ, cf. Isa. 40.12-14 σταθμῷ; ἐμέτρησεν; Isa. 40.26 במספר צבאם/κατὰ ἀριθμὸν τὸν κόσμον αὐτοῦ)'. Wis. 11.22, 'Because like a tipping of the scales (ὡς ῥοπὴ ἐκ πλαστίγγων, cf. Isa. 40.12 σταθμῷ . . . ζυγῷ – במאזנים . . . בפלס) the whole world before you, and like a drop of morning dew that falls upon the ground', cf. Isa. 40.15, 'Behold, the nations are like a drop from a bucket (σταγὼν ἀπὸ κάδου), and are accounted as the dust on the scales . . . (ὡς ῥοπὴ ζυγοῦ)'. The nations represent a 'droplet in the scales', in contrast with the vast 'waters' of creation which God 'weighed in the scales' in 40.12.

156   Compare τίς ἄνθρωπος γνώσεται βουλὴν θεοῦ (Wis. 9.13) and βουλὴν σου τίς ἔγνω (9.17a) with Isa. 40.13 τίς ἔγνω νοῦν κυρίου καὶ τίς αὐτοῦ σύμβουλος ἐγένετο.

7.5.3.5 *Concluding remarks*

Those proposing that the πνεῦμα-form of Isa. 40.13 is – or would have been – suitable for 1 Cor. 2.6-16 offer no argument (Section 7.4, above). Some consider πνεῦμα and νοῦς to be synonymous in 1 Cor. 2.6-16.[157] I have shown that πνεῦμα and νοῦς generally have distinct meanings in Greek Jewish scripture and also that the use of νοῦς ('mind') for רוח ('spirit') in Isa. 40.13 is exceptional. Moreover, Paul has distinct rhetorical and exegetical reasons to distinguish these terms and to make use of the πνεῦμα- and νοῦς-forms of Isa. 40.13 in 1 Corinthians 2. I argue, therefore, that Paul's writing in 1 Corinthians 2 reveals his awareness and use of two forms of Isa. 40.13.

That Paul and Wisdom 9 share an exegetical tradition (that appeals to the pM- and OG-forms of Isa. 40.13) shows that Paul's interest in the πνεῦμα- and νοῦς-forms of Isa. 40.13 does not witness to his interest in the lexical variation between 'text-types', but rather forms part of a wider exegetical conversation. Significantly, however, while Paul partakes in a traditional perception of the πνεῦμα- and νοῦς-forms of Isa. 40.13, he is directly aware of these two semantic forms, rather than merely replicating language of Wisdom 9. Paul's appeal to two forms of Isa. 40.13 belongs to his reading of this passage in conversation with the Genesis creation narratives, again reflecting his appeal to two semantic forms of Isa. 40.13 as part of a wider exegetical conversation between two traditional works – Isaiah and Genesis. As we saw above, Paul's appeals to Isa. 8.14pM and 25.8pM similarly reveal his engagement in an exegetical conversation among his sources; in Rom. 9.33 he reads a common traditional 'rock' motif, particularly characteristic of Deuteronomy 32 and the Psalms, in light of Isa. 8.14pM together with Isa. 28.16. Likewise, in 1 Cor. 15.56 he reads Genesis 2–3 in light of Isa. 25.8pM.

In the three examples discussed in this chapter – Paul's appeals to Isa. 8.14 (Rom. 9.33), 25.8 (1 Cor. 15.54), and 40.13 (1 Cor. 2.16) – two important conditions converge. In each case, the passage significantly structures his logic (a type B case, cf. Section 2.2.2, above) *and* his appeal to the passage forms part of a broader exegetical conversation. This last point underscores the presence of the discursive exegetical contextualization in Paul's practice, which I have argued to be so basic to the ancient exegetes' use of scripture. In Paul's appeal both to Isa. 8.14pM and to 25.8pM, only the *cited* pM-form is semantically integral to his argument, and the alternative OG-form was semantically irrelevant (indeed, counter-productive), so we could not expect to see any trace of those OG-forms in his writing. By contrast, in the case of Isa. 40.13 in 1 Cor. 2.16, both of the available sense contours were useful for his rhetorical project in 1 Corinthians 1–2. Both forms structure his thought. However, the rhetorical impact of 1 Corinthians 1–2 does not depend on an audience perceiving his private exegesis of two sense contours here.

---

157   See Footnote 152, above.

7.6 *Chapter conclusion*

The 'suitability argument' is frequently invoked against the possibility of Paul's preference for a given form of a passage. Taking each of Paul's citations to structure his thought to the same degree, commentators often assume that, were Paul aware of alternatives, he would invariably prefer the one most suitable to his logic. I have highlighted two problems with this reasoning. First, a particular form of a passage structures the logic of Paul's argument only on some occasions. In other cases, other factors, such as the rhetorical or aesthetic qualities of a passage, make it appropriate for citation. Therefore, with respect to his logic, the need for a particular form of a passage often does not arise. Second, preoccupations with lexical suitability obscure the issue. Lexical fidelity to sources is rarely his concern. Paul makes copious lexical changes to his cited material. Such changes, however, often do not affect the sense contour in which he is interested.

Sometimes a particular semantic form of a source-passage is integral to his logic. That is to say, Paul's reasoning relies on the semantic shape of the passage (its sense contour) rather than on its lexical shape. While Paul might make lexical changes to such a passage in order to increase rhetorical congruence, the sense contour that structures his thought remains unchanged (e.g. Isa. 8.14^{pM}). In these cases a convergence of conditions makes his preference for a particular form of a passage possible. Such a convergence in some cases pertained to Paul's use of Isaiah^{pM} discussed in this chapter. Moreover, Paul's use of Isa. 8.14^{pM} and 28.5^{pM} belongs, in each case, to a more inclusive exegetical process, in which Paul reads the Isaiah passage in conversation with other passages from Jewish scripture. It cannot be proved that he actually chose the pM-form in these cases, as his text does not explicitly indicate his simultaneous use of alternative forms. However, because his appeals to logically structural passages appear within inclusive exegetical processes, these appeals reflect Paul's interest in their location within the semantic context of a given conversation, rather than a detached interest in lexical variations as such. This inclusive exegetical process is also evident in the final example (Isa. 40.13), in which Paul's writing supplies direct ideological and lexical evidence that Paul knew and used different forms of the same passage (pM, πνεῦμα; OG νοῦς).

8

CONCLUSIONS

At the outset (Chapter 1) I presented two distinct positions, broadly represented by two scholars, Ellis and Koch. Despite differences in their conclusions, both broach the question at hand in the same terms. This shared framework is indicative of a general tendency to conceive of ancient Jews' awareness of first-century textual variation in terms of modern text-critical categories. As a result, the text-critical method has become a heuristic device, which solves the problem in the very terms in which the problem is posed, resulting in a tautology. I have argued that historical discussion of ancient awareness and exegetical use of textual variation must not be framed in terms of these categories, but rather in terms that are commensurate with exegetical patterns recognizable in the ancient literature in question.

Our question of attitudes to ancient Jewish scripture is a historical one. A historical study cannot be guided by the analytical priorities of the text-critical programme. When Paul's practice is judged according to text-critical standards, discussion of lexical material divorced from its semantic context becomes the ground for assessing his awareness and use of textual plurality. However, here I have shown that lexical fidelity to sources is often not Paul's concern. Rather, his lexical manipulations are frequently incidental to his engagement with the semantic currency of a given exegetical conversation.

The predominance of textual material available to us, and the contingent literary paradigms, should not lead to the construction of an overly literary picture of antiquity. While one can only guess at the role of memory in ancient citation practice, the extant textual evidence reveals the signs of the ongoing oral conversation in first-century Jewish exegetical communities. Awareness of text-forms and use of citation must therefore be understood as belonging to this conversation. When viewed as part of an ancient exegetical repertoire, awareness and use of textual plurality can be appreciated as a practice current among ancient Jewish exegetes.

Paul's practice reflects an erudite exegetical familiarity with Israel's scriptures. Notwithstanding uncertainties about his education, the use of textual plurality among Paul's exegetical contemporaries shows that the practice must be seen as part of the environment within which Paul learned his exegetical skills. Therefore, special appeal to the circumstances of individuals cannot bear load here. Only if we assume that Paul engaged with his ancestral scripture in isolation, can we consider his awareness and use of textual plurality impossible. However, I have shown that, despite the privileged literary situation of specialist *Yaḥad* writers, the work of *Yaḥad* literati exhibits the same oral exegetical patterning as Paul's own writings. That is, we can locate Paul's writing within this broader oral discourse.

I have argued that the modern text-critical typology is a misplaced framework for analyses of ancient exegetical practice and attitude. This typology reflects the material availability and classification of texts that belong to the nineteenth and twentieth centuries, but not to antiquity. It is also a product of the atomistic attention to lexical variation, integral to the text-critical approach. In Chapter 2 I have shown that ancient exegetes did not speculate on 'text-types' (or «texts», as I designate them). Therefore, inquiry into their perception of texts in their own context, cannot be framed in terms alien to it.

I have argued that historically more sensible analysis begins with establishing categories meaningful for ancient exegetes themselves. In order to do so, our method needs to shift from the lexical anatomy of textual criticism to the study of the semantic relationship between a literary passage and a given exegetical project. That is, rather than speaking of an exegete's awareness of a particular «text» (such as a particular version of Isaiah), we can only discuss the exegete's use of passages as units meaningful within the context of his writing. I have suggested that the exegetical use of alternative forms of the same passage can be discussed in terms of 'sense contours', which are distinct semantic properties of alternative forms of the same passage. This approach frees the discussion from questions regarding ancient exegetes' awareness of *our* textual categories. Moreover, exegetical appeals to and use of meaningful units are part of an exegetical conversation (the focus of Chapters 5 and 6). I have placed ancient awareness of textual plurality on an analytical continuum which, in expressing the mutual penetration of text and exegesis, shows that the limits of exegesis are not exclusively dictated by available copies.

Chapter 3 has looked at Josephus' use of scripture. I have shown that he is aware of varied forms of the same passage. Not only is he aware of a given passage in different languages, he can make exegetical use of semantic differences between alternative forms of the passage, and even generate his own varied forms of passages. His discussion of weights and measures, sacrifices, and priestly garments reflects this awareness and use of such different forms. His appeal to two forms of a passage relating to these matters is a choice that reveals the social motivations dictated by his daily life rather than his desire to undertake a text-critical exercise. That is, the lexical manipulation is subsumed by semantic concerns.

In Chapter 4 *Yaḥad* exegetical compositions show that some Jewish exegetes, working in a Hebrew linguistic milieu, negotiated multiple semantic forms of a traditional passage. The distinct sense contours apparent in their compositions reflect known ancient textual traditions. That is, the exegetes are working with known alternatives. Just as Josephus' appeals to textual variation reflect his daily concerns, the work of *Yaḥad* exegetes echoes their social concerns. In Chapter 5 I have argued that their work – both their 'scribal' copying of traditional works and exegetical composition – reveals an oral patterning indicative of live exegetical conversation. Therefore, their exegetical practice is comparable to that of their non-specialist contemporaries.

That is, their use of textual plurality should not be viewed as a 'scribal' anomaly, but rather as indicative of practice current within their wider environment.

The common assumption that the *Yaḥad* could engage in textual variation presupposes that, as scribes who could compare multiple copies, their mode of operation is broadly equivalent to that of the modern analyst. However, as part of a conversation, their exegetical use of textual plurality should not be viewed as a process contingent exclusively on comparison of individual variant copies, but rather as a discursive exchange of ideas associated with a given literary passage. The various kinds of exegetical use of textual plurality observed in Josephus' writing and *Yaḥad* literature provides a framework within which to assess Paul's participation in this practice. Just as we have seen the Dead Sea sectarians draw on their repertoire of traditional text-forms, we can conceive of Paul, their contemporary, as working in similar ways.

Chapter 6 has shown that Paul's thought and communication are orally structured. Paul's use of scripture, therefore, emerges from the same kind of discursive environment presupposed in *Yaḥad* writings, whose authors make use of textual plurality. This observation calls into question discussions that frame Paul's use of scripture in purely written-textual terms. In this chapter I have argued that Paul's citation of scripture often amounts to a rhetorical demonstration of personal authority. Paul's alerting his audience to his citations reveals more about the rhetorical role played by these citations than about his interest in the literary origins of his citations. Hence, Paul's documents need to be viewed as part of a discussion – within their social and rhetorical context.

In Chapter 7 I have examined Paul's use of scripture, and in particular his exegetical use of textual plurality, within this discursive authorial context. I argue that citation plays a wide variety of roles in Paul's writing. Lexical fidelity to his source is rarely Paul's concern; the urgency for Paul's preference of a 'most suitable' form is absent in many cases. This observation dispels the commonly made argument that, because he sometimes fails to select the most suitable form, he was never in a position to do so. I make a broad distinction between those of Paul's invocations of scripture that are integral to his logic and those that are rhetorical. Many of Paul's rhetorically used citations are not integral to the logic of his argument. In both uses he may make lexical changes, but these are peripheral to his semantic agenda. In examples where appeal to scripture is logically integral to Paul's argument I have argued that choice would be imperative, were Paul aware of alternatives. In light of case studies; that is, his citation of Isa. 8.14ᴾᴹ and 25.8ᴾᴹ, such preference would reflect current practice. Where Paul cites Isa. 40.13 in 1 Corinthians 2, I show that the text clearly indicates his awareness and use of alternatives.

I have proposed a shift in our approach to the question of Paul's awareness of textual plurality. This entails a broader methodological adjustment. Expedients of text-critical enquiry must not be allowed arbitrarily to constrict historical efforts to understand Paul's attitudes, and the awareness and uses of texts by ancient people at large. Historically, a purely literary vision of exegetical practice has proven untenable. And my study shows that this practice was located within the environment of an ongoing oral discussion. To understand this discussion, we need to invoke terms that are commensurate with the approaches reflected in the literature that grew out of this discussion. I have therefore argued that understanding Paul's awareness and use of textual plurality entails location of his references to scripture within the semantic framework of ancient exegeses. Within this framework I have found that exegetical use of textual plurality is entirely possible.

BIBLIOGRAPHY

Aberbach, M. and B. Grossfeld. 1982. *Targum Onkelos to Genesis: A Critical Analysis Together with an English Translation of the Text.* Hoboken, NJ: Ktav Publishing House.

Achtemeier, P. 1990. '*Omne verbum sonat:* The New Testament and the Oral Environment of Late Western Antiquity', *Journal of Biblical Literature* 109, 3–27.

Adams, E. 2000. *Constructing the World: A Study in Paul's Cosmological Language.* Edinburgh: T&T Clark.

Aeschylus. 1960. *Aeschylus II, Agamemnon, Libation-Bearers, Eumenides, Fragments* (Loeb Classical Library, No. 146). Smyth, H.W. and H. Lloyd-Jones (trans.). Cambridge, MA: Harvard University Press.

Aharoni, Y. 1961. 'Expedition B', *Israel Exploration Journal* 11, 23-40.

Aland, K. *et al.* 1994. *The Greek New Testament.* Stuttgart: Biblia-Druck.

Allegro, J.M. (ed.). 1968. *Qumran Cave 4.1 (4Q158-4Q186)*, volume 5. Oxford: Clarendon Press.

Anderson, B. 1983. *Imagined Communities: Reflections on the Origin and Spread of Nationalism.* Boston: Verso.

Aristotle. 1930. *Aristotle II, Posterior Analytica, Topica* (Loeb Classical Library, No. 391). Tredennick, H. and E.S. Forster (trans.). Cambridge, MA: Harvard University Press.

Asher, J.R. 2000. *Polarity and Change in 1 Corinthians 15* (Hermeneutische Untersuchungen zur Theologie 42). Tübingen: Mohr Siebeck.

Athenaeus. 1969. *Athenaeus IV, The Deipnosophists VIII–X* (Loeb Classical Library, No. 465). Glick, C.B. (trans.). Cambridge, MA: Harvard University Press.

Attridge, H.W. 1976. *The Interpretation of Biblical History in the 'Antiquitates Judaicae' of Flavius Josephus.* Missoula, MT: Scholars Press.

——1984. 'Josephus and His Works', in Stone, M.E. (ed.) *Jewish Writings of the Second Temple Period.* Philadelphia: Fortress Press, 185–232.

Baillet, M., J.T. Milik *et al.* (eds). 1962. *Les 'petites grottes' de Qumran*, volume 3. Oxford: Clarendon Press.

Barclay, J.M.G. 1992. 'Thessalonica and Corinth: Social Contrasts in Pauline Christianity', *Journal for the Study of the New Testament* 47, 49–74.

Bar-Ilan, M. 1988. 'Illiteracy in the Land of Israel in the First Centuries CE', in Mulder, M.J. (ed.). *Mikra: Text, Translation, Reading and Interpretation of the Hebrew Bible in Ancient Judaism and Early Christianity.* Philadelphia: Fortress Press, 46–61.

Barr, J. 2003. 'Did the Greek Pentateuch Really Serve as a Dictionary for the Translation of the Later Books?', in Baasten, M.F.J. and W.Th. van Peursen (eds). *Hamlet on a Hill: Semitic and Greek Studies Presented to Professor T. Muraoka on the Occasion of his Sixty-Fifth Birthday.* Leuven: Peeters, 523–544.

Barrett, C.K. 1968. *A Commentary on the First Epistle to the Corinthians*, second edition. London: A&C Black.

Barthélemy, D. 1950. 'Le grand rouleau d'Isaïe trouvé près de la Mer Morte', *Revue Biblique* 57, 530–549.

——1963. *Les devanciers d'Aquila.* Leiden: Brill.

Barthélemy, D. and J.T. Milik (eds). 1955. *Qumran Cave 1*, volume 1. Oxford: Clarendon Press.

Baumgarten, J.M. *et al.* (eds). 1997. *Qumran Cave 4*, volume 18. Oxford: Clarendon Press.

Baur, F.C. 1876. *Paul, the Apostle of Jesus Christ: His Life and Work, His Epistles and Doctrine: A Contribution to the Critical History of Primitive Christianity.* Zeller, E. (trans.). London: Williams & Northgate.

Begg, C.T. 2000. *Flavius Josephus: Translation and Commentary, volume 4: Judaean Antiquities, Books 5–7.* Leiden: Brill.

Begg, C.T. and P. Spilsbury. 2005. *Flavius Josephus: Translation and Commentary, volume 5: Judaean Antiquities, Books 8–10.* Leiden: Brill.

Ben-Yehuda, E. 1939. *Dictionary of the Hebrew Language.* New York: Doubleday.

Berliner, A. 1884. *Targum Onkelos: Herausgegeben und Erläutert.* Berlin: Gorzelanczyk & Co.

Bleek, F. 1828. *Brief an die Hebräer erlautert durch Einleilung, Ubersetzung, und fortlaufenden Commentar*, volume 1. Leipzig: Metzger & Wittig.

Bloch, H. 1897. *Die Quellen des Flavius Josephus in seiner Archaeologie*. Leipzig: Metzger & Wittig.

Bonner, S.F. 1977. *Education in Ancient Rome: From the Elder Cato to the Younger Pliny*. London: Methuen.

Bowman, A.K. and G. Woolf (eds). 1994. *Literacy and Power in the Ancient World*. Cambridge, MA: Cambridge University Press.

Branick, V.P. 1982. 'Source and Redaction Analysis of 1 Corinthians 1–3', *Journal of Biblical Literature* 101, 251–269.

Bratsiotis, N.P. 1966. 'נֶפֶשׁ – ψυχή. Ein Beitrag zur Erforschung der Sprache und der Theologie der Septuaginta', in *Volume Du Congrès, Genève 1965* (Supplements to *Vetus Testementum*, volume 15). Leiden: Brill, 58–89.

Brenner, A. 1982. *Colour Terms in the Old Testament*. Sheffield: Journal for the Study of the Old Testament Supplement Series 21.

Brenton, L.C.L., Sir. 1844. *The Septuagint Version of the Old Testament, According to the Vatican Text, Translated into English: With the Principal Various Readings of the Alexandrine Copy*. London: Samuel Bagster & Sons.

Broich, U. and M. Pfister (eds). 1985. *Intertexualität, Formen, Funktionen, anglistische Fallstudien*, IX. Tübingen: Max Niemeyer.

Brooke, G.J. 1985. *Exegesis at Qumran: 4QFlorilegium in its Jewish Context*. Sheffield: Society of Biblical Literature.

——1987. 'Biblical Texts in the Qumran Commentaries: Scribal Errors or Exegetical Variants?', in Evans, C.E. and W.G. Stinespring (eds). *Early Jewish and Christian Exegesis: Studies in Memory of William Hugh Brownlee*. Atlanta, GA: Scholars Press, 85–100.

——1998. 'Shared Intertextual Interpretations in the Dead Sea Scrolls and the New Testament', in Stone, M.E. and E.G. Chazon (eds). *Biblical Perspectives: Early Use and Interpretation of the Bible in Light of the Dead Sea Scrolls*. Leiden: Brill, 35–58.

——2000. '*E Pluribus Unum*: Textual Variety and Definitive Interpretation in the Qumran Scrolls', in Lim T. *et al.* (eds). *The Dead Sea Scrolls in Their Historical Context*. Edinburgh: T&T Clark, 107–122.

——2002. 'The Rewritten Law, Prophets and Psalms: Issues for Understanding the Text of the Bible', in Herbert, E.D. and E. Tov (eds). *The Bible as Book: The Hebrew Bible and the Judaean Desert Discoveries*. New Castle, DE: Oak Knoll Press, 31–40.

Brooke G.J. *et al.* (eds). 1996. *Qumran Cave 4.XVII: Parabiblical Texts, Part 3*, volume 22. Oxford: Clarendon Press.

Brown, F., S.R. Driver *et al.* (eds). 1979. *The New Brown-Driver-Briggs-Gesenius Hebrew and English Lexicon*. Peabody, MA: Hendrickson Publishers.

Brownlee, W.H. 1948. 'The Jerusalem Habakkuk Scroll', *Bulletin of the American Schools of Oriental Research* 112, 8–18.

——1949. 'Further Light on Habakkuk', *Bulletin of the American Schools of Oriental Research* 114, 9–10.

——1950. 'A Comparison of the Covenanters of the Dead Sea Scrolls with Pre-Christian Jewish Sects', *The Biblical Archaeologist* 8, 49–72.

——1951. 'Biblical Interpretation among the Sectaries of the Dead Sea Scrolls', *The Biblical Archaeologist* 14, 54–76.

——1959. *The Text of Habakkuk in the Ancient Commentary from Qumran*. Philadelphia: Journal of Biblical Literature Monograph Series.

——1964. *The Meaning of the Qumran Scrolls for the Bible*. New York: Oxford University Press.

——1979. *The Midrash Pesher of Habakkuk*. Montana: Scholars Press.

——1987. 'The Background of Biblical Interpretation at Qumran', in Evans, C.A. and W.F. Stinespring (eds). *Early Jewish and Christian Exegesis: Studies in Memory of William Hugh Brownlee*. Atlanta, GA: Scholars Press, 183–193.

Bruce, F.F. 1959. *Biblical Exegesis in the Qumran Texts*. London: Tyndale.

——1961 [1956]. *Second Thoughts on the Dead Sea Scrolls*, second edition. London: Paternoster.

——1983. 'Biblical Exposition at Qumran', in France, R.T. and D. Wenham (eds). *Gospel Perspectives, Volume III: Studies in Midrash and Historiography*. Sheffield: Sheffield Academic Press, 77–98.

Bultmann, R. 1969. 'Karl Barth, *The Resurrection of the Dead*', in *Faith and Understanding*. Philadelphia: Fortress Press, 70–72.

Burrows, M. 1948. 'Variant Readings in the Isaiah Manuscript' [Part One], *Bulletin of the American Schools of Oriental Research* 111, 16–24.
——1949a. 'Variant Readings in the Isaiah Manuscript' [Part Two], *Bulletin of the American Schools of Oriental Research* 113, 24–32.
——1949b. 'Orthography, Morphology, and Syntax of the St. Mark's Manuscript', *Journal of Biblical Literature* 68, 195–211.
Buth, R. 2000a. 'Aramaic Language', in Evans, C.A. and S.E. Porter (eds). *Dictionary of New Testament Background* (IVP Bible Dictionary Series). Nottingham: InterVarsity Press, 86–91.
——2000b. 'Aramaic Targumim: Qumran', in Evans, C.A. and S.E. Porter (eds). *Dictionary of New Testament Background* (IVP Bible Dictionary Series). Nottingham: InterVarsity Press, 91–93.
Callimachus. 1980. *Callimachus' Iambi*. Clayman, D.L. (trans.). Leiden: Brill.
Campbell, J.G. 1995. *The Use of Scripture in the Damascus Document 1–8, 19–20*. Berlin: Walter de Gruyter.
——2005. '"Rewritten Bible"' and "Parabiblical Texts": A Terminological and Ideological Critique', in Campbell J.G., J. Lyons and L.K. Pietersen (eds). *New Directions in Qumran Studies: Proceedings of the Bristol Colloquium on the Dead Sea Scrolls, 8–10 September 2003*, Library of Second Temple Studies 52. London: T&T Clark, 43–68.
Carruthers, M.J. 1992. *The Book of Memory: A Study of Memory in Medieval Culture*. Cambridge: Cambridge University Press.
Cathcart, K., M. Maher *et al.* (eds). 1992. *The Aramaic Bible*. Edinburgh: T&T Clark.
Chadwick, H. 1969. 'Florilegium', in Klauser, T. and E. Dassmann (eds). *Reallexicon für Antike Christentum: Sachwörterbuch zur Auseinandersetzung des Christentums mit der antiken Welt*, volume 7. Stuttgart: Hiersemann, 1131–1160.
Chamberlain, J.V. 1955. 'The Functions of God as Messianic Titles in the Complete Qumran Isaiah Scroll', *Vetus Testamentum* 5, 366–372.
Chow, J.K. 1992. *Patronage and Power. A Study of Social Networks in Corinth* (Journal for the Study of the New Testament Supplement Series 75). Sheffield: JSOT Press.
Chyutin, M. 2006. *Architecture and Utopia in the Temple Era*. Edinburgh: T&T Clark.
Cicero. 1970. *Cicero II, De Inventione, De Optimo Genere Oratorum, Topica* (Loeb Classical Library, No. 386). Hubbell, H.M. (trans.). Cambridge, MA: Harvard University Press.
Clark, D.L. 1957. *Rhetoric in Greco-Roman Education*. Morningside Heights, NY: Columbia University Press.
Clarke, A.D. 1993. *Secular and Christian Leadership in Corinth: A Socio-historical and Exegetical Study of 1 Corinthians 1-6* (Arbeiten zur Geschichte des antiken Judentums und des Urchristentums 18). Leiden: Brill.
Clarke, E.G. 1984. *Targum Pseudo-Jonathan of the Pentateuch: Text and Concordance*. Hoboken, NJ: Ktav Publishing House, Inc.
Cohen, S.J.D. 1979. *Josephus in Galilee and Rome: His Vita and Development as a Historian*. Leiden: Brill.
Collins, J.J. 1984. *The Apocalyptic Imagination*. New York: Crossroad.
——1995. *The Scepter and the Star: The Messiahs of the Dead Sea Scrolls and Other Ancient Literature*. London: Doubleday.
Collins, R.F. 1999. *First Corinthians* (Sacra Pagina Series 7). Collegeville and Minneapolis: Liturgical Press.
Colson, F.H. 1940. 'Philo's Quotations from the Old Testament', *Journal of Theological Studies* 41, 237–251.
Conzelmann, H. 1969. *Der Erste Brief an die Korinther*. Göttingen: Vandenhoek & Ruprecht.
——1972. *Die Apostelgeschichte: Handbuch zum Neuen Testament* 7. Tübingen: Mohr.
——1975. *1 Corinthians: A Commentary on the First Epistle to the Corinthians*. Philadelphia: Fortress Press.
Cook, S.E. 1913. '1 Esdras', in Charles, R.H. (ed.). *The Apocrypha and Pseudepigrapha of the Old Testament in English*, in two volumes. Oxford: Clarendon Press, 1–58.
Cross, F.M. 1958. *The Ancient Library of Qumran and Modern Biblical Studies*. New York: Doubleday & Co., Inc.
——1966. 'The Contribution of the Qumran Discoveries to the Study of the Biblical Text', *Israel Exploration Journal* 16, 81–95.
Crown, A. D. and L. Cansdale. 1994. 'Qumran: Was it an Essene Settlement?', *Biblical Archaeology Review* 20, 24–35, 73–74, 76–78.
Dahl, N.A. 1967. 'Paul and the Church at Corinth according to 1 Corinthians 1–4', in Farmer, W.R.,

C.D.F. Moule and R.R. Niebuhr (eds). *Christian History and Interpretation, Studies Presented to John Knox.* Cambridge: Cambridge University Press, 313–335.

Das, A.A. 2007. *Solving the Romans Debate.* Minneapolis: Fortress Press.

Daube, D. 1973. 'Alexandrian Methods of Interpretation and the Rabbis', in Fischel, H.A. (ed.). *Rabbinic Literature and Greco-Roman Philosophy: A Study of Epicurea and Rhetorica in Early Midrashic Writings.* Leiden: Brill, 165–182.

Davies, P.R. 1995. *Scribes and Schools: The Canonization of the Hebrew Scriptures.* Louisville, KY: John Knox Press.

Davies, W.D. 1970. *Paul and Rabbinic Judaism: Some Rabbinic Elements in Pauline Theology.* London: S.P.C.K.

——1983. 'Reflections about the Use of the Old Testament in the New in its Historical Context', *Jewish Quarterly Review* 74, 105–137.

Davila, J. 1993. 'Text Type and Terminology: Genesis and Exodus as Test Cases', *Revue de Qumran* 16, 3–37.

Deissmann, A. 1905. *Die Septuaginta-Papyri und andere altchristliche Texte der Heidelberger Papyrus-Sammlung.* Heidelberg: Heidelberg.

——1925. *Paulus: eine kultur- und religionsgeschichtliche Skizze.* Tübingen: Mohr-Siebeck.

——1926. *Paul: A Study in Social and Religious History,* second edition. Wilson, W.E. (trans.). London: Hodder & Stoughton Ltd.

——1978 [1927]. *Light from the Ancient East.* Lionel, R. and M. Strachan (trans.). New York: George H. Doran.

Delitzsch, F. 1920. *Die Lese – und Schreibfehler im Alten Testament; nebst den dem Schrifttexte einverleibten Randnoten klassifiziert.* Berlin: W. de Gruyter.

Dimant, D. 1984. 'Qumran Sectarian Literature', in Stone, M.E. (ed.). *Jewish Writings of the Second Temple Period.* Philadelphia: Fortress Press, 483–550.

——1995. 'The Qumran Manuscripts: Contents and Significance', in Dimant, D. and L. Schiffman (eds). *Time to Prepare a Way in the Wilderness: Papers on the Qumran Scrolls by Fellows of the Institute of Advanced Studies of the Hebrew University, Jerusalem, 1989–1990.* Leiden: Brill, 23–58.

Dio Chrysostom. 1940. *Dio Chrysostom III: Discourses XXXI–XXXVI* (Loeb Classical Library, No. 465). Crosby, H.L. and J.W. Cohoon (trans.). Cambridge, MA: Harvard University Press.

Dionysus of Halicarnassus. 1976. *Critical Essays I* (Loeb Classical Library, No. 465). Usher, S. (trans.). Cambridge, MA: Harvard University Press.

Dodd, C.H. 1965. *According to the Scriptures: The Sub-structure of New Testament Theology.* London: Collins/Fontana.

Dorival, G., M. Harl and O. Munnich (eds). 1988. *La Bible grecque des Septante.* Paris: Les Éditions du Cerf.

Driver, G.R. and A. Neubauer (eds). 1876–1877. *The Fifty-third Chapter of Isaiah according to the Jewish Interpreters, I-II.* Oxford: J. Parker.

Duhm, B. 1906. *Das Buch Habakuk: Text, Übersetzung und Erklärung.* Tübingen: Mohr Siebeck.

Dunn, J.D.G. 1988. *Romans 1–8* (Word Biblical Commentary volume 38a). Dallas, TX: Word Books Publisher.

Ehrlich, A.B. 1912. *Randglossen zur Hebräischen Bibel: textkritisches, sprachliches und sachliches.* Volume 5. Leipzig: J.C. Hinrichs.

Eisenman, R. 1983. *Maccabees, Zadokites, Christians and Qumran.* Leiden: Brill.

——1986. *James the Just in the Habakkuk Pesher.* Leiden: Brill.

Elliger, K. 1953. *Studien zum Habakuk-Kommentar vom Toten Meer.* Tübingen: Mohr-Siebeck.

Ellis, E.E. 1957. *Paul's Use of the Old Testament.* Edinburgh: Oliver & Boyd.

——1978. *Prophecy and Hermenteutic.* Tübingen: Mohr.

——1986. 'Traditions in 1 Corinthians', *New Testament Studies* 32, 481–502.

Ernesti, I.A. 1756. *Exercitationum Flavianarum prima de fontibus Archaeologiae.* Leipzig: Metzger & Wittig.

——1776. *Opuscula Philologica Critica.* Leiden: Samuel & Johannes Luchtmans.

Euripides. 1971. *Euripides III, Bacchanals, Madness of Hercules, Children of Hercules, Phoenician Maidens, Suppliants* (Loeb Classical Library, No. 11). Way, A.S. (trans.). Cambridge, MA: Harvard University Press.

Fee, G. 1987. *The First Epistle to the Corinthians.* Grand Rapids: Eerdmans.

Feldman, L.H. 1984. *Josephus and Modern Scholars (1937–1980).* Berlin: Walter de Gruyter.

——1988. 'Use, Authority and Exegesis of Mikra in the Writings of Josephus', in Mulder, M.J. (ed.).

Mikra: Text, Translation, Reading and Interpretation of the Hebrew Bible in Ancient Judaism and Early Christianity. Philadelphia: Fortress Press, 455–518.

——1996. 'Josephus, *Jewish Antiquities* and Pseudo-Philo's *Biblical Antiquities*', in Feldman, L.H. (ed.). *Studies in Hellenistic Judaism*. Leiden: Brill, 56–82.

——1997. 'Josephus' Portrait of Isaiah', in Broyles, C.C. and C.A. Evans (eds). *Writing and Reading the Scroll of Isaiah: Studies of an Interpretive Tradition*, in two volumes. Leiden: Brill, 583–608.

——1998a. *Josephus's Interpretation of the Bible*. Berkeley: University of California Press.

——1998b. *Studies in Josephus' Rewritten Bible*. Leiden: Brill.

——2000. *Flavius Josephus: Translation and Commentary, volume 3: Judaean Antiquities, Books 1–4*. Mason, S. (ed.). Leiden: Brill.

Finkel, A. 1963–1964. 'The Pesher of Dreams and Scriptures', *Revue de Qumran* 4, 357–370.

Fishbane, M. 1985. *Biblical Interpretation in Ancient Israel*. Oxford: Clarendon Press.

——1988. 'Use, Authority and Interpretation of Mikra at Qumran', in Mulder, M.J. (ed.). *Mikra: Text, Translation, Reading and Interpretation of the Hebrew Bible in Ancient Judaism and Early Christianity*. Philadelphia: Fortress Press, ch. 10.

Fitzmyer, J. 1961. 'The Use of Explicit Old Testament Quotations in Qumran Literature and in the New Testament', *New Testament Studies* 7, 297–333.

——1970. 'The Languages of Palestine in the First Century A.D.', *Catholic Biblical Quarterly* 32, 507–518.

——1993. *Romans: A New Translation With Introduction and Commentary* (The Anchor Bible). London: Doubleday.

Flesher, P.V.M. 1992. *Targum Studies: Textual and Contextual Studies in the Pentateuchal Targums*, in two volumes. Atlanta, GA: Scholars Press.

Francis, J. 1980. 'As Babes in Christ: Some Proposals regarding 1 Corinthians 3.1-3', *Journal for the Study of the New Testament* 7, 41–61.

Funk, R.W. 1966. *Language, Hermeneutic and Word of God*. New York: Harper & Row.

Gager, J. 1985. *The Origins of Anti-Semitism*. Oxford: Oxford University Press.

Gamble, H.Y. 1995. *Books and Readers in the Early Church: A History of Early Christian Texts*. New Haven: Yale University Press.

García Martínez, F. and E.J. Tigchelaar. 1997. *The Dead Sea Scrolls Study Edition*, volume 1. Leiden: Brill.

——1998. *The Dead Sea Scrolls Study Edition*, volume 2. Leiden: Brill.

Gärtner, B.E. 1967–1968. 'The Pauline and the Johannine Idea of "To Know God" Against the Hellenistic Background', *New Testament Studies* 14, 209–231.

Gerhardsson, B. 1961. *Memory and Manuscript*. Sharpe, E.J. (trans.). Copenhagen: Munskgaard.

Gillespie, T.W. 1990. 'Interpreting the Kerygma: Early Christian Prophecy according to 1 Corinthians 2:6-16', in Goehring, J.E. *et al.* (eds). *Gospel Origins and Christian Beginnings: In Honor of James M. Robinson*. Sonoma, CA: Polebridge, 151–166.

Gilliard, F.D. 1993. 'More Silent Reading in Antiquity: Non Omne Verbum Sonabat', *Journal of Biblical Literature* 111, 689–696.

Ginsberg, H.L. 1975. *Legends of the Bible*. Philadelphia: Jewish Publication Society of America.

Ginsburger, M. 1899. *Das Fragmententhargum: Thargum jeruschalmi zum Pentateuch*. Berlin: S. Calvary & Co.

Golb, N. 1980. 'The Problem of the Origin and Identification of the Dead Sea Scrolls', *Proceedings of American Philological Society* 124, 1–24.

——1985. 'Who Hid the Dead Sea Scrolls?', *Biblical Archaeologist* 48, 68–82.

——1995. *Who Wrote the Dead Sea Scrolls?: The Search for the Secret of Qumran*. London: Scribner.

Gooding, D.W. 1955. *Recensions of the Septuagint Pentateuch*. London: Tyndale Press.

——1976. 'An Appeal for a Stricter Terminology in the Textual Criticism of the Old Testament', *Journal of Semitic Studies* 21, 15–25.

Goodman, M. 1983. *State and Society in Roman Galilee, A.D. 132–212*. Totowa, NJ: Rowman & Allanheld.

——1994a. *Mission and Conversion: Proselytizing in the Religious History of the Roman Empire*. Oxford: Clarendon Press.

——1994b. 'Texts, Scribes, and Power in Roman Judaea', in Bowman, A.K. and G. Woolf (eds). *Literacy and Power in the Ancient World*. Cambridge: Cambridge University Press.

——1999. 'A Note on Josephus, the Pharisees and Ancestral Tradition', *Journal of Jewish Studies* 50, 17–20.

Goudge, H.L. 1903. *The First Epistle to the Corinthians*. London: WC.

Grabbe, L.L. 1992. 'The Translation Technique of the Greek Minor Versions: Translations of Revisions?', in Brooke, G. and B. Lindars (eds). *Septuagint, Scrolls and Cognate Writings: Papers Presented to the International Symposium on the Septuagint and Its Relations to the Dead Sea Scrolls and Other Writings*. Atlanta, GA: Scholars Press, 505–556.

Grintz, J.M. 1960. 'Hebrew as the Spoken and Written Language in the Last Days of the Second Temple', *Journal of Biblical Literature* 79, 32–47.

Gundry, R.H. 1967. *The Use of the Old Testament in Matthew's Gospel*. Leiden: Brill.

Haenchen, E. 1968. *Die Apostelgeschichte*, Kritisch-exegetischer Kommentar über das Neue Testament 3. Göttingen: Vandenhoeck & Ruprecht.

Hammershaimb, E. 1959. 'On the Method, Applied in the Copying of Manuscripts in Qumran', *Vetus Testamentum* 9, 415–418.

Hani, J. 1972. *Consolation d'Apollonius*. Paris: Editions Klincksieck, 30–50.

Hanson, A.T. 1974. *Studies in Paul's Technique and Theology*. Grand Rapids: Eerdmans.

Hanson, P.D. 1979. *The Dawn of Apocalyptic*, revised edition. Philadelphia: Fortress Press.

Harris, W.V. 1989. *Ancient Literacy*. Cambridge, MA: Harvard University Press.

Hata, G. 1975. 'Is the Greek Version of Josephus' Jewish War a Translation or a Rewriting of the First Version?', *Jewish Quarterly Review* 66, 89–108.

Hatch, E. 1889. *Essays in Biblical Greek*. Oxford: Clarendon Press.

Hatch, E., H.A. Redpath *et al.* (eds). 1998. *A Concordance to the Septuagint and Other Greek Versions of the Old Testament (Including Apocryphal Books)*. Grand Rapids: Baker Books.

Hays, R. 1988. 'Review of *Die Schrift als Zeuge des Evangeliums* by D.-E. Koch', *Journal of Biblical Literature* 107, 331–333.

——1989. *Echoes of Scripture in the Letters of Paul*. New Haven: Yale University Press.

Heinrici, C.F.G. 1900. *Die Korinther Briefe*, Kommentar II. Göttingen: KEK.

Helmbold, W.C. and E. O'Neill (eds). 1959. *Plutarch's Quotations* (American Philological Association Monographs 19). Oxford: Blackwell.

Hengel, M. 1969. *Judentum und Hellenismus: Studien zu ihrer Begegnung unter besonderer Berücksichtigung Palästinas bis zur Mitte des 2. Jh. v. Chr.* Tübingen: Mohr.

——1991a. *Der vorchristliche Paulus* in *Paulus und das Antike Judentum*. Tübingen: Mohr-Siebeck, 177–193.

——1991b. *The Pre-Christian Paul*. Bowden, J. (trans.). Philadelphia: Trinity Press International.

Hiebert, R.J.V. 2007. 'Genesis', in *A New Translation of the Septuagint*. The International Organization for Septuagint and Cognate Studies. Oxford: Oxford University Press. Online: http://ccat.sas.upenn.edu/nets/edition (accessed 29 September 2010).

Hobsbawm, E. and T. Ranger (eds). 1992. *The Invention of Tradition*. Cambridge: Cambridge University Press.

Hock, R.F. 1980. *The Social Context of Paul's Ministry: Tentmaking and Apostleship*. Philadelphia: Fortress Press.

——2005. 'The Educational Curriculum in Chariton's *Callirhoe*', in Brant, J.-A.A., C.W. Hedrick and C. Shea (eds). *Ancient Fiction: The Matrix of Early Christian and Jewish Narrative*, Symposium 32. Atlanta, GA: Scholars Press, 15–36.

Hölscher, G. 1916. 'Josephus', in Pauly, A. and G. Wissowa (eds). *Realencyclopädie der klassischen Altertumswissenschaft* 9, columns 1934–2000.

Hooker, M.D. 1990a. 'Beyond the things which are written', in Hooker, M.D. (ed.). *From Adam to Christ: Essays on Paul*. Cambridge: Cambridge University Press, 106–112.

——1990b. 'Beyond the things that are written? St. Paul's use of scripture', in Hooker, M.D. (ed.). *From Adam to Christ: Essays on Paul*. Cambridge: Cambridge University Press, 139–154.

Horbury, W.A. 1985. 'The Messianic Associations of "the Son of Man"', *Journal for the Study of the New Testament* 1986, 503–527.

——1998. *Jewish Messianism and the Cult of Christ*. London: SCM Press.

Horgan, M.P. 1979. *Pesharim: Qumran Interpretations of Biblical Books*. Washington, DC: Catholic Bible Association of America.

Horowitz, W. 1998. *Mesopotamian Cosmic Geography*. Winona Lake, IN: Eisenbrauns.

Horrell, D.G. 1996. *The Social Ethos of the Corinthian Correspondence: Interests and Ideology from 1 Corinthians to 1 Clement* (Studies of the New Testament and Its World). Edinburgh: T&T Clark.

Horsley, R.A. 1976. '*Pneumatikos* vs. *Psyuchikos*: Distinctions of Spiritual Status among the Corinthians', *Harvard Theological Review* 69, 269–288.

Horst, F. and T.H. Robinson. 1938. 'Die zwölf kleinen Propheten', *Handbuch zum Alten Testament*. Tübingen: Mohr-Siebeck.

Howard, G.E. 1973. 'The "Aberrant" Text of Philo's Quotations Reconsidered', *Hebrew Union College Annual* 44, 197–209.

Hübner, H. 1984. *The Law in Paul's Theology*. Edinburgh: T&T Clark.

——1993. *Biblische Theologie des Neuen Testaments. Band. 2: Die Theologie des Paulus und ihre neutestamentliche Wirkungsgeschichte*. Göttingen: Vandenhoeck & Ruprecht.

Hull, M.F. 2005. *Baptism on Account of the Dead (1 Cor 15:29): An Act of Faith in the Resurrection*. Atlanta, GA: SBL.

Hurvitz, A. 2000. 'Was Qumran Hebrew a "Spoken" Language? On Some Recent Views and Positions', in Muraoka, T. and J.F. Elwolde (eds). *Diggers at the Well: Proceedings of a Third International Symposium on the Hebrew of the Dead Sea Scrolls and Ben Sira*. Leiden: Brill.

Isaacs, M.E. 1976. *The Concept of Spirit* (Heythrop Monograph Series 1). London: Heythrop Monographs.

Jaffee, M.S. 2001. *Torah in the Mouth: Writing and Oral Tradition in Palestinian Judaism, 200 BCE–400 CE*. Oxford: Oxford University Press.

Jastrow, M. 1903. *A Dictionary of the Targumim, the Talmud Babli, and Yerushalmi, and the Midrashic Literature; with an Index of Scriptural Quotations*. London: Luzac & Co.

Jeremias, J. 1923–1937. *Jerusalem zur Zeit Jesu; eine kulturgeschichtliche Untersuchung zur neutestamentlichen Zeitgeschichte*. Göttingen: Vandenhoeck & Ruprecht.

Johnson, F. 1895. *The Quotations in the New Testament from the Old Testament*. London: Baptist Tract and Book Society.

Joosten, J. 2000. 'The Knowledge and Use of Hebrew in the Hellenistic Period: Qumran and the Septuagint', in Muraoka, T. and J.F. Elwolde (eds). *Diggers at the Well: Proceedings of a Third International Symposium on the Hebrew of the Dead Sea Scrolls and Ben Sira*. Leiden: Brill, 115–130.

Kahle, P.E. 1915. 'Untersuchgen zur Geschichte des Pentateuchtextes', *ISK* 88, 399–439.

——1954. 'Die im August 1952 entdeckte Lederrolle mit dem griechischen Text der kleinen Propheten und das Problem der LXX', *TLZ* 79, 1–29.

Kaiser, O. 1983. *Isaiah 1–12: A Commentary*. Bowman, J. (trans.). London: SCM.

Kasher, R. 1988. 'The Interpretation of Scripture in Rabbinic Literature', in Mulder, M.J. (ed.). *Mikra: Text, Translation, Reading and Interpretation of the Hebrew Bible in Ancient Judaism and Early Christianity*. Philadelphia: Fortress Press, ch. 15.

Katz, P. 1964. *The Seed of Wisdom*. Toronto: University of Toronto Press.

Kautzsch, E. 1869. *De Veteris Testamenti Locis A Paulo Apostolo Allegatis*. Leipzig: Metzger & Wittig.

Kenyon, F. 1932. *Books and Readers in Ancient Greece and Rome*. Oxford: Clarendon Press.

Kister, M.K. 1998. 'A Common Heritage: Biblical Interpretation at Qumran and its Implications', in Stone, M.E. and E.G. Chazon (eds). *Biblical Perspectives: Early Use and Interpretation of the Bible in Light of the Dead Sea Scrolls*. Leiden: Brill, 101–111.

Kittel, R. (ed.). 1997. *Biblia Hebraica Stuttgartensia*, Fünfte verbesserte Auflage. Stuttgard: Deutsche Biblegesellschaft.

Klein, M.L. 1980. *The Fragment-Targums of the Pentateuch according to their Extant Sources*, in two volumes. Rome: Biblical Institute Press.

Knox, B.M.W. and P.E. Easterling. 1985. 'Books and Readers in the Ancient World', in Knox, B.M.W. and P.E. Easterling (eds). *Cambridge History of Ancient Literature*, in two volumes. Cambridge: Cambridge University Press, volume 1, 11–25.

Knox, W.L. 1940. 'A Note on Philo's use of the Old Testament', *Journal of Theological Studies* 41, 30–34.

Koch, D.-A. 1980. 'Beobachtungen zum christologischen Schriftgebrauch in den vorpaulinschen Gemeinden', *Zeitschrift für Neutestamentliche Wissenschaft* 71, 174–191.

——1985. 'Der Text von Hab 2:4b in der Septuaginta und im neuen Testament', *Zeitschrift für Neutestamentliche Wissenschaft* 76, 68–85.

——1986. *Die Schrift als Zeuge des Evangeliums*. Tübingen: Mohr-Siebeck.

König, F.E. 1881–95. *Historisch-kritisches Lehrgebaude der hebräischen Sprache*. 2 volumes. Leipzig: J.C. Hinrichs.

Kooij, A. van der. 1981. *Die Alten Textzeugen des Jesajabuches: Ein Beitrag zur Textgeschichte des Alten Testaments*. Göttingen: Vanderhoek & Ruprecht.

——1989. 'The Septuagint of Isaiah: Translation and Interpretation', in Vermeylen, J. (ed.). *The Book of Isaiah, Le Livre d'Isaïe*. Leuven: Peeters.

——1989–1990. '1QIsaᵃ Col. VIII, 4-11 (Isa 8, 11-18): A Contextual Approach of its Variants', *Revue de Qumran* 14, 569–581.

——1992. 'The Old Greek of Isaiah in Relation to the Qumran Texts of Isaiah: Some General Comments', in Brooke, G. and B. Lindars (eds). *Septuagint, Scrolls and Cognate Writings: Papers Presented to the International Symposium on the Septuagint and Its Relations to the Dead Sea Scrolls and Other Writings*. Atlanta, GA: Scholars Press, 195–213.

Kraft, R.A. 2003. 'Some Newly Identified LXX/OG Fragments among the Amherst Papyri at the Pierpont Morgan Library in New York City', in Paul, S.M., R.A. Kraft *et al.* (eds). *Emanuel: Studies in Hebrew Bible, Septuagint, and Dead Sea Scrolls in Honor of Emanuel Tov*. Leiden: Brill, 542–551.

Kümmel, W.G. 1975. *Introduction to the New Testament*. Kee, H.C. (trans.). Nashville: Abingdon Press.

Kutscher, E.Y. 1974. *The Language and Linguistic Background of The Isaiah Scroll (1QIsaᵃ)* (Studies on the Texts of the Desert of Judah 6). Leiden: Brill.

Lagarde, P. A. de. 1882. *Ankündigung einer neuen Ausgabe der griechischen Übersetzung des Alten Testaments*. Göttingen: Dieterischen Univ.-Buchdruckerei.

Lange, A. 2002. 'The Status of Biblical Texts in the Qumran Corpus and the Canonical Process', in Herbert, E.D. and E. Tov (eds). *The Bible as a Book: The Hebrew Bible and the Judaean Desert Discoveries*. New Castle, DE: Oak Knoll Press, 21–30.

Lapide, P. 1972–1975. 'Insights from Qumran into the Languages of Jesus', *Revue de Qumran* 8, 483–501.

Levine, L.I. 2000. *The Ancient Synagogue: The First Thousand Years*. New Haven and London: Yale University Press.

Levy, J. 1924. *Chaldäisches Wörterbuch über die Targumim*, in two volumes. Berlin: B. Harz.

Liddell, G., R. Scott *et al.* (eds). 1992. *A Greek-English Lexicon*. Oxford: Clarendon Press.

Lieberman, S. 1965. *Greek in Jewish Palestine: Studies in the Life and Manners of Jewish Palestine in the II–IV Centuries C.E.* New York: Feldheim.

Lim, T.H. 1991. *Attitudes to Holy Scripture in the Qumran Pesharim and Pauline Letters*. D.Phil. thesis (Oxford).

——1997. *Holy Scripture in the Qumran Pesharim and Pauline Letters*. Oxford: Clarendon Press.

——2002. *Pesharim, Companion to the Qumran Scrolls 3*. Sheffield: Sheffield Academic Press.

Lindars, B. 1961. *New Testament Apologetic: The Doctrinal Significance of the Old Testament Quotations*. London: SCM Press.

——1992. 'Introduction', to Brooke, G. and B. Lindars (eds). *Septuagint, Scrolls and Cognate Writings: Papers Presented to the International Symposium on the Septuagint and Its Relations to the Dead Sea Scrolls and Other Writings*. Atlanta, GA: Scholars Press, 1–7.

Lord, A.B. 1960. *The Singer of Tales*. Cambridge, MA: Harvard University Press.

Louw, T.A.W. van der. 2008. 'The Dictation of the Septuagint Version', *Journal for the Study of Judaism* 39, 211–229.

Lührmann, D. 1965. *Das Offenbarungsverstandnis bei Paulus und in paulinischen Gemeinden*. Wissenschaftliche Monographien zum Alten und Neuen Testament, 16. Neukirchen-Vluyn: Neukirchener Verlag.

Lust, J., E. Eynikel *et al.* (eds). 1992–1996. *A Greek-English Lexicon of the Septuagint*. Stuttgart: Deutsche Bibelgesellschaft.

Mann, J. 1940. *The Bible as Read and Preached in the Old Synagogue: A Study in the Cycles of the Readings from Torah and Prophets, as Well as from Psalms, and in the Structure of the Midrashic Homilies*, volume 1. Cincinnati: Mann-Sonne Publication Committee.

——1996. *A Greek-English Lexicon of the Septuagint*. Stuttgart: Deutsche Bibelgesellschaft.

Marcos, N.F. 2000. *The Septuagint in Context: An Introduction to the Greek Version of the Bible*. W.G.E. Watson (trans.). Leiden: Brill.

Marcus, R. (trans.). 1952. *Josephus VII, Jewish Antiquities Books XII–XIV* (Loeb Classical Library, No. 365). Cambridge, MA: Harvard University Press.

——1978. *Josephus VI, Jewish Antiquities Books IX–XI* (Loeb Classical Library, No. 326). Cambridge, MA: Harvard University Press.

Marcus, R. and A. Wikgren (trans.). 1980. *Josephus VIII, Jewish Antiquities Books XV–XVII* (Loeb Classical Library, No. 410). Cambridge, MA: Harvard University Press.

Marrou, H.I. 1956. *A History of Education in Antiquity*. Lamb, G. (trans.). New York: Sheed & Ward.

Marshall, P. 1987. *Enmity in Corinth: Social Conventions in Paul's Relations with the Corinthians* (Wissentschaftliche Untersuchungen zum Neuen Testament, 2. Riehe 23). Tübingen: Mohr Siebeck.

Marti, K. 1904. *Das Dodekapropheton, Kurzer Handcommentar zum Alten Testament*. Tübingen: Mohr Siebeck.

Martin, D.B. 1995. *The Corinthian Body*. New Haven: Yale University Press.

Martin, M. 1958. *The Scribal Character of the Dead Sea Scrolls I–II*. Louvain: Publications Universitaires.

Martyn, J.L. 1997. *Theological Issues in the Letters of Paul*. Nashville: Abingdon Press.

Mason, S. 1991. *Flavius Josephus on the Pharisees*. Leiden: Brill.

——1994. 'For I am not Ashamed of the Gospel (Rom 1.16)', in Jervis, L.A. and P. Richardson (eds). *Gospel in Paul: Studies on Corinthians, Galatians and Romans for Richard N. Longenecker*. Sheffield: Sheffield Academic Press, 254–287.

——1996. '*Philosophiai*: Graeco-Roman, Judaean and Christian', in Kloppenborg, J.S. and G. Wilson (eds). *Voluntary Associations in the Graeco-Roman World*. London, New York: Routledge 1996, 31–58.

——2000. 'Introduction', to Mason, S. (ed.). *Flavius Josephus: Translation and Commentary, volume 3: Judaean Antiquities, Books 1–4*, XIII–XXXVI.

——2001. *Flavius Josephus: Translation and Commentary, volume 9: Vita, Books 5–7*. Leiden: Brill.

——2002. 'Josephus and his Twenty-Two Book Canon', in Herbert, E.D. and E. Tov (eds). *The Bible as a Book: The Hebrew Bible and the Judaean Desert Discoveries*. New Castle, DE: Oak Knoll Press.

McNamara, M. 1966. *The New Testament and the Palestinian Targum to the Pentateuch*. Rome: Pontifical Biblical Institute.

——1992. (trans.). *Targum Neofiti 1: Genesis* (The Aramaic Bible, volume 1B). Edinburgh: T&T Clark.

Meeks, W.A. 1982. '"And Rose Up To Play": Midrash and Paraenesis in 1 Corinthians 10:1-22', *Journal for the Study of the New Testament* 16, 64–78.

Metzger, B.M. 1958–1959. 'The Furniture in the Scriptorium at Qumran', *Revue de Qumran*, 509-15.

Mez, A. 1895. *Die Bibel des Josephus, untersucht für Buch v-vii der Archäologie*. Basel: Jaeger and Kober.

Michel, O. 1929. *Paulus und seine Bibel*. Gütersloh: C. Bertelsmann.

Milik, J.T. 1957. *Dix ans de découvertes dans le desert de Juda*. Paris: Les Éditions du Cerf.

Mitchell, M.M. 1991. *Paul and the Rhetoric of Reconciliation: An Exegetical Investigation of the Language and Composition of 1 Corinthians*. Louisville, KY: John Knox Press.

Molin, G. 1952. 'Der Habakukkommentar von 'En Fešha in der alttestamentlichen Wissenschaft', *Theologische Zeitschrift* 8, 340–357.

Moo, D.M. 1996. *The Epistle to the Romans* (New International Commentary on the New Testament). Grand Rapids: Eerdmans.

Morgan, R. 1997 [1995]. *Romans*. Sheffield: Sheffield Academic Press.

Morgan, T. 1998. *Literate Education in the Hellenistic and Roman Worlds*. Cambridge: Cambridge University Press.

Munck, J. 1959. *Paul and the Salvation of Mankind*. London: ET.

Murphy-O'Connor, J. 1986. 'Interpolations in 1 Corinthians', *Catholic Biblical Quarterly* 48, 81–94.

——2005. 'Review of *Paul and First-Century Letter Writing: Secretaries, Composition and Collection* by E. Randolph Richards', *Revue Biblique*, 112–114, 628–633.

Nägeli, T. 1905. *Der Wortschatz des Apostels Paulus*. Göttingen: Vandenhoeck & Ruprecht.

Nanos, M.D. 1996. *The Mystery of Romans: The Jewish Context of Paul's Letter*. Minneapolis: Fortress Press.

Nestle, E. *et al.* 1994. *Novum Testamentum Graece*. Stuttgart: Biblia-Druck.

Nodet, É. 1996. *Flavius Joséphe, les Antiquités juives*, volume 1: Livres I à III. Paris: Les Éditions du Cerf.

——1997. 'Josephus and the Pentateuch', *Journal of Jewish Studies* 28, 154–194.

——2000–2001. *Les Antiqités juives Josèphe*. Paris: Les Éditions du Cerf.

——2006. 'Josephus and the Books of Samuel', in Cohen, S.J.D. *et al.* (eds). *Studies in Josephus and the Varieties of Ancient Judaism: Louis H. Feldman Jubilee Volume*. Leiden: Brill, 141–167.

Norton, J. 2009. 'The question of "scribal exegesis" at Qumran', in Petersen, A.K., T. Elgvin *et al.* (eds). *Northern Lights on the Dead Sea Scrolls: Proceedings of the Nordic Qumran Network 2003–2006*. Leiden: Brill, 135–154.

Nowack, D.W. (ed.). 1897. *Die kleinen Propheten, Handkommentar zum Alten Testament*, III, 4. Göttingen: Vandehoeck & Ruprecht.

Oesch, J.M. 1979. *Petucha und Setuma, Untersuchungen zu einer überlieferten Gliederung im hebräischen Text des Alten Testament*. Göttingen: Freiburg.

Olofsson, S. 1990. *God Is My Rock: A Study of Translation Technique and Theological Exegesis in the Septuagint*. Stockholm: Almqvist & Wiksell International.

Ong, W.J. 1982. *Orality and Literacy: The Technologizing of the Word*. London: Methuen.

Orlinsky, H.M. 1950. 'Studies in the St. Mark's Isaiah Scroll', *Journal of Biblical Literature* 69, 149–166.

——1960. 'The origin of the Kethib-Qere system: A new approach', *Vetus Testamentum* (Supplemental Series) 7, 184–192.

Orton, D.E. 1989. *Understanding the Scribe: Matthew and the Apocalyptic Ideal.* Sheffield: JSOT Press.

Parry, M. 1971. *The Making of Homeric Verse: The Collected Papers of Milman Parry.* Parry, A. (ed.). Oxford: Oxford University Press.

Parsons, P.J. 1990. '7. The scripts and their date', in Tov, E. *et al. The Greek Minor Prophets Scroll from Nahal Ḥever (8HevXIIgr), DJD,* volume 8. Oxford: Clarendon Press, 19–26.

Pearson, B.A. 1973. *The Pneumatikos-Psychikos Terminology in 1 Corinthians: A Study in the Theology of the Corinthians Opponents of Paul and Its Relation to Gnosticism* (Society of Biblical Literature Dissertation Series 12). Missoula, MT: Society of Biblical Literature.

Pérez-Fernández, M. 1981. *Tradiciones Mesiánicas en el Targum Palestinense: Éstudios exegéticos.* Jerusalem: Valencia.

Perrin, N. 1976. *Jesus and the Kingdom of God.* Philadelphia: Fortress Press.

Pervo, R.I. 1987. *Profit with Delight: The Literary Genre of the Acts of the Apostles.* Philadelphia: Fortress Press.

Philo. 1935. *Philo VI, On Abraham, On Joseph, Moses* (Loeb Classical Library, No. 289). Colson, F.H. (trans.). Cambridge, MA: Harvard University Press.

——1937. *Philo VII, On The Decalogue, On The Special Laws* (Loeb Classical Library, No. 289). Colson, F.H. (trans.). Cambridge, MA: Harvard University Press.

Pliny the Younger. 1923. *Pliny's Letters* (Loeb Classical Library, No. 55). Melmouth, W. (trans.), Hutchinson, W.M.L. (rev.). Cambridge, MA: Harvard University Press.

Ploeg, J.P.M. van der. 1951. *Bibliotheca Orientalis,* VIII, No. 1.

Pogoloff, S.M. 1992. *Logos and Sophia: The Rhetorical situation of 1 Corinthians.* Society of Biblical Literature Dissertation Series 134. Atlanta, GA: Scholars Press.

Pope, M.H. 1992. 'Bible, Euphemism and Dysphemism in the Bible', in Freedman, D.N. *et al.* (ed.). *The Anchor Bible Dictionary.* New York: Doubleday, volume 1, 720–725.

Porter, S.E. 1997. 'Paul of Tarsus and his Letters', in Porter, S.E. (ed.). *Handbook of Classical Rhetoric in the Hellenistic Period 330 B.C.–A.D. 400.* Leiden: Brill, 532–585.

Procksch, O. 1937. 'Habakkuk', in Kittel, R. and P. Kahle (eds). *Biblia Hebraica,* third edition. Leipzig: J.C. Hinrichs, 946–950.

Pulikottil, P. 2001. *Transmission of Biblical Texts in Qumran: The Case of the Large Isaiah Scroll 1QIsaᵃ.* Sheffield: Sheffield Academic Press.

Qimron, E. 1986. *The Hebrew of the Dead Sea Scrolls.* Atlanta, GA: Scholars Press.

Rabin, C. 1955. 'Notes on the Habakkuk Scroll', *Vetus Testamentum* 5, 148–162.

——1958. 'The Historical Background of Qumran Hebrew', *Scripta Hierosolymitana* 4, 144–161.

Rahlfs, A. 1921. 'Über Theodotion-Lesarten im Neuen Testament und Aquila-Lesarten bei Justin', *Zeitschrift für die Neutestamentliche Wissenschaft und die Kunde der Älteren Kirche* 20, 182–199.

——1931. *Psalmi cum Odis: Septuaginta Vetus Testamentum Graecum Auctoritate Societis Litterarum Gottingensis,* volume 10. Göttingen: Vandehoeck & Ruprecht.

Rajak, T. 1974. *Flavius Josephus: Jewish History and the Greek World.* D.Phil. thesis (Oxford).

——1983. *Josephus: The Historian and his Society.* London: Duckworth.

Randolph Richards, E. 2004. *Paul and First-Century Letter Writing: Secretaries, Composition and Collection.* Downers Grove, IL: InterVarsity Press.

Rappaport, S. 1930. *Agada und Exegese bei Flavius Josephus.* Vienna: Kohut.

Reich, R. 1995. 'A Note on the Function of Room 30 (the "scriptorium") at Khirbet Qumran', *Journal of Jewish Studies* 6, 10–19.

Rese, M. 1997. 'Intertextualität: Ein Beispiel für Sinn und Unsinn "Neuer" Methoden', in Tuckett, C.M. (ed.). *The Scriptures in the Gospels.* Leuven: Leuven University Press, 431–439.

Revell, E.J. 1984. 'LXX and MT: Aspects of Relationship', in Pietersma, A. and C. Cox (eds). *De Septuaginta: Studies in Honour of John William Wevers on His Sixty-Fifth Birthday.* Mississauga, Ontario: Benben Publications.

Richards, G.C. 1939. 'The Composition of Josephus' Antiquities', *Classical Quarterly* 33, 36–40.

Rieder, D. (ed.). 1974. *Pseudo-Jonathan: Targum Jonathan Ben Uziel on the Pentateuch* (copied from the London MS, British Museum add. 27031). Jerusalem: Salomon's Printing Press.

Roberts, C.H. and T.C. Skeat. 1983 [1954]. *Birth of the Codex.* Oxford: Oxford University Press.

Roepe, G. 1827. *De Veteris Testamenti locrum in apostolorum libris allegatione.* n.p.

Ruiten, J. van and M. Verenne (eds). 1997. *Studies in the Book of Isaiah: Festschrift Willem A.M. Beuken*. Leuven: Leuven University Press.

Runia, D. 1986. *Philo of Alexandria and the Timaeus of Plato*. Leiden: Brill.

—— 2005. *On the Creation of the Cosmos according to Moses*. Atlanta, GA: SBL.

Russell, D.A. and M. Winterbottom (eds). 1998. *Classical Literary Criticism: Edited with an Introduction and Notes by D. A. Russell and Michael Winterbottom*. Oxford: Oxford University Press.

Safrai, S. 1990. 'The Origins of Reading the Aramaic Targum in Synagogue', in Lowe, M.F. (ed.). *The New Testament and Christian-Jewish Dialogue: Studies in Honor of David Flusser*. Immanuel Series 24/25. Jerusalem: Ecumenical Theological Research Fraternity in Israel, 187–193.

Saldarini, A.J. 1988. *Pharisees, Scribes and Sadducees in Palestinian Society*. Edinburgh: T&T Clark.

Salvesen, A. 1991. *Symmachus*. Manchester: University of Manchester Press.

——2004. 'Midrash in Greek? An Exploration of the versions of Aquila and Symmachus', unpublished paper presented at the Meeting of the British Association of Jewish Studies, Yarnton Manor, Oxford, August 2004.

Sanders, E.P. 1983. *Paul, the Law and the Jewish People*. Minneapolis: Fortress Press.

——1985. *Jesus and Judaism*. London: SCM Press.

——1991. *Paul* (Past Masters Series). Oxford: Oxford University Press.

——1992. *Judaism: Practice and Belief 63 BCE–66 CE*. London: SCM Press.

Schalit, A. 1968. 'Namenwörterbuch zu Flavius Josephus', in Rengstorf, K.H. (ed.). *A Complete Concordance to Flavius Josephus*. Leiden: Brill.

——1976. *Introduction to the Hebrew Translation of the Antiquities*. Jerusalem: Mosad Bialik.

——1982. 'Josephus', in Seckbach, F. and H. Wiseberg (eds). *Encyclopaedia Judaica*, volume 10. Jerusalem: Encyclopaedia Judaica, 251–263.

Schaller, B. 1980. 'Zum Textcharakter der Hiobzitate im paulinischen Schriftum', *Zeitschrift für Neutestamentliche Wissenschaft* 71, 21–26.

——1984. 'ἥξει ἐκ Σιὼν ὁ ῥυόμενος: Zur Textgestalt von Jes 59:20-21 in Rom. 11.26-27', in Pietersma, A. and C. Cox (eds). *De Septuaginta: Studies in Honour of John William Wevers on His Sixty-Fifth Birthday*. Mississauga, Ontario: Benben Publications.

Schams, C. 1998. *Jewish Scribes in the Second Temple Period*. Sheffield: Sheffield Academic Press.

Scharfenberg, J.G. 1780. *Prolusio de Iosephi et versionis Alexandrinae consensu*. Leipzig: Metzger & Wittig.

Schlier, H. 1956. *Die Zeit der Kirche, Exegetische Aufsätze und Vorträge*. Frieburg: Herder.

Schmithals, W. 1975. *Der Römerbrief als historisches Problem* (SNT 9). Gütersloh: Gerd Mohn.

Schoeps, H.-J. 1959. *Paulus: Die Theologie de Apostels im Lichte der jüdischen Religionsgeschichte*. Tübingen: Mohr Siebeck.

——1961. *Paul: The Theology of the Apostle in the Light of Jewish Religious History*. Knight, H. (trans.). London: Lutterworth Press.

Schürer, E. 1886–1911. *Geschichte des jüdischen Volkes im Zeitalter Jesu Christi*, in three volumes. Leipzig: Metzger & Wittig.

Schürer, E., G. Vermes *et al.* (eds). 1973–1987. *The History of the Jewish People in the Age of Jesus Christ (175 B.C.–A.D. 135)*, in three volumes. Edinburgh: T&T Clark.

Scroggs, R. 1967–1968. 'Paul: ΣΟΦΟΣ and ΠΝΕΥΜΑΤΙΚΟΣ', *New Testament Studies* 14, 33–55.

Seeligmann, I.L. 1984. *The Septuagint Version of Isaiah: A Discussion of its Problems*. Leiden: Brill.

Seeligmann, I.L., R. Hanhart and H. Spieckermann (eds). 2004. *The Septuagint Version of Isaiah and Cognate Studies*. Tübingen: Mohr-Siebeck.

Segal, M.H. 1936. *Grammar of Mishnaic Hebrew*. Tel Aviv: Dvir.

Shutt, R.J.H. 1961. *Studies in Josephus*. London: SPCK.

——1971. 'Biblical Names and Their Meanings in Josephus Jewish Antiquities, Books I and II, 1-200', *Journal for the Study of Judaism* 2, 167–182.

Sider, R.J. 1977. 'St. Paul's Understanding of the Nature and Significance of the Resurrection in 1 Corinthians XV1-19', *Novum Testamentum* 19, 124–141.

Siegel, J.P. 1975. *The Severus Scroll and 1QIsaᵃ*. Missoula, MT: Scholars Press for SBL.

Slusser, M. 1992. 'Reading Silently in Antiquity', *Journal of Biblical Literature* 111, 499.

Smit, G.A. 1900. *De Prophetie van Habakuk*. Utrecht. Erven J. Bijleveld.

Smith, M. 1978. *Jesus the Magician*. London: Victor Gollancz Ltd.

Splitter, L. 1779. *De usu versionis Alexandriesis apud Josephum*. Göttingen: Vandehoeck & Ruprecht.

Stanley, C.D. 1990. 'Paul and Homer', *Novum Testamentum* 32, 48–56.

——1992. *Paul and the Language of Scripture*. Cambridge: Cambridge University Press.

——1993. '"The Redeemer will Come ἐκ Ζιων": Romans 11: 26-27 Revisited', in Evans, C.A. and J.A. Sanders (eds). *Paul and the Scriptures of Israel*. Sheffield: Sheffield Academic Press, 118–142.

——1997a. 'The Social Environment of "Free" Biblical Quotations in the New Testament', in Evans, C.A. and J.A. Sanders (eds). *Early Christian Interpretation of the Scriptures of Israel*. Sheffield: Sheffield Academic Press, 18–27.

——1997b. 'The Rhetoric of Quotations: An Essay in Method', in Evans, C.A. and J.A. Sanders (eds). *Early Christian Interpretation of the Scriptures of Israel*. Sheffield: Sheffield Academic Press, 44–58.

——1998. 'Biblical Quotations as Rhetorical Devices in Paul's Letter to the Galatians', *Society of Biblical Literature 1998 Seminar Papers. 134th Annual Meeting, November 21–24 1998*. Part One. Atlanta, GA: Scholars Press, 700–730.

——1999. '"Pearls Before Swine": Did Paul's Audiences Understand His Biblical Citations?', *Novum Testamentum* 41.2, 124–144.

——2004. *Arguing with Scripture*. New York: T&T Clark International.

Stegemann, H. 1969. 'ΚΥΡΟΙΣ Ο ΘΕΟΣ und ΚΥΡΟΙΣ ΙΗΣΟΥΣ: Aufkommen und Ausbreitung des relilgiösen Gebrauchs von ΚΥΡΙΟΣ uns siene Verwendung im Neuen Testament'. Unpublished Habilitationsschrift. Göttingen: Georg-August Universität.

——1996. '1QS, 1QSa, 1QSb and Qumran Messianism', *Revue de Qumran* 17, 479–505.

Stendahl, K. 1954. *The School of St. Matthew*. Copenhagen: Munskgaard.

Sterling, G.E. 1992. *Historiography and Self-Definition: Josephus, Luke-Acts and Apologetic Historiography*. Leiden: Brill.

Steudel, A. 1994. *Der Midrasch zur Eschatologie aus der Qumrangemeinde (4QMidrEschat(ᵃᵇ). Materielle Rekonstruktion, Textbestand, Gattung und traditionsgeschichtliche Einordnung des durch 4Q174 ("Florilegium") und 4Q177 ("Catena A") repräsentierten Werkes aus den Qumranfunden* (Studies on the Texts of the Desert of Judah, 13). Leiden: Brill.

Stonehouse, G.G.V. 1911. *The Book of Habakkuk*. London: Rivingtons.

Stowers, S.K. 1994. *A Rereading of Romans*. New Haven: Yale University Press.

Strabo. 1967. *The Geography of Strabo III* (Loeb Classical Library, No. 182). Jones, H.L. (trans.). Cambridge, MA: Harvard University Press.

Strack, H.L. and P. Billerbeck (eds). 1922–1928. *Kommentar zum neuen Testament aus Talmud und Midrasch*, volumes 1–4. München: Verlag C.H. Beck.

Strecker, G. 1976. 'Befreiung und Rechtfertigung', in Friedrich, J., W. Pöhlmann and P. Stuhlmacher (eds). *Rechtfertigung: Festschrift E. Käsemann*, Tübingen: J.C.B. Mohr.

Struycken, P. 2003. 'Colour Mixtures according to Democritus and Plato', *Mnemosyne*, Fourth Series, volume 56, 273–305.

Swete, H.B. 1900. *An Introduction to the Old Testament in Greek*. Cambridge: Cambridge University Press.

Tachauer, G. 1871. *Das Verhältniss von Flavius Josephus zur Bibel und Tradition*. Berlin: Junge & Sohn.

Tal, A. 1994. *The Samaritan Pentateuch: Edited according to Ms 6 (C) of the Shekhem Synagogue*. Tel Aviv: Tel Aviv University, The Chaim Rosenberg School of Jewish Studies.

Talmon, S. 1964. 'Aspects of the Textual Transmission of the Bible in Light of the Qumran Manuscripts', *Textus* 4, 95–132.

——1975. 'The Textual Study of the Bible – A New Outlook', in Cross, F.M. and S. Talmon (eds). *Qumran and the History of the Biblical Text*. Cambridge, MA: Harvard University Press, 321–400.

Thackeray, H. St. J. 1961 [1930]. *Josephus IV, Jewish Antiquities Books I–IV* (Loeb Classical Library, No. 242). Cambridge, MA: Harvard University Press.

——1967. *Josephus: The Man and the Historian*. New York: Ktav.

Theissen, G. 1982. *The Social Setting of Pauline Christianity: Essays on Corinth*. Philadelphia: Fortress Press.

——1987. *Psychological Aspects of Pauline Theology*. Philadelphia: Fortress Press.

Thiselton, A.C. 1978. 'Realized Eschatology at Corinth', *New Testament Studies* 24, 510–526.

——2000. *The First Epistle to the Corinthians: A Commentary on the Greek Text*. Grand Rapids: Eerdmans.

Tov, E. 1981. *The Text-Critical Use of the Septuagint in Biblical Research*. Winona Lake, IN: Eisenbrauns.

——1986. 'The Orthography and Language of the Hebrew Scrolls Found at Qumran and the Origin of These Scrolls', *Textus* 13, 31–57.

——1988. 'Hebrew Biblical Manuscripts from the Judaean Desert: Their Contribution to Textual Criticism', *Journal of Jewish Studies* 39, 5–37.

——1992. *Textual Criticism of the Hebrew Bible*. Minneapolis: Fortress Press.

——1997. 'The Scribes of the Texts Found in the Judaean Desert', in Evans, C.A. and S. Talmon (eds). *The Quest for Context and Meaning: Studies in Intertextuality in Honor of James A. Sanders*. Leiden: Brill, 131–152.

——2001. *Textual Criticism of the Hebrew Bible*, second revised edition. Augsburg: Fortress.

——2004. *Scribal Practices and Approaches Reflected in the Texts Found in the Judaean Desert, Studies on the Texts of the Desert of Judah*. Leiden: Brill.

——2008. *Hebrew Bible, Greek Bible, and Qumran*. Tübingen: Mohr Siebeck.

Tov, E. *et al.* (eds). 1990. *The Greek Minor Prophets Scroll from Naḥal Ḥever (8ḤevXIIgr)*, volume 8. Oxford: Clarendon Press.

——2002. *The Text from the Judaean Desert: Indices and an Introduction to the Discoveries in the Judaean Desert Series*, volume 39. Oxford: Clarendon Press.

Toy, C.H. 1884. *Quotations in the New Testament*. New York: Scribner.

Trever, J.C. 1950. 'The Isaiah Scroll', in Burrows, M. *et al.* (eds). *The Dead Sea Scrolls of St. Mark's Monastery, volume I: The Isaiah Manuscript and the Habakkuk Commentary*. New Haven: American Schools of Oriental Research, xiii–xviii.

Tuckett, C.M. 1996. 'The Corinthians Who Say "There is no resurrection of the dead" (1 Cor 15:12)', in Bieringer, R. (ed.). *The Corinthian Correspondence*. Leuven: Leuven University Press, 247–275.

——2000. 'Paul, Scripture and Ethics: Some Reflections', *New Testament Studies* 46, 403–424.

Turner, E.G. 1968. *Greek Papyri: An Introduction*. Oxford: Clarendon Press, 91–92.

Ulrich, E. 1979. '4QSam^c: A Fragmentary Manuscript of 2 Samuel 14-15 from the Scribe of *Serek Hayyahad* (1QS)', *Bulletin of the American Schools of Oriental Research* 235, 1–25.

——1990. 'A Greek paraphrase of Exodus on Papyrus from Qumran Cave 4', in *Mitteilungen der Septuaginta-Unternehmens der Gesellschaft*. Göttingen: Akademie der Wissenschaften, 287–298.

——1998. 'The Dead Sea Scrolls and the Biblical Text', in Flint, P. and J. VanderKam (eds). *The Dead Sea Scrolls after Fifty Years: A Comprehensive Assessment*, volume 1. Leiden: Brill, 79–100.

——1999a: 'Appendix I: Index of Passages in the Biblical Scrolls', in Flint, P. and J. VanderKam (eds). *The Dead Sea Scrolls after Fifty Years: A Comprehensive Assessment*, volume 2. Leiden: Brill, 649–665.

——1999b. *The Dead Sea Scrolls and the Origins of the Bible*. Leiden: Brill.

Unnik, W.C. van. 1973. 'Tarsus or Jerusalem, the City of Paul's Youth', in Unnik, W.C. van. *Sparsa Collecta: The Collected Essays of W.C. Van Unnik*. Leiden: Brill, 259–320.

VanderKam, J.C. 1994. *The Dead Sea Scrolls Today*. London: SPCK.

——1998. 'Authoritative Literature in the DSS', *Dead Sea Discoveries* 5, 382–402.

——2002. 'The Wording of Biblical Citations in Some Rewritten Scriptural Works', in Herbert, E.D. and E. Tov (eds). *The Bible as a Book: The Hebrew Bible and the Judaean Desert Discoveries*. New Castle, DE: Oak Knoll Press, 41–56.

VanderKam, J.C. and P. Flint (eds). 2002. *The Meaning of the Dead Sea Scrolls: Their Significance for Understanding the Bible, Judaism, Jesus, and Christianity*. New York: HarperOne.

Van't Land, F.A.W. and A.S. van der Woude (eds). 1954. *De Habakkuk-rol von 'Ain Fašha, Tekst en Vertaling*. Van Gorcum Assen.

Vaux, R. de. 1961. *L'archéologie et les manuscrits de la Mer Morte*. London: British Academy.

Veenker, R.A. 1999–2000. 'Forbidden Fruit: Ancient Near Eastern Sexual Metaphors', *Hebrew Union College Annual 70–71*, 57–73.

Vermes, G. 1973a. *Jesus the Jew: A Historian's Reading of the Gospels*. London: Collins.

——1973b. *Scripture and Tradition in Judaism*. Leiden: Brill.

——1975a. *Post-Biblical Jewish Exegesis*. Leiden: Brill.

——1975b. *The Dead Sea Scrolls in English*. Harmondsworth: Penguin Books.

——1976. 'Interpretation, History of: B. At Qumran and in the Targums', in Krim, K.R. *et al.* (eds). *The Interpreter's Dictionary of the Bible*, supplementary volume. Nashville: Abingdon Press, 428–443.

——1997. *The Dead Sea Scrolls in English*. Harmondsworth: Penguin Books.

Vollmer, H. 1895. *Die Altestamentlichen Citate bei Paulus textkritisch und biblisch-theologisch gewürdigt nebst einem Anhang über das Verhältnis des Apostes zu Philo*. Freiburg: Mohr.

Walker, W.O., Jr. 1992. '1 Corinthians 2.6-16: A Non-Pauline Interpolation?', *Journal for the Study of the New Testament* 47, 75–94.

Watson, F. 1991. 'The two Roman congregations: Romans 14:1-15:3', in Donfried, K.P. (ed.). *The Romans Debate*. Edinburgh: T&T Clark, 203–215.

Wedderburn, A.J.M. 1987. *Baptism and Resurrection* (Wissenschaftliche Untersuchungen zum Neuen Testament 44). Tübingen: Mohr.

——1988. *The Reasons for Romans*. Edinburgh: T&T Clark.

Wellhausen, J. 1892. *Die kleinen Propheten übersetzt, mit Noten, Skizzen und Vorabeiten*, V. Berlin: Reimer.

Wernberg- Møller, P. 1957. *The Manual of Discipline: Translated and Annotated with an Introduction*. Leiden: Brill.

Wettstein, J.J. 1751. *Novum Testamentum Græcum editionis receptæ, cum Lectionibus Variantibus Codicum MSS., Editionum aliarum, Versionum et Patrum, necnon Commentario pleniore ex Scriptoribus veteribus, Hebræis, Græcis, et Latinis, historiam et vim verborum illustrante*, in two volumes. Amsterdam: Amstelædami.

Wevers, J.W. 1954. *Septuaginta: Vetus Testamentum Graecum*. Göttingen: Vandenhoeck & Ruprecht.

——1974. *Genesis*. Göttingen: Vandenhoeck & Ruprecht.

——1982. *Numeri: Septuaginta Vetus Testamentum Graecum Auctoritate Societis Litterarum Gottingensis*, volume 3.I. Göttingen: Vandehoeck & Ruprecht.

——1986. *Leviticus*. Göttingen: Vandenhoeck & Ruprecht.

Whiston, W. 1722. *An Essay toward Restoring the True Text of the Old Testament*. London: J. Senex.

White, J.R. 1997. '"Baptized on account of the dead": The meaning of 1 Corinthians 15,29 in its context', *Journal of Biblical Literature* 116/3, 487–499.

Widmann, M. 1979. '1 Kor 2 6-16: Ein Einspruch gegen Paulus', *Zeitschrift für die neutestamentliche Wissenschaft* 70, 44–53.

Wiefel, W. 1991. 'The Jewish Community in ancient Rome and the origins of Roman Christianity', in Donfried, K.P. (ed.). *The Romans Debate*. Edinburgh: T&T Clark, 85–101.

Wildberger, H. 1991. *Isaiah 1–12. Volume 1*. Continental commentaries. Trap, T.H. (trans.). Minneapolis: Fortress Press.

Wilk, F. 1998. *Die Bedeutung des Jesajabuchen für Paulus*. Göttingen: Vandenhoeck & Ruprecht.

Wilkens, U. 1959. *Weisheit und Torheit* (Beiträge zur historischen Theologie 26). Tübingen: Mohr.

Williams, T.F. 2001. 'Towards a Date for the Old Greek Psalter', in Hiebert, R.J.V., C.E. Cox and P.J. Gentry (eds). *The Old Greek Psalter: Studies in Honour of Albert Pietersma*. Sheffield: Sheffield Academic Press, 248–276.

Wilson, G.H. 1985. *The Editing of the Hebrew Psalter*. Chico, CA: Scholars Press.

Witherington III, B. 1995. *Conflict and Community in Corinth: A Socio-rhetorical Commentary on 1 and 2 Corinthians*. Grand Rapids: Eerdmans.

Wright, J.E. 2000. *The Early History of Heaven*. Oxford: Oxford University Press.

Wuellner, W. 1970. 'Haggadic Homily Genre in 1 Corinthians 1–3', *Journal of Biblical Literature* 101, 251–269.

Xenophon. 1923. *Xenophon IV, Memorabilia, Oeconomicus, Symposium, Apology* (Loeb Classical Library, No. 168). Marchand, E.C. and O.J. Todd (trans.). Cambridge, MA: Harvard University Press.

——1952. *Xenophon VI, Cyropaedia II* (Loeb Classical Library, No. 52). Miller, W. (trans.). Cambridge, MA: Harvard University Press.

——1998. *Xenophon III, Anabasis* (Loeb Classical Library, No. 90). Brownson, C.L. and J. Dillery (trans.). Cambridge, MA: Harvard University Press.

Yadin, Y. 1962. *The Scroll of the War between the Sons of Light and the Sons of Darkness*. Batya and C. Rabin (trans.). Oxford: Oxford University Press.

Zangenberg, J. 2000 'Wildnis unter Palmen? Khirbet Qumran im regionalen Kontext des Toten Meeres', in Mayer, B. (ed.). *Jericho und Qumran: Neues zum Umfeld der Bibel*. Regensburg: Eichstaetter Theologische Studien.

Ziegler, J. 1939. *Isaias: Septuaginta Vetus Testamentum Graecum Auctoritate Societis Litterarum Gottingensis*, volume 14. Göttingen: Vandehoeck & Ruprecht.

——1942. *Duodecim Prophetae: Septuaginta Vetus Testamentum Graecum Auctoritate Societis Litterarum Gottingensis*, volume XI13. Göttingen: Vandehoeck & Ruprecht.

——1959. 'Die Vorlage der Isaias: LXX und die erste Isaias-Rolle von Qumran 1QIsa A', *Journal of Biblical Literature* 78, 34–60.

Zimmermann, J. 1998. *Messianische Texte Aus Qumran: Konigliche, Priesterliche Und Prophetische Messiasvorstellungen in Den Schriftfunden Von Qumran* (Wissenschaftliche Untersuchungen zum Neuen Testament, 2. Reihe, 104). Tübingen: Mohr.

Index of Ancient Literature

Index of Ancient Literature

INDEX OF MODERN AUTHORS

INDEX OF SUBJECTS

Italics indicate the principal or most important references to a subject.

14–16, 19, 22–5, 29–33,
36–7, 48–9, 178
dictation of letters 158
education 6–7, 16–17, 22–4,
26–7, 31–3, 49
introductory citation
formulae *see under*
citation
knowledge of Aramaic 11,
22–4
knowledge of Greek 7,
16–17, 21–4, *36*, *49*
knowledge of Hebrew / use
of Hebrew sources 1, 5, 7,
10–11, 17, 19–25, 30, 36,
45, 49, *50*, 161–2
memory 5–8, 11–12, 14–18,
20–2, 24–30, 33–4, 37,
153
preference for a form of
a passage *see under*
passage
private exegetical process
128, 141, 150, 162, 176
Rabbinic characteristics 6–8,
22, 24, 33, 128, 137
status as scribe *see under*
scribe
textual character of his
sources *see* sources,
Paul's
use of wax tablets *see* wax
tablets
verbal alteration of his
written source 28, 37,
124, 137
pesharim 35, 44, 53–5, 82–8,
94–105, 108, 115, 119, 125
Pharisees 20, 23–4, 30–2, 34,
36, 57
pM-stream *3*, 42, 51–3, 140–8,
150–7, 160–3, 166, 171–4,
176–7, 180
private exegetical process *see
under* Paul's

Qumran
scribal practice (Tov) 103,
107, 114, 117
scriptorium 55, 105–7, 113

rabbinic
awareness of textual
plurality/variation 27, 40,
43, 53, 105, 113–14
canon 2–3, 39, 43–4, 46, 60,
67, 92, 108, 130
injunctions on copying
113–14

standardization of Masoretic
Text 2–3, 27, 40, 43,
113–14
reader-centred approaches
to citation *see also*
author-centred
reading
aloud 34, 53, 104, 110,
112–14, 116–17, 122–3
privately 29, 49, 110,
112–13, *116, 123*
of Torah in synagogues 53,
110, 158
rhetorical impact of citations
see citations

scribal
awareness of textual
plurality 49, 105–6, 108,
110–11, 179–80
collaboration 107, 111
error 68, 86, 88, 105, 111,
113, 143
exegesis 104–8, 110–11,
116, 119
realia 106–7
sloppiness 114
scribe
1QIsa^a
scribe A 111, 113
scribe B 111
1QS scribe 111
Baruch 112
Ezra 112
Josephus 107
Moses 112
Paul 23, 32–3, 36, 48,
105–7
Shaphan 116
Teacher of Righteousness
111
scribes
ability to memorize scripture
33, 113–14
access to copies 48–9, 87,
105–8, 110–11, 180
collaborating *see* scribal,
cooperation
connected with Levites 108
exegetes/Torah experts 33,
49, 104–8, 110–11, 116
historical perspectives on
106
soferim 23, 43
technicians 33, 107
scriptorium *see* Qumran
scroll
of Rabbi Meir (Severus
scroll) 53, 105 113

of the Teacher of
Righteousness 105
scrolls
expense of 4, 12, 31
mnemonic devices 114
Paul's portable collection of
12, 22
tools for oral performance
29–30, 49, 53, 104, 108,
111–17, 122, 179
unwieldiness of 4, 19, 24,
31, 48
'Sectarian', definition of *see
under* Dead Sea Sectarian
semantic
definition of 47, *51–2*
distinct from lexical 52–2,
138–41, 145, 147, 153–4,
161, 176–80
form of a passage *see*
passage 47, 50, 52–4,
82, 103, 106–8, 112, 121,
142, *161–2, 166–77*,
179
units *55–6*, 70, 81–2, 87, 91,
94, 98, 103, 106, 109
sense contours *52–6*, 67, 70–1,
81–4, 88, 91, 94–6, 98–9, 102,
106, 141, 144–8, 151–6, 161,
166, 175–7, 179
analytically distinct from
textual variants *49–56*, 82,
147, 154–5
Josephus' use of 67, 70–1,
81
Paul's use of 141, 144–8,
151–6, 166, 175–7
Yahad use of 82–4, 87–8,
91, 94–6, 98–9, 102–3
Septuagint
influence on Paul's language
and thought 7, 16–17,
21–2
revisions of 1, 3, 5, 10–11,
13, 22–3, 26, 27, 34, 36,
39–42, 45–6, 49–50, 62,
76, 85, 96, 98, 125–7, 142,
147, 155, 161, 170
translation of 2, 39, 41–2,
44, 46, 58, 60, 62, 68,
134
Severus scroll (Rabbis Meir's
Torah) 53, 105, 113
sources, Paul's
Isaiah source(s) 5, 9–13,
19, 21–3, 33–4, 45–6, 48,
50, 147
textual character of 1, 8–10,
28